Investigating Upper Mesopotamian Households using Micro-Archaeological Techniques

Lynn Rainville

BAR International Series 1368
2005

This title published by

Archaeopress
Publishers of British Archaeological Reports
Gordon House
276 Banbury Road
Oxford OX2 7ED
England
bar@archaeopress.com
www.archaeopress.com

BAR S1368

Investigating Upper Mesopotamian Households using Micro-Archaeological Techniques

ISBN 1 84171 810 6

Printed in England by The Basingstoke Press

All BAR titles are available from:

Hadrian Books Ltd
122 Banbury Road
Oxford
OX2 7BP
England
bar@hadrianbooks.co.uk

The current BAR catalogue with details of all titles in print, prices and means of payment is available free from Hadrian Books or may be downloaded from www.archaeopress.com

Contents

List of Figures

Tables

Appendices

Acknowledgements

The research presented in this volume would not have been possible without the support and assistance of my Ph.D. supervisors, fellow graduate students, Turkish colleagues and workers, and supportive friends. It is my pleasure to thank them here. Most of the work discussed in this book was completed as part of my dissertation research. I owe a debt of gratitude to my committee: Henry Wright, Norman Yoffee, Carla Sinopoli, Patricia Wattenmaker, and Piotr Michalowski. Their diverse perspectives added immensely to my understanding of ancient society. I am particularly grateful to Henry Wright, Arlene Rosen, and Wendy Matthews for their methodological and theoretical input in the early stages of my micro-archaeological research. I also owe a special thanks to the excavation directors who graciously permitted me to work on their sites and subsequently provided me with information on excavated units: Guillermo Algaze and Timothy Matney (co-directors of Titriş Höyük), Patricia Wattenmaker (director of Kazane Höyük), and Mitchell Rothman and Jesus Fuensanta (co-directors of Tilbes Höyük).

My peers took the brunt of my questions and pleas for assistance, most notably Kathryn Keith, Julie Solometo, Andrea Seri, Rana Özbal, Britt Hartenberger, and Kamyar Abdi. In addition, Richard Redding, John Alden, and Geoff Emberling provided crucial assistance early on in my research when I was a graduate student at the University of Michigan. I would like to express my thanks to several colleagues and friends who agreed to read earlier drafts of the manuscript: Kathryn Keith, Scott MacEachern, Régis Vallet, and, most notably, Michael Roaf, who read and thoroughly critiqued the final draft of this book. All remaining errors and omissions are mine alone.

I am also very appreciative of the collegial and technical support I received while a visiting instructor at Dartmouth College in 1999 and 2000. Special thanks are due to Dale Eickelman and Hoyt Alverson for sharing their ethnographic expertise with me and to Richard Barton, Mark O'Neil, and Gurcharan Khanna for assistance with statistics and computer graphing software. Thanks are also due to the University of Virginia and Sweet Briar College where I have spent time revising the dissertation manuscript into the present book. At the former, I wish to thank Adria LaViolette for her encouragement over the past several years and Sevil Baltalı who translated the abstract into Turkish.

The research discussed in this book was made possible by the dozens of trench supervisors and local workers who agreed to help collect micro-debris samples. Most of the work was conducted in Urfa province where I have had the great pleasure to work alongside Necmı Yaşal and Mustafa Kılıçal, our invaluable site managers (the cook and driver, respectively) at several of the sites where I collected micro-debris samples. I am immensely appreciative of the feedback and assistance I received from the many colleagues that I have worked with in the field.

I am also grateful to a variety of institutions for financial support that enabled me to conduct this research: The Wenner-Gren Foundation for Anthropological Research (Hunt Fellowship), American Research Institute in Turkey (ARIT Department of State Fellowship), Curtis T. and Mary G. Brennan Foundation, Sigma Xi, The Scientific Research Society (Grants in Aid of Research), and an assortment of fellowships and travel grants from the University of Michigan and Sweet Briar College.

Above all, thanks and love to my parents whose support and inspiration have been essential in this, as in many other, endeavors. And thanks to Carbon for being an archaeologist's best friend.

English Abstract

I undertook the research discussed in this volume between 1995 and 1999 as part of my Ph.D. research conducted at sites located in southeastern Turkey (ancient Upper Mesopotamia) (Rainville 2001). My research originated with an interest in household archaeology. It soon became clear that the excavation techniques commonly employed at urban sites were not adequate for recovering the ephemeral evidence from daily activities. Instead, I integrated archaeological and geological techniques (more frequently used at prehistoric sites) and developed a method that I refer to here as "micro-archaeology" or "micro-debris analysis." I apply this technique to a study of domestic life at two urban sites in Upper Mesopotamia, Titriş Höyük and Kazane Höyük, and, for comparison, a rural settlement, Tilbes Höyük. In total, 370 micro-debris samples were taken from a diversity of contexts that date to the Early Bronze Age, ca. third millennium B.C.E. In this book I present the results from this test of the applicability of micro-archaeology to urban sites in the ancient Near East.

Generations of archaeologists have devised models to explain the functioning of cities in ancient Mesopotamia. Implicit in many models is a focus on the elites and historic events. In this research, I analyze wealthy and commoner households to test current models of domestic economy, family structure, house types, and residential organization within rural and urban communities. I take a bottom-to-top approach and analyze daily domestic activities and the interactions between households and urban processes.

In order to recover additional evidence for domestic life, I apply micro-debris analysis (the study of artifacts under 10 mm in size) to identify the residues from daily activities. Micro-archaeology involves the collection and quantification of small artifactual remains that are not recovered by traditional dry-sieving techniques. Whereas the large finds may be scavenged, discarded, or curated in periods of abandonment, smaller debris is often swept into corners or trampled into floor surfaces. The distribution of micro-debris often correlates with primary activity areas. For example, micro-archaeology provides an effective way to identify activity areas within settlements (such as areas of lithic retouching or production) and points to households of greater or lesser economic status (through variable ceramic assemblages).

Micro-archaeology complements the traditional analysis of features, macro-artifacts, and architecture. Together with the architectural study of domestic forms, micro-archaeology provides important insights into ancient Upper Mesopotamian households.

Turkish Abstract

Bu kitap içerisinde anlatılan araştırma 1995 ile 1999 yılları arasında Güneydoğu Anadolu'da yer alan arkaeolojik yerleşim merkezlerinde yaptığım doktora tezi çalışmaları sonucu ortaya çıkmıştır (Rainville 2001). Araştırmalarım ilk önce ev arkeolojisine duyduğum ilgiyle başladı. Antik şehirleri anlamaya yönelik kullanılan kazı teknikleri evler içerisindeki güncel faaliyetleri anlamamıza yardımcı olamamıştır. Bu yüzden ben tarih öncesi devirlere ait yerleşim merkezlerinde kullanılan jeolojik ve arkeolojik teknikleri kullanarak yeni bir 'mikro-arkeoloji' ya da 'mikro-kalıntı' yöntemi geliştirdim. Bu metodu yukarı Mezopotamya yani Türkiye'nin güney doğusunda bulunan iki antik şehirde, Titriş ve Kazane Höyükte'ki ev yaşantısını incelemek için uyguladım, ve sonuçları diğer bir şehir, Tilbes Höyük ile karşılaştırdım. Erken Tunç çağına ait yerleşim merkezlerinden toplam olarak 370 mikro-arkeoloji örneği topladım. Bu kitapta araştırmalarımın sonuçlarını ve dolasıyla mikro-arkeoloji metodunun yakın doğuda bulunan antik şehirlere uygulanılabilir olucağını açıkladım.

Arkeologlar uzun yıllardan beri eski Mezopotamya da bulunan şehirlerin foksiyonunu anlamak icin çesitli metodlar geliştirmişlerdir. Ancak bu modeler daha çok elit halkları ve tarihi olayları anlamaya yönelik geliştirilmiştir. Bu araştırmada ise, ben hem zengin tabakaya hemde halk tabakasına ait evleri, aile yapısı, ev ekonomisi, ev tipi ve de şehirlerde ve kırsal kesimlerdeki oturum organizasyonu ile ilgili teorik modelleri test etmek için kullandım. Benim yaklaşımım halk tabakasını ve bu tabakanın şehir oluşumu içerisindeki rolünü anlamak için ev içerisindeki güncel hayatı araştırmak olmuştur.

Ev yaşantısını anlamak için mikro-kalıntı analizi metodu ile 10 mm altında olan arkeolojik buluntuları güncel faaliyetlerle ilgili kalıntıları bulmak için topluyorum. Mikro-arkeoloji geleneksel kuru elek teknigi ile tespit edilemeyen küçük buluntuların toplanmasından ve miktarlarının ölçülmesinden ibarettir. Evler içerisindeki büyük kalıntılar terk edilme dönemlerinde genellikle çöpe atılma ve diğer yollarla yer degiştirir. Mikro-kalıntılar ise köşelere süprülür ve tabanların üzerinde bulunur. Mikro-kalıntıların bulunduğu yerler aktivite bölgelerinin olduğu yerleri gösterir (taş alet yapımı bölgesi gibi). Mikro-arkaeoloji yerleşimler içerisindeki aktivite alanlarını bulmamazı sağlayan etkili bir yöntemdir. Ayrıca bu metod ile buluntuların yüzeydeki yayılımından değişik ekonomik statüye sahib insanların yaşadığı yerleri belirliyebiliriz.

Mikro-Arkeoloji geneleksel mimari ve buluntu analizine katkıda bulunur. Ev formlarının mimari analizi ile birlikte mikro-arkeoloji eski Mesopotamya şehirlerindeki güncel yaşamı anlamamızı sağlar.

Chapter 1: Introduction: debris and domiciles

Mesopotamia was home to many of the world's first states. Much has been written about their emergence, characteristics, and functioning, including their decline and collapse. Early Bronze Age (EBA) polities have been characterized as state-level societies based on the presence of a complex administrative hierarchy, palaces, and monuments to ruling lineages (Wright 1977: 220-221, Wright 1986, Yoffee 1995: 288-89). Other traits include centralization, dense populations, social and economic hierarchies, and monumental architecture. Several of these traits first emerged in the preceding Uruk period, in the fourth millennium B.C.E.

Implicit in many models of early Mesopotamian states is a focus on the lives and actions of the economic and political elites, such as kings, priests, officials, and wealthy landowners. Little is known of the lives of commoners. Most studies have taken a "top-down" approach to the study of ancient society, focusing primarily on the structure of central institutions (Childe 1951, Oppenheim 1964, Lloyd 1978, Kuhrt 1995, Van De Mieroop 1997). Less work has been done on the social and economic basis of ancient settlements, namely, households. An alternative, and in some ways, more interesting approach is a conjoint top-down/bottom-up investigation, considering all aspects of the role of households in early states. In the present study the form and function of ancient Near Eastern households is investigated through a detailed analysis of domestic architecture, features, and artifacts recovered from diverse contexts at Early Bronze Age sites dating to the mid and late third millennium B.C.E.

Households from three Upper Mesopotamian sites will be discussed in detail in this book: Kazane Höyük and Titriş Höyük (two ancient cities) and, for comparison, Tilbes Höyük (an ancient village) (Figure 1.1). These sites contain layers dating to the EBA, between 3100 and 2250 B.C.E (Table 1.1).

Domestic Activities

This volume analyzes several lines of evidence to better understand the diversity of domestic activities within Mesopotamian households. The identification and analysis of activity areas provides the foundation for an understanding of domestic production, class distinctions, gender relations, and the presence of ethnic, religious, and economic variability within ancient urban neighborhoods. Over the past several decades the study of households has been increasingly incorporated into excavation strategies. However, most investigators search for regularly occurring domestic activities and fail to analyze the variability of social and economic activities within individual households. In other words, a handful of households are studied to provide a representative sample of domestic activities. As a result, a detailed study of activity areas is rarely conducted and the recognition of the potential variability in household organization is unattainable. In the following chapters I analyze multiple levels of evidence to explore fully the variability in Early Bronze Age, ca. third millennium B.C.E., Mesopotamian households.

Two dozen domestic and non-domestic structures were selected from three sites in southeastern Turkey for consideration in this study. We know that cities emerged in this area in the fourth millennium, but we do not know how cities were organized or the extent of household variability within these urban centers. The Early Bronze Age is a particularly appropriate period for study because multiple lines of evidence suggest that domestic units produced a surplus amount of food (both in plant and animal products). Additional work is necessary to determine the extent to which the production and distribution of these goods were controlled or supervised by political leaders. In my research I analyze architectural and artifactual data to understand the role of household labor and products in these early Near Eastern cities. In addition, a relatively new method, called micro-debris analysis, is applied to recover *in situ* evidence for past domestic activities.

Household Archaeology

Richard Wilk and William Rathje first introduced the term "household archaeology" in 1982 in their article entitled "Household Archaeology" published in a special issue of *American Behavioral Scientist*: "Archaeology of the Household: Building a Prehistory of Domestic Life." Earlier, Flannery (1976) had called attention to the

Figure 1.1. Geographical focus: southeastern Turkey

Kazane	Titriş	Tilbes	Dates, B.C.E.	Southern Mesopotamia
EBA I	Early – EBA	**EBA I**	c. 3000 – 2700	Early Dynastic, c. 2900 - 2750
EBA II	Mid – EBA	EBA II	c. 2600 / 2500 – 2400 / 2300	Early Dynastic, c. 2750 - 2600
EBA III and IIIa	**Late – EBA**	EBA III	c. 2300 – 2200 / 2100	Early Dynastic, c. 2600 – 2500
EBA IV, IIIb		EBA III		Early Dynastic, c. 2500 – 2371
	Late – EBA / Early MBA		c. 2100 – 1800	
Tablet (not found *in situ*)			c. 1813 – 1781	

Table 1.1. Chronology of the layers sampled from the three sites discussed in the text. The acronym "EBA" stands for "Early Bronze Age" and will be used throughout the book. The periods highlighted in bold were the most intensively sampled.

importance of analyzing household activities by including a chapter on this subject, co-authored with Marcus Winter, in his influential book, *Mesoamerican Village*. Over the next decade, household archaeology became a recognized sub-field, as explained by Wilk and Ashmore (1988:1): "The remains of houses are among the most common and obtrusive of archaeological sites. It is for these reasons, we believe, that something called household archaeology has begun to emerge as an area of research in various parts of the world." Today this sub-field is referred to as "domestic archaeology" or "household archaeology." In a recent review article, Steadman (1996: 54) defined the field as "address[ing] the most elemental unit within the socioeconomic structure, where the 'most primary functions of society' take place" (quoting Sharer and Ashmore 1987: 439). The results of more than two decades of household research are summarized in a variety of articles (Hendon 1996, LaMotta and Schiffer 1999, Beaudry 1999).

I build on the insights from these studies and test whether these models are applicable to the Upper Mesopotamian Early Bronze Age. In addition, I present a new method — micro-archaeology — for identifying household activities which, in turn, allows us to refine our understanding of the role of households in ancient communities. I utilize several lines of evidence (material culture, texts, ethnographic observations, and the results from ethnoarchaeological studies) to understand domestic activities and relations. Although many anthropologists, historians, and ethnographers have examined artifacts, features, and texts found in houses, few have incorporated this information into models of daily life. Moreover, almost all have neglected household-level data in building models of the emergence of urbanism.

This work is based on two assumptions: (1) the everyday lives of individuals, regardless of class, are relevant to understanding broader social, political, and economic processes, and (2) the built environment is both the arena for and a participant in the construction and conveyance of culturally specific ideas and beliefs. Two hurdles have prohibited researchers from fully exploring these ideas. First, for decades anthropologists and archaeologists have defined (and thereby trivialized) "daily life" to mean purely private, and often exclusively female, pursuits. In contrast, I interpret "daily life" as including actions that impact both the domestic and public spheres by individuals of both genders. A second, more fundamental challenge is the difficulty in interpreting past behavior from poorly preserved material culture, such as highly eroded mudbrick architecture and related features. To better interpret the archaeological evidence for everyday life, I combine an architectural approach encompassing vernacular and public architecture with a study of artifacts (both macro and micro) and features distributed within rooms.

I use both architectural and artifactual analyses to consider evidence for several categories of human behavior, from the smallest unit of space (i.e., individual loci and activity areas) to rooms, houses, and, finally, to supra-household environs (i.e., neighborhoods). All these analyses revolve around household activities because the house serves as the physical stage for a majority of individual actions. Finally, I compare the types of tasks conducted by rural and urban households. For each unit of analysis it is important to consider, as much as archaeologically possible, the individuals behind the resultant material culture. It is these social actors, not abstract entities such as adaptive mechanisms, who create material culture and live in the resulting society (Hendon 1996: 55). Towards this end, "material culture" is treated in this book in the "Hodderian" sense, not because it reflects culture, but because it actively constitutes it (Hodder 1987).

Although households are the fundamental economic and social building blocks of society, they are often considered of little importance in traditional research designs and, subsequently, in interpretations of socio-economic relationships and the emergence of states. As Tringham (1995: 79) succinctly phrased it:

> We [archaeologists] write a lot about *architecture, spatial patterns, buildings, dwellings, shelters,* and we make inferences about *houses*. Only recently have we even begun to make explicit inferences about *households* (original emphasis).

This lacuna may, in part, be due to the difficulty in identifying the boundaries between and among the physical structures that make up ancient houses. Another source of confusion lies in the terminology: The shared activities of the household are often separate from the physical structure of the house which, in turn, is separate from the kinship relations among the family. Unfortunately, these three terms are often used indiscriminately and serve to confuse the form, function, and activities associated with each. The following section suggests working definitions for each and will be the foundation for my discussion of domestic activities.

The study of houses and households is a necessary component to understanding ancient society. In this volume I rethink several common assumptions about domestic life. Instead of treating households as a simplistic and bounded "domestic sphere," I consider the role of households within cities and villages. First, houses serve as a stage for the interrelations among buildings, people, and ideas. Second, domestic labor contributes to urban economies. Third, social norms and beliefs are often revealed through daily household activities and organization of space.

Houses

Cross-culturally houses serve several functions: a shelter from the elements, a gathering space for social groups, and a center for daily social and economic activities. Despite these universal aspects, houses vary in form according to the climate, available building materials, cultural preferences for design and architectural forms, and the resources of the house owner. Most houses contain a mixture of public and private areas that are variously used for work, play, sleep, socializing, storage, and the performance of religious rituals. In many societies, the maintenance of the house is a daily chore that includes sweeping, cleaning, trash disposal, and (less often) rebuilding and adding or deleting rooms. Contrary to conventional interpretations, most spaces within the house are multifunctional and serve as the stage for more than one daily activity (Horne 1994, Kramer 1979a). Moreover, domestic activities can take place in both interior and exterior spaces, including associated courtyards, streets, and roofs (Rothschild 1991).

In archaeology, the study of houses is a relatively recent and far from universal phenomenon. In many excavations the residential areas have been ignored or, if excavated, never fully published nor incorporated into anthropological models designed to explain inter- and intra-site activities. One of the first studies to analyze the physical structure of houses was Amos Rapoport's work on the "built environment." Rapoport (1969, 1982) argued that the built environment represented an important avenue of nonverbal communication within a society. Specifically, builders and residents transmitted cultural beliefs through the construction and modification of houses; this physical environment, in turn, triggered culturally appropriate behavior (Rapoport 1982: 61). In other words, "structures are both the medium and the outcome of social practices" (Pearson and Richards 1994: 3). The subsequent analysis of structural plans by Hillier and Hanson is also applicable to archaeological remains. In their book, The Social Logic of Space, Hillier and Hanson (1984) searched for identifiable regularities in architecture. They tried to interpret the socio-cultural meaning of these regularities through an analysis of access patterns, nodes, and connectivity. Around the same time, a handful of archaeologists began to analyze the distribution of activities within houses (Ciolek-Torrello 1984, Kent 1984, Manzanilla and Barba 1990, Rothchild 1991). Susan Kent (1990: 1) summarized the main question to be answered by these studies: how does the use of space affect domestic architectural design and vice versa? In the last decade, other scholars have attempted to "read" houses and domestic symbols as texts (Carsten and Hugh-Jones 1995, Allison 1999). All these perspectives are useful and, taken together, inform us about the dynamics of houses.

Households

Whereas the domestic structure is often recognizable by the presence of certain artifacts (grinding stones, utilitarian pottery, and cookware), features (hearths and middens), and architectural patterns (mud-brick walls constructed on stone foundations), defining household membership and activities is more difficult. The term "household" refers primarily to shared activities and residence (as opposed to the term "families" which are "kinship groupings that need not be localized") (Netting, Wilk and Arnould 1984: xx). These shared activities include production, distribution, transmission of property, rights, or roles, and reproduction (Wilk and Rathje 1982: 622-631). Other activities include food sharing, cohabitation, and child rearing and enculturation. Hammel (1980: 251) synthesized the nature of the household as the "smallest social group that participates in the maximum number of functions." Nass and Yerkes (1995: 69) argue further that the household lineage is a domestic strategy designed to meet the social, material, and subsistence needs of their membership. If this is an accurate definition of the household's role, the spatial configuration of household activities should provide insight into its economic, social, and political organization.

The household is, archaeologically, the smallest social arrangement within the settlement pattern. Three categories of household data are visible in the archaeological record: (1) At a minimum, we hope to recover information on daily activities, such as sleeping, cooking/eating, and possibly craft production, (2) less frequent activities, such as burials, and (3) the size of the domestic unit, in terms of the physical structure and the composition of the household.

My interest in households is to elaborate models about household decisions and actions. For over 100 years, anthropologists have studied family lineages, the division of labor, resource controls, marriage patterns, and the developmental cycle of households in order to create a model for how households functioned. From these studies, anthropologists realized that shifting economic and political pressures were made evident in changing kinship structures and residence patterns (e.g., Kuper 1982, Comaroff 1980). In other words, the "household" is of variable structure: "it is both outcome and channel of broader social processes; and it is the site of separable, often competing interests, rights, and responsibilities" (Guyer and Peters 1987: 210). As a result, social identities such as gender, age, clan, and ethnicity may be revealed through household praxis.

Families

While households can be composed of kin and non-kin, the family is traditionally defined as a group of people related by descent or marriage. It should be stressed that the term family does not necessarily denote a co-residential domestic group. Unfortunately, analyses of "the family" are often ignored in the study of state-level societies because of a prevailing assumption that kinship relations are no longer central to economic or political goals in these societies (e.g., Wirth 1938). To the contrary, I would suggest that there is no absolute dichotomy between kin-based and non-kin-based societies. Rather, kinship forms the basis of social relations within all types of societies (Yoffee 1997: 262). It should go without saying that social relations are fundamental in both states and non-states.

A second popular yet misleading dichotomy is between "public" and "private" spheres. In many models, men inhabit the public and women the private. As a result, "women's work" is considered irrelevant to the non-domestic sphere. As Silverblatt correctly observed, even in state societies, men's and women's lives do not neatly fall into categories of public and domestic spheres. An example from the 18th-Century parish in Santa Catarina, Mexico, demonstrates the overlapping nature of domestic and public spheres where "women were more often than not heads of households and principal providers...[and thus]... homes functioned as both domiciles and work sites, while work sites, like factories, also functioned as nurseries" (Silverblatt 1995: 642). Moreover, gender can only be understood as a social category within other social identities, including class, religion, and ethnicity. Thus, an understanding of daily activities or household composition and management is a necessary component to understanding the functioning of these ancient societies at both the domestic and political level.

Societal traditions, marriage patterns, and child-rearing practices have an impact on family structure. Types of family arrangements include: nuclear families, which contain a husband and wife and their offspring; joint family households, which contain two or more families (not necessarily related to each other); extended families, which contain relatives by descent and marriage belonging to several generations, and polygamous families that contain an individual with more than one spouse and their offspring (Laslett 1972: 28-29, Fortes 1971). Many researchers have argued that certain kinds of societies contain specific family types. For example, many researchers equate extended families with "simple societies" and argue that nuclear families only become the norm after the creation of states. Conversely, Melvin and Carol Ember (1983: 219-21) argue that the introduction of agricultural practices served as an impetus for extended families due to the advantages of large numbers of workers. They also suggest that in a society lacking slaves or hired workers, women would demand or prefer extended families to provide assistance with child rearing. From an economic perspective, Sjoberg (1960: 160) argued that members of lower classes are economically unable to maintain large families and thus are restricted to small family units. Clearly the type of criteria prioritized, whether status, societal type, or labor needs, influences the explanation for the distribution of different family types.

Archaeologically these scenarios are even more difficult to evaluate. There is no universal association between house type or size and family type. For example, a small but wealthy family may inhabit a large house, while a large, but poor, family may inhabit a small one. Another possibility is that house size correlates with the age of the neighborhood. Jacobs (1979: 188) concurs that variability in compound size may not correlate with wealth, but rather old and new sections of a settlement. For example, at Tell-i Nun, a contemporary Iranian village, the newer houses were all, on average, smaller than the older houses, regardless of the wealth of the individual inhabitants.

Individuals

Although many authors have discussed families, houses, and households, many of the anthropological and archaeological studies have devalued the importance of the individual social actors. Some researchers ignore the individual entirely, some insert individuals into models as "faceless blobs," and still others theorize individuals as "rational actors." Thoroughly critiqued by sociologists, economists, and some archaeologists (Shennan 1991), this last model ignores the importance of emotions and moral sentiments in influencing individual actions (see further Schutz 1964). Cowgill (1993) suggests a different way to conceptualize human actors. He acknowledges that people are rationale "quite a bit of the time" while maintaining unpredictable responses guided by emotions, sentiments, and unmeditated responses, or "nonrational propensities" (Cowgill 1993: 556). I explore the utility of this fourth perspective for understanding the daily life of ancient people.

Without texts, fortuitous finds, and careful excavations, it is almost impossible for archaeologists to talk about specific individuals. It is therefore more practical to be more precise. I analyze "social types" such as mothers, commoners, or craftspeople (Ortner 1984: 149). Through a careful analysis of the material remains from particular houses, I build an argument for the household membership of certain domestic structures at ancient Near Eastern sites. By emphasizing the role of the individual I do not deny the fundamental importance of the social organization. Instead, I develop a model that includes people as social actors within their specific cultural traditions (Giddens 1984).

Beyond Houses and Households: Neighborhoods

Household archaeology provides the foundation for discussing supra-familial and supra-household organization including neighborhoods, villages, and cities. Although a popular topic among sociologists and geographers, urban anthropologists have only recently turned their attention to intra-city or neighborhood-level patterning. One reason for this lack of interest is the assumption that an urban neighborhood exists only as an intangible concept, composed of a psychological "unity" or social relationships, that might be difficult to see in the archaeological record. Taking a slightly different approach, I emphasize the daily activities and resultant physical plan of these intangible social relations. Just as the built environment of the house can convey signals as to appropriate behavior and the rhythms of family life, so too can the spatial layout of houses, the distribution of streets, entrances, and types of houses convey messages about levels of privacy, the social relations among neighbors, and economic or class distinctions within neighborhoods.

Neighborhoods may be particularly important in pre-industrial, state-level societies where, as I argue, kinship relations are important. For example, neighbors may help each other in labor-intensive agricultural tasks such as harvesting, especially if the predominant family type is the nuclear one. Or neighbors may create and maintain socially acceptable behaviors. I find this model much more satisfying than the argument, often implicit, that "states" somehow suggest and/or enforce ethical and moral standards. Again, these intangible values and norms may be difficult to recover archaeologically, but this should not negate the attempt to identify both the physical boundaries to these social units and the types of social, economic, and political relations among neighbors. Beyond the composition of neighborhoods, the next logical level of analysis is the larger socio-political entities of cities and, in the case of rural adaptations, villages. Households form the socio-economic base within these settlements. I suggest that urban and rural settlements do not exist in opposition to each other. Rather, I explore the interrelations between these two types of communities. One intriguing scenario is the possibility that a rural village is the equivalent of an urban neighborhood: roughly self-sufficient with a diversity of socio-economic members who live and work within a larger political framework. Accordingly, Chapter 7 will assess the evidence for daily life at Tilbes Höyük, a rural village in southeastern Turkey.

Households within States

> To understand how a state maintains its power, it is of interest to know to what extent the state enters various domains, especially at the fundamental level of the domestic unit. (Hastorf 1990: 263)

I analyze households within complex, or state-level, systems. Traditionally, models of state formation and consolidation have assumed a uniform enforcement of state control or power. Accordingly, existing models often take a top-down approach and assume that households had no choice but to acquiesce to state demands. But new research suggests that rural or hinterland areas were relatively autonomous from the coordination efforts of local states. For example, Stein (1987) analyzed the extent of control over pastoral production and discovered that while the medieval rural site of Gritille (in southeastern Turkey) was integrated into a regional economy, the village followed a "resilient" strategy whereby it retained a degree of economic flexibility under the supposedly comprehensive control of urban elites (Stein 1987: 102). We see this strategy in modern-day Turkey, where villagers organized a grass-roots cooperative to protect themselves from state-determined prices (Kandiyoti 1974: 210). Another example of resistance to state demands, in this case by shopkeepers in medieval Cairo, was the practice of closing shops in protest against high buying or low selling prices (Southall 1998: 232). Clearly the assumption that states operate as monoliths and, moreover, are effective in their policies, must be examined more closely. Not only do state policies impact households, but

> Research has continued to show the effect of taxation, land control, family law market institutions, and so on, on a whole range of 'domestic processes' (Guyer and Peters 1987: 199).

Household actions also shape state policies:

> Domestic relationships are often so inextricably intermeshed with relationships of political alliance that to separate the domestic aspects from the political aspects is to misconstrue these relationships (Yanagisako 1979: 191).

Despite this relationship between "domestic" and "political" units, only a handful of researchers have explicitly looked at the interaction between households and states. One of the few models for the impact of political concerns on household economy was presented by Sahlins (1972). He suggested that household production in "tribal societies" was, in part, determined by political pressure (Sahlins 1972: 82). The elements of this "Domestic Mode of Production" (DMP) included a division of labor by sex, the use of tools to increase productivity, and a pooling of resources within the family unit. Unfortunately, a similar type of analysis for the relations between households and political pressures does not exist for state-level societies. This is due, in large part, because scholars presume that kinship ties are no longer significant. Economic models for domestic productivity have focused instead on the extent of craft specialization, often ignoring the social and political dimensions to household economy. A popular model for understanding craft specialization within states is Brumfiel and Earle's (1987) argument that household members can engage in craft production that is either independent from or dependent on state support. A less economically focused approach suggests that goods may communicate social information and thus serve more than simply an economic function (Wattenmaker 1998a: 10). These messages may be particularly relevant as state societies emerge and expand. Regardless, in both "simple" and "complex" societies, domestic economy is motivated by more than simply a means to an end — i.e., to satisfy the domestic group. Moreover, DMP cannot be reduced to an equation (e.g., Chayanov's "law") whereby individuals optimize their output (beyond their livelihood requirements) relative to the numbers of consumers and producers (Sahlins 1971). Instead, multiple kinds of "labor mobilization" may have been simultaneously employed, including family/household, extended kin group, elite retinues or retainers, the community, the state, and religious institutions. Within each of these groups the workforce is both obligated to state directives and, simultaneously, able to circumvent state control through periods of occasional non-compliance (e.g., Brumfiel 1991, Sinopoli 1994).

One household-based approach is the *oikos* model based on Max Weber's theories that *oikoi* (Greek for "households") form the basis of economic production and consumption within societies. For Mesopotamia we have a rich textual corpus that reveals the economic and social importance of households that ranged from temples and large estates to the smaller, and often dependent, kin-based households (Gelb 1979, Grégoire and Renger 1988). This model was recently applied to provide an insightful discussion of third millennium society in a recent overview of Mesopotamian civilization (Pollock 1999: 117-148).

I suggest that social and economic relations within households are as relevant as "political" relations within palaces and temples for obtaining a full understanding of ancient society. Thus, I build a model of interactions between households and supra-household units that considers social, economic, and political variables.

In the second half of this chapter, I (1) provide an overview of the environmental setting and the distinctions among Southern Mesopotamia, Northern Mesopotamia, and Upper Mesopotamia in terms of subsistence and exchange strategies, (2) briefly discuss the chronological setting, and (3) describe the environmental, economic, social, political, and religious context for domestic life in Upper Mesopotamian EBA society.

Environmental Setting and Subsistence Strategies

The term "Mesopotamia" is used by scholars to refer to at least three regions, each with a distinctive topography, climate, and, most likely, cultural traditions (Figure 1.2). The earliest documented use of the term "Mesopotamia" dates to the late second century B.C.E. and refers to parts of Syria between the Euphrates and Tigris Rivers. Finkelstein (1962: 73-4) suggested that the noun, literally "between the rivers" is a Greek translation of an Akkadian antecedent, *māt birītim*, translated as "between-land" and found in a second millennium economic document. For a sophisticated historical overview of terms used to describe this region (e.g., Mesopotamia, Near East, Middle East versus Iraq or Iran, see Bahrani 2003: 50-72). Usually the term "Mesopotamia" refers to the land between the Euphrates and Tigris Rivers. Practically speaking, however, the Zagros foothills north and east of the Tigris and the desert margins to the south were culturally a part of Mesopotamia. Mesopotamia can be divided into two regions: a lower or southern zone in which agriculture relies on irrigation, and an upper or northern zone in which agriculture relies upon rainfall. During the third millennium, the upstream or northwest part of Lower Mesopotamia was termed "Akkad" and the downstream or southeast part was termed "Sumer." Later this area was termed "Babylonia." Third millennium writers also referred to Upper Mesopotamia with several toponyms including "Subartu," (Postgate 1992: 32) but the geographical referents of these toponyms are far from clear. In this study, the term "Upper Mesopotamia," including parts of southeastern Turkey, northern Syria, and northeastern Iraq, is interchangeable with the term "Syro-Anatolia."

Three Third Millennium Sites in Upper Mesopotamia

In the archaeological record, I studied three sites from southeastern Turkey in detail: Titriş Höyük (excavations directed by Guillermo Algaze, University of California at San Diego, and Timothy Matney, University of Akron), Kazane (excavations directed by Patricia Wattenmaker, University of Virginia), and Tilbes Höyük (excavations directed by Mitchell Rothman, Widener University). As I elaborate below, based on size and administrative complexity, these sites were a rural village (Tilbes, Kurdish for "beautiful land"), an urban center located on a trade route (Titriş, English translation unknown), and a second urban center, located on the strategically important upper Balikh Valley (Kazane, Turkish for "forked mound"). In my research I analyzed 370 sediment samples (approximately 10 liters each) from over 20 structures (public and domestic) and 73 individual rooms at the three sites (Figure 1.3). The layers sampled from Kazane and Tilbes are earlier, by perhaps 300 to 500 years, than the Titriş layers. Within these samples, 70% (n = 257) were collected from domestic contexts and 30% (n = 107) were taken from non-domestic contexts (including public structures, a lithic workshop, and a set of rooms within a defensive wall).

Titriş may have been the center of a small EBA state that emerged and collapsed between the mid- and late-EBA (ca. 2600-2100 B.C.E.; Algaze et al. 1996: 129). Titriş owes its prominence and size to its advantageous location along an important east-west overland trading route "focused on the historical Euphrates river crossing point at Samsat" (Matney, Algaze, and Pittman 1997: 61). At its largest extent, the walled portion of Titriş covered 33 hectares, including areas that the excavators have termed upper town, lower town, and outer town. Excavations have revealed two main building phases that contain domestic architecture (Matney and Algaze 1995). Four large compounds were excavated from the earlier phase (Algaze and Mısır 1995b: 133), and ten compounds were exposed from the later phase (Matney and Algaze

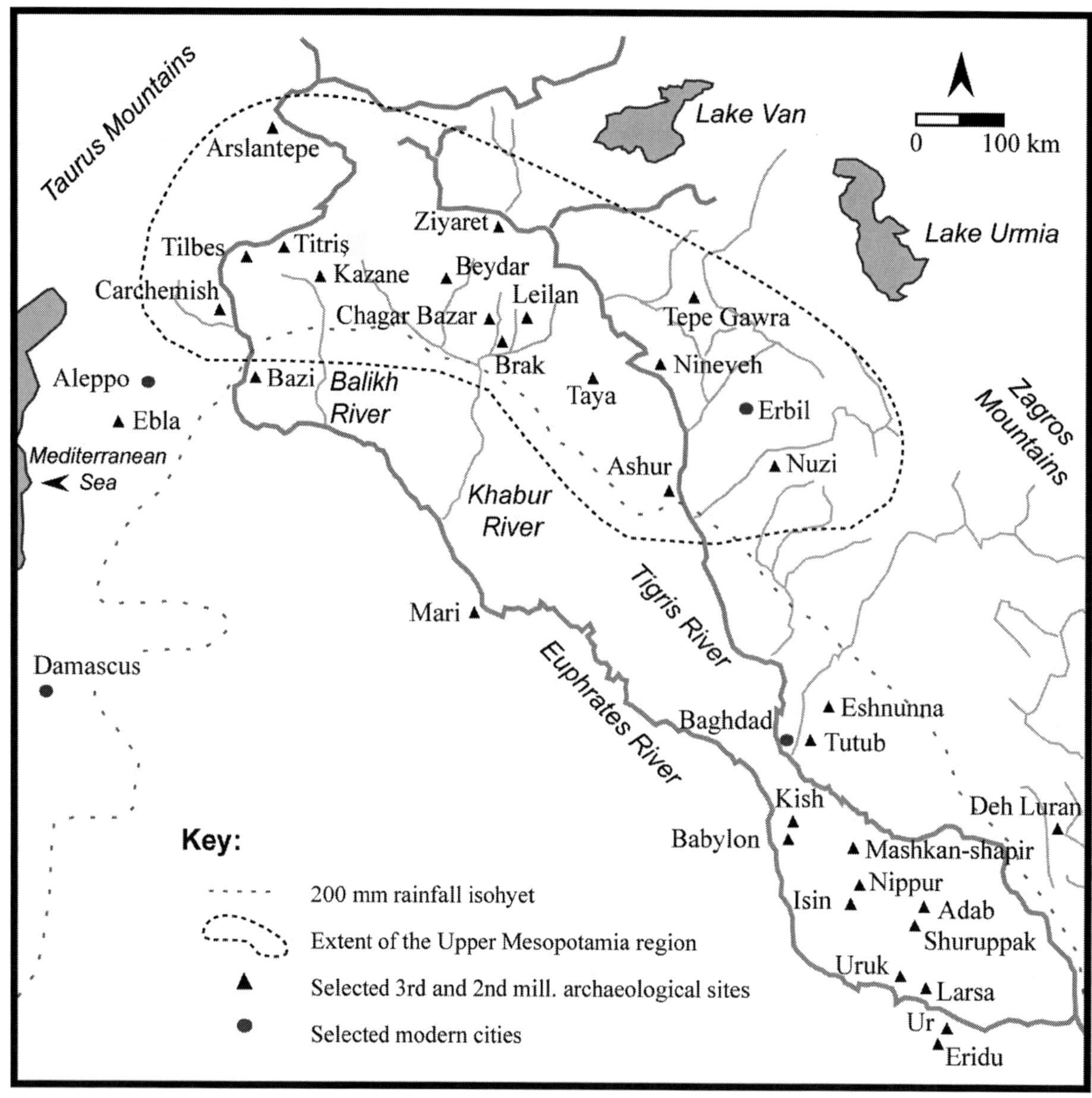

Figure 1.2. Map of Ancient Mesopotamia.

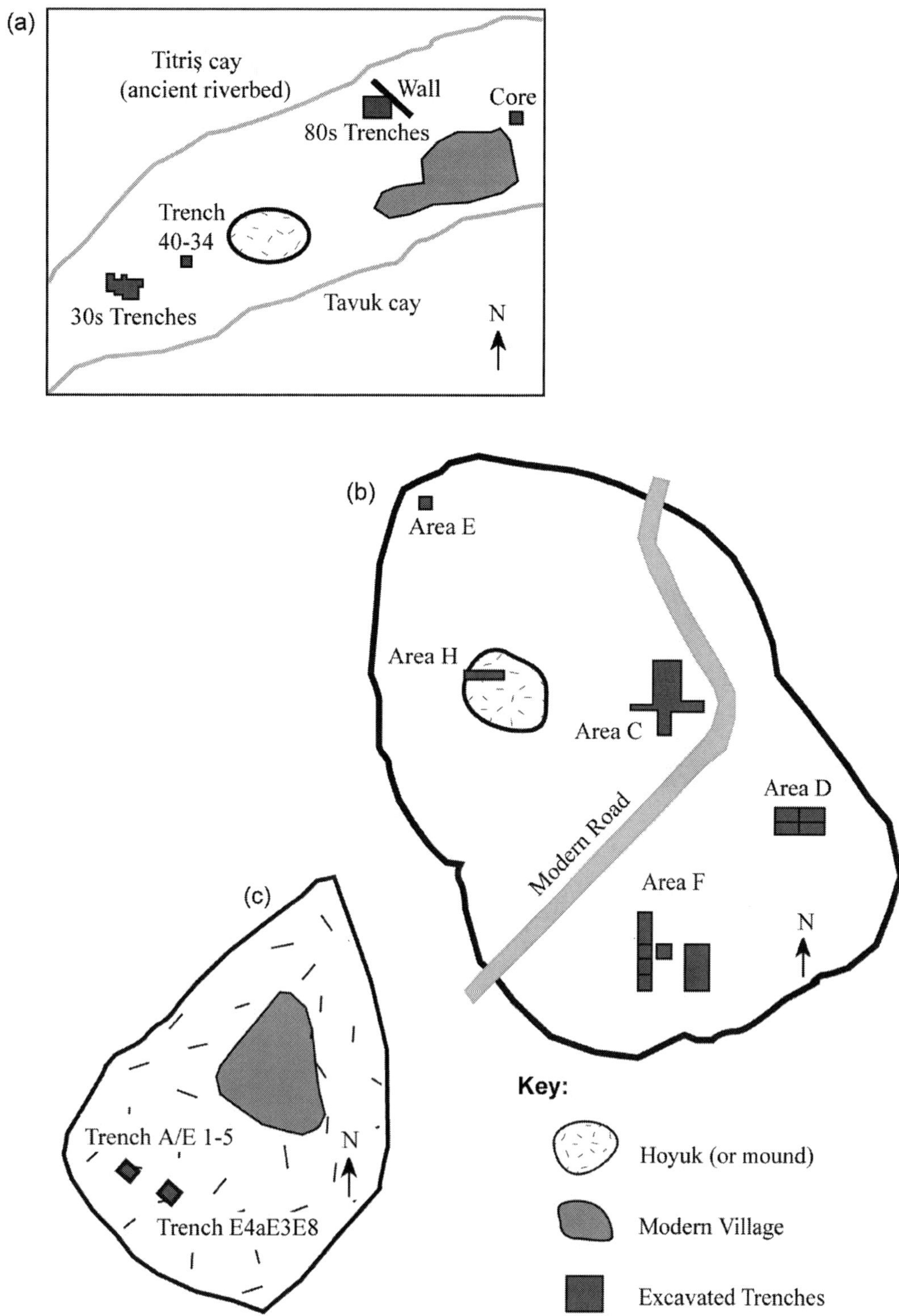

Figure 1.3. Site plans for the three sites discussed in the study: (a) Titriş Höyük, (b) Kazane Höyük, (c) Tilbes Höyük. The trenches are not to scale.

1995: 40). The excavated structures include large and small domestic residences, a lithic workshop, rooms in a defensive wall, and a large-scale mudbrick structure, possibly a public building. The architecture is described in more detail in Chapters 4 and 5 together with the micro-debris samples and analyses.

Kazane was a large EBA center located in southeastern Turkey and was probably the capital of a regional state that dominated much of the rich upper Balikh Valley. Kazane lies "at the border between the Taurus foothills and lowland steppe region, at the entrance to the Urfa Plain" (Wattenmaker and Mısır 1994: 177). The site is surrounded by a fortification wall, which encloses an upper town and a lower town. Kazane was continuously occupied from the Halaf period (ca. sixth millennium B.C.E.) until its abandonment in the early second millennium B.C.E. (Wattenmaker and Mısır 1994: 177-178). Kazane's period of greatest growth occurred in the mid-third millennium B.C.E. (EB II-IV), when the site reached its maximum size of 100 hectares (Wattenmaker and Mısır 1994: 179). Excavated structures include large-scale elaborate residences or public buildings, small-scale domestic complexes, and a defensive wall. Excavations are still ongoing at this site and only preliminary reports have been published to date.

Both Kazane and Titriş must have relied on their rural hinterlands to support their populations (Wilkinson 2003: 125-6). Assuming, for the moment, at least 100 people per hectare of settlement, Titriş may have contained approximately 3,300 people and Kazane about 10,000 at their maximums. Clearly, these sites relied on a large amount of off-site farmland. Thus, nearby rural sites may have supplied these urban centers with agricultural surpluses. While regional survey data are not presently available, supporting lines of evidence for this conclusion include a larger proportion of sherds from large storage vessels at regional centers (such as Titriş) as compared to smaller sites. At the same time the centers contained an under-representation of botanical remains from grain processing stages (Wattenmaker 1998a: 188), suggesting that such work took place elsewhere.

The third site in the sample, Tilbes, provides an example of an Upper Mesopotamian rural settlement. Located along the Euphrates, Tilbes Höyük is perhaps as large as 6 hectares. The results from excavations at this site are still being analyzed; the final report is scheduled to be published in an upcoming volume (Rothman and Fuensanta, in progress). Excavated structures include a series of EB IV and III buildings, a burnt EB III building with possible ritual functions, a large terracing wall, and a significant amount of EB I architecture (Fuensanta, Rothman, Bucak 2000). However, analysis of the Tilbes material has only just begun. The site was flooded in C.E. 2000 as a result of the construction of the Birecik Dam.

Environmental Setting

The three discussed above can only be understood within their geographical and environmental contexts. Subsistence production was limited by such geographical factors. There are six main environmental zones within the area depicted in Figure 1.2: (1) the Tigris and Euphrates River valleys; (2) the arid desertic short-grass steppe, only cultivable if irrigated, and used mostly for horizontal transhumance; (3) the lusher, tall-grass steppe and foothill valleys, where rain-fed cultivation is possible; (4) the mountain front ranges, the "Cedar Mountains," where patchy cultivation, grazing, and forestry exploitation is possible; and (5) the high mountains and adjacent plateau, the "Silver Mountains," where cultivation is limited by water and frost, transhumance and mining are prominent; (6) the fresh water marshes in Lower Mesopotamia (Matthews 2003: 145, Larsen 1979: 79). In sum, the topography varied dramatically from temperate uplands, intramontane valleys, river valleys, desertic plains to marshes. The temperature and rainfall tables in six modern Middle Eastern cities demonstrate this climatic variability (Table 1.2). In the modern Turkish province of Urfa, near to where my research is focused, the annual precipitation is between 263 and 771 millimeters. In the 1960s, only 1.4% of the farming was irrigated (Urfa 1967: 126); the rest was rain fed. In contrast, modern-day Baghdad receives 140 mm of rain a year and the majority of the crops are irrigated. Because of the limited annual rainfall, the inhabitants a long time ago developed a complex irrigation system, utilizing the waters of the Diyala (a perennial river which flows down from the mountains), Euphrates, and Tigris (via the Nahrawan Canal). Throughout the Near East, two- and even three- year droughts occur, and all farmers must store surplus food to survive such disasters. In short, the Middle East is characterized by a Mediterranean climate with hot, dry summers and cold, wet winters. In general, rainfall increases as one heads north or as the land rises. Thus, the northern foothills (rising from 380 to 914 meters above sea level) receive approximately 510 to 760 mm of rain each year (Brice 1966: 234), whereas the southern plains (in Mesopotamia and the Levant) receive approximately 140 mm of rain a year.

Farming Techniques and Subsistence Products

The variable rainfall discussed above had crucial implications on the necessity for and extent of irrigation systems. The settlements along the plains were dependent upon elaborate irrigation systems. In contrast, the inhabitants of regions that received more than 200 millimeters of rain each year (the "200 mm isohyet") used rainfed agriculture for cereals, referred to as "dry-farming" techniques. The Oates' have argued the 300 mm isohyet is a more reliable indicator (Oates and Oates 1976b). Regardless, in the north there is a dividing line

	Average Maximum Daily Temperature (in degrees Celsius)		Average Precipitation (in millimeters)		
	Annual	Warmest Month	Annual Rain	Wettest Month	Driest Month
Erzurum, Turkey	11.7	26.7	450	79	23
Mosul, Iraq	27.8	43.3	390	79	< 3
Baghdad, Iraq	30.6	43.3	154	28	< 3
Basra, S. Iraq	30.6	40.6	187	36	< 3
Damascus, Syria	29	N / A	250 to 300	N / A	N / A
Tehran, Iran	N / A	29.5	200	N / A	N / A

Table 1.2. Temperature and rainfall in six modern Middle Eastern cities. Modified from Larsen and Evans 1978: 233, Pitard 1987: 1, and Madanipour 1998: 106.

B.C.E.	Upper Mesopotamia	Lower Mesopotamia
1600	Late Middle Bronze Age	Old Babylonian
1800	Mid Middle Bronze Age	Isin Larsa
2000	Early Middle Bronze Age	Ur III
2200	Late Early Bronze Age	Akkadian
2400	Mid Early Bronze Age	Early Dynastic II/III
2600		
2800	Early Early Bronze Age /	Early Dynastic I
3000	Ninevite 5	Jemdet Nasr
3200		
3400	Late Chalcolithic / Uruk	Late Uruk
3600		
3800	Late Chalcolithic	Early Uruk
4000		
4200	Late Northern 'Ubaid	'Ubaid 4
4400		
4600		'Ubaid 3
4800	Early Northern 'Ubaid	
5000		
5200	Late Halaf	'Ubaid 2
5400	Middle Halaf	
5600	Early Halaf	'Ubaid 1
5800	Ceramic Neolithic / Hassuna	'Ubaid 0
6000		

Table 1.3. Near Eastern chronologies for periods discussed in the text. Modified from Wilkinson 2000: 225. See Wright and Rupley 2001 and Evin 1995 for calibrated dates. Radiocarbon dates for EBA levels range from ca. 3,400 B.C.E. to 1,900 B.C.E. (Ehrich 1992: 219).

north of which rain-fed agriculture is possible. Each type of farming required a different set of techniques. Postgate (1992: 18) explained that "the southern farmer needed constant vigilance to control and exploit the irrigation system," whereas the northern farmers relied upon natural rainfall. Two important exceptions to these general environments are the marshes of southern Iraq (inhabited by "marsh dwellers" who construct their houses out of reeds) and the front range valleys and ridges of western Iran (in part, inhabited by pastoral nomads). All three of the sites discussed in this book fall within the northern, dry-farming area.

The third millennium Upper Mesopotamian subsistence economy was based on agricultural production, primarily cereal harvests. In addition, horticulture, arboriculture, and animal husbandry (principally cattle, sheep, goats, and pigs) were practiced. In Upper Mesopotamia during the third millennium B.C.E., perhaps due to deforestation, grazing species such as sheep and goats dominate the third millennium faunal assemblages (in contrast to the abundance of pig remains from fourth millennium assemblages; Stein and Wattenmaker, in Marfoe 1986). These domesticates were supplemented by hunting and fishing (especially in settlements located along the primary rivers), grains including wheat and barley, and pulses such as lentils. At Titriş there is also evidence for viticulture (grape production) and acorn and pistachio consumption.

Early Bronze Age Chronology in Upper Mesopotamia

Although the first experimentations with bronze probably predate the "Bronze Age," one of the hallmarks of the third millennium was the increased production of copper alloys and the introduction of bronze tools, weapons, and assorted implements. Bronze is an alloy of copper and arsenic or tin (Moorey 1994: 250-1). The last ingredient, tin, is not found in southeastern Turkey. Instead, trade contacts were initiated with sites to the northwest where tin was mined, e.g., Gülhan, near Niğde, which was used during the third millennium. The increased efficiency in bronze tools expedited the construction of massive public buildings within early cities (Knapp 1988: 63). In addition to copper, objects of gold, silver, electrum, and lead were also produced during the EBA. For example, a mold for casting lead (made of either chlorite / steatite or serpentine) was found in a domestic courtyard and several lead rods were excavated in houses and intramural burials at Titriş Höyük (Matney et. al 1997: 68-69). Table 1.3 provides an overview of the chronological periods referred to in the following chapters. Most chronological boundaries are approximate. The radiocarbon dates for the EBA levels at Upper Mesopotamian sites range from c. 3400 B.C.E. to 1900 B.C.E. (Ehrich 1992: 219). See also Elvin 1995 for calibrated dates.

Economic and Social Contacts Between Upper and Lower Mesopotamia

The environmental context shaped resource availability. One of the sharpest contrasts between Upper and Lower Mesopotamia can be seen in the presence of timber and abundant stone in the north, whereas both are rare in the south. One of the exceptions to this statement was the discovery of a limestone outcrop in southern Iraq, used in the construction of buildings at Uruk during the fourth millennium B.C.E. (Potts 1997: 101). Conversely, date palms and reeds were available in the south and lacking in the north. The availability of building materials influenced the form of structures in each area. Whereas southern sites contained structures built primarily of reeds (seen in the *sarifa* huts of modern-day Iraq), mud-brick, or baked bricks, Syro-Anatolian structures contained stone footings capped with a mudbrick superstructure. Both had mud roofs supported by wooden beams on which brush or mats were laid. In exceptional cases, limestone was used (e.g., the Uruk period temple at Warka).

While Lower Mesopotamia was rich in wool, grain, and mud, Anatolia contained additional resources such as obsidian, limestone, copper, iron, antimony, silver, and some gold. In addition, Anatolia exported leather goods, sewn textiles, and possibly jewelry. Anatolia's primary imports were raw cloth and tin, along with smaller amounts of carnelian and lapis lazuli. This unequal distribution of natural resources probably provided one of the initial stimuli for trade between the two regions (Algaze 1989: 572). Although we lack clear evidence for Near Eastern markets, goods were clearly exchanged, possibly in harbors (in the south), at city gates, or via workshops (Stone 1995: 242).

This exchange between Lower and Upper Mesopotamia dates to the time of the earliest villages (Cauvin 1996: 3). For example, obsidian and metal objects were found in southern 'Ubaid layers; these items originated in eastern or central Anatolia. During the Uruk period, there was increasing movement of semiprecious stones and of copper (Stein 1999: 109). In the third millennium, long-distance exchange between Upper and Lower Mesopotamia may have been one of the prime catalysts for the growth of settlements (Algaze 1989: 588, Wilkinson 2000: 241).

While Upper Mesopotamia should be considered separately from Lower Mesopotamia (due to distinct climatic, political, religious, and most likely, social traditions), the inhabitants of both regions did share certain types of material culture, including cylinder seals, administrative iconography, cuneiform writing, and ceramic styles. For example, by the late 'Ubaid, Lower and Upper Mesopotamia shared some building techniques, such as comparable temple and house plans (e.g., Eridu X-VII with those of Gawra XIII, Perkins 1949: 68; Safar et al 1981: Figure 39, Temple VII).

During the later Uruk Period there was a renewal of these long-standing relations. Indeed, some Late Uruk buildings in the north contain certain ceramic styles, seals, mace heads, tokens, etc. that are not merely "analogous," but "identical" to those in the south (Algaze 1986, Lupton 1996: 2, Stein 1999: 138-45).

By the end of the Early Dynastic period, distinctive southern Mesopotamian art styles, manifested in cylinder seals and statues of worshippers, appeared in Upper Mesopotamia. These objects and cuneiform texts found as far north as Ebla suggest a degree of exchange (both in terms of trade goods and ideas) over a very long time span between Lower Mesopotamia and the Upper regions of the Euphrates and Tigris rivers.

Whether these shared styles were due to migrations north (i.e., colonies of southerners), northern acculturation from a southern "core," or independent invention remains a matter of debate (see further Algaze 1986, Stein 1999). In this study, I investigate Upper Mesopotamian households separately on their own terms, and not venture into the complicated and much debated terrain of northern-southern relations and contacts.

Upper Mesopotamian Society

A detailed overview of Upper Mesopotamian society remains to be written. In this brief summary I synthesize what is known to date from archaeological excavations and the limited number of excavated cuneiform tablets. For the first two-thirds of the 20th Century, archaeological research was concentrated at southern sites. In contrast, Upper Mesopotamia was dismissed as backwards and primitive. For example, in his book titled *The Archaeology of Mesopotamia*, Seton Lloyd titled his chapter on the north: "Illiterate Peoples of Northern Mesopotamia" (Lloyd 1978: 65-87). When the north was credited with "complex traits," it was argued that they were borrowed or had diffused from the presumably more advanced southern "heartland." To the contrary, recent research suggests that some cultural elements, such as urbanism, may have emerged in the north prior to the south (e.g., at Tell Brak in Syria in the first half of the fourth millennium, see Emberling et al. 1999: 1).

Ancient Near Eastern Urbanism

The focus of this book is the role of households within early Upper Mesopotamian cities. More broadly, ancient Near Eastern urbanism has been a focus of research since the early part of the last century (e.g., Childe 1951, Frankfort 1950, Adams 1966). Adams (1981: 248) highlighted the importance of studying cities because they are "the most visible and enduring realities of social life," which is in turn, "coterminous with the underlying conditions of civilized life." Zeder (1991: 19) defined urbanism as "the process by which the abstract relations among state-level governance, economy, and society find concrete expression in the arrangement of people and activities over space." In cities, domestic and manufacturing activities, and the laborers that perform them, are specialized, integrated, and organized on a large scale (Blanton et al. 1981). Mesopotamian cities played a particularly important role as centers of religion and learning (Van De Mieroop 1997: 222). By the EBA, Mesopotamian rulers governed administrative bodies whose purview included laws, taxes, and elaborate bureaucracies. Texts from the south inform us that Sumer (southern Iraq) was divided into about 30 city-states, each with a patron deity and a ruler generally called an *en, ensi,* or *lugal* (Charpin 1995: 809). While much research has been conducted on southern Mesopotamian urbanism (Oppenheim 1964; Adams 1966; Van De Mieroop 1997), we lack adequate evidence from third-millennium sites in Upper Mesopotamia to describe urban and rural relations. We do know that as early as the fourth millennium we find evidence for urbanism (Tell Brak, Emberling et. al 1999) and fortified cities and towns in the north (e.g., Gawra, Tobler 1950; Habuba Kabira, Strommenger 1980). And in the third millennium additional large centers existed at Ebla (Matthiae 1980), Leilan (Weiss 1983), Taya (Reade 1982), and Kazane (Wattenmaker 1997).

Writing facilitated these complex urban systems through which people and ideas were organized and controlled. The earliest proto-cuneiform texts date to the Uruk IV period (Englund and Grégoire 1991, Nissen, Damerow, and Englund 1990). In the third millennium we find tablets written in the Sumerian language using cuneiform signs. Cuneiform tablets have been excavated from several Upper Mesopotamian sites including Ebla (dating to ca. 2450-2350; Milano 1995), Tell Beydar (with over 140 texts dating to roughly the same period; Ismail 1996), and Tell Brak (Oates and Jasim 1986).

Research suggests that these early cities contained an ethnically diverse population. Issues of ethnic affiliation in the third millennium were reviewed by Emberling (1997). Briefly defined, an "ethnic groups," includes people who share basic cultural values and are engaged in communication and interaction that results in self-defined membership that is distinguishable from other groups (Barth 1981:200). This group affiliation must be identifiable by others as constituting a distinct category. Unfortunately, most work has been conducted on southern Mesopotamian groups and, conversely, little on Syro-Anatolian groups. At the sites under consideration in this book, there was limited archaeological evidence for multiple ethnic groups. Lacking texts, we can suggest that differences in domestic architectural styles or material culture within houses may be attributable to different social, professional, religious, or economic affiliations. The study of household variability may be a particularly rich avenue to explore. House form is one of the more sensitive indicators of a foreign presence, due to the limited construction costs and time necessary to build mudbrick houses. Moreover, as a "folk tradition," house design and decoration may exhibit more variability than more formal and standardized temple or palace forms. I will return to the importance of ethnic affiliation in my discussion of urban migration (Chapter 7), a process which often increases social solidarity within groups. Although difficult to see archaeologically, we should not overlook the possibility, especially in heterogeneous urban settings, that certain groups maintained identities separate from the prevailing rulers or urbanites.

Central governance is one of the hallmarks of state-level societies. While we know much more about southern Mesopotamian temples and palaces, excavations at Upper Mesopotamian sites have uncovered several palaces (e.g., at Beydar, Mozan, and Mari) and temples (e.g., at Tell Brak and Taya). Additional palaces and temples are probably buried underneath meters of later deposits on Upper Mesopotamian high mounds. In terms of named leaders, we have texts from Ebla that refer to *ÁBBA.ÁBBA*, translated as "elders" (Milano 1995: 1222). Some scholars argue that these city elders were in charge of distributing barley to cultivators, organizing the digging of canals, and selling land (Westenholz 1984: 21). They may have supervised the economic productivity of large households. Other northern texts refer to *LUGAL.LUGAL,* or "leading families" who held state responsibilities. Diakonoff (1991b: 74) interpreted this term as "chiefs who were military commanders." Lupton (1996: 8) suggested that, in Anatolia, these elites probably gained socio-political power through land ownership. Van Driel (2000: 277) concurred that a "basically aristocratic land-holding elite" wielded control over agrarian lands. A similar process occurred in the south, where land consolidation in the hands of the members of the ruling elite provided them with increased social and economic prestige (Renger 1995: 278). If the resulting northern network of city-states resembled the southern model, we would expect to find small states ruled by kings who frequently engaged in military conflicts. Northern temples and palaces likely owned land, sponsored trading expeditions, redistributed products and goods, and demanded labor from urban residents. Due to a limited number of northern sites with excavated texts, we do not fully understand the roles that kings or priests played in these cities, with one exception: Ebla.

Upper Mesopotamian Settlement Systems

After two decades of work, we have a better understanding of the Upper Mesopotamian settlement systems (Whallon 1979, Wilkinson 2000 and 2003). In the 1970s the beginning of construction on the Karakaya and Atatürk Dams resulted in numerous salvage projects designed to excavate a series of tells along the upper reaches of the Euphrates River. Coupled with archaeological surveys (e.g., Serdaroglu 1977, Özdogan 1977), excavations revealed a number of third millennium cities in the Habur Valley, Karababa Basin, and Balikh Valley. Table 1.4 groups select northern sites into a four-tier settlement hierarchy, ranging from small hamlets to large, regional centers (see further Maigret 1981, cited in van Driel 2000: 269; Wilkinson 2000).

Upper Mesopotamian Regional Variations

The economic, political, and social relations between these sites remain uncertain. Some archaeologists suggest that these settlements formed part of a single political and / or cultural unit — the so-called "Kranzhügel"— culture (Schwartz 1987: 417-18). This term is used to describe Upper Mesopotamian cities with distinct circular Lower and Upper Cities, a fortification wall, monumental stone architecture, and inhabited by users of metallic wares (Orthmann 1986: 62). The term itself, "Kranzhügel" (roughly translated from the German as "wreathed hill") refers to the standard shape of these sites which include a high mound with a central depression, an outer town, and, finally, an outer wall. Additional excavations and analyses of existing material culture may enable us to distinguish among culture areas within these various river valleys. For example, sites in the Balikh Valley shared certain features: horseshoe shaped hearths and painted Karababa ware (Wattenmaker, personal communication). And similar ceramic assemblages from the Karababa Basin and Upper Balikh Valley suggest that these sites belonged to the same socio-political system (Wattenmaker 1996: 26). For example, both areas contain Karaz wares that may originate beyond Turkey's eastern boundary (Algaze, Breuninger, and Rosenberg 1991: 182, Algaze 1990: 289). In addition, these sites contained monumental structures built on stone terraces (distinct from southern cult buildings) and an urban complex of upper and lower towns (a characteristic Upper Mesopotamian urban feature). The results of an extensive regional survey (Özdogan 1977: 171-72) suggest that the northern boundary for these shared traits during the third millennium is the Karababa Basin. Accordingly, this volume will not consider sites to the north of the Karababa (e.g., sites in the Karakaya Basin, such as Arslantepe).

Upper Mesopotamian Craft Specialization

Craft specialization is one of the foundations of the specialized economies found in state-level societies. The term "craft specialization" implies that workers produce goods (such as ceramics, textiles, metals, etc.) in quantities beyond their consumption needs and use them for exchange. As such production becomes regularized and increases in scale, it is expected that these goods, thought to be produced in workshops by specialists, will be "standardized" and less heterogeneous than goods produced by unspecialized household workers (Brumfiel and Earle 1987, Costin 1991). Many of the cities and villages in Upper Mesopotamia included evidence for craft specialists, such as manufacturing facilities (i.e., workshops), standardized artifact types across large areas, and evidence for exchange of these products between

Regional Centers (> 70 ha)		**70 – 20 ha**	**20 – 10 ha**	**< 10 ha**
Kazane	*Mari* / Hariri	Titriş	Kurban	Tilbes
Chuera	Carchemish	Sweyhat	Lidar	Hayaz
Nagar / Brak	*Urkish* / Mozan	*Nabula* / Beydar		Gritille
Shehua / Leilan	Hamoukar			Hassek
Taya	*Ebla* / Mardikh			Yaslica

Table 1.4. Settlement hierarchy for select EBA, Upper Mesopotamian sites. Ancient names for archaeological sites are in italics. The abbreviation "ha" stands for hectare.

sites. For example, a structure at Lidar (in the Karababa Basin) contained 19 kilns (Hauptmann 1984: 205-6). And at the contemporary site of Leilan in the Khabur Valley, kiln wasters were analyzed with neutron activation and scanning-electron microscopy. The results show that the utilitarian ceramics were mass produced by a specialized workshop (Blackman, Stein, and Vandiver 1993: 76). Texts from Ebla mention a "house of carpenters," occupational terms for weavers, smiths, and carpenters, and give the quantity of palace craftsmen (Wattenmaker 1998b: 49). At one of the sites under consideration in this volume, Titriş, a Canaanean blade workshop was excavated that contained over 1500 lithic cores and debris from stone tool production.

Upper Mesopotamian Social Differentiation

In the South, by the end of the Early Dynastic period there is evidence for at least a four-tier social hierarchy including kings and officials, both high and low, temple estates, traders, dependents, community members, and slaves (Jacobsen 1970: 132-72, Diakonoff 1991: 39-40). Although we lack these emic terms for Upper Mesopotamian social classes, differential burial goods (see Laneri 1999) and house size (Matney et al, 1997: 70-71) suggest that these communities were also socially stratified. For example, the necropolis at Lidar Höyük contained two discrete areas of graves: closely packed, simple stone cist graves versus larger and more elaborately constructed graves (Hauptmann 1983: 227). In addition, some Upper Mesopotamian houses contained intramural burials, but it is unclear what attributes determined who was to be buried under house floors and who in extramural cemeteries. Social differentiation at Upper Mesopotamian sites is also indicated by differences in house sizes, from large, multi-roomed residences to two to three roomed structures (see Figures 5.10 and 5.11).

Upper Mesopotamian Domestic Worship and Funerary Activity

Since this volume is focused on domestic units, I leave aside the complex discussion of formal Syro-Anatolian religion. Instead, I provide a brief overview of the rituals practiced in the domestic sphere by family members (presumably without the intervention of religious specialists), in particular of religious practices focused on beliefs about ancestors and ghosts. Evidence for ancestor rites (or at least a tradition of bringing offerings to graves) is found throughout the ancient Near East. In addition to fasting, wearing special forms of dress, and public mourning / lamenting, family members were expected to provide the deceased with a continuous series of funerary offerings (Scurlock 1995: 1888). Non-royal deceased were provided with cold water, bread, hot broth, beer, flour, oil, wine, honey, and occasionally the ribs from a sacrificed animal (Scurlock 1995: 1889).

Outline of Chapters

Utilizing a bottom–to–top perspective, we can address several important questions concerning the socio-economic dynamics of Early Bronze Age Anatolia. This chapter presented a framework for a fuller understanding of the cultural context of Upper Mesopotamian households. In the following chapters, I analyze these households to test current models of domestic economy, family structure, house types, and residential organization within urban communities in the Early Bronze Age. In my conception of urbanism and domestic affairs, the social, political, and economic context are all crucial.

In Chapter 2, I examine a relatively new archaeological method to provide better information about past daily activities: micro-debris analysis or micro-archaeology. I apply this technique to an analysis of 370 sediment samples taken from diverse domestic contexts at three Early Bronze Age sites in southeastern Turkey: Kazane and Titriş (two urban sites) and Tilbes (a village site). In Chapter 3, I provide evidence for micro-signatures from different loci types and incorporate the results from these patterns to identify discrete activity areas within rooms.

In Chapter 4, I analyze the variability among houses in terms of room functions and structural form. I use these results to discuss differences and similarities among 22 sampled structures. The amount of household variability within a site may indicate wealth, ethnicity, or social identity. Moreover, the organization of space within the house may correspond to beliefs, family type, or socio-economic status. Despite the wealth of data preserved in architectural and household form, few Mesopotamian archaeologists have studied individual room functions (for two notable exceptions see Franke 1987 and Verhaaren 1989). Instead, researchers have labeled domestic units as "courtyard" forms with hearths and middens. In the second half of the chapter, I investigate individual domestic structures in order to analyze the variability of architectural form, craft production, socio-economic status, and membership among households. The chapter concludes with a diachronic summary of ancient Near Eastern house forms from the Neolithic to the early historic periods. This brief overview is included in order to refute the commonly held opinion that Near Eastern house form has remained unchanged for millennia.

In Chapter 5, I contextualize these houses within their respective neighborhoods and suggest methods for identifying neighborhoods and understanding the importance of these socio-economic groups in the lives of Mesopotamian urbanites. By studying the amount of activities, such as chipped stone tool production, cooking, or meat processing per household, we gain a much better understanding of the composition of neighborhoods.

Chapter 6 includes a discussion of Early Bronze Age urbanism in Upper Mesopotamia. To date, very little is known about upper Mesopotamian urbanism. Instead, many of our models rely on untested hypotheses derived from examples in southern Mesopotamia. I demonstrate how patterns of everyday life relate to broader trends of urbanism, economic production, and politics within urban settlements.

Chapter 7 analyzes the frequently cited dichotomy between urban and rural society. To date, very little is known about upper Mesopotamian urbanism. Most of our models are untested southern versions. Moreover, most models of urbanism ignore the necessary component to urbanism, rural settlements, and the subsequent interaction between the two communities. To test these assumptions, I collected architectural and micro-debris data from a rural site, Tilbes, in order to compare urban activity areas to rural ones. Although we have no evidence that Tilbes exchanged products with either Titriş or Kazane, Tilbes represents a typical farming community, situated on a small, circumscribed mound. In this chapter I identify the traits associated with Anatolian urbanism and evaluate to what extent villages included craft specialists and social elites.

In Chapter 8, Concluding Remarks, I demonstrate how patterns of everyday life relate to broader trends of urbanism, economic production, and politics within rural and urban settlements.

Chapter 2: Micro-Archaeological Methods

Architectural remains and associated features are becoming increasingly well understood (Watson 1979, Kramer 1982a and b, Cameron 1991), but the debris left by activities performed within structures are usually disturbed and often discarded far from the loci of activity (Schiffer 1972, Binford 1978, Schiffer 1996). While large finds may be scavenged, discarded, or curated in periods of abandonment, smaller debris is often swept into corners or trampled into the surface of a floor or courtyard (Deal 1985, Matthews 1995). Ethnoarchaeological research at U.S. campgrounds revealed that even if an activity area is periodically cleaned, smaller remains are more likely to become primary refuse, while larger items are removed in the process of cleaning (Schiffer 1983: 679; he named this phenomena after one of his students, the McKellar Hypothesis). This straightforward premise is the rationale behind the collection and analysis of small artifacts.

Research into Micro-Archaeology and Micro-Debris Analysis

Micro-debris analysis (also referred to as micro-artifact analysis or micro-archaeology) is a growing field (Table 2.1). The study of micro-debris was first attempted in the early twentieth century with the detailed analysis of Californian shell middens. For example, Gifford (1916) tested the proposition that small items may not be represented in larger sizes and thus must be collected separately. After a hiatus of several decades, further micro-debris studies were conducted on Native American sites in California (Cook and Treganza 1947, 1950). Only micro-artifacts remained at these sites due to the poor preservation of macro-artifacts. In the 1970s, archaeologists and geologists analyzed the distribution of small artifacts in order to identify primary activity areas and to recover evidence for activities that would

Date	Researcher	Artifacts Analyzed	Size Collected
1916	Gifford	shell middens	all sizes
1947	Cook & Treganza	middens, chemicals	all sizes
1956	Meighan	ceramics, bones, lithics	all sizes
1978	Hassan	sediments	x<1 mm
1979	Rathje	contemporary garbage	x<90 mm
1982	Fladmark	lithic debitage	x<1 mm
1983	McKellar	campsite ethnoarchaeology	x<30 mm
1983	Schiffer	all types	x<20 mm
1983	Hull	lithic debitage	x<1 mm
1986	Rosen	charcoal, bone, phytoliths	x<30 mm
1989	Courty et al.	sediments	x<10 mm
1989	Dunnell & Stein	general micro-artifacts	x<2 mm
1990	Metcalfe & Heath	plant, bone, lithic debitage	x<25 mm
1990	Manzanilla & Barba	chemicals, pollen, phytoliths, bones	all sizes
1992	Matthews	sediments, chemicals, phytoliths	x<1 mm
1994	Kemp	cereals	all sizes
1995	Sherwood et al.	ceramics, bones, lithics, shell, daub	x<2 mm
1996	Manzanilla	sediments, chemicals, phytoliths	x<1 mm
1997	Matthews	thin sections, chemicals, phytoliths	x<1 mm
2001	Rainville	ceramics, bones, lithics, shells	x<10 mm
2001	Özbal	ceramics, bones, lithics	x<10 mm
2003	Cessford	ceramics, bones, lithics	x<4 mm and larger

Table 2.1. Previous micro-debris research.

otherwise not be visible in the archaeological record (Lange and Rydberg 1972, Baker 1978, Henry, Haynes, and Bradley 1976, Fehon and Scholtz 1978, Gifford 1978, Hassan 1978, Wilk and Schiffer 1979). Most of these early studies were experimental, testing the deposition and preservation of micro-ceramics, lithics, and faunal remains.

In the 1980s and 1990s, the earlier micro-artifact studies were refined and expanded upon (Goldberg 1980, Fladmark 1982, Rosen 1986, Courty, Goldberg, and McPhail 1989, Manzanilla and Barba 1990, Metcalfe and Heath 1990, Matthews 1992, Kemp et al. 1994, Manzanilla 1996, Matthews 1997). These studies evaluated the methodological feasibility of microanalysis and proposed a variety of techniques for collecting and analyzing micro-debris. Methodologically, there were variations in the debris size collected (ranging from .063 mm to 30 mm). There was also a distinction between researchers who counted debris as opposed to those who estimated percentages of debris categories. And while some researchers located debris that was otherwise unobservable, others tested the concordance between macro- and micro-remains. In these studies, most researchers focused on only one category of data, such as lithics or ceramics.

The questions posed by these researchers included the identification of primary versus secondary deposits, the impact of formation processes on micro-artifacts, and the impact of preservational processes on macro- and micro-debris. These studies were significant in that they tested the methodological feasibility of various techniques, but few asked anthropological questions of their data. The results of past studies will be discussed below in order to consider the deposition, preservation, and patterning of micro-remains in the archaeological record.

Micro-Morphology

A complementary approach to studying micro-artifacts is the field of micromorphology. Micromorphologists usually focus on the analysis of thin sections taken from sediment samples to describe the geological and chemical composition of sediment samples. One of the first researchers to apply this technique to Near Eastern sites is Wendy Matthews. She has spent over a decade taking samples from ancient surfaces and analyzing the microscopic sequences that contain organic and cultural remains (Matthews et al. 1994, Matthews et al. 1996, Matthews 2001, Matthews 2003, Matthews 2004). Most recently, she has applied this technique to the Neolithic site of Çatal Höyük in Turkey (directed by Ian Hodder).

Her results have improved our understanding of the material and technology used in floor construction, the activities that were conducted within structures and on adjacent outdoor surfaces, the distribution of artifacts, organics, and sediments within occupational deposits, and the impact of post-depositional forces on the archaeological record. Matthews' work belongs to a much larger field of research into archaeological sediments and microscopic remains that has been successfully applied at sites around the world (e.g., Courty et al. 1989, Courty et al. 1991, Sherwood et al. 1995, Goldberg et al. 1993). I consider this approach as distinct, but complementary, to micro-archaeology (defined here as a focus on the micro-artifacts, rather than the surrounding sedimentary matrix and organic remains). Accordingly, I will apply the insights from micromorphology where appropriate, but this volume does not present a comprehensive overview of the technique or the researchers involved in this work.

Geo-Physical Techniques

Chemical

Middleton and Price (1996) and Manzanilla and Barba (1990) convincingly demonstrated the utility of chemical tests. Tests include soil phosphate analysis, inductively coupled plasma-atomic emission spectroscopy, atomic absorption spectroscopy, and colorimetry of acid extracts of soils. These tests help locate the residues from ancient activities. For example, wood ash contributes potassium, magnesium, and phosphate to the surrounding soils, possibly indicating the location of an ancient hearth. Simple tests, such as tests for soil acidity and pH levels, would also help distinguish between preservation factors and variable levels of activities and cleanliness. At each site, samples should be taken from sterile layers and off-site areas in order to compare geological matrices to culturally modified levels.

The study of activity area analysis is improved by the incorporation of soil tests that identify chemical residues, such as single element analysis (e.g., phosphate, potassium, magnesium, or organic matter) that reveals signatures that correspond to ancient activities such as cooking (e.g., Barba and Ortiz 1992, Parnell et al. 2002). For this technique, samples are taken from well-preserved floor surfaces, areas of modern and ancient fields, and outdoor surfaces within uncertain activity area designations. Each sample is collected with a stainless steel scoop (approximately 2 cups) and then exported to a laboratory for chemical tests. These tests include measurements for phosphate (P), potassium (K), nitrogen (N), organic matter (OM), and soil pH levels (Middleton and Price 1996, Middleton 1998). The results from these tests reveal a series of chemical signatures for different activity areas. For example, modern agricultural features contain very low levels of potassium and phosphate, whereas ancient areas of settlement display the opposite. This suggests that soil samples could help identify locations around an archaeological site that contain areas of ancient settlement within modern fields (Schuldenrein 1995).

Petrographic Thin Sections

For the past several decades, geoarchaeologists have successfully applied many standard geological methods of materials analysis, including petrography, particle-size analysis, x-ray diffraction (XRD), scanning electron microscope (SEM), Instrumental Neutron Activation Analysis (INAA), and other geochemical methods to the study of undisturbed soils and sediments and artifacts from archaeological sites (Bullock et al. 1985, Stein 1987, Courty *et al.* 1989). In particular, earth materials analysis can be used to identify the source of an artifact, its subsequent transport and environmental deposition, and any post-depositional alteration. For example, many geoarchaeologists have used petrography, XRD, and geochemistry to successfully provenance ceramic vessels and stone tools (Peacock 1970, Williams 1983). Soil micromorphology, as determined by petrography and SEM, can be used to define the nature of human activities at different parts of a site (Goldberg 1980, Goldberg and Sherwood 1994). SEM has also been used to examine wear patterns on lithic artifacts and tool marks on bones. One advantage of XRD, SEM/EDS, and petrographic analysis is the small sample size required, perfectly suited for micro-artifacts.

Three of the *most popular* techniques include electron microscopy, neutron activation analysis, and thin section analysis.

Optical and electron microscopy of the materials within soil samples are invaluable for understanding household variability in terms of artifact sources, types, and composition. For example, the micro-ceramics can be viewed using a scanning electron microscope and x-ray diffraction to analyze fine-grained material and inclusions within the sherds.

Obsidian and chert can be analyzed with neutron activation analysis and the newer ICP-MS (inductively coupled plasma-mass spectrometer) technique (Speakman and Neff 2004). This method is well suited for pieces of lithic debitage because it only requires 100 milligrams of sampled material (Glascock 1998).

Sediment samples can be collected for thin section analysis. This technique involves a variety of geoarchaeological analyses, including mineralogy and texture, use and wear, and site soil characteristics. Such tests provide important information for determining the context in which objects were manufactured and used. Over the past decade, this technique has been increasingly applied at archaeological sites, providing valuable insight into activity areas at ancient settlements (Goldberg and Sherwood 1994, Matthews 2001, 2004, Sherwood 2001a and b).

Chemical and mineralogical characterization of ceramic sherds using petrography, XRD, and SEM/EDS reveals the extent of variability in clay sources and temper or grog types. These techniques allow archaeologists to determine the assemblage of vessel types found within households, what, if any, variability existed among the households in terms of vessel standardization, and whether access to clay sources varied by site size or household status. This analysis also provides the foundation for future clay provenance studies that would further increase understanding of the patterns of household ceramics trade and use.

Application of petrography, XRD, SEM/EDS, and particle-size analysis methods provides information about the morphology, mineralogy, and chemical composition of artifacts that can be used to solve geoarchaeological problems such as identifying a given material's source, transport, environmental deposition, and post-depositional alteration (Whitbread 1989). Answers to these questions are fundamental in understanding the production of artifacts (craft production), their function, and their differential use by different members of a society.

In a future research design, separate sediment samples could be collected at each locus in order to study any extant phytoliths and to analyze chemical traces (Heizer 1960). Phytolith analysis may often be the only source of information on diet and plant utilization in the absence of carbonized botanical material (Matthews et al. 1996: 306-308). Similarly, the chemical analysis of sediment samples, discussed above, is very useful in locating activity areas (Hassan 1978, Middleton 1998). This method could also include a test of the sediment pH at each location that could be correlated with micro-artifact preservation. And finally, sediments could be collected for morphological examination (i.e., soil morphology). This method usually includes the preparation and later interpretation of thin sections from sediment samples (Bullock et al. 1985, Davidson et al. 1992). I mention these additional approaches as a program for future work, but they were not incorporated into the current study.

Micro-Debris Technique

In the research presented here I focus on the collection and interpretation of micro-artifacts from EBA features, floors, and outdoor surfaces. To obtain a broad range of data, sediment samples were collected from randomly sampled units within rooms and from discrete features to document the functional use of public and domestic architecture within the sites. These samples ranged from 2 to 30 liters of sediment. Depending on the horizontal exposure, I took systematic samples in order to document changing densities of debris across horizontal space. For discrete rooms, I laid out a grid (divided into 50 cm by 50 cm squares) across the surface and took carefully measured samples from three to eight of the 50 cm^2 squares. Within smaller areas, such as hearths and burials, I took representative samples. Finally, in vertically deep loci, such as middens, I took samples from the tops and bottoms of features.

After collection in the field, the samples were floated with a mechanical flotation machine (Figure 2.1). The "flots" or "light fractions" (containing botanical matter) were set aside for analysis by the botanical specialists.

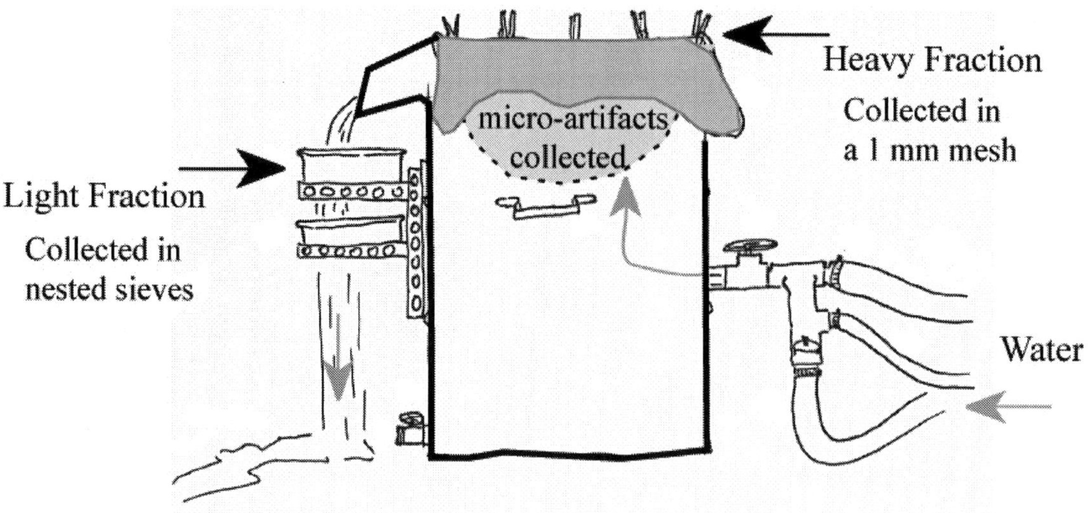

Figure 2.1. Flotation machine used to process the sediment samples. Drawn by R. Vallet.

Figure 2.2. Sorting micro-artifacts. (a) Taking a sediment sample from in front of a threshold. (b) Sorting through a heavy fraction. The small circular dishes contain small fragments of sherds, animal bones, chipped stone, shell, plaster, and mudbrick. (c) Micro-sherds recovered from the sample, ranging from 3 to 8 square millimeters. The black and white boxes in the photograph are 1 square centimeter.

The materials left over from flotation are referred to as the "heavy fractions." I added a small amount of phosphate to these samples to dissolve remnant clay and silt, and rinsed the sample through a 1 mm mesh. After the remaining debris dried, it was sifted through a series of 4 screens of variable mesh: 6.30 mm, 4.75 mm, 2 mm, and 1 mm. For debris under 1 mm I use the term "microscopic" to denote a size that is impossible to see with the naked eye. Sorting the debris into size categories made it much easier to identify and separate archaeological remains from unmodified pebbles. With the aid of 3.5x magnifying binoculars, delicate tweezers, and large sorting trays, I picked out pieces of pottery, bone (animal and human), chipped and ground stone, baked brick, plaster, shell (both aquatic and terrestrial), bitumen, charcoal, and botanical matter (which was occasionally lodged underneath the heavier materials in the "heavy fraction"), and the occasional bead or bit of sealing clay (Figure 2.2)

For each sample, I calculated the weight and count density by dividing the raw count or weight by the total number of liters in the sample, producing a ratio that could be compared among the 370 samples. These densities were mapped onto site plans and visually inspected. The data were also entered into one of two computer programs (JMP for graphing and SPSS for cluster analysis) and analyzed with a variety of non-parametric tests of association. I examined distributions of micro-debris within each site, considering distributions in the kinds and relative frequencies of micro-debris at the level of individual features or collections of loci, households, and neighborhoods or "communities" (Chang 1958: 303). I then considered inter-site variation in the kinds and frequencies of goods. The results are discussed in subsequent chapters.

In addition to studying the density of micro-debris types at each locus, the debris was sorted into finer categories including ceramic wares (fine, sandy, and cooking), biological taxa (including medium and large mammals and rats and mice), chipped stone colors (tan, dark gray, and the less common pink, white, and clear; these categories were determined by comparison with the macro lithic production debris and tools, Hartenberger, 2003: 91), and shell (aquatic and terrestrial). This qualitative sorting more precisely revealed different ancient activities. For example, the co-occurrence of EBA cooking ware with burned, non-intrusive mammal bone strongly suggested that the correlations resulted from specific culinary activities.

The results of the debris analysis were also tested against independent inferences based on architectural structures and fixed features such as hearths, bins, or benches.

My analysis of micro-debris was limited to counts and weights of materials between 1 and 10 mm in dimension. This enabled me to avoid the use of percent estimates and retain the debris for future analyses. Recording the liters of sediment from each sample enabled me to calculate densities of artifacts per sample and, subsequently, to compare the quantity of cultural materials collected from across a site. Data from architecture, features, and macro-debris associated with these locations were used to evaluate the patterns observed in the micro-samples.

In the next several chapters, the term "artifact" refers to any object found using traditional excavation techniques, most likely 3 cm or larger in size (large enough to be noticed by an observant excavator who is not screening). The term "macro-artifact" refers to an item larger than 1 cm in size, large enough to be caught in most screens. The term "micro-artifact" or "micro-debris" refers to an artifact or ecofact between 1 and 10 mm.

Physical Properties of Micro-Debris Types

In order to interpret the patterning of micro-artifacts, I determined the micro-debris signature of the different loci. This, in turn, was contingent upon the deposition and preservation of the various components, and what activities correlated with each signature. Through my own ethnoarchaeological work and from other studies, I developed micro-debris signatures for specific activities. This helped differentiate between accidental associations and artifacts that were used together in the same activity. Here I will discuss the patterning of only the most common micro-debris categories: ceramic, bone, chipped stone, and shell. Within each of these categories, qualitative types were identified and counted. The ceramics were sorted by wares (fine, sandy, and cooking) and by thickness (thin, medium, and thick, Figure 2.3a). The bones were preliminarily sorted into burned and unburned bones, and rodent teeth were separated and counted (Figure 2.3b). The chipped stone was separated into colors: tan, dark brown, gray, white, clear, and pink (Figure 2.3c). These colors corresponded to the colors found among the macro flakes and chipped stone tools. And finally, different types of shell were recovered. I estimated the amount of mudbrick and plaster per sample by absence, presence, or abundance.

Micro-Ceramic Debris

Early EBA ceramic forms include "barrel-shaped goblets, outflaring cups, hole-mouthed jars with incised decoration, and jars with diagonal reserve slip decoration" and bowls (Algaze, Breuninger, and Knudstad 1994: 12). Chronologically these vessels correlated locally with Kurban Höyük Period V and Hassek Höyük EB I-II and with Phases G-H of the 'Amuq sequence (Braidwood and Braidwood 1960). The Mid-EBA includes mass-manufactured metallic-ware conical cups and handmade, burnished cooking pot wares with everted rims and triangular lug handles (Algaze, Breuninger, and Knudstad 1994: 13) (Figure 2.4). These correlate with Kurban Period IV and Amuq I. Late-EBA ceramic forms were difficult to distinguish from Early-

Figure 2.3. Qualitative types of micro-debris. (a) Micro-ceramic wares. (b) Fragments of skeletal elements from animals. (c) Micro-chipped stone debitage colors.

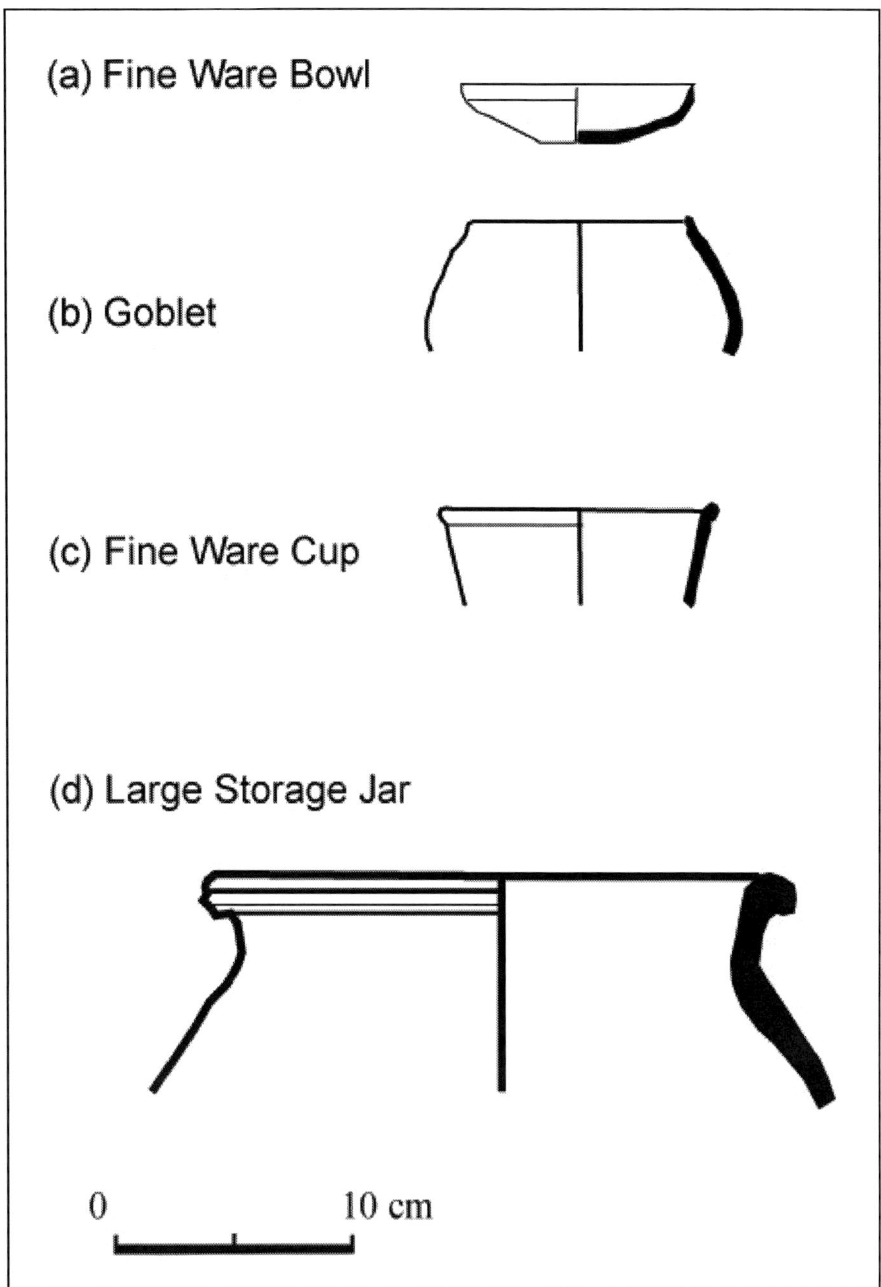

Figure 2.4. A sample of mid to late Early Bronze Age ceramic vessel forms. (a) and (d) modified from Wilkinson 1994: 494; (b) and (c) modified from Algaze et al. 1994: 88.

Middle Bronze Age vessels, but included globular jars with band rims and "Hama Goblets" (Algaze, Breuninger, Knudstad 1994: 14).

The micro-sherds recovered from third millennium contexts mirrored the vessel types discussed above. The wares represented include "Plain Simple Ware," "Sandy Ware," and "Coarse Ware" or "Cooking Ware" (Algaze 1990: 311-21). In Wilkinson's (1994: 494) terminology, these correspond to "Fine (or Table) Wares," "Medium Wares," and "Large Storage Jars." A paste that included sand-sized mineral inclusions identified the sandy wares, while the fine wares contained a paste with a uniform texture (Pollock and Coursey 1995: 116). The cooking wares were heavily burnished. Thickness provides the best indication of vessel type, with thin sherds belonging primarily to cups and bowls, medium sherds to jars and larger bowls, and thick sherds to storage and cooking containers. For this research I use the term "fine ware" to refer to thin-walled vessels, often with painted designs, and a fine paste. In contrast, "sandy wares" refers to medium-thick vessels with a greater number of inclusions in the paste.

As one of the more indestructible micro-remains, micro-ceramics have often been used to determine the degree of trampling within a given room (Bradley and Fulford 1980, Gifford-Gonzalez et al. 1985, Nielsen 1991). Fewer small-sized fragments are usually attributed to lower intensity of foot traffic (Kirkby and Kirkby 1976: 237, Rosen 1993: 147). However, before coming to this conclusion, the possibility of different firing conditions among the ceramics (and thus friability) must be ruled out (DeBoer and Lathrop 1979). The analysis of micro-ceramics also provided an interesting window on fine ceramic wares (mostly cups and bowls) which, because of the small size of the original vessel and variations in firing temperatures in the area of study, tended to break into small (3 to 10 mm) pieces. Micro-debris is often the only source of these fine ceramic wares (unless screening is 100%).

Samples with high densities of micro-ceramics may indicate areas of food preparation (and accompanying accidents), food serving in bowls or cups (also dropped on occasion), or vessel storage. If macro- and micro-ceramics co-occurred, it may indicate roof collapse. But if micro-ceramics occur alone, they may point to breakage and subsequent removal of the broken fragments, leaving behind only the smallest pieces. These various scenarios will be tested in Chapter 3 using the spatial distribution of micro-ceramics within rooms and fixed features.

Micro-Bone Debris

Small fragments of bone have rarely been studied because they are often very difficult to identify. Accordingly, I sorted the bones in my study into broad categories of large animals, small commensal animals, human, and burned bones. While I could not distinguish among cow, sheep, and goat, the relative concentrations of bones were relevant to identify primary cooking and eating contexts where these animals were either slaughtered, cooked, eaten, or discarded. Table 2.2 lists the most abundant animal species present in Syro-Anatolian sites of the third millennium. Most of the animals listed in the table were consumed.

Samples with high bone densities may indicate areas of food preparation or consumption (where small bones were discarded when encountered in meat consumption and subsequently trampled into a mud floor), food storage (either directly from unused butchered pieces of meat that decayed, leaving the bones, or from rat or mice corpses that are sometimes found in storage rooms). For example, at the site of Kahun (a workers village in Egypt), rat skeletons were found in the corners of store rooms with the remains of rags stuffed into the holes. Large-sized bone fragments (10 - 30 mm) were very rare in all of the sediment samples. One explanation for this pattern is that "most bones that are dropped on the floor are swept away or eaten by dogs and other scavengers, small bones or fish scales as well as fragments of larger animal bones are often trampled into the living surface" (Rosen 1991: 100). In addition, Isaac (1967: 39-40) demonstrated, using experimental archaeology among the contemporary Masai, that "all pieces [of bone] of any appreciable size had been removed" from a bone scatter area (laid down by the archaeologist and resurveyed a couple months later). This is a strong argument for the collection of small pieces of bones. These scenarios will be tested in later chapters.

Micro-Chipped Stone Debris

Although copper and bronze implements are common at EBA sites, chipped stone industries still predominate in the tool assemblages. A majority of these tools were chipped from cryptocrystalline materials (e.g., flint / chert). At the sites studied in this research, obsidian occurred very rarely in the archaeological record. One of the most abundant tool types during the EBA were long prismatic blades, referred to as "Canaanean blades" (S. Rosen 1989, Figure 2.5). These blades were struck from large, very carefully shaped, uniplatform cores and primarily used for sickle manufacture (Hartenberger et al. 2000: 51). A Canaanean blade workshop was excavated at Titriş, "Core" Trenches 1 through 5. Other EBA tools included scrapers, notched pieces, knives, borers, and choppers. These tools were used for a wide variety of functions including hide scraping, cutting, plant processing, pounding, and chopping. Most of the raw materials used for these tools were local, except the very gray and tan-colored chipped stone (Hartenberger 2003: 91). Tan- and dark brown-colored tools dominated the assemblages at Titriş, followed by gray, and even less frequent, pink-colored tools. Cream-colored tools occurred less frequently in the lithic assemblages.

Micro-debitage, produced during stone tool production, was one of the first artifact types to be thoroughly studied

Large Sized Mammals		
	Dama dama	Fallow Deer
	Cervus elephus	Red Deer
	Bos taurus	Domestic Cattle
	Ovis aries	Domestic Sheep
	Capra hircus	Goat
	Sus scrofa	Wild Pig
	S. domesticus	Domestic Pig
	Equus	Donkey
	Gazella sp.	Gazelle
Medium Sized Mammals		
	Dog, Fox, Jackel, Wolf, Cat, Mongoose, Badger, Beaver, Hare	
Small Sized Mammals		
	Mouse, Rat, Mole, Squirrel, Weasel	
Small Sized Non-Mammals		
	Birds: quail, chukar, mallard, white stork	
	Snakes, Lizards, Scorpions, Frogs	
	Turtles	
	Fish	
	Bees, Locusts	

Table 2.2. Early Bronze Age animal species. Compiled from Gilbert 1995 and Allentuck 2004.

Figure 2.5. Canaanean blades: an Early Bronze Age tool type. Photograph taken by B. Hartenberger.

at the microscopic level. Because of its durability, chipped stone is one of the best artifact categories to study at the micro-level (Shea and Klenck 1993). Fladmark (1982) was one of the first archaeologists to test the proposition that micro-lithics were embedded into the surfaces where they were generated. He demonstrated this by collecting chipped stone debitage from knapping experiments. Next, Hull (1987) collected lithic debris from northern plains tipi rings in order to investigate the spatial concordance between macro- and micro-debitage. He tested the proposition that micro-debris is more likely than macro-debris to be situated in its original location. As a reductive technology, lithic remains are one of the most prevalent and useful types of micro-debris. Furthermore, chipped stone debris provides accurate evidence for a limited number of activities: tool production, retouching, or, simply, tool use. In contrast, there are several possible explanations for the presence of micro-ceramics or bones.

Shell

Over 70% of the samples contained small pieces of crushed shells. These remains are probably a background noise from the composition of the soils. Almost all archaeologically recovered shell was micro, averaging between 1 and 8 mm in size. These remains would not have been recovered with traditional excavation methods. Shell was removed from both the ancient and modern sediment samples (Figure 2.6). The ancient samples had a relatively high density of snail shell, whereas the four samples I took from the modern village of Kazane contained no shell. The absence of shell from the modern village may be due to recent environmental change (i.e., a drier climate) or increased herbicide use. The denser concentration of shells in the more ancient samples may indicate a more pluvial climate (Hassan 1978: 210). In order to appear in the ancient household samples, these snails must have been brought into the houses from along local rivers as components of mudbrick, mud plaster, water carried in animal skins (Figure 2.7; Hole, Neely, and Flannery 1969: 329), or possibly along with the roots of aquatic plants. The relatively high density of shell in mudbricks (higher than floors and other constructed features) suggests the first scenario is most applicable here. The shell may have been in the dirt collected along rivers and subsequently used to make bricks. A search conducted by the author along a modern riverbank at the site of Titriş turned up one of the shell types commonly found in the ancient samples (a pyriform-shaped shell; Claassen 1998: 20). The modern example was much darker than the ancient one, raising the possibility that intrusive shell might be identifiable in archaeological deposits based on color.

Mudbrick / Plaster

Mudbrick is a ubiquitous building material in both ancient and modern Middle Eastern structures. The low cost and ease of construction makes mudbrick an ideal building material. Mudbricks are a combination of clayey soil, sand, water, and, if desired, a binder such as straw, chaff, sand, or grit (Pamuklu villagers, personal communication). The resulting mixture is placed in wooden molds. The bricks are left to dry in the sun, or if fuel resources are available, slightly baked in ovens. Ethnoarchaeological studies reveal that a mudbrick structure will last for about 15 years before improvements are necessary and up to 100 years before collapsing completely (Torraca et al. 1972). Abandoned and rebuilt mudbrick structures are one of the primary components of tells that rise above the plains. Mudbrick structures provide a good balance between insulation (during the winter months) and air flow (during the summer months). Specifically, the mud absorbs daytime heat and radiates it during the night, when the temperature decreases. Moreover, the thick, flat mud roofs insulate against summer heat and winter cold. During the winter, layers of snow may add to the insulation of the house (Kramer 1982a: 91).

A layer of plaster can be added to mudbrick walls in order to preserve them longer and/or for aesthetic reasons. Although the types of plaster vary, contemporary Middle Eastern villagers normally add straw to the mud plaster (Kramer 1982a: 137). Archaeologically, plaster frequently contained lime; this is recognizable as a faint white surface. Ethnographic observations suggest that both quantity and quality of plaster may correlate with economic status (due to the cost of straw, whitewash, and the additional labor involved).

Organic Remains

The occupants of many EBA sites in southeastern Anatolia practiced a mixed economy of grain and legume cultivations, supplemented by crops such as grapes, acorns, and nuts. Table 2.3 lists the plant species found at Titriş. A similarly large quantity of barley, as opposed to wheat, was reported at other mid to late EBA sites such as Hassek Höyük and Arslantepe. In contrast, wheat was the more common domesticate at Kurban and Korucutepe (Miller 1986). Although organic materials were occasionally recovered from the heavy fractions in this study, these remains are still being studied by paleobotanical specialists.

Advantages to Collecting Micro-Debris

Micro-debris complements the study of architecture and features. The analysis of micro-debris has four additional advantages over the study of macro-artifacts.

(1) Due to the difficulty in removing small debris with traditional cleaning methods, small items are more likely than large items to remain where they were dropped.

(2) Small remains are less likely to be affected by post-depositional disturbances.

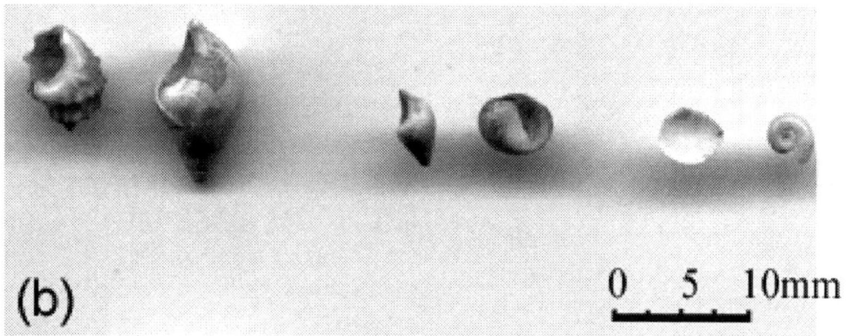

Figure 2.6. Shell types found at Titriş Höyük. (a) Front and (b) Reverse.

Figure 2.7. Woman carrying a goat-skin bag. Photograph modified from English 1966: Plate 5b.

Cereals	hulled barley (*Hordeum sativum*) – either 2 or 6 row less common: wheat grains, emmer & free-threshing (*Triticum durum / aestivum*)
Pulses	lentils (*Lens culinaris*), grass vetchling (*Lathyrus cf. circea/sativus*)
Fruits	domesticated grape (*vitis vinifera*), wild terebinth nuts (*Pistacia*) hawthorn (*crataegus sp*), almond/plum shells (*Prunus sp*), acorns (*Quercus)*
Weeds	calium, silene, lolium, aegilops
Animal Dung	to date, no evidence for dung has been recovered from Titriş Höyük
Wood Charcoal	ubiquitous in samples – oak and other species

Table 2.3. Early Bronze Age paleobotanical species. Identified in EBA Contexts at Titriş. Compiled from Schlee, in Algaze et al. 1995: 28-32.

(3) Micro-debris may provide information on activities that are rarely represented by larger artifacts.

(4) The systematic collection of sediment samples with a known volume improves our interpretation of the spatial distribution of artifact densities within architectural features.

In this section, I look more closely at these four propositions. Because of these characteristics of micro-remains, my research focused on the recovery and analysis of artifacts under 1 square centimeter in area. After interpreting the patterning of macro- and micro-debris, I study the use of rooms, the composition of households, and the roles of these households in cities and villages.

(1) The first advantage of micro-debris is that its small size often results in unintentional deposition (i.e., through loss or as an unintentional by-product) at the original location of the activity in which the materials were used (Fehon and Scholtz 1978, Schiffer 1983: 679, Deal 1985, Hull 1987). Moreover, these small items are often overlooked (or perhaps not relevant to the inhabitant's conception of "clean") in everyday housekeeping activities such as trash disposal or sweeping. First tested with ethnoarchaeological studies (Gifford 1978, O'Connell 1987, Simms 1988), many authors have concluded that the patterning of micro-debris on floors is a useful, and perhaps unique, source of information about past activities (Hayden and Cannon 1983, Rosen 1986, Simms and Heath 1990, Metcalfe and Heath 1990, Schiffer 1996). In contrast, decades of research on site formation processes suggests that many of the larger artifacts found in rooms were deposited as unstructured tertiary trash, deposited after the abandonment of a room or structure (Schiffer 1996). This artifact discard was often found in locations other than where the activity was performed due to safety, hygiene, space, or symbolic considerations, and is therefore not useful for interpreting locations of past activities.

In addition, site formation processes commonly include an abandonment episode, when the residents remove or "curate" (Schiffer 1983) anything usable from the premises (Lange and Rydberg 1972). Items under 10 mm^2 are rarely considered usable and thus often left behind. Hull (1987: 773) concurred: "The extremely small size of micro-debitage, specifically, precludes post-depositional cultural disturbance of the artifact-activity area relation through scavenging or reuse of materials." The identification of unintentionally discarded artifacts in their primary location allows archaeologists to document ancient activity areas. For example, while macro-debris was most often removed from production areas due to safety concerns or cleanliness, micro-debitage often remains, crushed into dirt-packed floor surfaces (Fladmark 1982, Baumler and Downum 1989). In contrast, the location of macro-debitage may indicate a secondary trash removal location, rather than the site of production or use. For example, at Tula, in Mexico, Healan (1983: 135) recovered significant amounts of microscopic obsidian debris from an area with only moderate quantities of macroscopic lithic debris. He was later able to identify this structure as a workshop located outside a habitation unit. Due to the safety concerns mentioned above, the macro-remains had been regularly disposed of at a different location, in refuse pits.

Future ethnoarchaeological work could also help differentiate between non-cultural associations, such as inclusions in mudbrick (possibly pebbles and snails) and activity-related artifacts (such as meat by-products and cutting tools). A recent and comprehensive volume on Turkish ethnoarchaeology will be a useful source for collecting additional data on everyday life (Yakar 2000). In Chapters 3 and 4, contemporary behavior and its resultant material culture are studied to help explain ancient micro-patterning observed at three Anatolian sites. Of course, different behaviors (occurring in the present as opposed to the past) may produce similar artifactual patterns. I have tried to consider this possibility by employing more than one line of evidence to connect ancient behavior with physical remains. In sum, I suggest that micro-artifacts were frequently primary refuse and undisturbed by anthropogenic agents.

These two characteristics make micro-debris a useful and rare type of evidence for locating ancient, daily activities.

(2) Because of their small size, micro-debris are unaffected by many of the post-depositional factors that commonly act upon larger remains (Isaac 1967: 40, Rosen 1986: 92-93, Schiffer 1996: 62). There are two broad categories of post-depositional or post-occupational disturbances: natural and cultural.

Cultural disturbances include the removal of larger items from their original disposal location, such as the reuse of sherds from a broken vessel for patching holes in mudbrick walls or the consumption of large pieces of bone by animal scavengers. While ethnographic and archaeological research often provides evidence for dogs, pigs, or rodents that gnawed at bones or carried away trash, tiny pieces of bone or trash are unlikely to have attracted the attention of scavengers and thus were left *in situ*. Similarly, sherds under 1 cm in dimension were less likely to be retrieved by people and used in repairs.

A second category of post-depositional forces that must be accounted for are the biogenic and geogenic agents that reduce the concordance between macro-artifact position and past activity areas (Murray 1980, Goldberg et al. 1993). These natural forces include water sorting, gravity movements, and wind erosion (Rosen 1986: 92). Experimental and geological studies support the contention that small remains are less likely to be affected by post-depositional forces and subsequent mixing of systemic contexts (Schiffer 1996: 62, J. Stein 1987). For example, an experiment initiated by Posnansky (reported by Isaac 1967: 40) demonstrated that although climatic forces caused the disintegration of large faunal remains, smaller fragments survived. Posnansky laid out a goat and a cattle skeleton in an area with alkaline soil and a dry climate (similar to Middle Eastern conditions). After several years, only the ridges, neck, and articular surfaces of the scapulae remained. The larger cranium, mandibles, and vertebra were cracked and friable, probably as the result of "foot"-falls (in this case animal ones).

Of course, not all micro-debris was untouched by post-depositional forces. Certainly a small percent of the micro-debitage consists of macro-remains that were reduced in size by chemical and physical weathering. In this case, micro-debris represents "shadows of larger objects" that have since decayed or been removed (Sherwood et al. 1995: 433). A second potential post-depositional disturbance included intrusive micro-remains from more recent deposits. Because of their light weight and small size, this scenario is unlikely to affect micro-artifacts unless the entire deposit has been disturbed. If this were the case, we would expect secondary refuse to be readily apparent based on its depositional context (such as a trash pit). In contrast, micro-debris is not easily removed by human or animal activity, except by the bulk removal of a matrix, such as the sediment displacement that occurs from the construction of burrows or pits. In each of these cases, the disturbance would be apparent when taking the micro-debris sample. An example of the utility of micro-debris for identifying disturbed contexts comes from Rosen's work in Israel. She analyzed a floor surface at Tel Miqne-Ekron (an Iron Age city site) that contained an unusually high concentration of tiny, crushed bone fragments. She concluded that they were the result of feces from either canine or porcine species. The presence of large numbers of scavengers indicated the room's secondary use as a trash-disposal location (Rosen 1989: 568).

Additionally, I monitored potential disturbance at the micro-level by sampling mudbricks, sterile soil, and multiple samples from each floor surface. Rosen (1986: 93) cautioned that mudbrick can be a source of secondary refuse, brought in from the sediment source, such as a riverbed. Accordingly, I sampled mudbricks to account for this background noise. Other items — for example, earlier or later diagnostic micro-sherds — can be recognized as intrusive. And finally, in all cases, an attempt was made to sample only well excavated and undisturbed contexts.

(3) Micro-debris analysis is a unique source for certain types of remains that are rarely preserved in a size recoverable by traditional screening methods. These include beads, pierced shells, small mammal teeth, or fish scales (Hayden and Cannon 1983, Simms and Heath 1990, Metcalfe and Heath 1990). In the present study, micro-debris samples contained pieces of sealing clay and bitumen, beads, rat or mice bones, and possible clay stamps that are infrequently recovered with traditional excavation techniques.

Often micro-debris provided the only surviving evidence of a past activity, even if the activity originally included the use of large items such as ceramic vessels or chipped stone tools. With each type of debris, macro remains were only preserved in a small percentage of the sediment samples (Table 2.4). In contrast, micro-remains occurred much more frequently within each sample.

The particularly low percentage of samples that contained macro-chipped stone supports the earlier contention that larger chipped stone debris maybe removed for safety reasons. And the small percentage of macro-faunal remains may be because of the impact of post-depositional forces that eroded large pieces of friable bone. The pottery, while more durable and thus preserved at the macro-size category in a larger percent of the samples, was still found in many fewer samples than the comparable micro sherds. Clearly, micro-remains reveal a more detailed signature of past activities than macro-remains.

(4) There is one additional advantage to collecting micro-debris samples. At large sites, where it is difficult or time consuming to record the volume of excavated sediment from each context, the systematic collection of

Micro-Debris	macro (10 – 30 mm)	micro (x < 10 mm)
ceramic	16% (n = 57)	57% (n = 208)
bone	6% (n = 23)	88% (n = 323)
chipped stone	2% (n = 7)	80% (n = 291)

Table 2.4. Percent of macro- and micro- remains recovered from 365 sediment samples. The "n" after each percentage represents the number of samples that contained the artifact type.

micro-debris samples (with a known volume) is crucial in order to calculate the density of debris and compare its distribution among houses.

A Model of Micro-Debris Deposition and Preservation

Building on two decades of micro-debris research, I devised a model to delineate the relationship between the quantitative and qualitative distribution of micro-remains and past activities. In addition to conducting my own brief ethnoarchaeological project in both an Indian and Turkish village, I compiled patterns from comparable ethnoarchaeological research in various parts of the world. The results from ethnoarchaeological projects were used to test various explanations for correlations between categories of artifacts — e.g., to control for the background effects of the source of the debris' matrix, the impact of cleaning and trampling activities, and the impact from natural or cultural post-depositional processes.

Note: in the following discussion the term *in situ* is only used in reference to objects that remained in the location where they were produced or stored, for example: stationary features, burials, and micro-debris that was not disturbed in cleaning procedures and thus lay on the floor where the artifact was created (as debitage), dropped (as broken pieces), or stored (as preserved remains).

Pathways for Micro-debris to Enter the Archaeological Record

In order to interpret the micro-debris signatures we must determine how and why the remains entered the archaeological record. Micro-debris enters the archaeological record by one of three main pathways:

(1) The item was dropped or lost at a particular location and then went unnoticed during cleaning efforts. "Lost" items include small items that were dropped intact, such as a small bead, and small pieces of a larger item that may have gone unnoticed after the vessel was dropped and broken. Slightly larger debris (between 5 and 10 mm) may have been unintentionally swept into a corner or over a threshold into another room (perhaps a socially less important one where a spotless surface was less relevant) or to an outside surface. Although less helpful for reconstructing activity areas, the presence of micro-debris in corners and directly outside doorsteps or room entrances is a better source of information about the original function of the room than macro-remains discarded after the rooms were abandoned, and thus unrelated to the original room use.

In situ micro-remains may be trampled and reduced to a smaller size. Trampling appeared not to affect objects that were smaller than 5 mm. For example, a 2 mm bead would, ironically, be unharmed by the sole of a shoe because it would be small enough to fit into the leather cracks. Moreover, if the piece of debris came into direct contact with a flat sole, it would simply be pushed further into the mudbrick surface. Conversely, larger objects had a greater chance of breakage than small pieces (Kirkby and Kirkby 1976).

(2) An item can enter the archaeological record as a result of a subtractive technology, such as stone tool retouching that produced small-sized flakes and, because of its small size (1 to 5 mm), may well have been overlooked in cleaning efforts. As a result, the micro-debris patterning may reflect the place of manufacture (especially in the case of chipped stone), the place of storage (especially for ceramics and bones), the place of use (especially for ceramics and chipped stone), or the place of discard (especially for bones) (Table 2.5).

(3) The micro-artifact may already be present in the make-up of the floor. For example, mud taken from elsewhere on the site may unintentionally transfer artifacts and/or trash from one area of the site to another.

Type of Material	Incorporation into the Archaeological Record	Size	Post-Depositional Forces	Predicted Context
Ceramic	dropped	> 30 mm	curated or abandoned	storage room kitchen / food preparation
		15 – 30 mm	secondary trash	
		10 – 15 mm	possibly secondary trash	
		5 – 10 mm	swept or kicked into corners	
		< 5 mm	ground into earthen surface	
Bone	left over food remains butchering dead rodent tool (e.g., awl)	> 30 mm	secondary trash	hearth / food preparation animal pen
		15 – 30 mm	secondary trash	
		10 – 15 mm	possibly secondary trash	
		5 – 10 mm	swept into corners or deposited from scavenger feces	
Chipped Stone	production debitage retouched tool	> 30 mm	depleted core or discarded tool	storage room tool production area midden
		15 – 30 mm	secondary trash	
		10 – 5 mm	secondary trash	
		< 5 mm	ground into earthen surface	
Shell	deposited from the river (e.g., the dirt source for the mudbricks)			mudbricks / floors
	re-deposited from a moist area such as a midden			fill / midden
	fallen from an animal skin that was used for carrying water			kitchen / outdoors

Table 2.5. Model for the deposition and preservation of micro-debris.

Ethnoarchaeological Case Study of Micro-Debris Remains: Kamalapuram, India

In 1997, while working on an archaeological survey at Vijayanagara directed by Carla Sinopoli (University of Michigan) and Kathleen Morrison (University of Chicago), I conducted an exploratory study on artifact disposal patterns in village households. In this study I collected micro-debris samples from a modern Indian village, Kamalapuram, in Karnataka. The results confirmed that sometimes micro-remains are the only source of information about certain activities. Moreover, this micro-debris can be studied to recover evidence for social distinctions, such as class or occupation, within a community (Rainville, in press). Kamalapuram contained a wide range of socio-economic classes, from the poorest "untouchables" who lived in very small lean-to shacks, to successful shopkeepers and businessmen who lived in multi-story houses. The household breadwinners in my study included a restaurant owner, a government employee, and three single women who were dependent on their extended families. I took sediment samples from the trash disposal areas of these three households to test whether I would find small objects not represented by macro-artifacts and if the micro-artifacts could tell me anything about the social or economic status of the household.

For each of the houses, I located and visually surveyed the household trash dump and noted the distribution of macro-debris such as clothes, rags, playing cards, shoes, matchbooks, food rinds or husks, dung, straw, and plastic wrapping (Figure 2.8a). Another category of macro-remains was straw and ash deposits. The straw provided food for the animals and the ash was derived from burned dung that was used as fuel. Within the trash disposal area, I cleared a 50 x 50 cm area of large debris and removed 1 kilogram of sediment to a depth of 3 cm. Finally, the earth was sifted through graduated screens as small as 1 mm. I recovered a variety of botanical matter, fabric bits, cardboard, plaster, plastic, charcoal, dung, pottery, shell, glass, bead, and the occasional piece of broken jewelry or bone (Figure 2.8b). Several of the refuse categories would not have been recovered with traditional screening methods.

From the restaurant owner's trash, I collected botanical matter that would not usually be recovered, including a whole clove, a shell from a nut, and several pieces of peanut shell. Other minuscule remains recovered by this method included a glass bead, ten pieces of eggshell, small pieces of newspaper and plastic, garlic clove skins, and threads from clothing. Small bits of the more commonly found plaster, pottery, and charcoal also occurred. In the second sample, from the employee's trash, a different selection of foods were recovered, including apple or watermelon seeds, green beans, and a small piece of bone. This was the only animal remain found among my three samples. The absence of bone may be due to vegetarianism (common in southern India), predation from animals, or the lack of resources to afford meat products. This sample also contained very small samples of plastic, rope, and thread. The third sample, from the widows' house, contained the largest number of seeds and the least amount of plaster (Table 2.6).

The micro-remains correlated with socio-economic status, dietary habits, literacy rates, and patterns of trash disposal. First, the highest density of pottery occurred in the first household. In such a small sample this was not very useful, but in a larger sample of refuse we might infer greater resources in the household that could afford to throw out larger quantities of pottery (as opposed to mending the pots) or who owned more pots. Second, the presence of garlic husks, found in each of the samples, might indicate that the households were not Brahmins, because they consumed this lower caste food product. Third, all of the samples contained a low density of paper or newspaper. Although most Kamalapuram families owned some papers, such as receipts or ownership agreements, these were saved for a long time and not found in the trash heaps. A limited number of households used and disposed of writing paper on a regular basis. In contrast, newspaper was fairly common in all trash dumps because of its function as a container for food.

Without a small screen and whole earth flots I would not have recovered many of the botanical remains. Furthermore, vegetable remains were most often consumed by animals or spread out on the fields as green fertilizer, manure, or ashes. Remnant phytoliths or carbonized macro-fragments were thus deposited far from where they were first discarded. This brief study of micro-debris is particularly useful in rural India, where most items are reused and recycled, limiting the quantity of disposed materials in the archaeological record.

A Comparison of the Spatial Distribution of Micro-Debris to Macro-Debris

After determining how the micro-debris entered the archaeological record, macro-artifact (10 to 30 mm) patterning must be compared to that of the micro-debris ($x<10$ mm) in order to develop models for activity areas. "Size unstable" remains (such as bone or shell) may be generated from the decay of larger macro-remains in secondary contexts. As a result, a model for the deposition, intentional or not, of micro-debris into the archaeological record must consider the association, or concordance relationships, between macro- and micro-remains (Sherwood et al. 1995). If micro-remains were simply the product of broken, larger remains and they always co-occurred, there would be no reason to collect the former. A bar chart of densities per sampled location at Titriş illustrates a more complex pattern: the presence of both macro- and micro-remains; the presence of macro but no micro; the presence of micro but no macro; and finally the absence of both sizes (Figure 2.8)

Micro- and macro-debris were distributed in four main patterns:

(a)

(b)

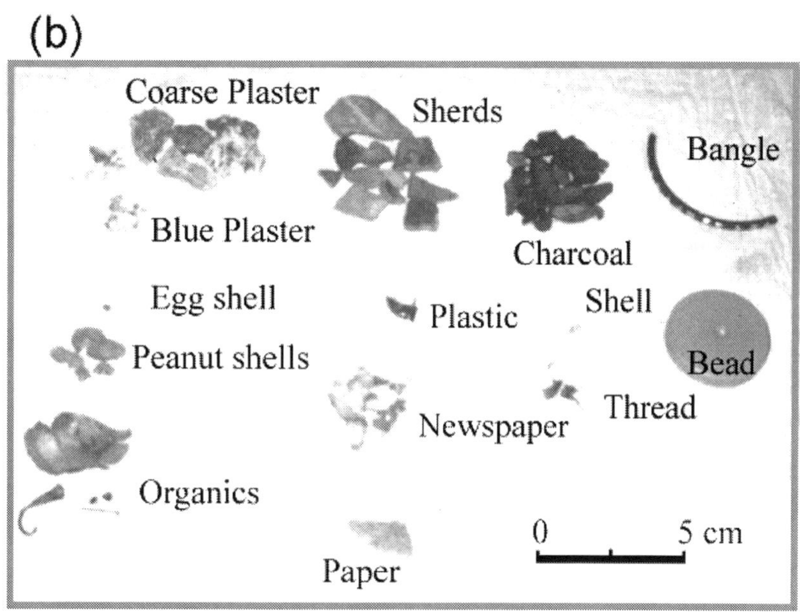

Figure 2.8. Macro- and micro-remains from a trash disposal area in an Indian village. (a) Trash disposal area and scattered macro-remains. (b) Micro-remains collected from a 5 liter sediment sample taken from (a).

		House 1	House 2	House 3
Category of Debris	*Debris Type*	*Restaurant Owner*	*Government Worker*	*Widows*
Building Materials	*Plaster, coarse*	.05	0	**.12**
	Plaster, fine	.22	**.31**	0
Kitchen Items	*Pottery*	**.1**	0	.08
	Charcoal	**.36**	.06	.12
Food Products	*Eggshell*	.07	**.14**	.04
	Peanut	.03	**.09**	0
	Garlic	.01	**.02**	.01
	Green Bean	0	**.03**	0
	Seed	0	.15	**.55**
	Bone	0	**.02**	0
Personal Adornment	*Bead*	**.01**	0	0
	Bangle	.01	**.02**	0
Recyclable Materials	*Paper*	.05	0	**.12**
	Plastic	**.03**	.02	.01
	Cardboard	0	**.06**	.01
	Glass	**.02**	0	**.02**
Miscellaneous	*Rope*	0	**.02**	0
	Thread	.04	**.08**	.02

Table 2.6. Micro-debris densities per household, Kamalapuram, India. The highest densities in each sample are highlighted in bold type.

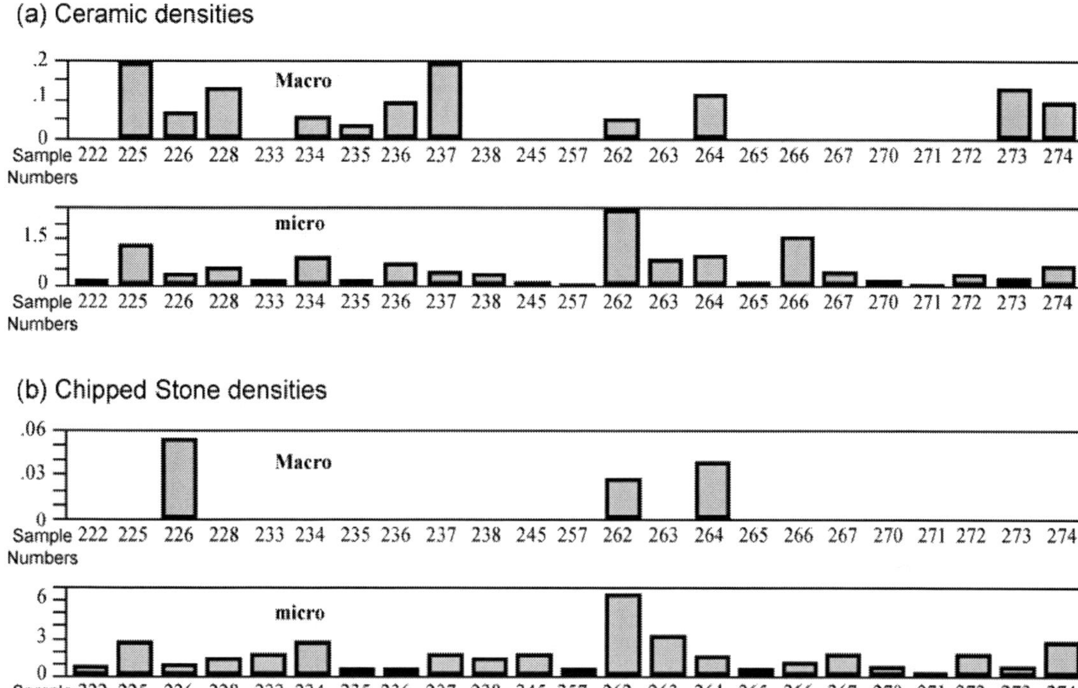

Figure 2.9. Comparison of macro- to micro-densities: ceramic and chipped stone. The samples were taken at Titriş from the 30s trenches. The vertical axis is the micro-artifact count per liter.

(1) High density of micro-debris; Low or absent macro-debris

If we subdivide the micro-debris into two size categories, we can suggest that items in the smallest category (1 to 5 mm) were rarely intentionally removed because they were too small to be seen or handled. This debris was most likely left at its original site of deposition, unless the deposit itself was removed (e.g., the construction of mudbricks out of older middens). Artifacts in the second category, 5 to 10 mm, include objects that were large enough to move through either sweeping or water transport (e.g., from washing courtyards), but that were still small enough to be trampled into mudbrick floors or swept into corners and ignored (Metcalfe and Heath 1990, Schiffer 1996). In contrast, macro-remains may be removed from floors as a result of cleaning activities, hygenic concerns, or curation when a site is abandoned. Thus, micro-debris is one of the only sources of information, beyond associated features, to inform us about the original location of activities.

(2) High density of macro-debris; Low or absent micro-debris

Conversely, the presence of macro-remains (lacking any micro-remains) often occurs in trash pits and streets. All excavators are familiar with the contents of trash pits: remains of vessels, discarded or broken tools, animal parts, and/or a variety of broken or spent artifacts. Trash pits are particularly informative when clearly associated with a specific house. In the case of communally used trash pits, the recovered artifacts are useful for the creation of ceramic typologies, chronologies, or to record the variety of subsistence resources consumed. In rare, very well excavated cases, the artifacts recovered from the various layers of the trash pit indicate the seasonality of activities and the nature of the administrative structure (Wright et al. 1980). While a trash pit may be in the same setting as the activities performed, modern ethnographic studies suggest that middens are often placed in outdoor courtyards or in nearby abandoned buildings (Kramer 1979b). Clearly such pits are not ideal for identifying activities within various rooms. It is important to realize that middens would contain some micro-artifacts, either from breakage incurred during the placement of the artifact into the midden or possibly from the decay of larger items over the centuries as post-depositional forces (such as water, acidic soil, etc.) acted upon the large remains. The larger "macro-debris" (10 to 30 mm) and the rest of the artifacts were most likely discarded in middens or disposal pits (Healan 1986), as building fill (Moholy-Nagy 1990, 1992) or in streets (Matthews et al. 1996b).

(3) High density of both micro- and macro-debris

In this study, Spearman's correlation was chosen (instead of Pearson's) because the samples were not normally distributed. To correct for this, Spearman's transforms the raw data into ranks before doing the correlation.

Among the Mesopotamian artifact types, a concordance between macro- and micro-debris occurred most often with ceramics (at a value of .38 using Spearman's correlation). The physical properties of ceramics influence this pattern. Pottery is likely to break into discrete pieces. In contrast, the bone is likely to be crushed. As a result, there was almost no correlation between macro- and micro-bones because the macro-faunal remains (10 to 30 mm) were rarely preserved *in situ*. The only contexts in which macro- and micro-lithics co-occurred were in large storage pits where tools may have been chipped or broken by improper storage or care while stacking (the two sizes correlated at a low value of .18 across the various loci).

(4) Low or absent micro- and macro-debris

I would expect low micro densities in sterile geological (as compared to cultural) deposits. To test this proposition, I collected samples from sterile soil beneath architectural levels. As expected, the control samples were very low in all cultural debris. In addition, there were no macro-artifacts in these samples. Instead, these samples had large amounts of shell, probably a background noise from the composition of the soils.

In each of the above patterns, macro (10 to 30 mm) and larger artifacts (>30 mm) were most likely to be recovered in secondary or tertiary contexts. A rare example of *in situ* macro remains is a burial with intentionally deposited grave goods.

Conclusion

Over the past several years (since this research was conducted in the late 1990s), several archaeologists have applied micro-archaeological techniques to the study of ancient activity areas (Ozbal 2000, Rainville 2001, Sherwood 2001b, Matthews 2003, Rainville 2003a and 2003b, Hodder and Cessford 2004). Taken collectively, these studies demonstrate variability in surface preparation and micro-artifact preservation and recovery. These results reveal that the causes of the micro-artifact patterns are subject to equifinality: a variety of actions and artifact pathways can produce the same end result. For example, in this study, exterior surfaces contained a much higher density of micro-chipped stone than interior ones. There are at least two explanations for this pattern. One, the patterning may reflect cleaning habits whereby a greater effort was made to clean interior surfaces due to the potential hazard from sharp micro-lithics. On the other hand, the superior outdoor light may have been preferred for tool retouching and/or production. I control for this effect by considering multiple lines of evidence and testing the micro-debris against the patterning of fixed features and architectural elements. However, some patterns will always retain more than one explanation.

Chapter 3: Archaeological Evidence for Everyday Life

In this chapter, the spatial distribution of micro-artifacts is analyzed to identify activity areas and room use. This scale of analysis, room-level activities, is usually not considered in any detail in studies of Near Eastern architecture (for notable exceptions see Franke 1987, Verhaaren 1989, Roaf 1989 and Matthews 2001 and 2003). In the research discussed here, the patterning of micro-debris within various contexts was studied to identify discrete micro-signatures. Then the results of micro-debris analysis were independently contrasted with architectural plans and fixed features. Additionally, ethnoarchaeological data from contemporaneous Anatolian and Syrian sites was used to test the rules of inference.

After the micro-debris model was tested with these multiple lines of evidence, a micro-signature was created for each locus type. Second, micro-debris analysis was applied to better identify the activities that occurred within fixed features and architecture. Third, activities within rooms were summarized, and fourth, activities among the different households were compared. Fifth, the composition of urban neighborhoods was studied. As Marcus (1983: 308) suggested (for ancient Mesoamerican city layouts), the location of houses within urban neighborhoods may reveal the household's position within a hierarchical network of political or social power. Along with the distribution of neighborhoods within the sites, the degree of town planning was examined. As Lampl (1968: 21) explained: "The city pattern develops from the house unit outward."

In sum, the levels of analysis considered in this research include:

1. Locus signatures (e.g., floors, features)
2. Activity Areas (e.g., tool production, food preparation)
3. Room Functions (e.g., kitchen, storage, craft production)
4. Households (e.g., wealthy, poor, nuclear family, extended family)
5. Neighborhoods (e.g., domestic, non-domestic, religious)
6. Sites (e.g., differences between urban and rural settlements)

These six levels of analysis were used to evaluate general propositions about activities and household organization in Near Eastern settlements. In the end, the variability of domestic architecture, household size, and distribution of craft activities was examined to determine how the arrangement of domestic space varied among Early Bronze Age cities in Upper Mesopotamia.

Mesopotamian Micro-Debris Samples

For this research, sediment samples were collected from three EBA sites in southeastern Turkey: Kazane, Titriş, and Tilbes. At each of these sites samples were taken from floor surfaces (both the fill and the direct, trampled floor surface), courtyard areas (both within the domestic compound and in publicly accessible spaces outside them), streets (cobbled and mud-packed), and more specific loci of activities, such as hearths, ovens, craft production areas, storage pits, and middens. Care was taken to collect samples away from disturbances such as rodent holes or churned sediments. For comparison, control samples were collected from non-cultural levels and from construction debris (Table 3.1).

Two Sampling Procedures: HF and LHF

Roughly one-third, 34% (n = 126), of the samples were heavy fractions previously floated using the same flotation machine. These samples were collected in earlier seasons, in 1995, 1996, and 1997, from floors, hearths, and pits for the analysis of botanical remains. Fortunately, the heavy fractions (HF) were set aside from these flotations. Many of the domestic units and debris samples were previously taken with larger block samples selected by the site supervisors, based on systematic surface collections and geophysical mapping of streets and buildings. Within these larger block excavations, flotation samples were selected from ashier floor deposits and the fill within feature in hopes of recovering more seeds, a bias that should favor less disturbed primary and secondary deposits. In these samples usually only the

(a)					
Site	**Total Number**	**Domestic Floor / Collapse**	**Exterior Domestic Surface**	**Non-Domestic Floor**	**Streets**
Kazane	n = 53	6 /4	8	17	1
Titriş	n = 276	173 / 15	18	0	20
Tilbes	n = 31	0 / 3	11	0	2
Mod. Vill.	n = 4	0	4	0	0
	n = 364	n = 179 / 22	n = 41	n = 17	n = 23

(b)					
Site	**Pit**	**Fire Installation**	**Mud-Brick**	**Burial**	**Vessel Contents**
Kazane	3	12	0	0	2
Titriş	22	11	8	5	4
Tilbes	5	2	0	5	1
	n = 30	n = 25	n = 8	n = 10	n = 7

Table 3.1. Summary of micro-debris samples. (a) Sampled from surfaces. (b) Sampled from features. In addition, two control samples were taken from sterile soil.

debris under 5 mm in dimension was saved in the heavy fraction.

The remaining two-thirds, 66%, (n = 238), of the samples were collected by the author during the 1998 and 1999 field seasons. These samples contained both the "light fraction" and "heavy fraction" (LHF), the former was set aside for analysis by the botanical specialist. I picked through the "heavy fractions" for all artifacts. Later, I separated these artifacts into "micro" (between 1 and 10 mm) and "macro" (above 30 mm) categories.

The location of the two sample types, HF and LHF, was mapped onto trench plans at one of two scales: the HF samples were mapped by room, while the LHF samples were mapped to a precise location within rooms. Table 3.2 illustrates the differences between the count density of HF and LHF samples. Note, the LHF are uniformly higher (by two or three times) in total micro-debris. When it was necessary to compare samples from the two methods, the differences were handled by using dichotomous (presence/absence) variables, by sorting the samples into quartiles (comparing the top 25% HF samples to the top 25% LHF samples), or by ranking the samples by density and then comparing the ranks instead of the raw densities.

Measurement Options

For each of the analyses presented in this and subsequent chapters, I selected which variables to study and how to measure them. The resulting statistical measurements were used to describe the distribution of micro-artifacts. Unless otherwise noted, I used the median (defined as the middle value in a distribution, above and below which lie an equal number of values), instead of the mean (defined as the value obtained by dividing the sum of a set of quantities by the number of quantities in the set), to avoid bias from statistical outliers. However, in samples with large numbers of "0" values, where the median would be "0," I used the mean to more accurately reflect the variability. Because the data were not normally distributed, non-parametric techniques were used. Accordingly, Spearman's coefficient was used for correlation analysis (Aldenderfer and Blashfield 1984).

The variables I measured included micro-count densities, micro-weight densities, macro-count densities, macro-weight densities, and micro-size distributions (e.g., the number of 1 mm pieces of debris, 2 mm pieces, etc). Most informative were the micro-count densities, since they were not so sensitive toward individual heavy objects. For example, one large piece of chipped stone might weigh 50 times that of the combined weight of 100 smaller pieces. Weight densities were used instead to measure the concentration of larger pieces of debris, especially in the 10 to 15 mm categories. Figure 3.1 displays the results obtained by plotting three different variables at each sampled location within Building Unit 4 at Titriş. Among the graphs, the micro-count and micro-weight densities shared some high concentrations (e.g., in the southwest corner of the structure), but several samples contained heavy objects while they lacked copious count concentrations (e.g., in the northeast and along the southwest border). And completely distinct from the micro-measurement results, the macro-artifacts concentrated in only one area: the southwest corner in a courtyard.

Levels of Analysis for Micro-Debris Data

Depending on the question being asked, I analyzed the micro-debris data with parametric or non-parametric techniques or visual inspection. For each analysis, a decision was made as to whether to use raw densities, ranked values, dichotomous variables, or quartiles. Each measurement has advantages and disadvantages for certain types of statistical analyses. The raw densities, although not normally distributed, allow for a fuller range of statistical tests. For example, the raw data (the density of micro-debris counts and weights divided by the total number of liters per sample) were used to calculate mean densities, standard deviations among the samples, correlation matrices, and frequency distributions. These descriptive statistics were performed in order to reveal the range, distribution, and interrelations of the debris densities.

After I transformed the data into ranks or quartiles, the data could be more easily compared among the three sites which otherwise had inherent variability in average densities (due, most likely, to variability in soil acidity, water sorting, or the length of occupation). The transformed data also enabled me to compare micro-densities among the three sites.

The different statistical measures and tests were used to evaluate data patterning at six levels: the locus, activity area, room, house, neighborhood, and intra-site.

(1) Locus Signatures

I collected samples from surfaces and features and calculated the mean density of debris by locus type. This debris density measure varied among the 15 types of loci. If micro-debris were not culturally significant, we would expect a similar density of micro-debris among locus types as background sedimental noise that would not vary by cultural feature. These results were one of the first tests of the reliability of micro-debris patterning. Correlation matrices were also used to identify associations between different types of artifacts. The results of these patterns will be discussed in Chapter 4.

(2) Activity Areas

I calculated the location and character of activity areas for the LHF samples by visually inspecting the density graphs. Areas of high or low debris concentrations suggested areas for cooking, eating, storage, craft production, animal husbandry, burial, and trash disposal. Similar types of activity areas were compared among

	Ceramic	Bone	Chipped Stone	Shell
Mean HF	0.5	2.4	2.2	0.4
Mean LHF	1.7	3.4	7.2	1.7
Median HF	0.4	1.6	1.8	0.3
Median LHF	0.8	2.5	4.0	1.2

Table 3.2. Comparison of count densities from the two sampling methods.

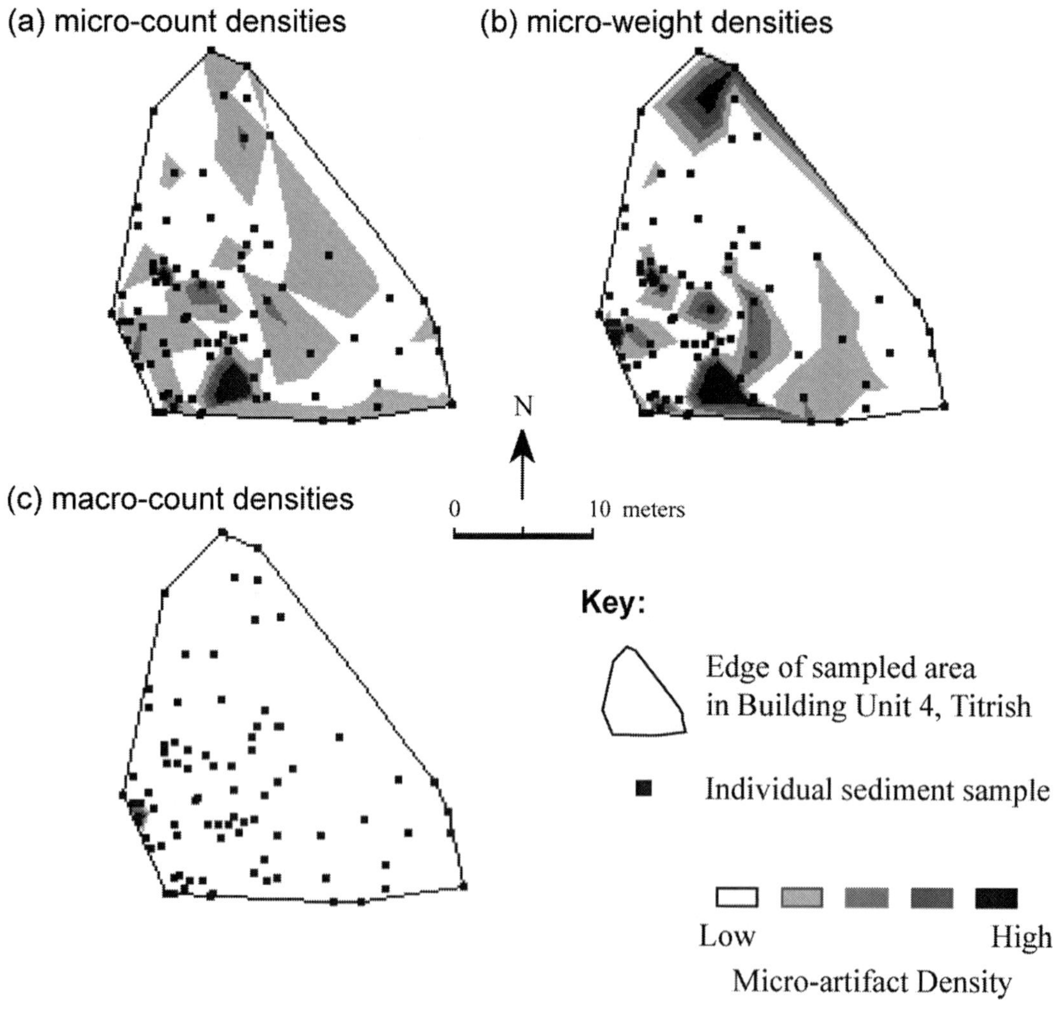

Figure 3.1. A comparison of measurement options for artifact densities. The contours represent low and high densities of micro-artifact counts per liter.

rooms to assess the relative significance of the activity within individual rooms.

(3) Room Functions

I studied ethnoarchaeological evidence, features, and architecture to suggest general room categories (such as courtyard, kitchen, storage, reception area, and private rooms). Next I applied more advanced inferential techniques. In particular I chose eight variables for discriminant analysis and used these to predict the degree of "fit" between expected room use (based on the presence of certain artifacts and features, such as hearths) and the one predicted by the discriminant model (built using the density of the various micro- and macro-remains; Huberty 1994). This modeling was an important result of my research because it suggests that micro-debris can be predictive, not simply descriptive. Unfortunately, there was an inherent bias in the construction of the discriminant model: it was weighted towards domestic and non-wealthy households. Thus the results were somewhat circular in tending to predict domestic and non-wealthy households for the identification of "gray areas" that were not easily categorized by excavators based on architecture or features alone. In the future, this method could be better applied if an effort were made to collect a larger number of samples from different house and neighborhood types.

(4) House Types

I synthesized the results of room functions and activity areas to suggest more and less wealthy households and to identify workshops, guardhouses, and public structures. I used cluster analysis to classify the structures and create homogenous groups or clusters, according to the above distinctions (Aldenderfer and Blashfield 1984, Whallon 1984). On average, five to six clear clusters of activity areas and room types emerged. These clusters were graphed and the patterning was summarized for individual houses to better understand the activities conducted by household members.

Next, I compared the house types found at Titriş and Kazane to house plans from other contemporaneous Upper Mesopotamian sites (including Brak, Bderi, Gawra, Leilan, Kurban, Chagar Bazar, and Taya). Utilizing data from other EBA sites enabled me to identify broader patterns in Upper Mesopotamian urbanism.

(5) Neighborhood Organization

I combined the levels of analysis presented above to evaluate the overall patterning of micro-artifacts at the various neighborhoods within the sites. Inherent in many models of Near Eastern urbanism is the assumption that neighborhoods were segregated by occupation or class. This remains to be fully tested. Chapter 5 is a preliminary attempt to investigate the nature and diversity of daily activities conducted within two different neighborhoods at Titriş Höyük. While not statistically significant (due to unequal and in some cases very low sample sizes from certain neighborhoods), some categories of micro-artifacts were absent from certain houses and neighborhoods. These micro patterns were combined with the presence/absence and distribution of craft activities, burial practices, size of the structures, and evidence for planning in order to analyze individual neighborhood traditions.

(6) Site Differentiation

Finally, I compared two types of third millennium communities: cities (Titriş and Kazane) and a rural village (Tilbes) in order to determine whether distinct activities occurred in each settlement type and how villages interacted with urban centers.

Ethnographic Insight into the Patterning of Daily Activity Areas

Because of potential differences between rural and urban house plans and the subsequent organization of daily activities, I conducted a brief ethnographic study of activities within a rural and urban settlement in Turkey. The rural household was located in the village of Pamuklu and the urban example was a house in the city of Urfa. Micro-debris samples were taken from the former. While neither ethnographic example is a perfect fit for ancient Tilbes (an EBA village) or ancient Kazane and Titriş (EBA regional centers), there are sufficient similarities in activities, building materials, and possibly family structure to merit investigation.

Rural Case Example: Pamuklu, a Contemporary Turkish Village

In 1998 I conducted a brief study of three village compounds in the modern village of Pamuklu (population approximately 2,000), located about 10 km from the southeastern city of Urfa. During my visit to the village, I analyzed the distribution of activities in three houses. The interviews were conducted in Turkish and English (my informant spoke some English). The villagers, however, were Arabic and Kurdish speakers. Before the rise of television, only "the village wise man" knew Turkish (an official report estimated approximately 10% of the people in Urfa province could read and write Turkish in 1960). My informant estimated that today over half the women and all the men in Pamuklu spoke Turkish.

The village contained "traditional" structures (constructed of sun-dried mudbrick) side-by-side with more recent ones constructed of concrete blocks. The village was supplied with electricity, and some families had televisions. Very few families owned cars. Most houses contained animal pens for sheep, goats, and donkeys. Most of the men were farmers; cotton and goats were particularly lucrative. Many took on additional jobs during the winter to supplement their farming income. The primary occupation of women was to care for children and their households. In contrast to their urban contemporaries, most of the women in the village still baked their own circular, flat bread, sometimes using specialized rooms for bread baking.

In this ethnoarchaeological study, spaces used for discrete activities—interior rooms, streets, ovens, courtyards, and workshops—were easy to identify (although they occasionally lacked clear boundaries). Thus the five sediment samples I collected were taken from known contexts: an oven, courtyards, an animal pen, and an informal drain that cut through the earth. Compared to the sediment samples taken from the ancient sites, the ethnoarchaeological samples contained many fewer chipped stones and ceramics (Figure 3.2). It is pretty clear that chipped stones and ceramics were less frequent because iron tools substituted for lithic ones and plastics and porcelains vessels substituted for ceramic ones. All four sites, three ancient and one modern, contained a high density of burned bone in hearths and ovens. But the ancient courtyards contained a higher density of micro-bones. The smaller number of pieces of micro-bones in the modern samples may be due to the fact that, for the most part, the cuts of meat arrived pre-processed from a village butcher or market. Because the modern villages are not abandoned, additional types of formation processes may have acted on the archaeological record and affected the size and distribution of the micro-debris. In the future, a greater diversity of modern samples would help to support interpretations of the micro-debris densities of ancient samples.

After taking the micro-samples, I recorded and mapped the distribution of architectural remains and activity areas (Figure 3.3). The results illustrate the importance of reconstruction, additions, and changes in family fortunes on domestic structures and organization. Twelve individuals, spanning three generations, lived in House 1: a father and mother, their six children (three brothers and three sisters), a spouse of one of the sons, and three grandchildren. During the summer, between April and December, the family moved 10 kilometers away to a second house to be near the agricultural fields owned by the father. In the village, the family's compound was built in three main construction phases that roughly paralleled the growth of the family and its fortunes. First, a mudbrick house (A) was built. This structure had few windows and an interior heater for the winter months. Second, in 1970, another mudbrick structure (B) was constructed with more windows. At the time I observed this structure it was whitewashed. Structure B also contained a television. More recently, a concrete house (C) was built and painted.

These three buildings surrounded a courtyard (approximately 10 x 20 meters). The courtyard contained a wooden frame for grapevines, an area of plaster debris (left over from the most recent building operations), and a surface that alternated between cobbles (10 to 30 cm in size) and baked brick. Courtyards in other Middle Eastern villages contained animal troughs, wells, and trees (Kramer 1982a: 108). Archaeologists often have difficulty in distinguishing between roofed and unroofed spaces. Micro-archaeology can help identify open-air courtyards: During the winter, rainwater pools and creates laminated silts that are observable with thin-section analysis (Rosen 1986: 113, Goldberg and Whitbread 1993). Time did not permit thin-section analysis of the ancient nor ethnographic samples, but future samples from known contexts could be sampled and would assist in the identification of ancient outdoor surfaces.

Activities conducted in the Pamuklu courtyard included bread making, grape growing, plaster mixing, and socializing. In addition, the courtyard was used to store dung (for fuel) and straw (for fodder). The sediment sample collected from the hearth in the courtyard, labeled number 57 in Figure 3.3, contained a variety of organic remains: straw, plaster, burned wood, twigs, food husks, and carbonized seeds. The sample also contained a piece of window glass, a bead, rusted metal, about 20 pieces of multi-colored thread, four pieces of blue plaster, and several pieces of colored foil (used in religious decorations). The second sample taken from the courtyard, labeled number 58 in Figure 3.3, included a large quantity of straw, nails, pieces of tape and cardboard, twigs, a candy wrapper, an orange peel, a green aluminum decoration, human hair, and several pieces of light blue paint. Both micro-samples revealed daily activities that would otherwise not be represented in the archaeological record: the use of tape, candy purchases, the consumption of fruit, remains from an impermanent religious decoration, and a past paint job (currently painted over in white).

My informant and his wife lived in House 2. They had been married for a year and did not have any children. They owned a several-month-old puppy. House 2 contained five whitewashed concrete rooms that surrounded a 10-meter long, 2-meter wide courtyard. At one end was an animal pen for the 44 goats owned by the husband; however, the animals were most often put out to pasture. Food was prepared in Rooms 2, 3, and 5, where utensils, water, and food were stored. Room 3 was also used for sleeping. The bread oven was located in Room 5, an unroofed, concrete chamber. Room 4 was used to store straw and wood. Room 1 was the more private room. The interior walls were painted blue approximately once every five years, while the exterior walls were whitewashed. The ceilings in Rooms 1, 2, and 3 were constructed using wooden beams with concrete poured on top. Overall, the construction materials used to build the house suggested that the owners were moderately wealthy. Furthermore, the house was large, compared to other ones in the village, especially considering that only two people lived there.

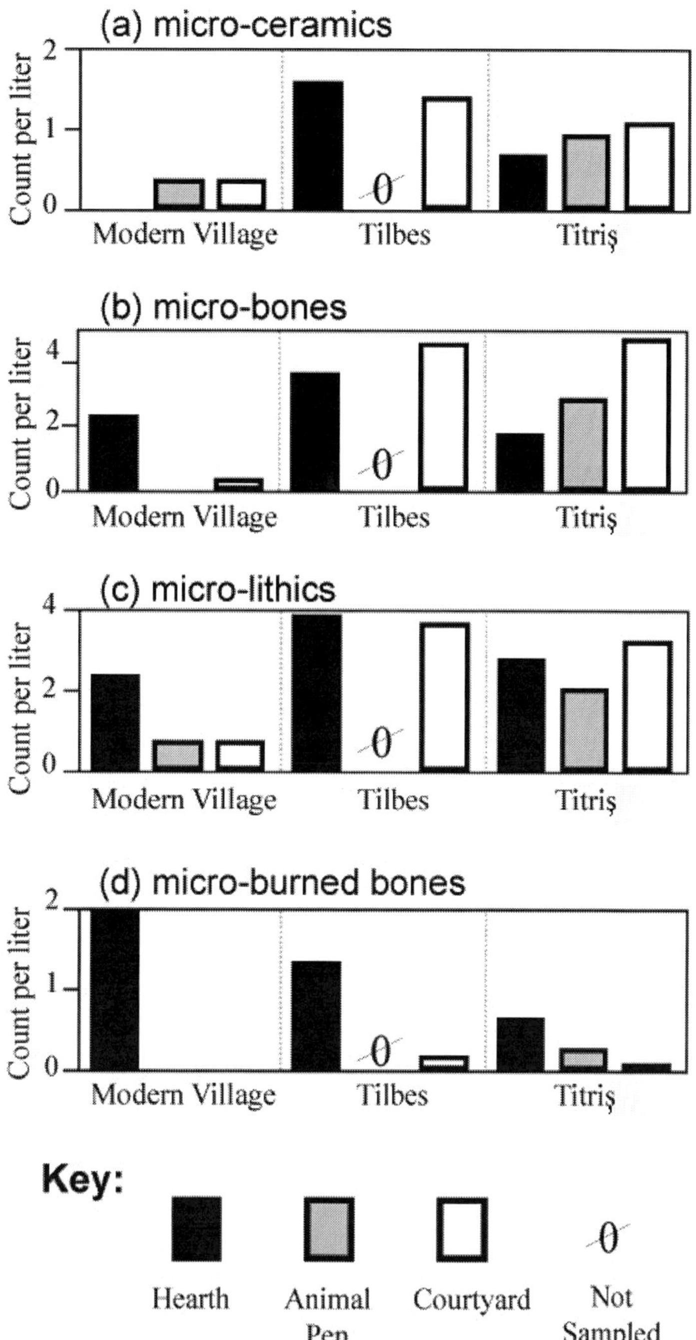

Figure 3.2. Modern micro-debris samples compared to ancient samples. Tilbes did not contain an "animal pen" hence the absence of measurements.

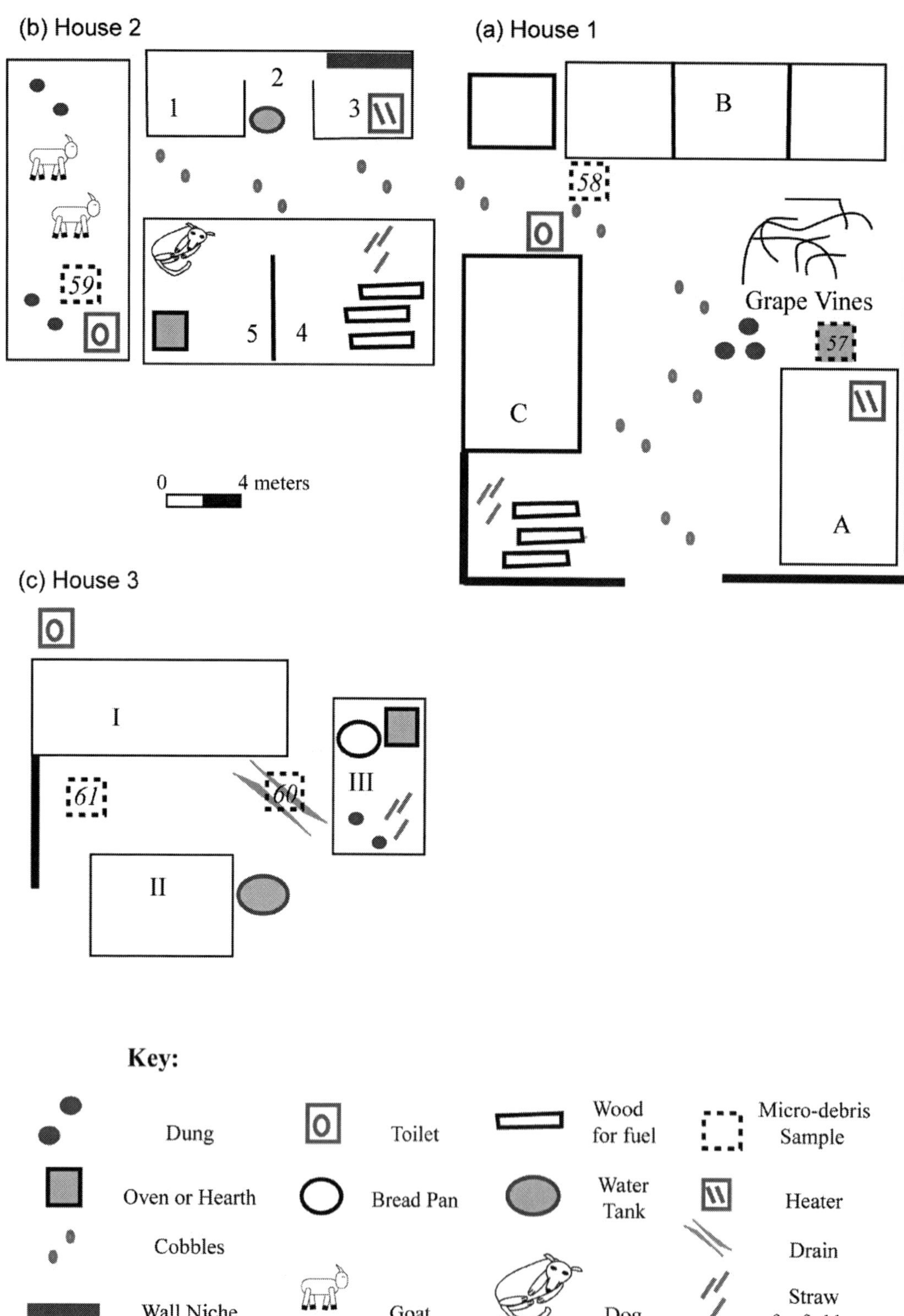

Figure 3.3. Three village compounds, Pamuklu, Turkey, C.E. 1998.

Because the courtyard was rather long and narrow (perhaps due to the fact that the house was a late addition to the village and thus squeezed into a long but narrow vacant lot), bread making and, presumably, socializing among women, occurred in Rooms 5 and 2, rather than outside. Although only one woman lived here, her relatives lived in nearby houses. Food and utensils were stored in a large wall niche in Room 3 that was covered by a hanging blanket. Dried peppers were hung across doorways, tied with thread. Clearly the five rooms were strategically built to face each other and allow for maximum privacy. This arrangement imitated courtyard plans, even though there was not sufficient space to open up the courtyard. The sediment sample, labeled number 59 in Figure 3.3, taken from the animal pen (after the initial layer of dirt containing fresh dung was scraped off) contained dung, straw, a clump of string, coarse hair, a purple sequin, four fragments of dried pepper, eggshell, a small sherd, pieces of pink paint, and a small, hard pellet that may have come from a chicken's gizzard. Because of the rich preservation of multiple items, the sample provides a window into the multiple activities that occurred in the animal pen: animals were stabled here (evidenced by the dung, straw, hair, presumably goat, and pellet), vegetables were hung to dry above the pen (perhaps evidenced by the string and the pepper fragments if they had broken off when the peppers were removed), and adjacent walls were painted pink. The sherd and sequin were probably swept into the pen while cleaning the narrow passage.

House 3 contained an extended family of at least 10 adults and children. There were several mudbrick and wood-roofed buildings, none of which were strong enough to support the weight of people for rooftop activities. The courtyard surface was very irregular in height and contained cobbles, trash accumulations, mudbrick, and a dirt drain for water running down its center. The sample labeled number 60 in Figure 3.3, taken from the courtyard, contained eggshells, pieces of thread, a stem of a dried pepper, dung, some plaster, and colored plastic. A second sample, labeled number 61 in Figure 3.3, was taken from the middle of the courtyard. It contained plastic sequins (nearby was a folk object that contained hanging threads decorated with sequins and styrofoam), pieces of pink and blue plaster, cardboard, and pieces of metal. In contrast to House 2, the inhabitants could not afford wood for their family cooking and instead used straw to start fires and burn dung. Watson (1978: 133) noted that the ability to burn wood was one indication of wealth among Iranian village households.

In sum, the micro-debris samples yielded useful evidence for daily activities. Coupled with architectural evidence, the macro and micro-artifacts provided insight into the organization and distribution of activities within village compounds. Four patterns emerged from this study.

First, the features within House 3 pointed to the limited economic resources of the household inhabitants. They could not afford to whitewash the house, own animals (other than a couple of chickens), or burn wood (instead they relied on manure). Moreover, the women in the household baked bread beyond household consumption to sell, which necessitated a relatively large room set aside for that specialized use. The bread was baked in a bread oven, or *tannur*. This Arabic word is related to the Akkadian term *tinūru* (Bottéro 1985: 39). Although the plan of House 3 resembled that of House 1 and 2, roughly a courtyard surrounded by rooms, the size (many fewer meters per person than either House 2 or 3) and building materials (mudbrick instead of concrete) were important indicators of the limited economic resources of the household. On the other hand, the glass-paned windows, concrete building, and the use of wood in House 1 suggested greater economic prosperity. Among the five micro-samples, the one taken from near Structure A in House 1 contained the highest density of micro-bones, a tantalizing suggestion that the household consumed more meat than the others did.

Second, my ethnographic observations suggested that several daily activities occurred in unroofed or outdoor areas, including animal husbandry, bread baking, socializing, and grape growing (see Kramer 1982a, Simms 1988: 204-205). Note, in a city, the grape growing might be restricted to urban gardens, instead of within houses. Because multiple activities were conducted in outdoor courtyards, the identification and analysis of outdoor or unroofed areas in the archaeological record is crucial. Conversely, interior rooms were used primarily to store kitchen implements, carpets, and clothes.

Third, my work confirms a set of signatures for bread making in Anatolia. Areas of bread making included walled rooms (perhaps erected because of safety concerns with young children and animals running loose or to give greater privacy to the women baking the bread), ovens, fuels (such as straw, animal dung, or wood), and convex circular bread pans made of iron. At the micro-level, fragments of burned wood, animal manure (identified by a greater proportion of wild plant seeds to domestic crops), and phytoliths (Matthews and Postgate 1994: 193-4) can identify these areas.

Fourth, the study identified gender-segregated areas. Each house contained at least one room that was primarily used by women: in House 1, structure B; in House 2, Room 3; and in House 3, Room III. While none of these rooms contained locked doors or, in the case of Houses 2 and 3, doors at all, it was clear that village customs restricted access to these rooms. My informant was related to the women in House 3, otherwise he would not have been allowed into the room. At the micro-level, this division would be unclear because the colored sequins and colored threads, found primarily on women's clothing, were distributed throughout the courtyard, rather than limited to one or two rooms, as a result of trash disposal patterns. However, the remains of women's labor, bread making, would be clearly observable with micro-archaeological techniques.

In short, detailed analyses of the distribution of activities within houses provided evidence for social and gender differentiation within the community.

Urban Case Example: Urfa, a Contemporary Turkish City

Although many ethnographic studies exist which describe life in modern Middle Eastern villages, there are very few ethnoarchaeological studies of houses within urban communities. Unfortunately, this results in the erroneous application of models derived from observations of modern village life to interpretations of daily activities in ancient cities. Important distinctions exist between modern villages and ancient cities. For example, ancient Titriş and Kazane contained contiguous houses, not the individual compounds that are found in modern villages. Perhaps most importantly, from an archaeological perspective, urban houses are much more likely to contain two or more stories. In order to investigate these differences between rural and urban houses, I studied a several-centuries' old house in modern-day Urfa.

Urfa is located in southeastern Turkey, just north of Aleppo, Syria, on an important trade route. Urfa was called Ruhua by the Assyrians, Edessa by the Romans, and Diyar-i Mudar by the Arabs (Ören 1997). In the 20th Century, Urfa was renamed Sanlıurfa or "glorious Urfa." In 1990, the population was over one million people, a six-fold increase from the 1914 population of 165,000 (Ören 1997). Located in the foothills, the climate includes high diurnal and seasonal temperature differences. Prior to the establishment of the Turkish Republic in 1923, Urfa contains a wide variety of ethnic groups. Today the inhabitants are primarily Muslim. As a result of population increase and, most recently, the relocation of rural populations into the city due to dam constructions, modern high-rise apartment buildings have been built, and many traditional, courtyard-style houses have been converted to fit the needs of the modern inhabitants. My brief ethnographic discussion focused on a more traditional house.

I observed architectural forms and daily activities in a house shared by a Kurdish family and a team of archaeologists. The house was built around 1780 and is now referred to by the Turks as "Alman Evi," translated as "the house of the German" (Wright, personal communication 1999). Although purchased and refurbished by German archaeologists in the 1980s, the original distribution of rooms around a courtyard remains. A small annex was added to the house at one point, which houses a Kurdish family of five (Figure 3.4). Based on several visits to other Kurdish houses, I concluded that the house size and attributes of the annex were fairly typical of a lower-middle class family in Urfa. The Kurdish house is contrasted to the larger and more expensive Alman Evi.

Because the house was constructed centuries ago, it is less influenced by European designs in architecture or by modern conveniences (such as indoor plumbing or toilets) than modern structures. The contemporary owners added each of these conveniences, but their awkward placement identifies them as later additions: one toilet is located in the very center of the courtyard and the other is under a stairway. The courtyard plan found at ancient Titriş is very similar to this more modern house (e.g., one row of rooms grouped around a central, unroofed courtyard). In the modern structure, there was a second floor, and, in addition, the roof was used for sleeping during the summer. Similar to Woolley's observations at the ancient site of Ur (Woolley 1929: 127), the ground floor of the Alman Evi contained storerooms and a kitchen. The storerooms were slightly subterranean, subsequently very cool, and, for the most part, lacked windows. By building thick stone walls, high ceilings, and a large open courtyard, the house was designed to be cool in the summer and warm in the winter. Moreover, several trees (one in a concrete planter and the others in old gas cans) and a fountain in the center of the courtyard point to the attempt to create a microclimate within the house, slightly cooler and moister than the environs.

The current furnishing in the rooms of the Alman Evi have been supplied by the archaeological team to accommodate work needs: tables, chairs, computers, bed frames, a refrigerator, and a German washing machine. The furnishings from the much smaller house next door, inhabited by the Kurdish family, more accurately reflect the furnishings of a lower-middle class house in Urfa. Most of the furnishings consisted of rugs, pillows, blankets, with only the occasional chair, chest, wooden cradle, table, or formal bed. In Egypt, one historian has suggested that "the role played by wooden furniture in European houses was taken [in modern Cairo] by textiles" (Hourani 1991: 127). If true for ancient Mesopotamian houses this is unfortunate because very few textiles have been preserved in the archaeological record.

In contrast to the large Alman Evi, the annex contained few rooms. In the small open courtyard (immediately accessible from the street, unlike the privacy afforded by the narrow hallway in the Alman Evi), food preparation, eating, and playing occurred (the children also spilled into the streets to play). A small narrow room near the stairs was used for food and clothes storage. The entrance into the main living room was also used to store clothes and, for the moment, a baby cradle. The very small kitchen was packed with a gas stove, refrigerator, and a small cabinet. The lack of working space resulted in the use of the open courtyard for food preparation. Guests were entertained in the living room and, at night, the family slept in it (the roof was not large enough for

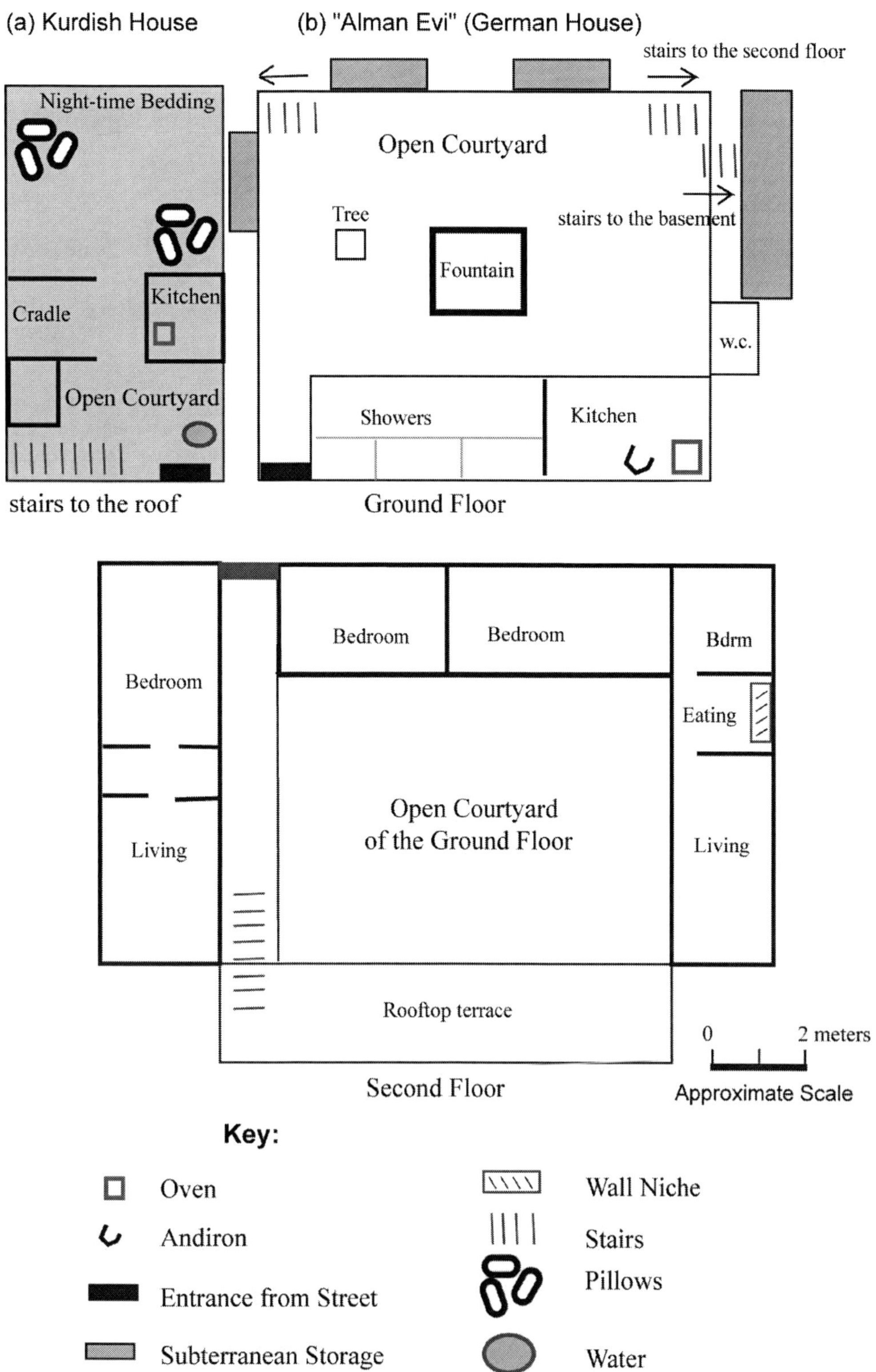

Figure 3.4. City house, Urfa, Turkey, C.E. 1999. German archaeologists own the large, two-story house on the right (b), while a Kurdish family lives in the adjacent and much smaller one-story house highlighted in light gray (a). Both households utilize the rooftop for storage, water tanks, and sleeping during the summer months.

clothes drying and food drying (e.g., red and green peppers). In sum, activities were more likely to overlap within the rooms in the smaller structure, and there was less opportunity to segregate men and women (for example, the presence of only one living room, instead of multiple ones). Although I collected no micro-debris samples from these structures, they do provide a useful illustration of the range of variation that can exist in urban contexts. Moreover, the structures and organization of activities are distinct from that of modern villages, as evidenced by the presence of a second story (some village compounds have two stories, but in the urban context this is the rule, not the exception), the increased architectural efforts to provide privacy in an otherwise crowded urban setting, and the organization of structures off narrow alleys.

Identifying Activity Areas with Micro-Debris

As discussed in Chapter 1, the domestic structure, or house, is often recognizable by certain artifacts (grinding stones, utilitarian pottery, cookware, and features (hearths and mudbrick walls constructed on stone foundations). In contrast, identifying specific household membership and activities is more difficult. Crawford (1991: 103) explains:

> The private houses tell us relatively little about the everyday life of the people who lived in them. They have few distinctive features and, generally speaking, are poor in small finds. This is not because the people who lived in them were poor and unsophisticated, but because objects tended to be reused until they fell apart and furniture and fittings were not widely used.

Thus identifying activity areas is the first step in assessing the degree of economic specialization and the nature of social relations within EBA households.

Until recently, chemical analysis of soils has been the most common method used to determine past activity areas. For example, Middleton and Price (1996) compared samples from a modern earthen house floor to an ancient one from Oaxaca to test whether activity areas could be distinguished on the basis of chemical characteristics of soils. Using inductively coupled plasma-atomic emission spectroscopy for various elements, they identified areas of burning (evidenced by phosphorous and potassium) and enclosed spaces (that contained high levels of calcium and strontium) (Middleton and Price 1996: 679). Similarly, Manzanilla (1996) recovered traces of past activities by chemically analyzing stucco floors within a household compound at Teotihuacan, Mexico. In addition, she mapped the distribution of pollen, phytoliths, and micro-botanical and faunal remains within households. From these data, she and her colleagues determined levels of craft specialization between households, differential patterning of high-status items, and the distribution of ritual areas within a courtyard (Manzanilla and Barba 1990).

In addition to chemical studies, micro-debris analysis is ideally suited for identifying past activity areas. As discussed earlier, micro-debris had a far greater chance than macro-remains of remaining in or near the original site of a past activity. The earliest application of micro-debris research to activity area identification was in analyses of Paleolithic and Neolithic cave deposits (Goldberg 1987, Courty et al. 1991). Only a handful of studies exist for later Near Eastern sites (Rosen 1986, 1989, Matthews 1992, 1995, Özbal 2000, Rainville 2001, 2003a, 2003b, in press).

Three promising studies demonstrate the utility of this approach. (1) Working at the Iron Age site of Tel Miqne-Ekron in Israel, Rosen analyzed micro-debris found on and within occupational surfaces in order to document past activities and the location of food-preparation areas, flint-knapping stations, and storage facilities. (2) Matthews' research at Abu Salabikh (a mid-third millennium B.C.E site) has added to our knowledge of urban life. One of her more interesting discoveries was the identification of possible mat or rug locations that she and her colleagues described as "strongly layered lenses of articulated phytoliths and occasionally charred remains or sediments preserving a void pattern suggestive of decayed matting" (Matthews and Postgate 1994: 190). In one room, the combined presence of a "rug signature" and the absence of any debris (including microscopic traces) supported the excavators' interpretation that the room may have been a sanctuary (Matthews and Postgate 1994: 197). (3) On-going work at Çatal Höyük demonstrates the significant contributions that micro-debris analysis can make to the identification and interpretation of activity areas (Matthews et al. 1996; micro-archaeological excavation reports posted on-line at the Çatal Höyük website, http://catal.arch.cam.ac.uk/catal/catal.html). In addition to analyzing the variable construction and composition of house floors (varying by plaster quality, the amount of plant remains, the presence of red ochre, and charred wood), Matthews and her team uncovered two categories of activity areas: domestic-related deposits and cleaner deposits (possibly associated with rituals) (Matthews et al. 1996: 325). In some cases these categories of activities, domestic and ritual, can be observed from room-to-room within a structure and, temporally, from level-to-level within a structure.

In addition to Matthews' micro-morphological work, other team members at Çatal have been analyzing heavy fractions from house floor samples (Cessford 2003, Hodder and Cessford 2004). Hodder and Cessford (2004: 25-26) concluded that while it was problematic to conclusively distinguish the difference between micro-artifacts lying "on" floors rather than "in" floors, there were noticeable differences in artifact densities within rooms. For example, the areas nearest to ovens contained high densities of charcoal, sherds, animal bones, and obsidian debitage. In contrast, areas further away from the hearths were cleaner, plastered surfaces (Hodder and Cessford 2004: 26). The ongoing micromorphological and microarchaeological research at Çatal Höyük is an excellent example of how to test the utility of these methods and apply the results to gain a better understanding of past behavior and daily practices.

In the study presented in this book, the identification of activity areas will serve as the foundation to understanding the composition and activities of EBA households located in Upper Mesopotamia. The methods used to identify and interpret these activity areas will be discussed below.

Beyond Micro-Debris: Artifacts, Features, and Architecture

Because work at these three sites is ongoing, the analysis of artifacts is not complete. Instead, the distribution of *in situ* features (including hearths, burials, food preparation surfaces, storage pits, middens, and intact vessels) was mapped and studied. These distributions were compared to the micro-debris as an independent test of the reliability of the micro-data. Building on the premise that the built environment changes in response to the needs and daily activities, or *habitus*, of the inhabitants (Carsten and Hugh-Jones 1995, Bourdieu 1973), I examined domestic architecture using a variety of techniques. First, I categorized rooms based on their location within the structure (front, center, or rear, Henrickson 1982). Second, I counted the number of access routes in and out of the room (i.e., doorways). Third, I measured room size and sorted rooms into small, medium, or large. These results are summarized and interpreted in Chapter 5.

Conclusion

I use multiple approaches to document the activities in domestic and non-domestic units in EBA society. Currently only a few Near Eastern archaeologists analyze the activities performed within structures (e.g., Matthews et al. 1997a, Rosen 1986). Of these studies, even fewer analyze one structure in detail (for an exception, see Roaf 1989). A better understanding of the form, variability, and the distribution of domestic units is the foundation to evaluating the social, economic, and political changes that accompanied the earliest Near Eastern urbanism.

There is an additional lacuna in our knowledge of third millennium society: data on the daily activities of the elites and ordinary people. By analyzing the data from macro-remains, micro-debris, ethnoarchaeological studies, textual sources, and architectural forms, we obtain a clearer picture of the Mesopotamian social hierarchy. These multiple lines of evidence provide a rich window into households — the economic and social building blocks of ancient states. The remainder of this chapter is divided into two sections, in order of magnitude from the smaller level of analysis (micro-debris signatures at individual loci) to a larger scale (analyzing clusters of loci into micro-debris signatures associated with certain types of activity areas). These two sections present the results from the micro-debris samples taken from three Near Eastern sites to test the correlation between micro-debris patterns and evidence for everyday life.

Locus Signatures

Using macro-artifacts, features, architecture, and texts some archaeologists have attempted to identify types of domestic activities and their spatial distribution within houses. These lines of evidence produce limited results because in most cases artifacts have been removed when the site was abandoned, features are often poorly preserved, architectural modifications may not have been observed, and texts contain the wrong sort of information. As argued earlier, the study of micro-debris may provide reliable additional information about activity areas. Accordingly, the next three chapters (4, 5, and 6) summarize the contributions of micro-debris to our understanding of domestic activities and subsequent community organization at the sites of Titriş, Kazane, and Tilbes.

While most archaeologists agree on associations between features and macro-artifacts (e.g., a burial should contain skeletal remains and possibly grave goods), few archaeologists have discussed the possible associations between *micro*-artifacts and features. In this section, I discuss a variety of micro-signatures that characterize certain locus types. I sampled 14 types of loci from three sites in southeastern Turkey. A variety of locus types was examined from each site and structure and an attempt was made to sample equal numbers from each (Table 3.3). During the excavating, the loci were identified by traditional methods: a floor was distinguished from a supra-floor (defined by the site supervisors as the fill located 10 cm above the floor surface) by changes in hardness, color, and texture. Interior surfaces were distinguished from exterior ones by the locus' location within buildings and/or by water-damaged surfaces. Exterior surfaces included outdoor courtyards associated with compounds and surfaces adjacent to structures. Interior courtyards, surrounded by other rooms, were not classified as exterior surfaces, even though, in some cases, they were unroofed and thus technically "exterior." I reserved this classification for rooms or surfaces that were adjacent to, or outside, a house.

The determination of domestic versus non-domestic surfaces was determined after the structure was completely analyzed (this will be discussed in detail in Chapter 4). And finally, the excavators identified features by their physical form and contents (including macro-artifacts). Features included trash pits, storage pits, hearths, ovens, plastered circular surfaces (labeled

Locus Type	Total	Sites		
		Kazane	Tilbes	Titriş
Surfaces				
Exterior floor	19	5	6	8
Exterior supra-floor	12	1	3	8
Interior domestic floor	98	7	1	90
Interior domestic supra-floor	76	4	4	68
Non-domestic floor	23	13	0	10
Non-domestic supra-floor	17	5	0	12
Street	22	0	2	20
Features				
Hearth	23	11	2	10
Preparation Surface (DPS)	7	0	0	7
Pit	29	3	5	21
Burial	10	0	5	5
Objects				
Vessel	7	2	1	5
Mudbrick	8	0	0	8
Non-Cultural				
Control from sterile levels	2	0	2	0
	353	51	31	272

Table 3.3. Samples collected per locus type.

"domestic preparation surfaces" by the excavators and subsequently abbreviated "DPS"; Matney, Algaze, Pittman 1997: 63), and burials. In addition, two other objects were sampled: intact vessels and mudbricks.

Macro-Debris Signatures per Locus Type

Before proceeding further with micro-archaeology, we must determine what characterized the *macro*-signature (composed of artifacts over 10 mm in size). A totally different macro- and micro-locus signature might indicate that the micro-debris was disturbed, while an identical set of signatures would negate the need to do micro-debris analysis. Figure 3.5 illustrates the median *macro*-signature of artifacts over 10 mm found within the 5 to 50 liter samples, per locus type. The "macro" category is not a substitute for the final count / weight of artifacts per locus. Those calculations will be in the final reports for each site. Although many of the loci contained no macro-artifacts, streets, interior floors, and exterior surfaces contained significant amounts of large artifacts. Figure 3.6 compares the micro-ceramic signature to the macro one for the 11 locus types found within one excavated trench at Titriş Höyük. While streets, domestic preparation surfaces, and exterior supra-floors contained a large amount of both macro and micro-debris, the rest of the loci contained very few macro-artifacts. Thus the micro-variability provided unique information about the constituent parts of hearths and mudbricks. As one would expect, the control samples, taken from sterile soil, contained neither macro nor micro-debris.

Micro-Debris Signatures per Locus Type

The association, if any, between the distribution of micro-debris and the locus type must be determined before we can use micro-archaeology to identify activity areas. Accordingly, I calculated the median density of micro-artifacts per locus type to determine if different loci were identifiable by a micro-signature. One of the first indications that micro-debris densities varied with human activity, not natural causes, was the variability of medians per locus type (Figure 3.7). If the micro-debris occurred naturally (i.e., non-cultural rocks or non-contemporary scavenger bones), the debris should not vary in interpretable ways across cultural categories. For example, samples taken from intact vessels contained a very small amount of micro-ceramics. Although a macro-artifact measurement would produce the opposite result (i.e., the count or weight of the vessel itself), the micro-measurement is understandable because the only source for ceramic debris would be the crushed pieces of the vessel itself. Moreover, each of the loci contained a recognizable profile of the relative amounts of micro-

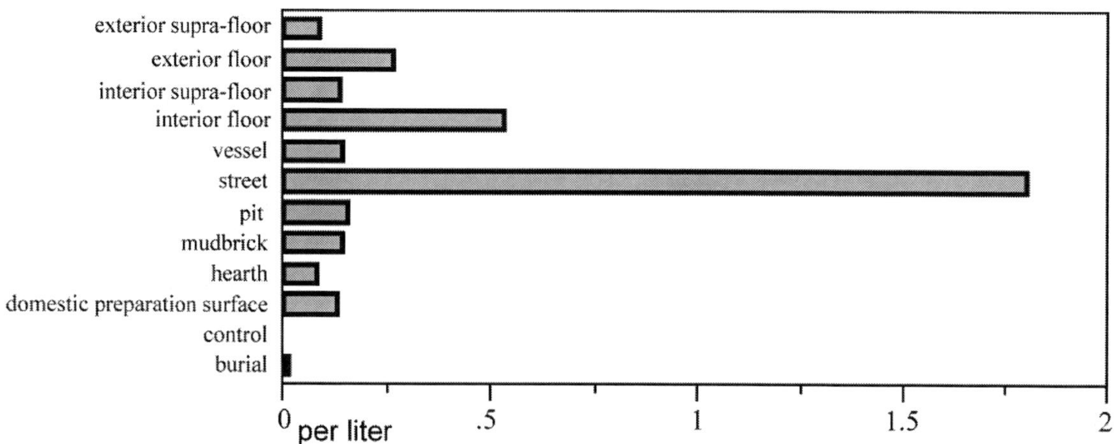

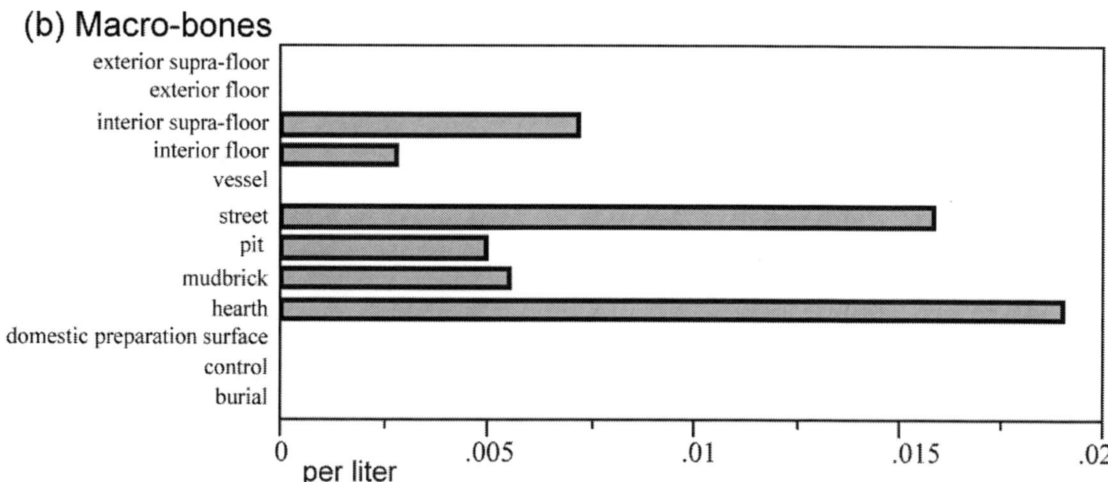

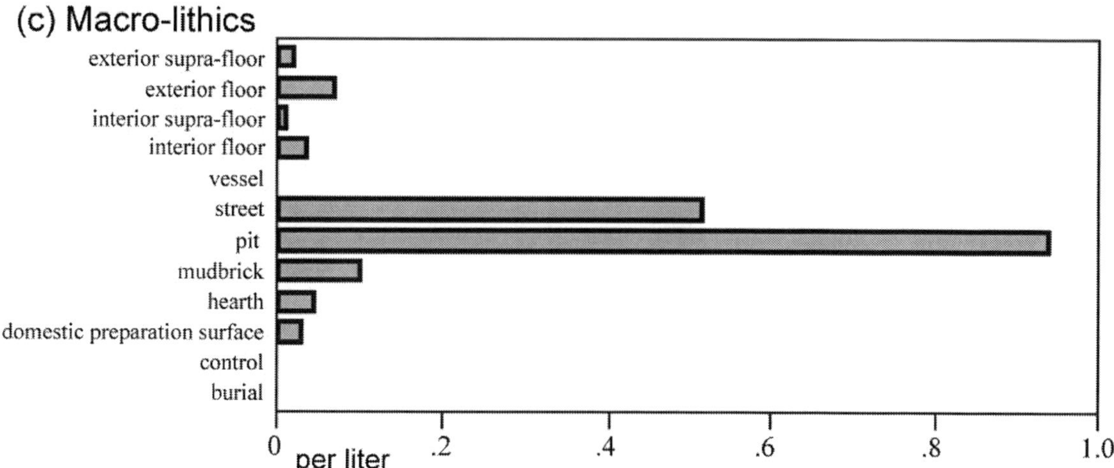

Figure 3.5. Macro-artifact densities per locus type. The abbreviation "DPS" stands for "Domestic Preparation Surface."

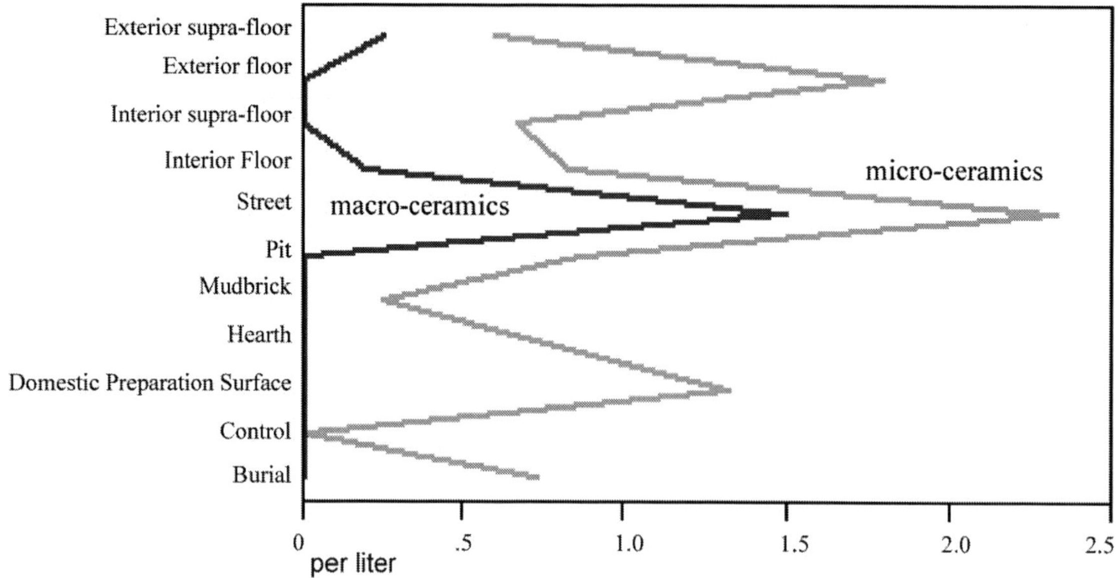

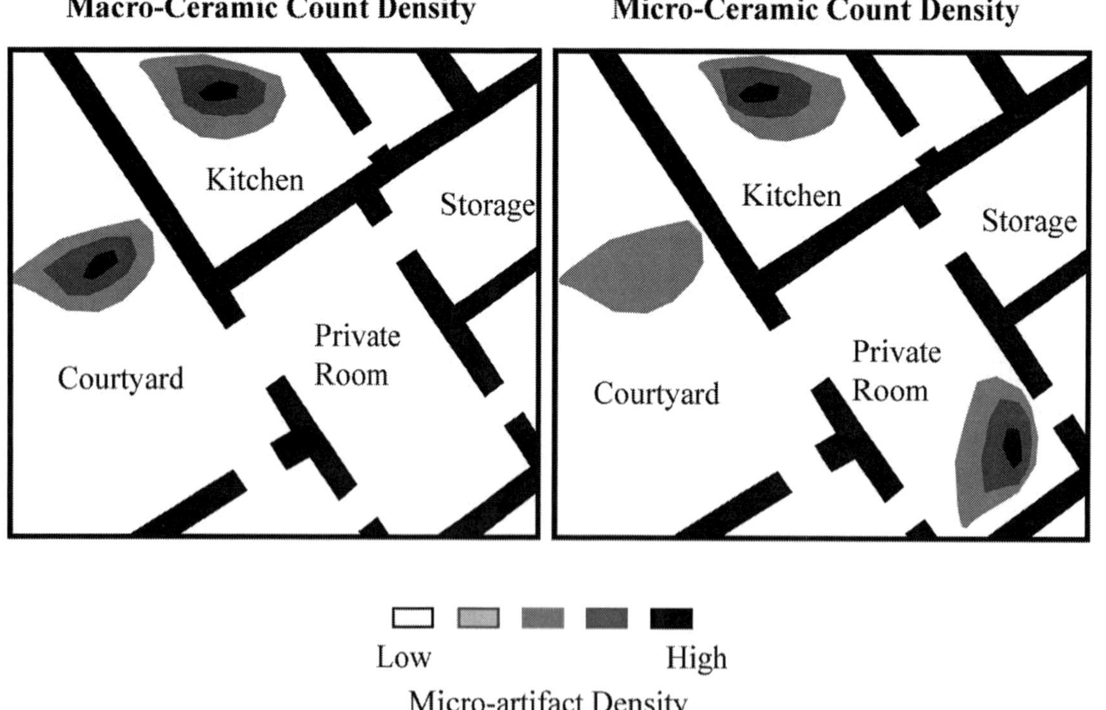

Figure 3.6. Micro- and macro-count ceramic densities within Trench 80/87, Titriş.

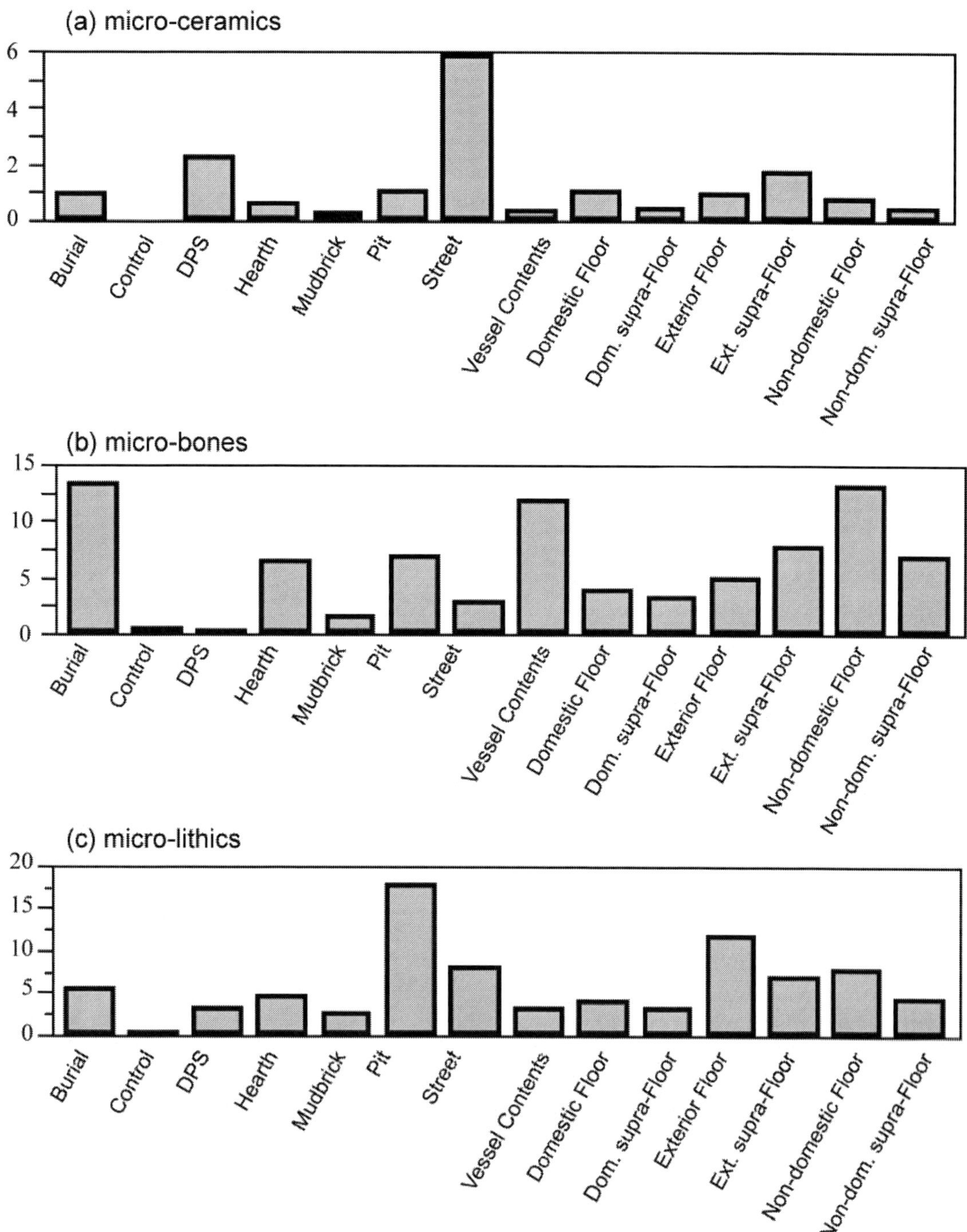

Figure 3.7. Micro-debris densities per locus type (combining samples from all three sites). The abbreviation "DPS" stands for "Domestic Preparation Surface."

pottery, bone, and lithic debris within the locus (Figure 3.8). For example, while the micro-profiles for streets and exterior floors were very similar, each of the features contained a distinct micro-profile. For example, DPSs contained high amounts of micro-chipped stones, a moderate amount of micro-ceramics, and no micro-bones, while the burials contained a high amount of micro-bones and chipped stones, with fewer pieces of ceramics.

Figure 3.7 and Figure 3.8 combine data from the three sites. This obscures potential differences among them. For example, all Kazane loci contained larger quantities of bone than identical locus types at Titriş or Tilbes. This may be caused by less acidic earth at Kazane, which allowed for better bone preservation. To correct for different preservation factors, I separated the median densities among the three sites (Figure 3.9). Although the median values changed from site to site (Table 3.4), there were recognizable patterns among the types of loci at each site (Table 3.5). Streets were uniformly high in micro-ceramics, while exterior surfaces were high in micro-lithics. More specifically (and eliminating further biases in preservation, recovery, or excavation technique), Figure 3.10 illustrates the median density of debris per locus type in one structure, Building Unit 4 at Titriş Höyük. Here the highest concentrations of micro-ceramics occurred on a circular, plastered, domestic preparation surface (DPS) and on an exterior surface. Meanwhile, small pieces of bones were highest on interior floors in hearths, burials, and exterior supra-surfaces. Finally, micro-lithics were highest in mudbricks and interior and exterior surfaces.

Explanations for these patterns, using the 273 samples from Titriş Höyük, are explored below.

Micro-ceramics

The micro-ceramic density was highest in the streets, supporting the contention that streets were used as dumping areas for broken vessels. Another possible explanation for the micro-pattern is that vessels were dropped in transit (e.g., off the backs of donkey caravans or by servants carrying food or goods in ceramic vessels). The next highest concentration of micro-ceramics was found on raised, circular preparation surfaces that were commonly found in Titriş kitchens and courtyards. These micro-sherds may have been used as a "temper" to make a hard surface. In addition, micro-debris from these surfaces exhibited a significant (.52, r < .01) correlation between chipped stone and bone. In this analysis a correlation was reported as significant if the Rho ("r") value was less than .05 and if the correlation value were over .5 (an agreed upon value in the social sciences, see Aldenderfer and Blashfield 1984).. This correlation suggested that lithic knives were used to chop meat into smaller pieces. These surfaces contained very few pieces of micro-burned-bone, suggesting that the meat was stewed or eaten raw, but not roasted. These two patterns supported the conclusion that DPSs were used for preparing food.

Conversely, construction materials (i.e., the actual mudbricks), the control samples taken from sterile soil, and domestic supra-floors were lowest in micro-ceramics. The low density of micro-ceramics in mudbricks and the control samples was to be expected if the mudbricks were made from soil collected off the site. And the supra-floors (debris 10 cm above the floor) contained layers of domestic collapse that were not compacted by foot traffic or swept, resulting in low micro-densities but high macro-densities (from discarded objects). The domestic collapse may include macro-artifacts that were left behind on pegs or hung from the roof and later fell to the ground.

The distribution of ceramic wares clarifies the interpretation of several locus signatures (Figure 3.11). While the streets were highest in sandy wares and lowest in cooking wares, the DPSs contained a large amount of both sandy and cooking wares. Of the six sampled burials, only one contained and one lacked micro-ceramics entirely. This latter burial was found in the lithic workshop at Titriş and contained four skulls, long bones, and equid remains. At the micro-level, the sediment included a large amount of micro-lithics and a moderate amount of micro-bones, presumably crushed human or equid ones. Among the other burials, the burial in Building Unit 4 at Titriş contained the largest amount of fine wares, while the two Tilbes burials, in Structure E, contained only sandy wares. This distinction in micro-ware distributions suggests that the two households were socially differentiated, supported by the quantity and quality of architectural forms at the two structures. Another explanation for the disparity in wares is a distinct rural ceramic tradition, whereby the residents preferred sandy wares.

Mapping the distribution of cooking wares per feature in one structure, Building Unit 4, verified the accuracy of the micro-debris distributions. If cooking wares were correctly identified in micro-debris samples and were associated with past human activities, the concentration of these wares should be highest in hearths and DPSs. Figure 3.12 demonstrates this pattern, with additional concentrations of cooking wares in streets (probably from trash disposal habits), domestic floors (mostly from kitchens), pits (again trash disposal or broken vessels), and hearths.

Micro-bones

At Titriş, the fill from human burials contained the largest amount of micro-bones, likely from crushed skeletons and/or intentionally disarticulated skeletons that were stuffed into ceramic vessels. Three of the burials at Titriş contained several pieces of burned micro-bone, suggesting partial cremation before burial. The second highest concentration of small fragments of bones was from exterior supra-floors. These surfaces may have been kept less clean than the interior floors. Pits also contained

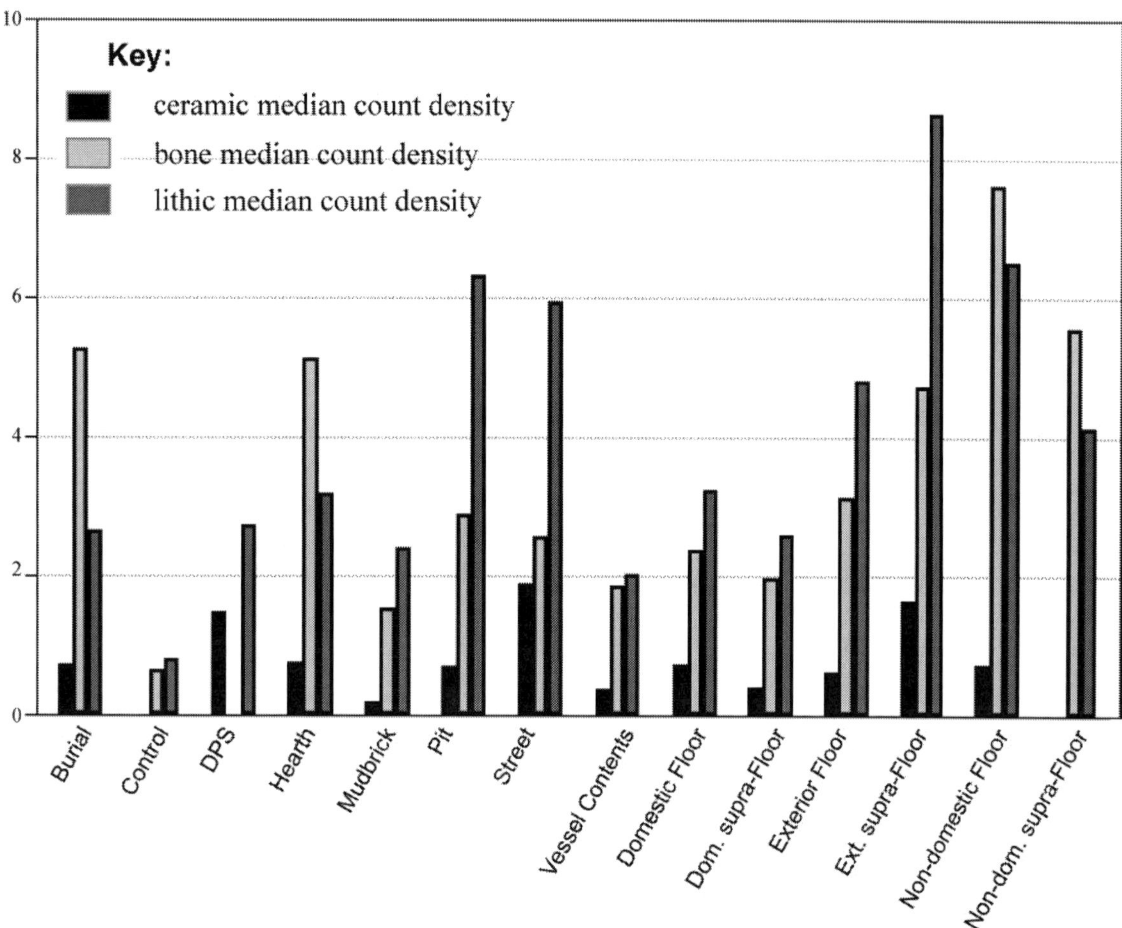

Figure 3.8. Micro-debris density profiles per locus type. The abbreviation "DPS" stands for "Domestic Preparation Surface."

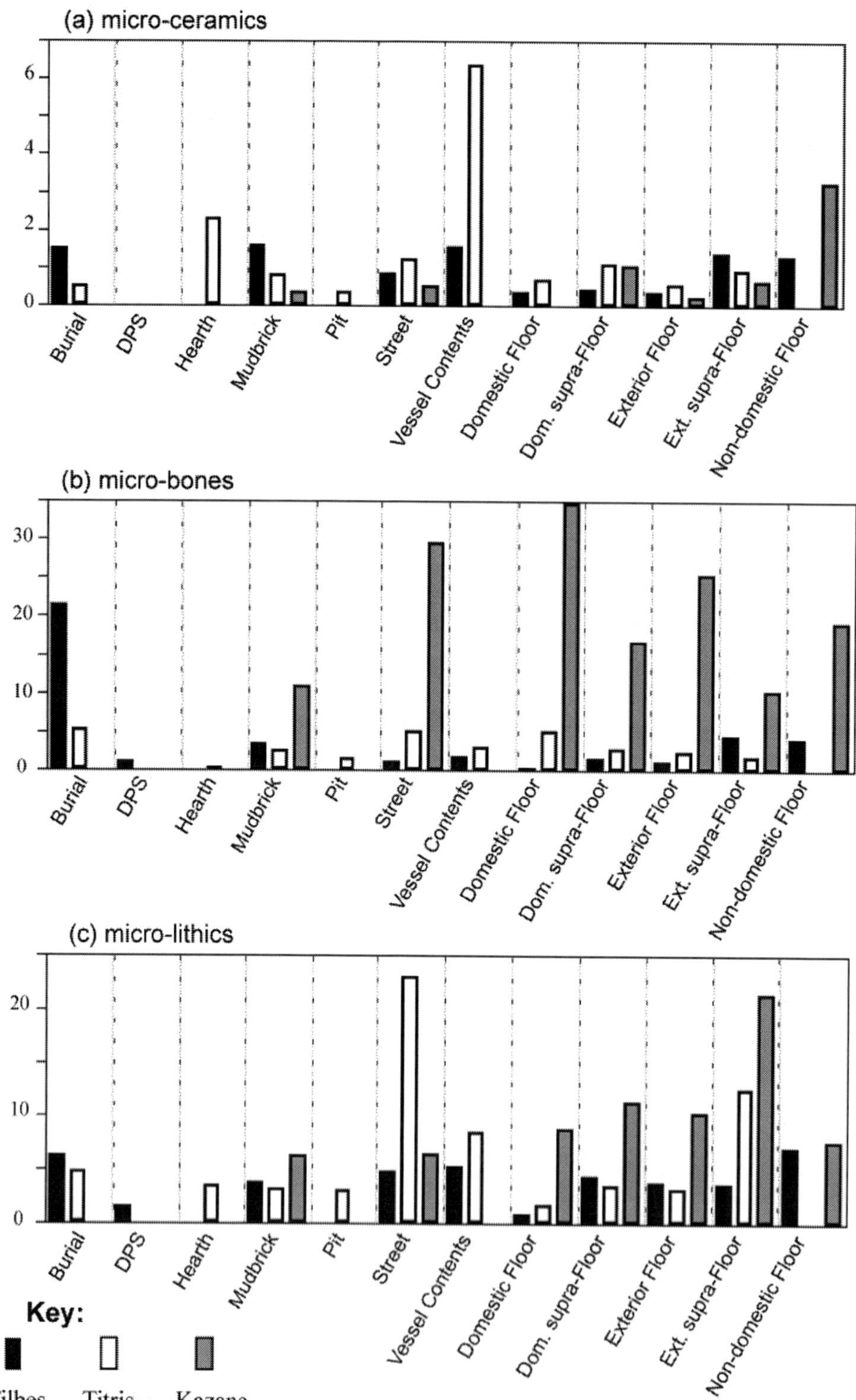

Figure 3.9. Micro-debris density per locus type at three sites. The abbreviation "DPS" stands for "Domestic Preparation Surface."

	Titriş			***Kazane***			***Tilbes***		
	ceramic	bone	lithic	ceramic	bone	lithic	ceramic	bone	lithic
Interior Floor	0.8	2.08	**2.95**	0.5	16.25	**11.5**	0.48	1.71	**4.57**
Interior supra-floor	0.39	2.0	2.55	0	21.5	7.29	0.37	1.27	3.35
Exterior Floor	0.78	2.26	0.67	0	8.0	10.6	1.05	2.49	4.50
Exterior supra-floor	.6	**3.2**	2.07	**3.3**	19.4	7.8	0	**3.47**	**9.54**
Non-domestic floor	0.75	0.67	0.75	0.5	13.33	**12.67**	n/a	n/a	n/a
Non-domestic supra-floor	n/a	n/a	n/a	0	20.0	5.5	n/a	n/a	n/a
Street	**1.9**	**2.58**	**5.96**	n/a	n/a	n/a	**1.58**	1.97	**5.39**
DPS	**1.32**	0	2.52	n/a	n/a	n/a	n/a	n/a	n/a
Mudbrick	0.21	1.56	2.41	n/a	n/a	n/a	n/a	n/a	n/a
Burial	0..73	**3.27**	2.18	n/a	n/a	n/a	**1.33**	**6.0**	4.33
Hearth	**0.81**	1.3	2.24	0.3	10.0	4.5	**1.62**	**3.68**	3.93
Pit	1.0	2.9	**6.33**	**0.62**	**33.33**	6.33	0.71	1.4	3.65
Vessel	0.66	1.49	1.78	0	**35**	9	0.4	0.6	1.0
Control	n/a	n/a	n/a	n/a	n/a	n/a	0	1.33	1.67

Table 3.4. Median micro-debris densities from three Upper Mesopotamian sites. Loci with the highest densities per micro-artifact category are in bold type. The abbreviation "n/a" indicates that the locus type was not sampled at the site.

	Highest Densities				Lowest Densities		
	Rank 1	Rank 2	Rank 3		Rank 12	Rank 13	Rank 14
Pottery	Street	DPS	≠Dom F		Vessel	Mudbrick	Control
Bone	Burial	Vessel	≠Dom F		DPS	Mudbrick	Control
Lithic	Pit	Ext F	≠Dom F		Dom F	Dom SF	Control
Shell	Control	≠Dom F	Vessel		Dom F	≠Dom SF	DPS
	"DPS"	Domestic Preparation Surface, associated with hearths and kitchens					
	"≠Dom F"	non-domestic floor					
	"≠Dom SF"	non-domestic suprafloor (10 cm above floor)					
	"Dom F"	domestic floor					
	"Dom SF"	domestic suprafloor (10 cm above floor)					
	"Ext F"	exterior surface associated with a domestic residence					
	"Control"	samples taken from sterile sediments					

Table 3.5. Micro-debris densities ranked by locus type. The samples were ranked from 1 to 14 among the locus types listed in Table 3.1.

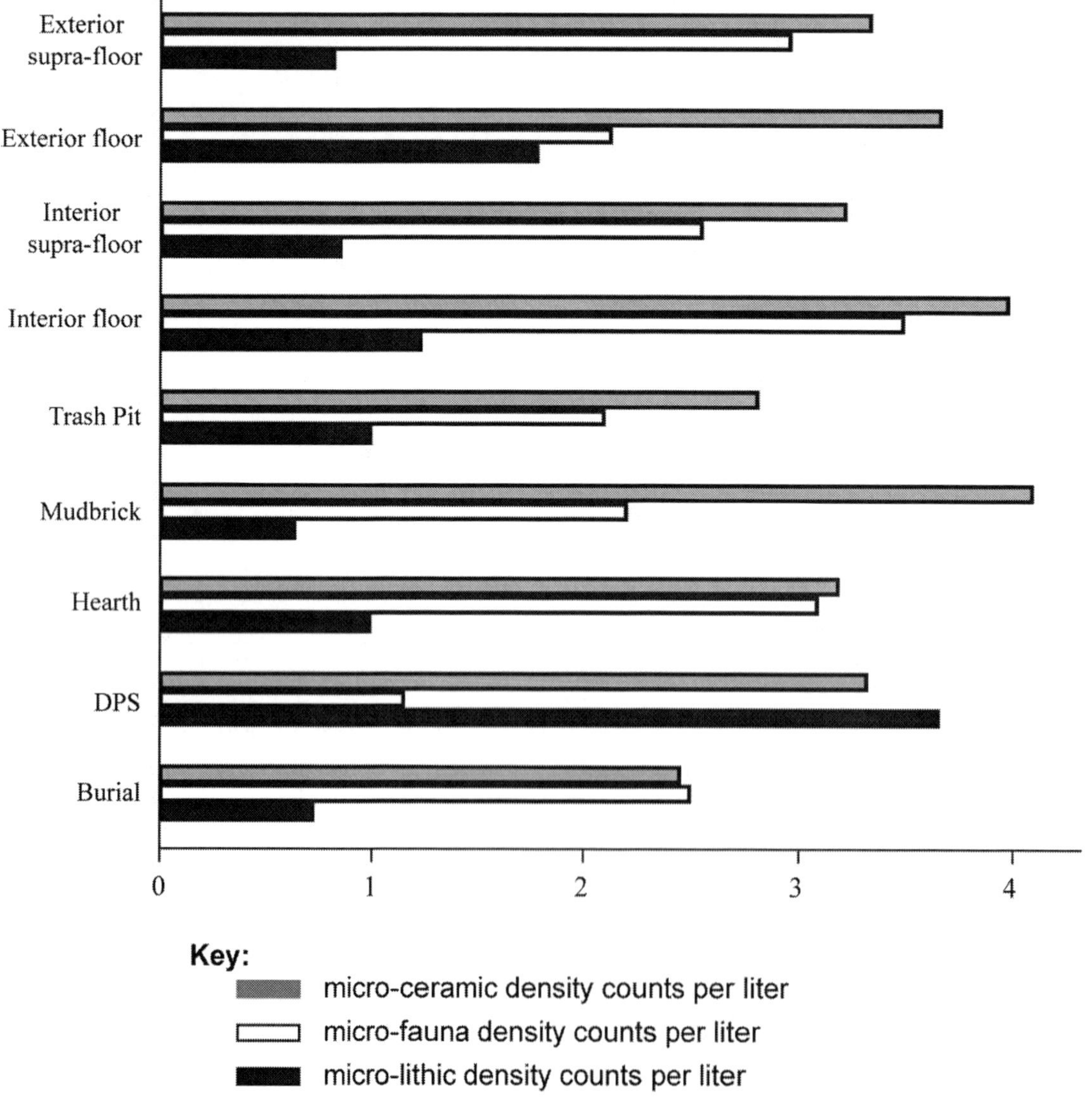

Figure 3.10. Densities per locus type in Building Unit 4, Titriş. The abbreviation "DPS" stands for "Domestic Preparation Surface." The horizontal axis indicates micro-artifact counts per liter.

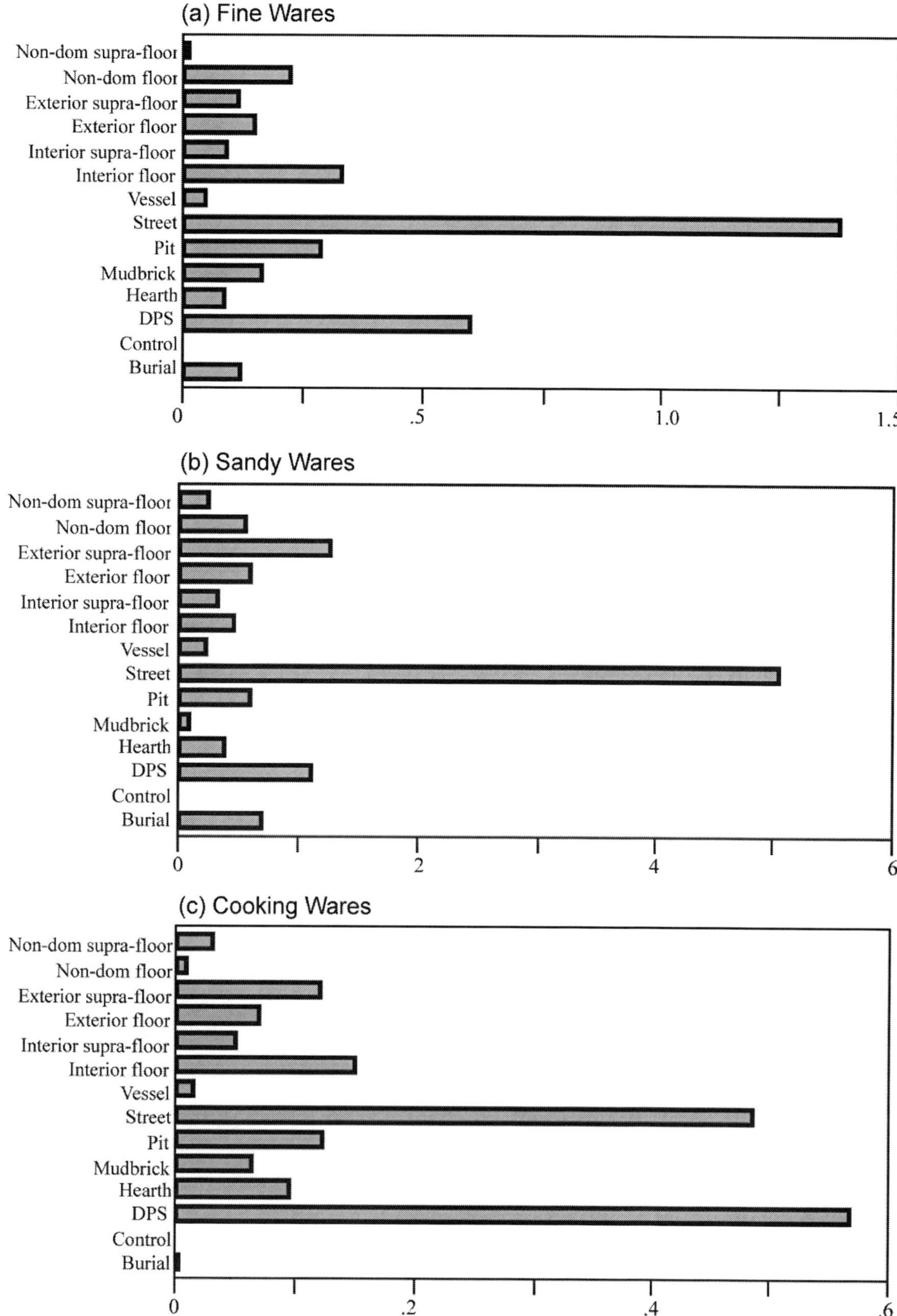

Figure 3.11. Distribution of micro-ceramic wares per locus type in Building Unit 4, Titriş. The abbreviation "DPS" stands for "Domestic Preparation Surface." The horizontal axis indicates micro-artifact counts per liter.

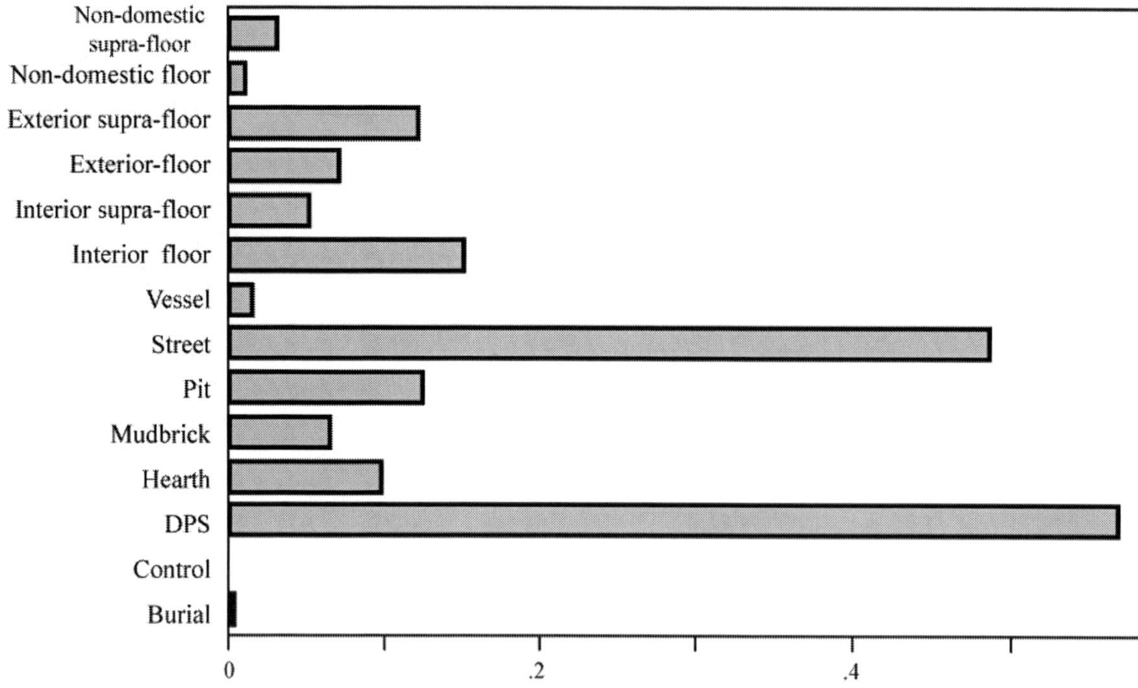

Figure 3.12. Distribution of cooking ware densities per locus type in Building Unit 4, Titriş. The abbreviation "DPS" stands for "Domestic Preparation Surface."

a large amount of micro-bones, suggesting food disposal patterns.

In contrast to these high concentrations, the lowest density of micro-bones occurred in DPSs, the control samples, and non-domestic floors. The small amount of micro-bones in DPSs and the control samples is not surprising. The DPSs were probably kept meticulously clean of food remains in order not to attract scavengers into household rooms. And the low density of bone fragments on non-domestic floors suggests that animals were not consumed or butchered in these rooms. The small pieces of bones were evenly distributed among the domestic floors, exterior surfaces, and street samples. There are at least two explanations for this pattern: either domestic dogs or other scavengers carried away and consumed the larger bones and/ or the small bones represent the remains of rats.

The distribution of burned bone provided an independent test of micro-debris reliability. Appropriately, in samples taken from two different sites, burned bone was highest in hearths (Figure 3.13). At Titriş, a secondary concentration occurred on domestic supra-floors in areas associated with meat preparation for household consumption.

Micro-chipped stones

The micro-chipped stones were highest in pits, streets, and on exterior surfaces. The low count from interior floors would suggest that extra care was taken to remove this sharp material from interior floors. Or perhaps the natural light found in outdoor work areas was preferred for flint knapping. Vessels, non-domestic floors, and the control samples contained the lowest amount of micro-lithics. Figure 3.14 distinguishes between loci from a house (Building Unit 4 at Titriş) and a lithic workshop (Core-5 at Titriş). Not surprisingly, the debitage pits at the workshop were highest in micro-lithic debris, while very low in micro-ceramics. The opposite held true for the domestic unit, where trash pits contained high amounts of micro-ceramics, but many fewer pieces of micro-lithics. In sum, while there were micro-signatures for certain locus types, the type of structure mitigated the micro-pattern.

Separating the chipped stone debris based on stone color produced interesting results. I sorted the micro-lithics into the macro-level color categories: tan, mixed tan/pink, gray, cream, and a locally available dark brown, following the categories established by the lithic specialist (Hartenberger 2003: 91-92). In addition, I identified a clear color. Obsidian occurred very rarely in the micro-debris samples and will be discussed separately in the section on house types. Table 3.6 illustrates the distribution of the chipped stone colors among the locus

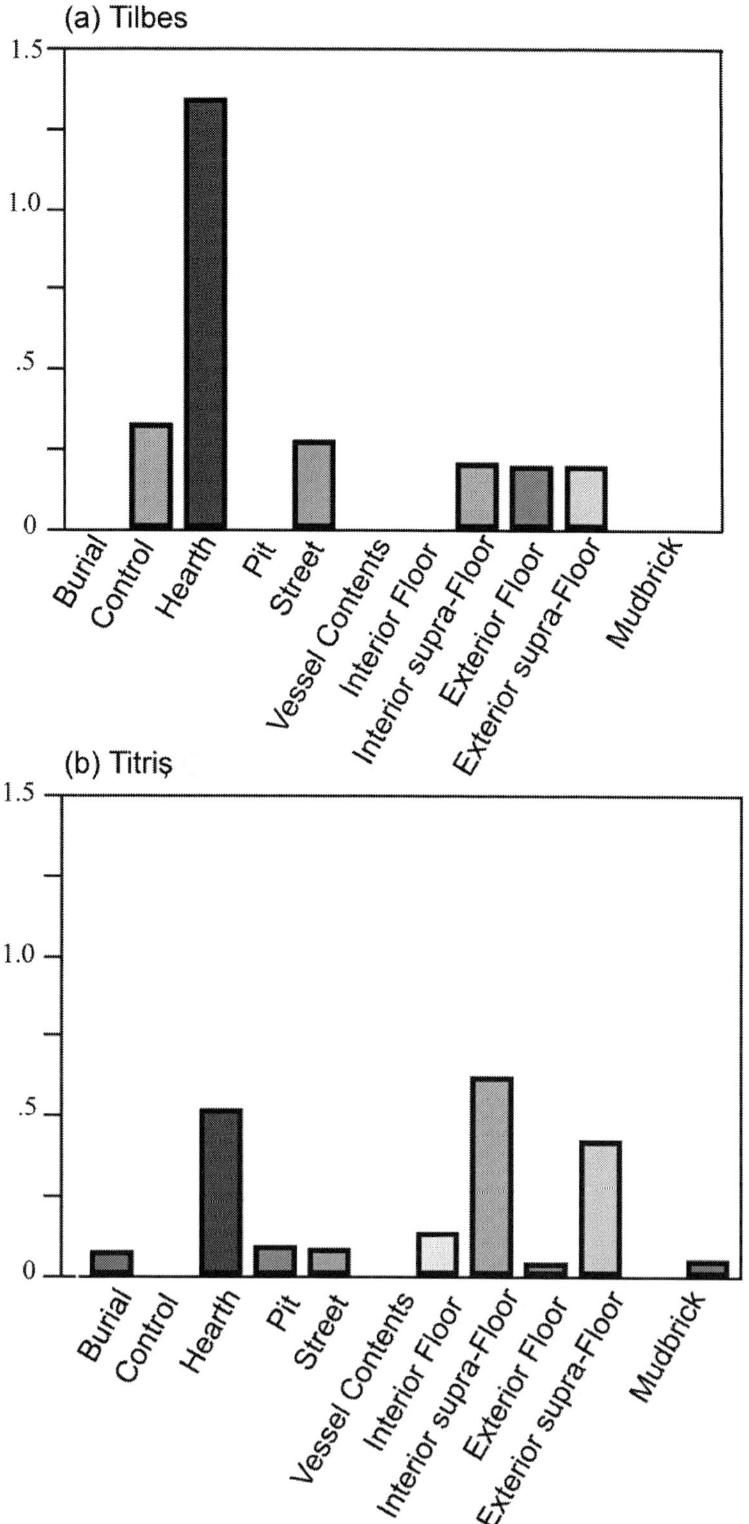

Figure 3.13. Distribution of burned bone densities per locus type at two sites.

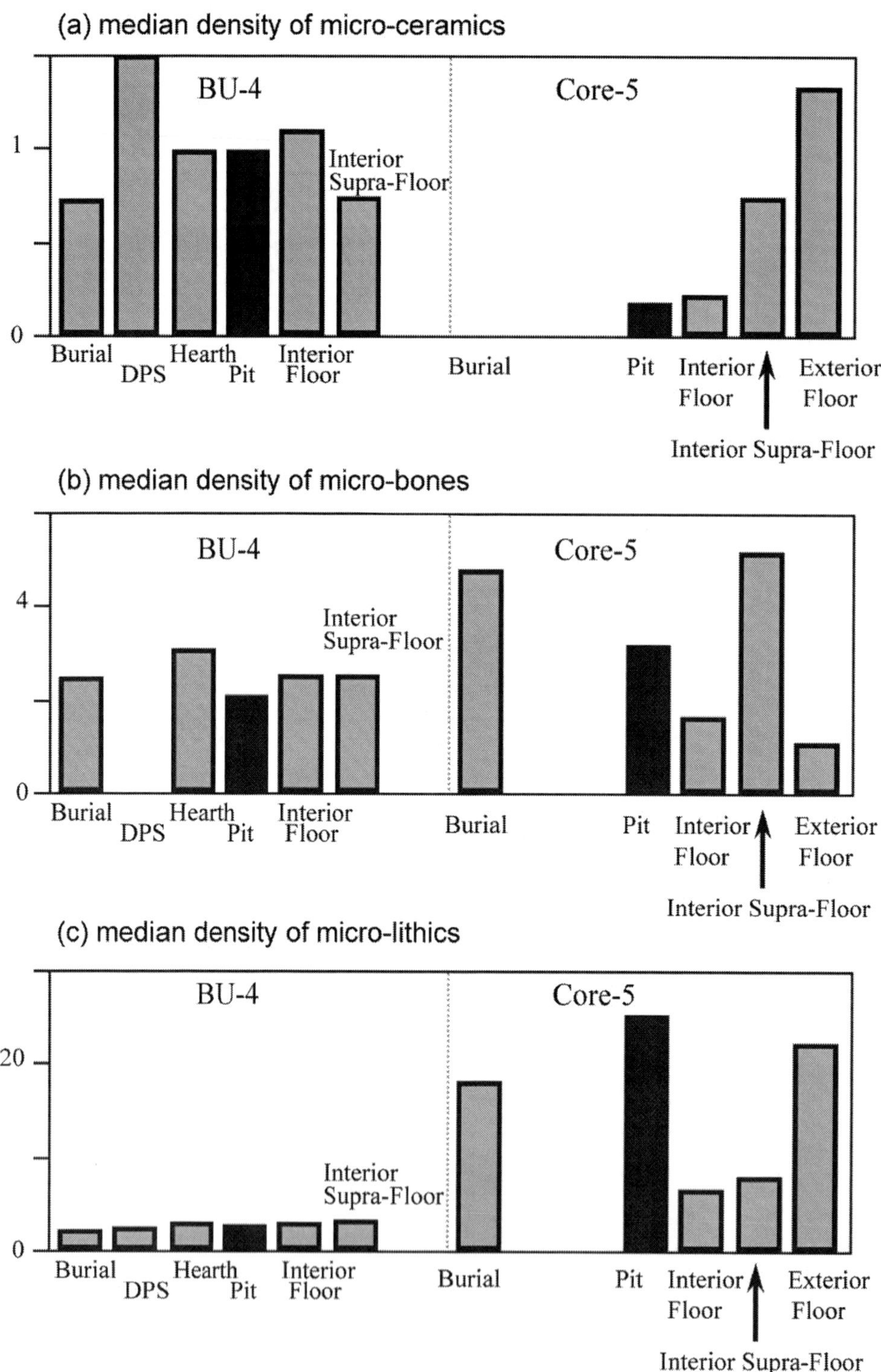

Figure 3.14. Comparison of locus types between Building Unit 4 and Core-5, Titriş.

	Among all Sites		Among Building Unit 4	
Stone Color	*Highest Density*	*Lowest Density*	*Highest Density*	*Lowest Density*
Tan	Ext F, Mudbrick, Burial, non-domestic F	Control, DPS	Rm 16 F	DPS
Gray	Ext F, Hearth	Control, DPS	Hearth, DPS	Ext F
Dark Brown	Hearth, DPS, Burial	Control, Mudbrick	DPS	Mudbrick
White	Mudbrick, Burial, Ext F, non-domestic F	Control, DPS	Storage F	Rm 23 Kitchen F
Clear	Control, Mudbrick	Hearth, Burial	Mudbrick	
Pink	DPS, Vessel, Hearth, non-domestic F	Control, Burial	DPS, Hearth	Mudbrick, Burial

	"DPS"	Domestic Preparation Surface, associated with hearths and kitchens
	"F"	floor surface
	"Ext F"	exterior surface associated with a domestic residence
	"Control"	samples taken from sterile sediments

Table 3.6. Distribution of chipped stone colors.

types from all sites and among the loci in Building Unit 4. The distribution of micro-lithics suggests that the dark brown material was used to make domestic implements, such as knives or scrapers, whereas the tan flint was preferred for agricultural tools, such as sickles. In support of this conclusion, dark brown micro-flints had the highest density in hearths, domestic courtyards, and DPSs (except the DPS in Building Unit 8, the defensive wall). All these locations were associated with food preparation or consumption. In contrast, only small numbers of dark brown flints were found in non-domestic floors and mudbricks. Conversely, trash and storage pits at the Titriş lithic workshop and mudbrick samples contained the largest amount of tan flints. The raw material collected for the 1500+ lithic cores found in the workshop was high-quality tabular or nodular tan flint. Canaanean blades were produced from these cores (Hartenberger et al. 2000: 3). An outcrop four kilometers from the site may have been the source for this raw material. Tan flint occurred in very low quantities in domestic contexts such as DPSs and a kitchen trash pit in Building Unit 4.

Patterns also existed among the other three stone colors: pink, white, and clear. Among all of the structures at Titriş, the white colored flint was highest in Building Unit 4, suggesting specialized use or a personal preference by some of the inhabitants of this large household. Within Unit 4, the highest concentration of white flint was found on floors within storage rooms, supporting the conclusion that white colored lithics were used to make a specific tool type. The pink colored flint was found almost exclusively in DPSs and hearths, suggesting a domestic tool type. It is important to note that within any given sample the high density of pink lithics never co-occurred with the high levels of dark brown flints, suggesting that the pink flints were used for distinct cutting implements. Finally, the clear-colored lithics were probably naturally occurring rocks because they were primarily found in control samples and mudbricks.

Shell

The largest quantities of shell appeared in "natural" matrices, such as the control samples and the natural deposition of sediment in an abandoned vessel. More specifically, the control was very low in *all* micro-debris except shell. In contrast, the human-constructed domestic preparation surfaces were lowest in shell, as were supra-floors from non-domestic contexts and domestic floor surfaces.

Mudbricks

When the mudbrick density was compared to other locus types, mudbricks were low in cultural debris, and moderately high in aquatic shell. This suggested that the earth for the mudbricks came from along riverbanks where snails lived or that the water used for making the bricks was brought from a river that contained snails. I sampled eight bricks at Titriş Höyük. Among the mudbricks, bone and pottery (.84, $r < .01$) and shell and chipped stone (.99, $r < .01$) co-occurred. This suggested that some of the earth for the mudbrick was taken from similar sources, such as a defunct midden, where the three types of debris might be found among household trash. This hypothesis is reinforced by the pattern illustrated in Figure 3.15: similar micro-profiles in two different mudbricks. Because the sediment samples were floated, these brick pieces must have been baked, suggesting that the builder or owner of the brick wall could afford baked brick, a sign of relative wealth.

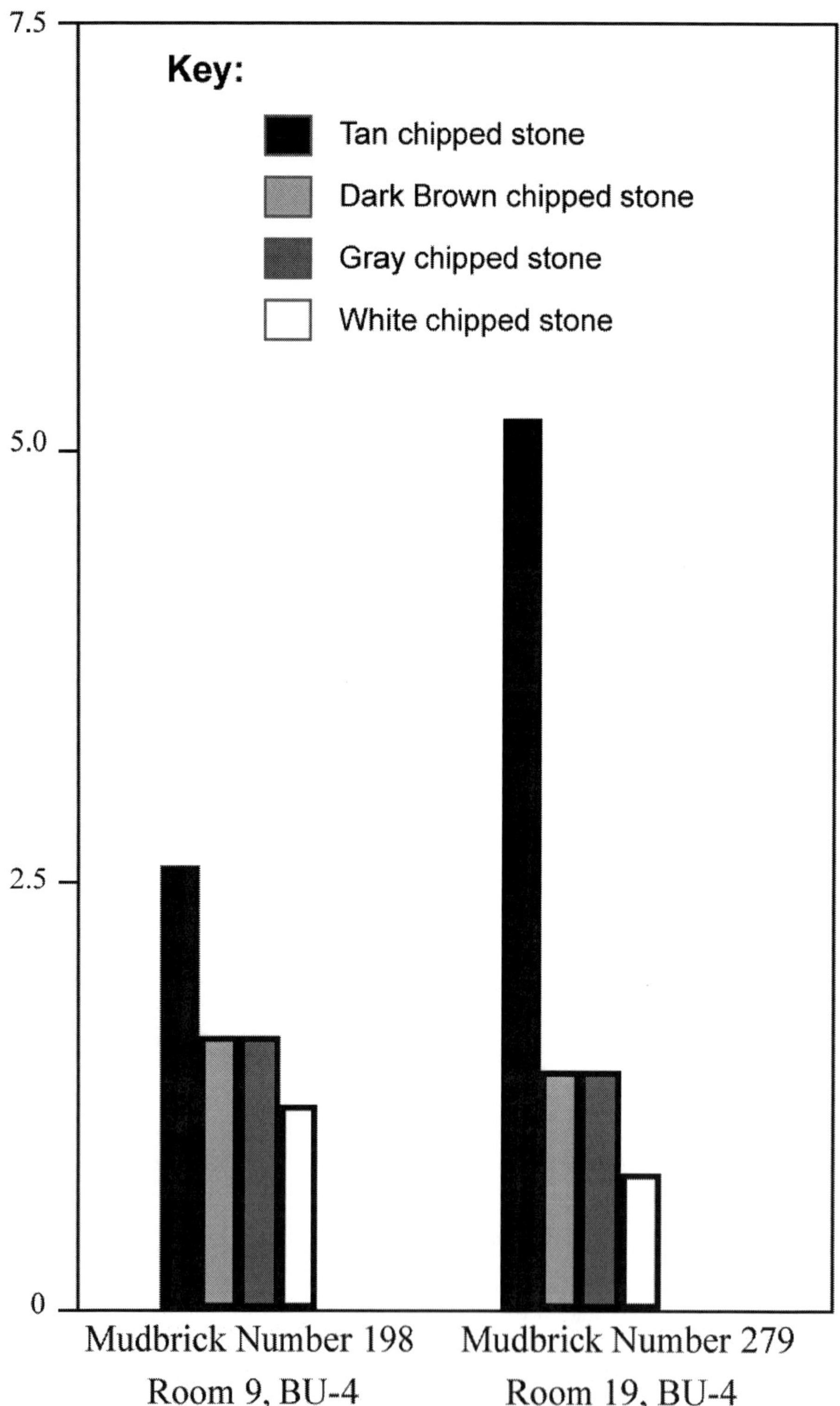

Figure 3.15. Two mudbrick profiles. "BU-4" is an abbreviation for "Building Unit 4." The pink and clear chipped stone were absent from the mudbrick samples. The vertical axis indicates the count density of micro-lithics per liter.

Figure 3.16 illustrates the micro-signature of the eight mudbricks sampled from Titriş. Each mudbrick had a large amount of micro-chipped stone pieces. An ethnographic example from a 20th Century Turkish village offers one possible scenario to explain the presence of micro-lithics in mudbricks. The lithics may have accumulated in the mudbricks from the use of straw to make the bricks stronger. Straw, in turn, was cut into small pieces using flints placed on the bottom of threshing sleds. Pierce (1964: 29) described the seasonal threshing of wheat in a Turkish village in the 1950s. A threshing sled (a piece of wood with sharp lithics embedded in its base) was dragged around a 30-foot diameter threshing floor (Figure 3.17). The villagers of the modern village at Titriş used a similar procedure, with tan tabular flint secured underneath the threshing sledge, up until the 1970s (Algaze, personal communication). The lithics, in the former case obsidian and chert, cut the straw into smaller pieces. These pieces of straw were later raked into a pile in the center of the room. While the wind blew the chaff away and left the grain behind on the floor (which was later collected and ground), the straw was swept up and either fed to animals or mixed with mud to make stronger mudbricks. This latter explanation would account for the presence of micro-lithics in the mudbricks and provides insight into the construction of the bricks.

Plaster

I estimated the quantity of white plaster per sample on a scale of absent, low, or high. Areas with higher amounts of plaster may indicate greater access to resources (Kramer 1979c: 148) or increased religious or festival observances (Boivin 2000: 370). The structures with the greatest amount of plaster (from the sediment samples) were Area C at Kazane and Building Unit 4 at Titriş; the size and quality of construction suggests that each of these structures belonged to wealthier residents. Among the room samples, rooms with burials contained the highest amount of plaster, suggesting religious rituals. In a rural Rajasthani village in modern India, floors were often replastered at annual village festivals or for special occasions such as weddings (Boivin 2000: 370). And in northeastern Iran, the replastering of interior walls occurred at the beginning of the Persian New Year, Nauruz, a symbolic day considered a time of "rebirth and refurbishing" (Horne 1994: 141). Thus the areas of high plaster at Titriş and Kazane may have correlated with either economic status or domestic rituals.

Micro-Debris Correlations among Loci

I tested the samples from the three sites for significant correlations among the three most common types of micro-debris: ceramics, bones, and lithics. First, I investigated the correlations among micro-artifacts found in features. Among all the hearths ($n = 23$), bone and chipped stone were significantly correlated (.75, $r < .01$). The bone and chipped stone probably co-occurred as a result of animal butchering or from cutting meat into smaller pieces. Since the Kazane hearths were located in a large public structure with, possibly, distinct artifact distributions, a second correlation analysis was conducted for Titriş. The hearths at Titriş ($n = 10$) displayed a high correlation between chipped stone and bone (.85, $r < .01$) and chipped stone and pottery (.66, $r < .05$). While Titriş shared the chipped stone / bone correlation with Kazane, the correlation between micro-lithics and micro-ceramics suggested that the meat was prepared in cooking vessels (i.e., stews rather than kebabs) and that serving vessels were regularly used around the hearth. We would expect micro-chipped stone and ceramics to co-occur in a domestic setting such as Building Unit 4, whereas the hearths at Kazane may have been used solely for chopping and roasting meat on skewers. Support for this interpretation comes from the distribution of ceramic wares among the hearths. Some of the hearths at Kazane lacked cooking wares, whereas the Titriş hearths contained moderate to high amounts of this ware. In sum, different sets of activities occurred at different hearths, depending on the use of the room or structure. These distinctions are difficult to observe at the macro-level because cooking pots and fine serving vessels were usually removed for from hearths for re-use when the structure was abandoned.

The micro-debris sampled from pits at Titriş and Tilbes indicated whether the pit was used for trash disposal or storage. In the lithic workshop pits ($n = 7$) at Titriş, chipped stone and bone co-occurred (.77, $r < .08$), while, in the Tilbes pits ($n = 6$), bone and pottery co-occurred (.77, $r < .08$). The two distinct correlations indicated the difference between a lithic workshop's storage pits and a domestic structure's daily trash disposal pits. The macro-chipped stone found in the workshop supported this conclusion. Based on the placement of still usable cores in concentric rings, rather than the disposal of exhausted cores in a haphazard manner, the excavator of Core-5, a lithic specialist, concluded that several of the workshop pits were used for storage (S. Rosen 1999, personal communication). When analyzed together ($n = 31$), the micro-debris from pits exhibited no significant correlations, indicating the diverse patterning of debris in these features.

The dirt within eight intact vessels was sampled. In general, the highest percent of micro-debris within the vessel was micro-bones, suggesting the final resting place of an ancient mouse or, perhaps, the residue of an ancient meal. A closer look at the vessel contents from Titriş suggested that two separate activities produced the remains. The two vessels in Building Unit 9 contained a high correlation between bone and pottery (.70, $r < .08$), while the other two, from Building Unit 4 and Building Unit 2, contained a high correlation of chipped stone to bone (.93, $r < .01$). The first two vessels were sampled from a domestic unit in the "30s neighborhood" (see Figure 5.10) and may represent meat storage in sandy-ware jars. The second two vessels, from two different

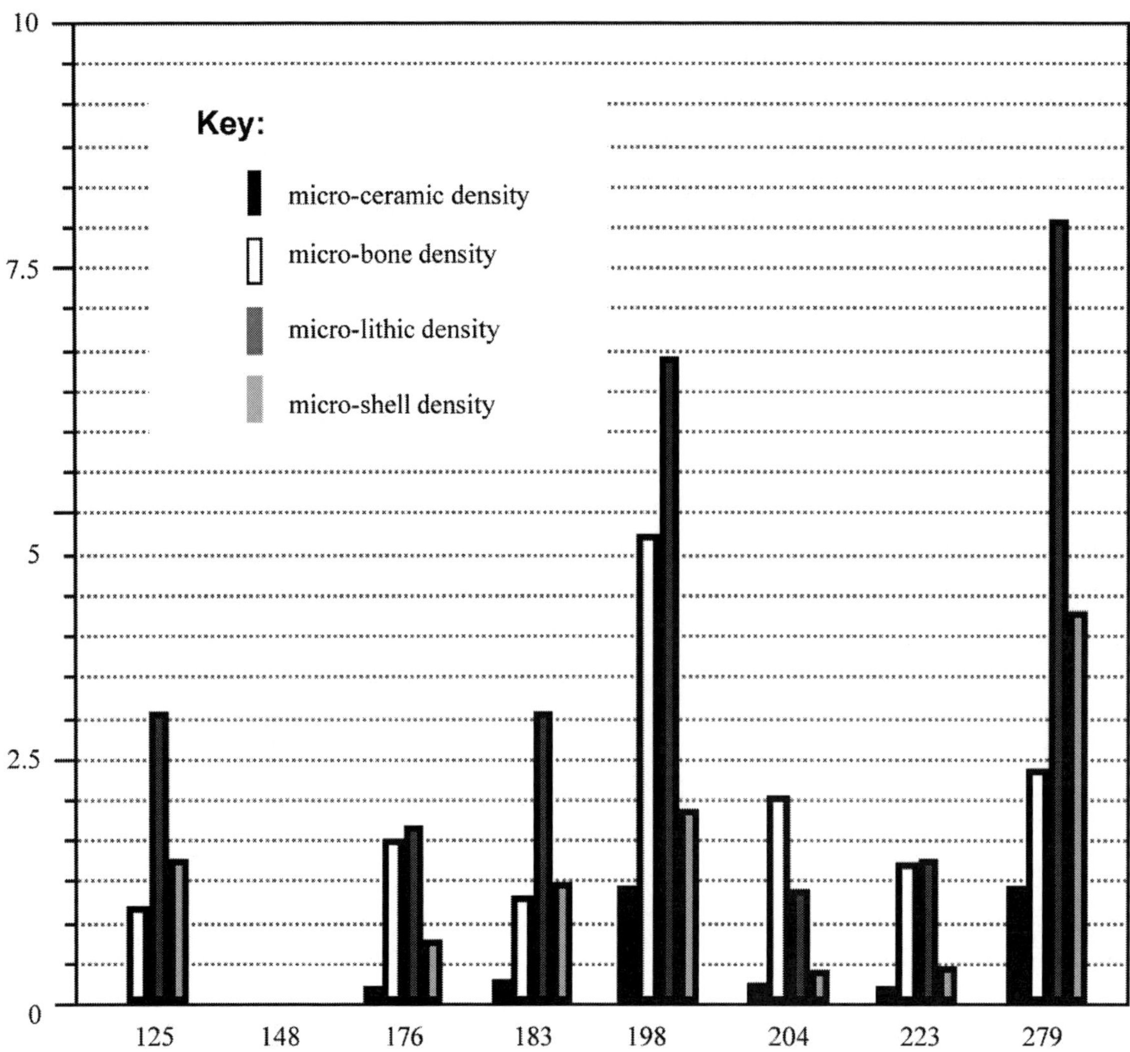

Figure 3.16. Quantity of micro-ceramics, bones, lithics, and shells per mudbrick. The vertical axis indicates the density of micro-artifact counts per liter.

(a) Threshing wheat in Qanaghistan, Iran in 1961

(b) Threshing machine used at Tell Toqaan, Syria, ca. 1954

Figure 3.17. Contemporary threshing sleds. (a) Modified from English 1966: Plate 10a. (b) Modified from Sweet 1974: 264, Figure 22; reproduced with permission from the University of Michigan, Museum of Anthropology Press.

houses in the "80s neighborhood" (see Figure 5.11), may have stored both meat and lithic tools.

To check the reliability of the above correlations, I tested the associations among micro-debris within burial fill. As expected, micro-bones (most likely human) and micro-ceramics co-occurred. This same association between human skeletal remains and ceramic grave goods occurred at the macro level.

Micro-Debris Tests

In order to test the reliability of the micro-debris samples, I compared densities from seven pits at Titriş (a – g) where two separate micro-debris samples were taken (Fig 3.18). The profiles between the two samples (separated into different rectangular boxes on Figure 3.18) were very similar. I also expected that, due to the effects of gravity, the bottom of pits would have a higher density of micro-debris. In the admittedly small sample, pit bottoms contained more ceramic and lithic debris, while the bone (the lightest material and perhaps relatively unaffected by gravity) exhibited no clear pattern (Figure 3.19).

Next I compared the median densities of supra-floor debris to floors. Contrary to the macro-remains, I expected floors to contain a higher amount of micro-debris than the collapsed levels of supra-floors. For micro-ceramics and micro-lithics this was the case (Table 3.7), but micro-bones were higher in supra-floors, suggesting contamination from subsequent burrowing animals. Supra-floors were also higher in shell, as expected from a deposit that contained natural fill deposited after the room was vacated.

Finally, micro-densities were calculated for each specific locus from one trench, Trench 80/87, at Titriş. While surface densities varied according to the type of room and the location within a room, general feature categories (such as hearths, pits, mudbrick, and burials) shared similar densities between two different loci (Figure 3.20).

Conclusion: Locus Signatures

This section demonstrated that micro-debris has patterned variability that characterizes different loci. More importantly, micro-debris provided a window into artifact variability that was unobservable at the macro level. The next section builds on the association between micro-debris and locus type and simultaneously graphs the distribution of micro-debris within rooms to try to identify specific areas of domestic activities.

Activity Areas

Decades of ethnographic research contribute to the anthropologist's understandings of everyday activities in Near Eastern households (Table 3.8). Identifying the nature of activities in discrete locations, such as individual houses, can provide insight into the type of residential group or the ethnic diversity of residents within an urban setting. Moreover, repeated sets of activities areas (such as associated cooking, sleeping, and eating areas) may reveal family units.

When left *in situ*, certain artifacts and features can help identify these ancient activity areas (Table 3.9). Unfortunately, ethnographic results demonstrate that few features permanently mark the location of past activities. For example, spinning and carding wool may be unobservable in the archaeological record: spindle whorls, rarely left *in situ*, are used to spin the wool, and the loom is often portable and leaves behind only small postholes which are quickly refilled (and only exceptionally would the loom weights be left behind and not re-used). Similarly, the area where food is consumed might be hard to recognize archaeologically: the cups and bowls from a meal might be stored in the kitchen rather than in the room where consumption occurred. Exceptions to these nomadic macro-artifacts are features such as hearths, bread ovens, drains, and large artifacts such as grinding stones or door sockets. In addition, a limited number of activities take place in marked-out areas: threshing (in packed-down threshing floors, as large as 30 feet in diameter), cooking (in ash-filled hearths or ovens), and grape processing (in large vats stained with tartar residue) (Horne 1994: 96). A further complication is the changing use of rooms depending on the time of day and the seasons (Figure 3.21).

Because of the difficulties outlined above, archaeologists rarely succeed in mapping the distribution of activities within houses. The very infrequent occurrence of a burned, but otherwise well preserved, house allowed Michael Roaf to record activity areas within a Late 'Ubaid (ca. 4500 B.C.E.) house at Tell Madhurr in northern Mesopotamia. In this rare case, although valuable items were removed, everyday household artifacts were left behind in the burned and deliberately leveled house. Abandoned artifacts included vessels, grinding stones and pestles, chipped flint tools, spindle whorls, bone tools, and burned organic remains (Roaf 1989). The distribution of these macro-artifacts, coupled with features, was used to identify activity areas throughout the rooms (Figure 3.22).

Micro-debris distributions can help to identify activity areas within unburned and mostly cleaned rooms. The location of activity areas within rooms may be determined by analyzing the locus densities discussed in the micro-signatures section and then by visual inspection of contour graphs mapping the distribution of high and low concentrations of micro-debris by individual sample. In interpreting these graphs, I evaluated several reasons for each pattern (Table 3.10).

Earlier in this chapter, I discussed the influence of sweeping on the patterning of micro-remains, suggesting that the smallest pieces of debris would accumulate in

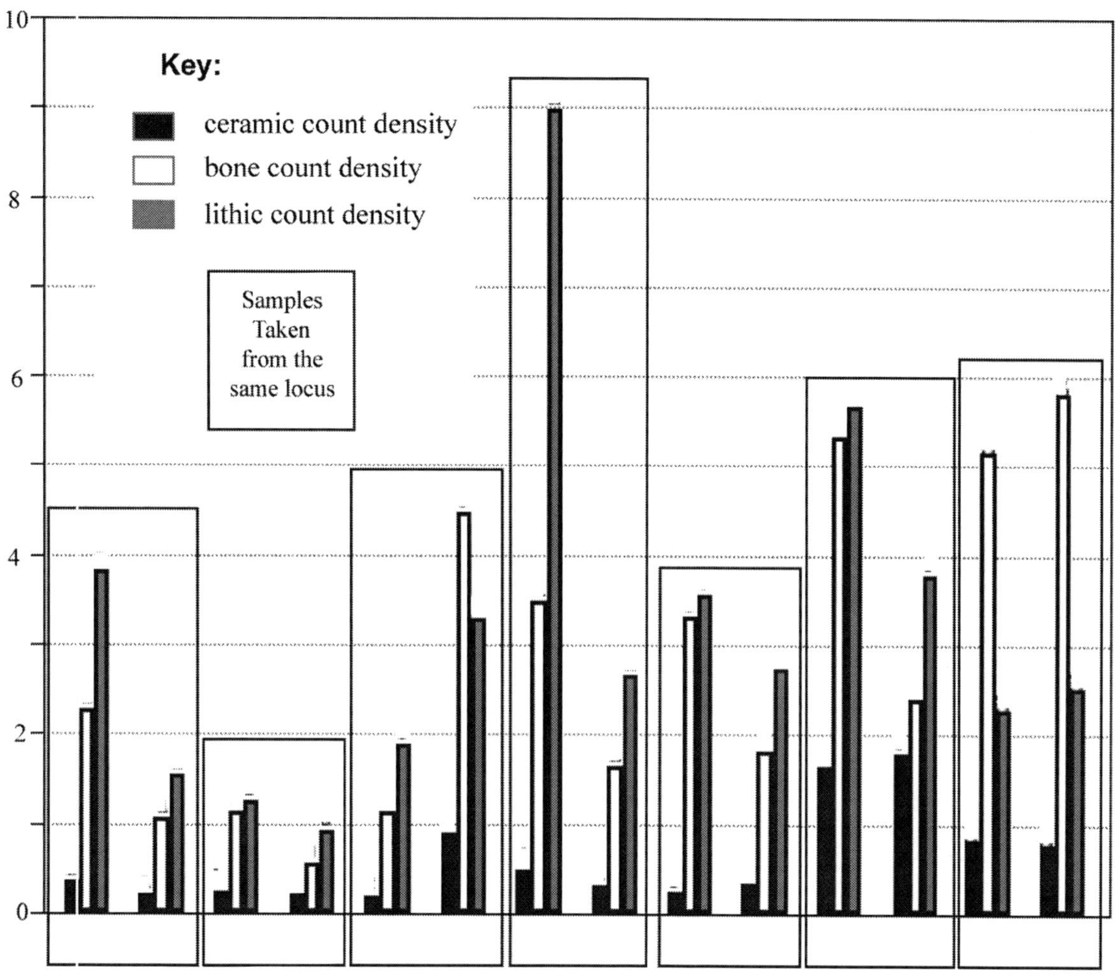

Figure 3.18. Profiles of samples taken from similar locations. The vertical axis indicates the density of micro-artifact counts per liter.

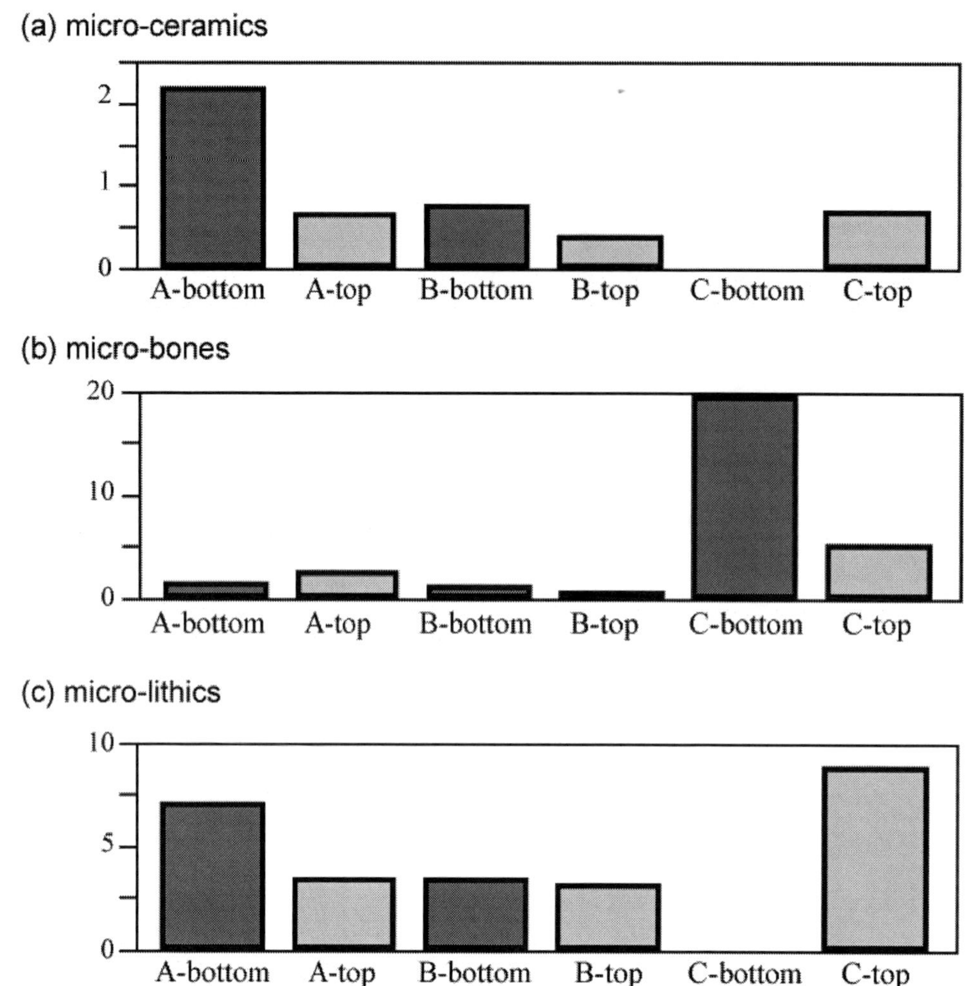

Figure 3.19. Micro-densities in pit samples. The vertical axis indicates the density of micro-artifact counts per liter.

	ceramic	bone	lithic	shell
supra-floors	0.70	3.13	3.44	2.59
floors	0.97	2.57	4.15	1.62

Table 3.7. Comparison between supra-floor and floor micro-debris densities.

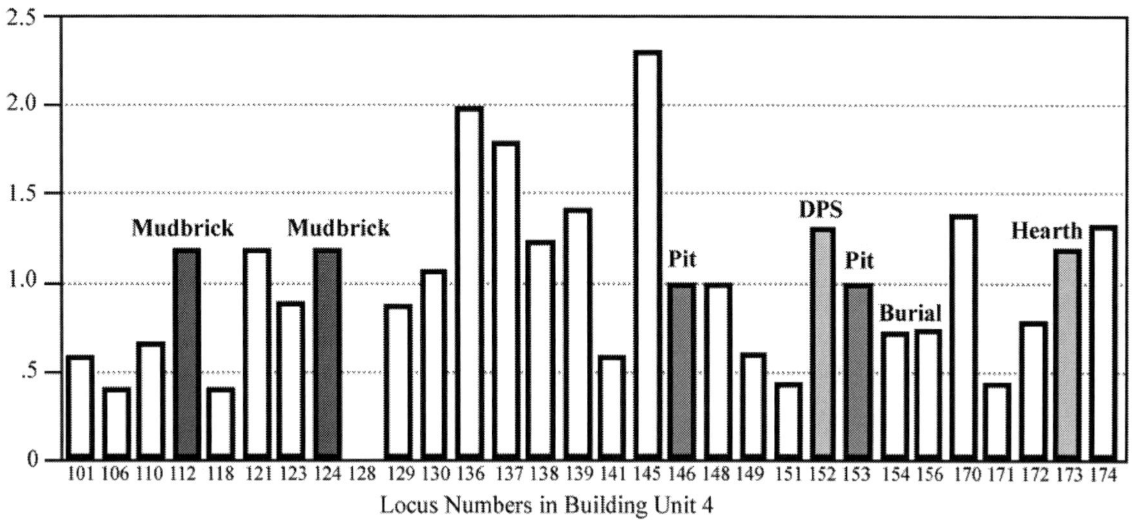

Figure 3.20. Micro-ceramics per individual locus number. The vertical axis indicates the density of micro-artifact counts per liter.

Daily Activity	Location of the Activity
• preparing food and cooking	kitchen
	exterior courtyard
note: the bread may be obtained from the local baker (*firin*)	communal oven
• making yogurt	courtyard, later stored under rugs outdoors
• eating	kitchen
	courtyard
note: men may also dine in a restaurant or tea house	reception rooms
• receiving guests	reception rooms
• socializing	men's room
	kitchen or courtyard
	streets
note: this occurs in the family or in all male / female groups	markets or tea houses
• religious rituals	separate room (chapel, shrine, etc.)
	amulets may hang on the walls
	neighborhood mosque
	cemetery
• gathering water	exterior well and stored in a room
note: the urban elites may have had water supplied by pipes	river / spring
• washing of bodies and clothing	kitchen or courtyard
	river
	separate facility (toilet / bathroom)
• sleeping	in the summer: roof
	in the winter: "living room"
• keeping domestic animals	pens or shed
	exterior courtyard

Table 3.8. Daily activities of contemporary Middle Eastern villagers. Compiled from the sources listed in Table 4.3.

Daily Activities	Features, Macro-artifacts, Ecofacts
• weaving / spinning	2 postholes in the floor
	spindle whorl
	loom weights
• cooking	oven
	hearth
	raised plaster surface
	dung cakes
• manufacturing (lithics, pottery, metalwork, etc.)	debris from subtractive technologies
• penning animals	trough
	straw (fodder)
	dung
• socializing	bench
	food remains from eating or drinking
	crockery
• storing food	bin / grain storage
	ceramic storage vessels
• storing water	waterproof container
	well / cistern
• performing biological functions	latrine (possibly indicated by green clay)
	drains or troughs
Occasional Activities	**Features, Macro-artifacts, Ecofacts**
• birth	"birthing stool" (?)
• puberty rituals	new clothing, figurines, food remains
• marriage	new house or room
• death	an abandoned house (?)

Table 3.9. Macro-signatures of ancient daily activities. Compiled from the sources listed in Table 4.3.

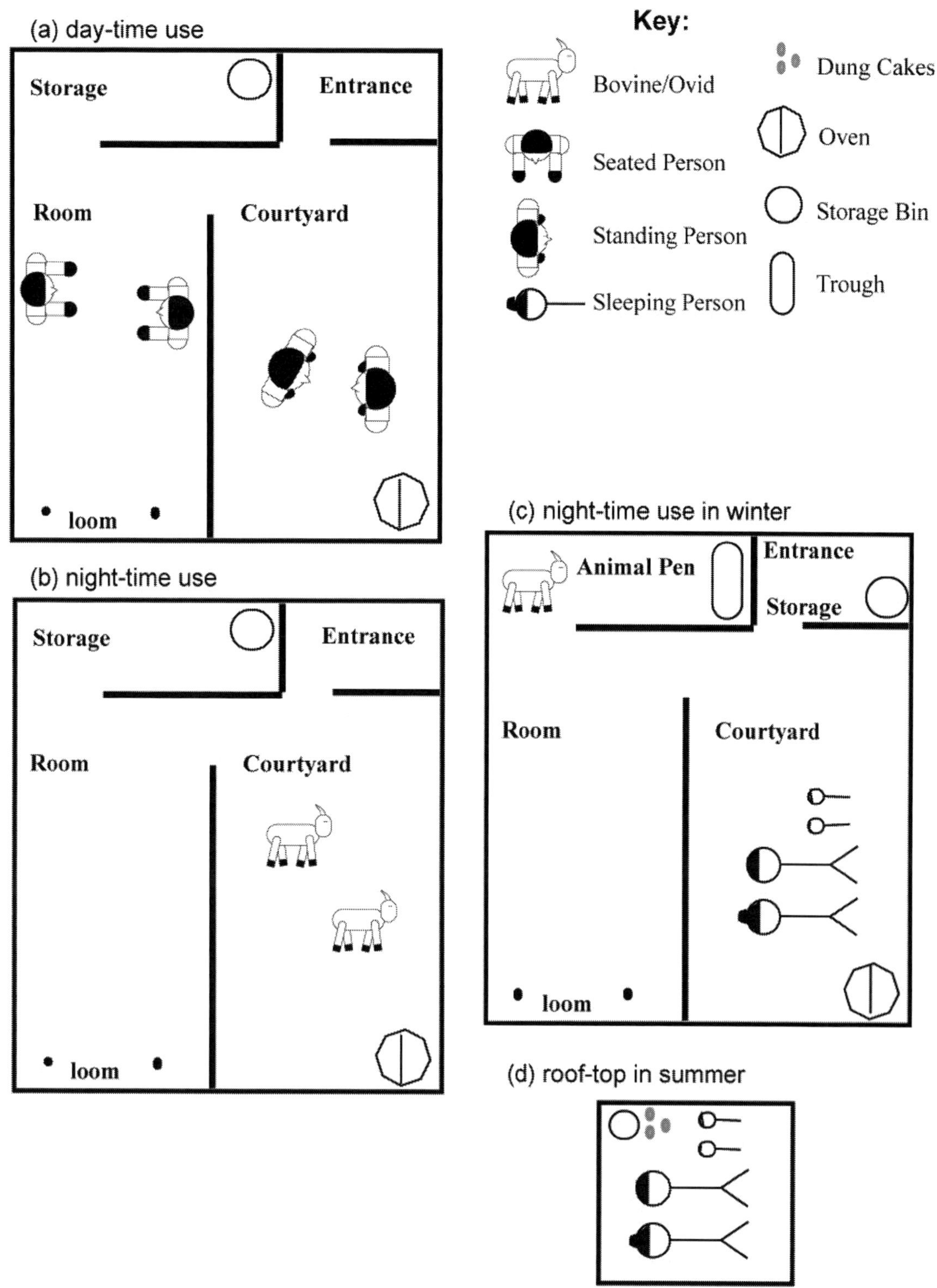

Figure 3.21. Changing room use throughout the day and between the seasons.

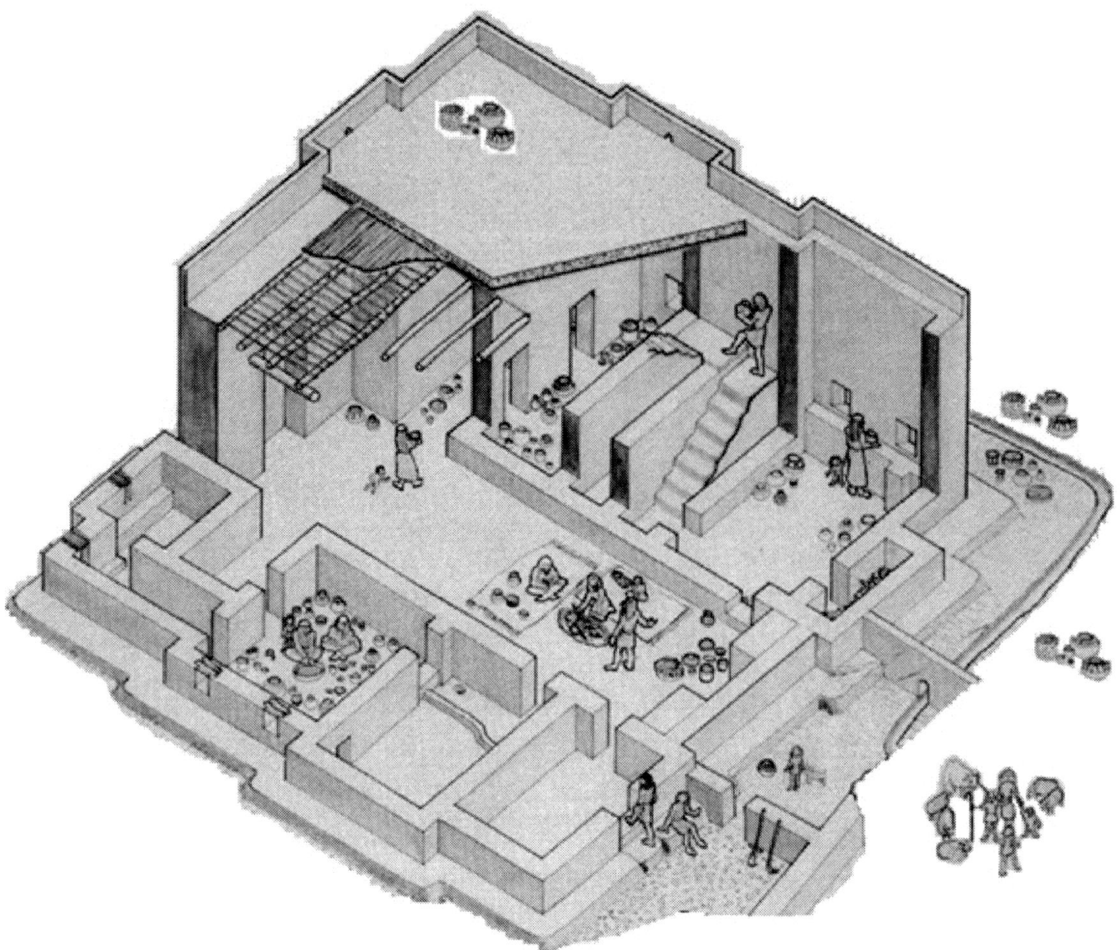

Figure 3.22. Distribution of daily activities in an 'Ubaid house at Tell Madhhur. Modified from Roaf 1990: 54-55. Drawn by Susan Roaf. The drawing has been modified to reflect the possibility of roof-top activities and additional artifact use and/or disposal locations adjacent to the house.

Daily Activities	Micro-Signatures
• weaving / spinning	broken spindle whorl fragments
	bead
• cooking	burned bone (from roasting)
	unburned bone (from stewing)
	broken cooking ware fragments
	ash
	burned organics
	chipped pieces from ceramic storage containers
• stone tool production and retouching	lithic debitage
• agricultural duties	wood fragments from pens
	straw phytoliths from fodder
	dung
• food consumption	broken ceramic wares
	unburned bones from meals
• water consumption	broken fragments from a water jug
	mollusc inclusions from waterproof skins
• construction	fragments of plaster
	fragments of mudbricks
• playing	tokens (whole and broken)
	figurine fragments

Table 3.10. Micro-signatures of ancient daily activities.

corners, edges, and possibly in front of raised thresholds. The 86 samples taken from Building Unit 4 at Titriş supported this contention. Among all floor samples, corners and edges were highest in micro-ceramic, bone, and lithic debris (Figure 3.23). Two additional case examples, discussed below, demonstrate this same pattern. In addition to sweeping patterns, the presence of floor coverings influenced the amount and distribution of micro-remains. In addition to packed, earthen floors, the surfaces at the three sites may have been covered by a combination of carpets (in wealthier houses), reed matting (attested at Third Dynasty Ur; Woolley 1965: 160; Matthews 1994: 190-1), or plaster. For example, the surfaces in Building Unit 5 at Titriş were uniformly low in all debris types. The presence of carpets or reed matting is one explanation for the low densities.

Case Example: Building Unit 8, Room 2, Titriş Höyük

The techniques discussed above were applied to two areas at Titriş where multiple samples were taken from one floor surface. Graphing micro-debris concentrations from Room 6 within the Titriş defensive wall illustrates the distribution of micro-debris within a room (Figure 3.24). Within the 2 meter by 1.5 meter room, eleven sediment samples were purposefully collected from corners and the threshold as well as from 50 by 50 centimeter units laid out across the room. Figure 3.25a illustrates the distribution of micro-debris by count density. The highest ceramic densities clustered along the edges of the room, while the only high concentration of bone occurred in the north corner, suggesting a more discrete and specific activity area. Perhaps someone sitting against a wall (creating a drop/toss zone as discussed by Binford 1978) scraped a hide in this corner. Or, perhaps bone tools were produced here. This interpretation is strengthened by the distribution of chipped stone debris, which was concentrated in that same corner.

Figure 3.25b graphs the same samples, but this time by weight, highlighting the larger pieces of debris. Here we observe that larger pieces of ceramic debris were missed by cleaning efforts only in the extreme corners and in front of sample 155, taken from in front of a raised threshold that made effective debris removal difficult. The heavier pieces of bone still pointed to an activity area in the north corner, while the larger pieces of chipped stone were concentrated along the southeastern edge of the room. This may correspond to a habitual west-east sweeping pattern or the presence of stored boxes, bins, or baskets or other restricting objects laid on the floor in the south-eastern half of the room, which made it more difficult to sweep in this area.

And finally, Figure 3.25c illustrates the distribution of ceramic wares within the room. The highest density of fine wares was concentrated in the south corner, especially in sample 215. This sample may have been the result of a one-time dropped fine plate or bowl. In contrast, micro-sandy wares were found throughout the edges of the room. The only cooking wares were found in the threshold sample (number 155). These pieces may have been swept into the room by mistake while cleaning out the southern room (Room 8.3, see Figure 3.24).

Case Example: Terrace, Room Y, Titriş Höyük

The pattern discussed above was not unique to Building Unit 8. Room Y, in the "Terrace trenches" at Titriş, illustrated a similar pattern. Again, the ceramics were highest in two of the corners (Figure 3.26a), while the bone indicated a functionally specific area. In this case, the concentration of bone fragments corresponded to a human burial in the center of the room. In contrast to the relatively benign ceramic and bone debris, the interior surface was kept clean of chipped stone, except in the northeast corner.

Figure 3.26b depicts the micro-ceramic ware distributions within Room 4. The high density of fine wares and cooking wares occurred at specific locations (sample 269 and 305, respectively), while the sandy wares were concentrated in the northeast and southwest corners. Interestingly, the concentration of cooking wares corresponded to the area of chipped stone concentration, and a concentration of burned bone occurred in roughly the same spot. These three overlapping patterns suggest an area where meat was carved, roasted, and consumed. Ancient texts confirm that some Mesopotamian recipes called for broiled or roasted meat (Bottéro 1985: 39).

Trampling

Micro-debris can also be used to assess the amount of traffic on a surface. Based on ethnographic and experimental studies, the rooms with the highest amount of foot traffic — i.e., trampling — should have a large amount of small debris. To test this hypothesis, the bone, chipped stone, and ceramics were sorted by size to quantify breakage. Within selected samples, the micro-debris was placed into 1 to 15 millimeter categories based on overall size. Several archaeologists have realized that the type of material affects the utility of analyzing the size distribution (Rosen 1986, Özbal 2000). For example, small pieces of chipped stone are unlikely to break simply because they are stepped upon. Rather, they enter the archaeological record in a variety of sizes based on the knapping that produced the debitage (for example, producing a handaxe from a core would produce many large pieces, whereas retouching a blade would only produce small flakes).

In contrast, ethnoarchaeological studies demonstrate that sherd size correlates with trampling (Bradley and Fulford 1980: 90-91). Bone can also be used for grain-size analysis because of its inherent friability and thus sensitivity to trampling. Another item that can be sorted by particle size is charcoal, both wood and grain (Rosen

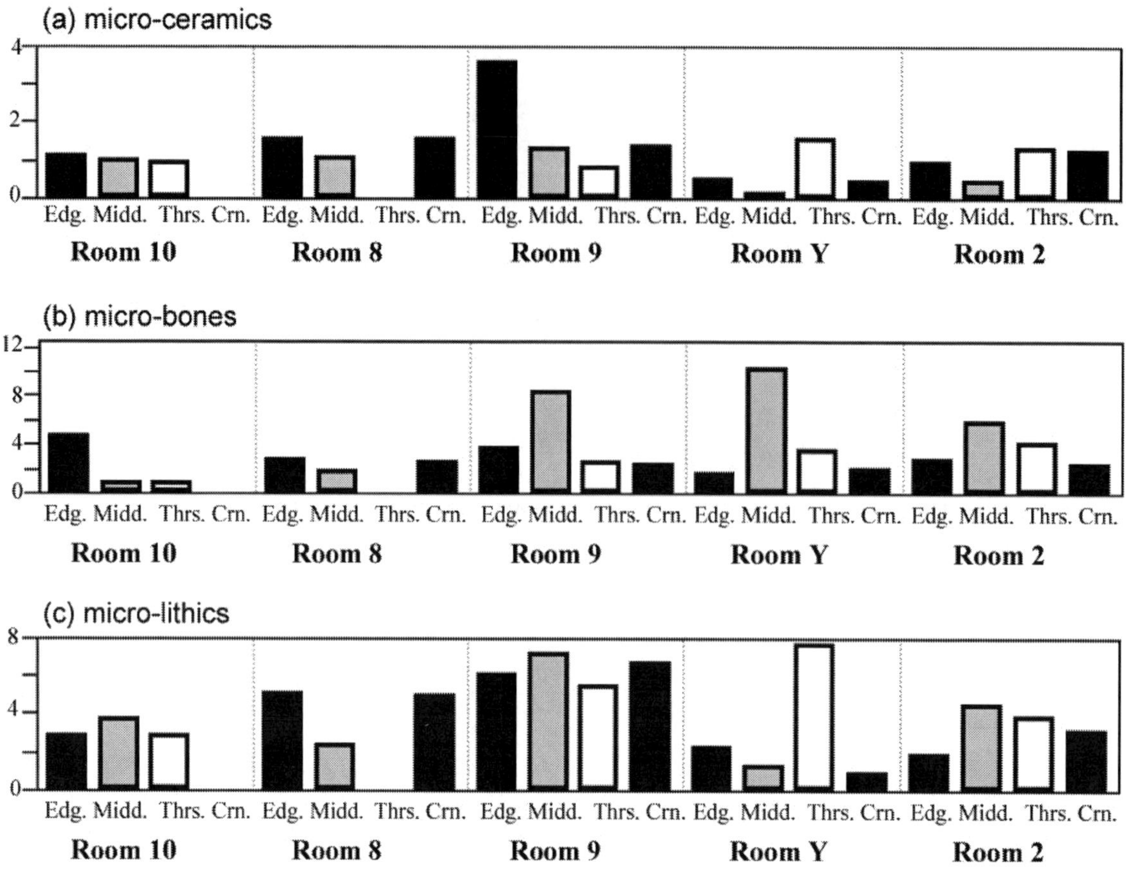

Figure 3.23. Micro-densities within rooms: edge (Edg.), middle (Midd.), threshold, (Thrs.) and corner (Crn.). The vertical axis indicates the density of micro-artifact counts per liter.

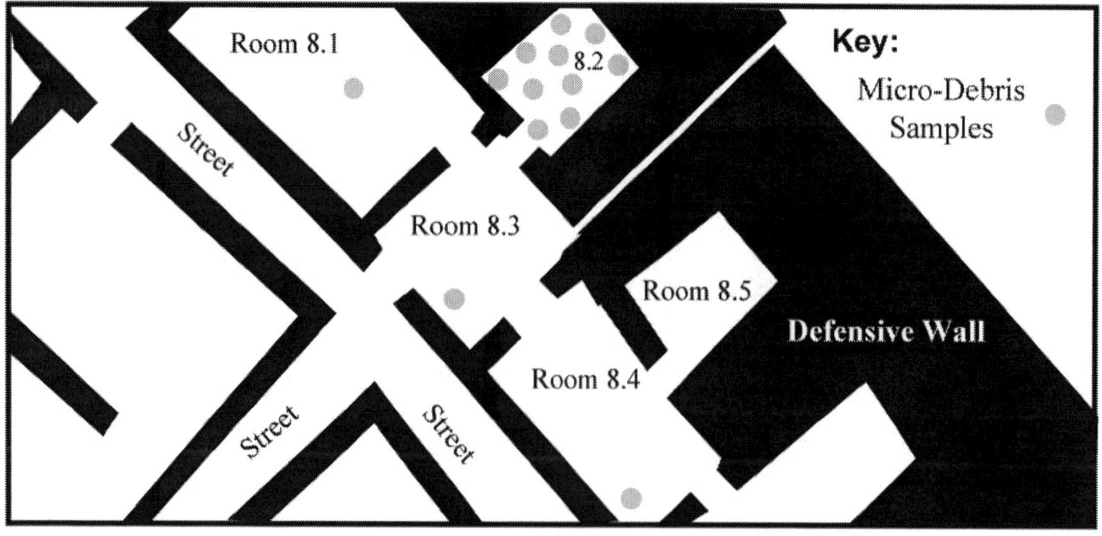

Figure 3.24. Building Unit 8: micro-debris samples.

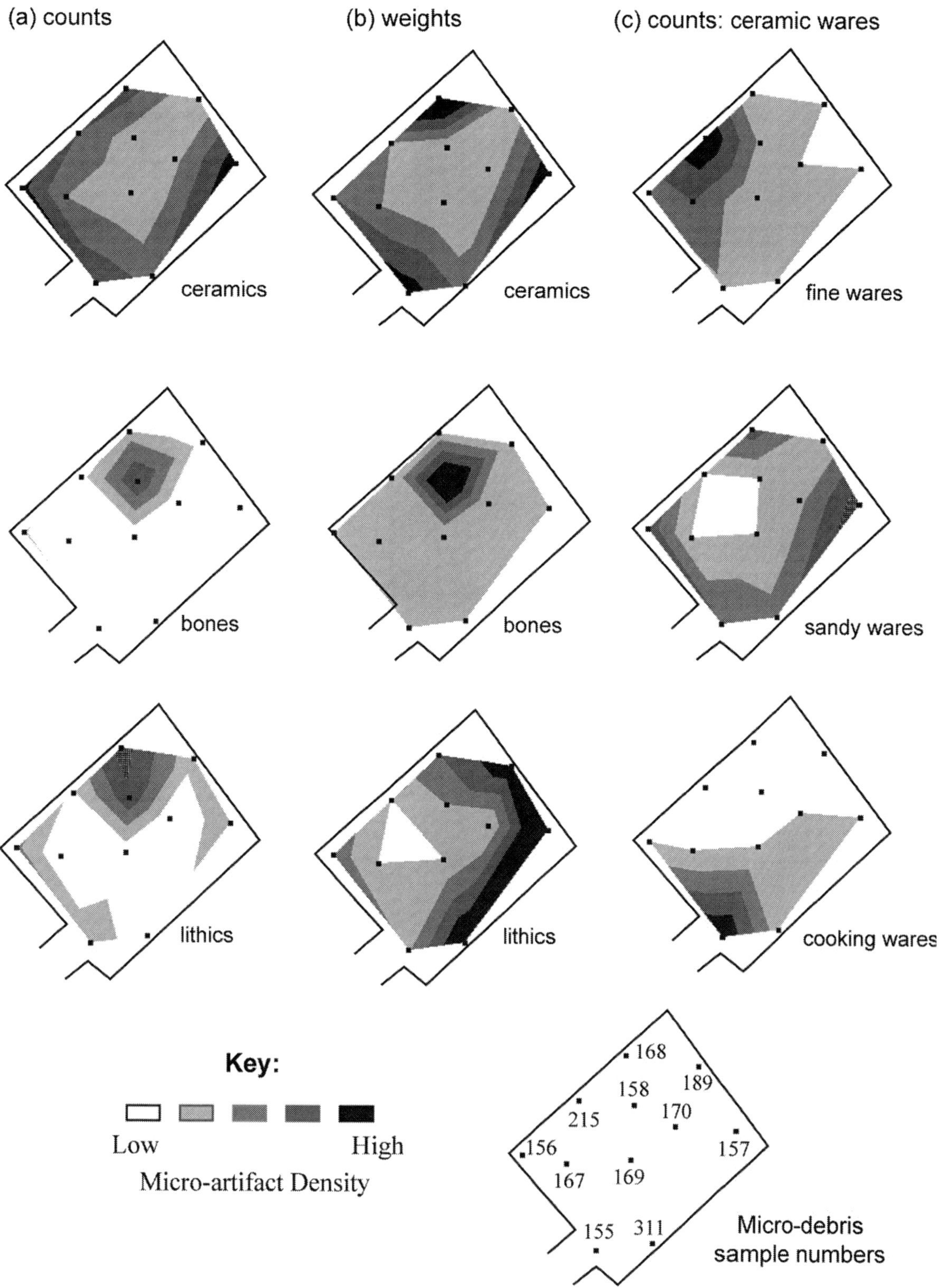

Figure 3.25. Building Unit 8: micro-debris densities within Room 2. For the architectural context of Room 2, see Figure 3.24.

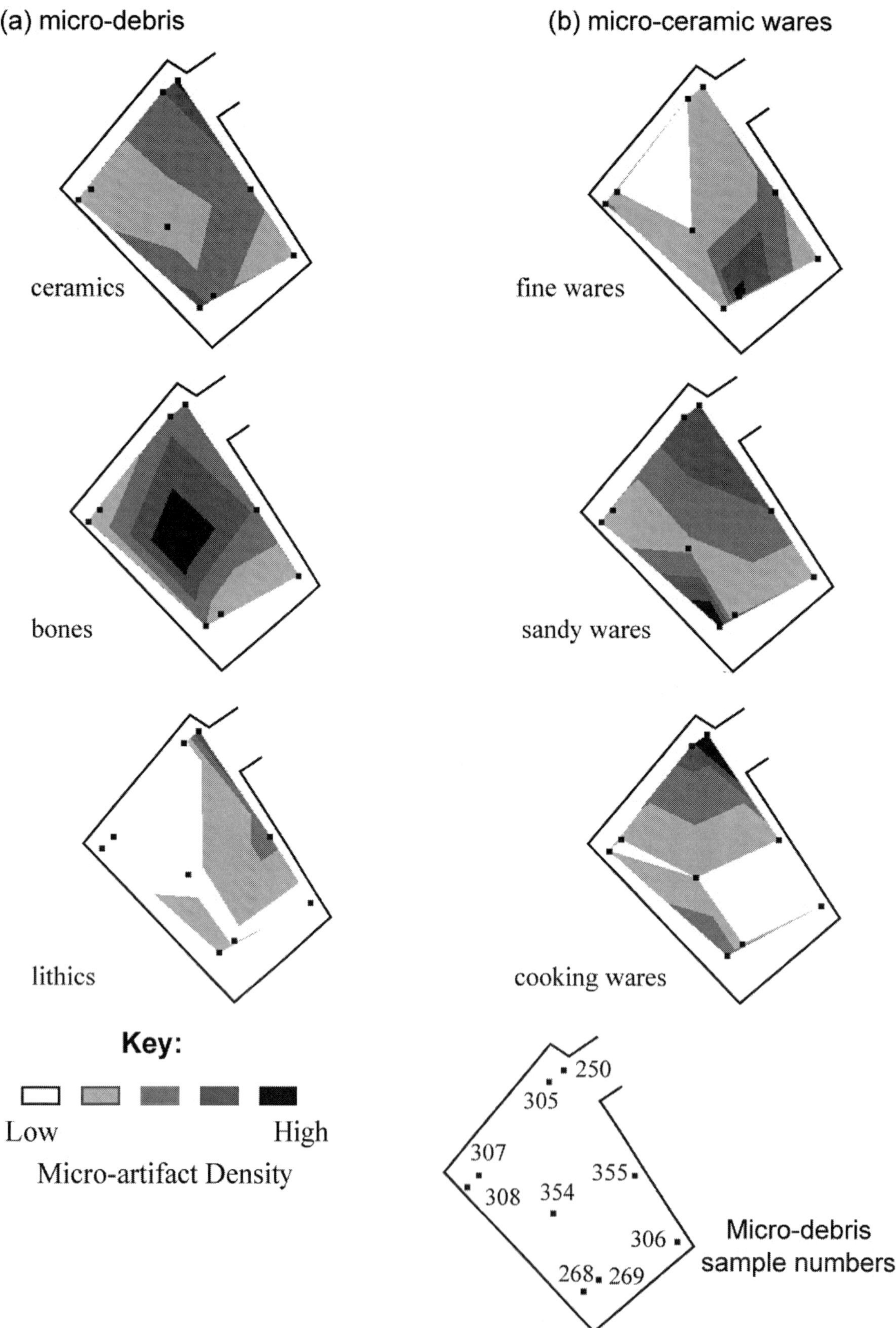

Figure 3.26. Terrace: micro-debris distributions within Room Y. For the architectural context of Room Y, see Figure 4.18.

1986: 104). Independent of debris type, the hardness and permeability of the surface influences the size of debris after trampling. Figure 3.27 demonstrates the difference in micro-artifact size between room corners and edges and the surface in the middle of a room. Room edges contained the greatest concentration of large pieces of bone: in the 6 to 10 mm and 11 to 15 mm categories. In contrast, the middle of the room, presumably the area with the most foot traffic, contained the greatest amount of small (1 to 5 mm) pieces of bone. Figure 3.28 demonstrates that domestic floors contained a larger proportion of small (less than 5 mm) debris than supra-floors. The smallest piece of bone in the supra-floors was 3 mm in size, while the floors contained pieces as small as 1 mm. This is expected from a supra-surface that contained untrampled fill.

Micro-Debris Correlations among Surfaces

Correlation results can further assist in identifying the activities that occurred on room surfaces. As mentioned earlier, streets contained very high amounts of micro-ceramics and lithics, and a lesser amount of micro-bones. Among these debris types, all types of debris were significantly correlated: bone and pottery (.50, r < .05), chipped stone and pottery (.83, r < .01), and chipped stone and bone (.50, r < .05). This is to be expected from a surface that contained an almost infinite variety of activities.

In contrast, among interior floors, the correlation profile varied from room to room. For example, in Rooms 10 and 11 in Building Unit 4 at Titriş, bone and pottery were significantly (r < .05) correlated (at .70 and .73 respectively). The former was as an entrance, while the latter a kitchen. In contrast, Room 8, a courtyard, contained significant correlations between bone and pottery (.54) and bone and chipped stone (.57). This suggested an additional set of activities, perhaps animal butchering, hide processing, or simply tool sharpening and meat consumption. Bone and chipped stone also co-occurred in Building Unit 8. For reasons discussed further in Chapter 4, I concluded that Unit 8 may have housed animals and been used to store agricultural tools. If correct, this hypothesis would account for the co-occurrence of bone and chipped stone. In the limited samples I took from the courtyard of the modern village of Kazane, chipped stone and bone co-occurred. This suggests that we can expect domestic courtyards to contain food processing remains. A different pattern characterized the floors in the Terrace at Titriş, where only chipped stone and pottery (.55, r < .01) co-occurred. And, finally, on Area H floors at Kazane, all three types of debris co-occurred, suggesting a variety of domestic activities: chipped stone and bone (1, r < .01), bone and pottery (.8, r < .05), and chipped stone and pottery (.8, r < .05). In contrast to floor surfaces, supra-floors contained the highest (among the 14 locus types) amount of rodent bones (Figure 3.29a). This suggests disturbances by mice and burrowing animals. Among floor surfaces, large quantities of rodent bones were restricted to areas of food preparation or storage (Figure 3.29b).

Of course, all the above correlations may have a different or more than one explanation. For example, animal bone and chipped stone may co-occur because of related activities (such as meat preparation or consumption), or related conditions (such as adequate light, heat, or ventilation). Or debris may co-occur because people preferred to undertake those activities in social groups resulting in a cluster of debris from separate activities.

Case Example: Building Unit 4 , Titriş Höyük

The two previous examples — Unit 8 and the Terrace — focused on the distribution of activity areas within a single room. In addition to revealing activity areas within one room, micro-debris can reveal connections between rooms. Building Unit 4 at Titriş Höyük provided a good example of this technique. Figure 3.30 depicts the macro and micro distribution of chipped stone from micro-debris samples taken within one trench (the southwestern corner of Building Unit 4). Relative to the other rooms, all the samples in Room 4.9 contained a large amount of micro-lithics, suggesting that the room's activities centered on stone tool production or retouching. The samples in Room 4.4 contained a similar quantity of micro-debitage. Room 4.4 may have been used to store the products of, or the raw material for, the activities conducted in Room 4.9. As illustrated in Figure 3.31, a greater effort was made to keep the northwest entrance into the room (from the courtyard) free of micro-flakes (indicated by the lower density marked in light gray). The only other high concentrations of micro-chipped stones in the trench were, not surprisingly, in a courtyard pit (Room 4.8), next to a hearth and a DPS (Room 4.11), and in storage areas (Rooms 4.12 and 4.13). Figure 4.28 depicts the distribution of micro-chipped stone throughout the rest of Building Unit 4. Room 9 still contained the highest concentration of chipped stone, reinforcing the hypothesis that this was a room with regular lithic activities (including production, retouching, and/or tool use). In addition, Rooms 13, 14, and 16b contained high densities of lithic debitage. Room 13 might have been used to store kitchen utensils. Room 16b was the entry into a possible animal byre (Room 16), thus hide processing with lithic scrapers or straw storage may have occurred here. Moderate areas of micro-lithic debris included Room 10 (in burial samples), Room 20 (a courtyard where chipped stone tools may have been used), Room 11 (a kitchen), and Room 19 (a possible storage room associated with Room 9).

Micro-ceramic and bone distributions in Building Unit 4 can also be analyzed. Figure 3.32 illustrates that the micro-ceramics were distributed very differently to the chipped-stone. The highest concentrations of ceramics occurred in isolated samples, perhaps indicating the

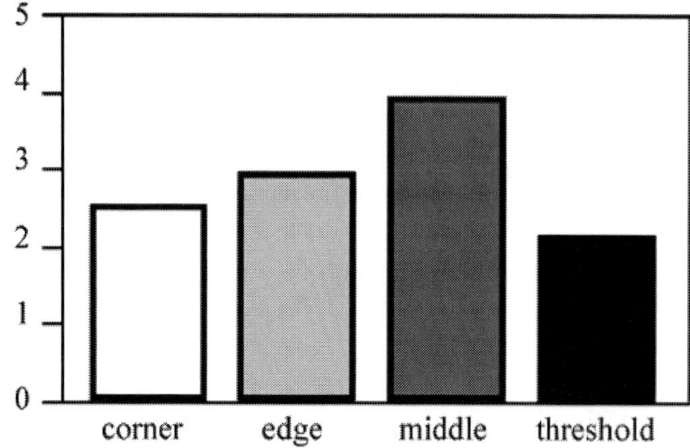

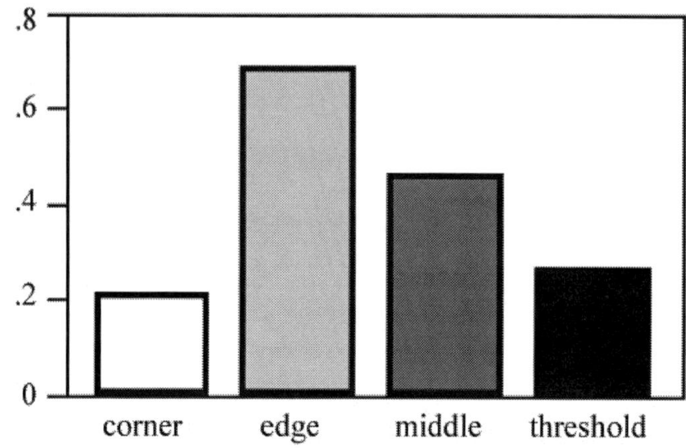

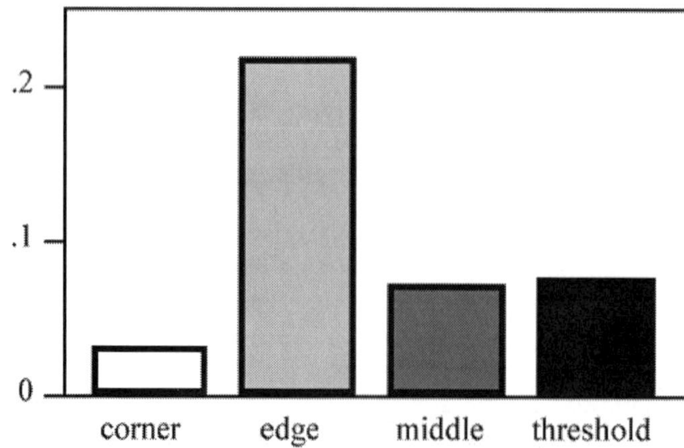

Figure 3.27 Bone size distribution within rooms. The vertical axis indicates the density of micro-bone counts per liter.

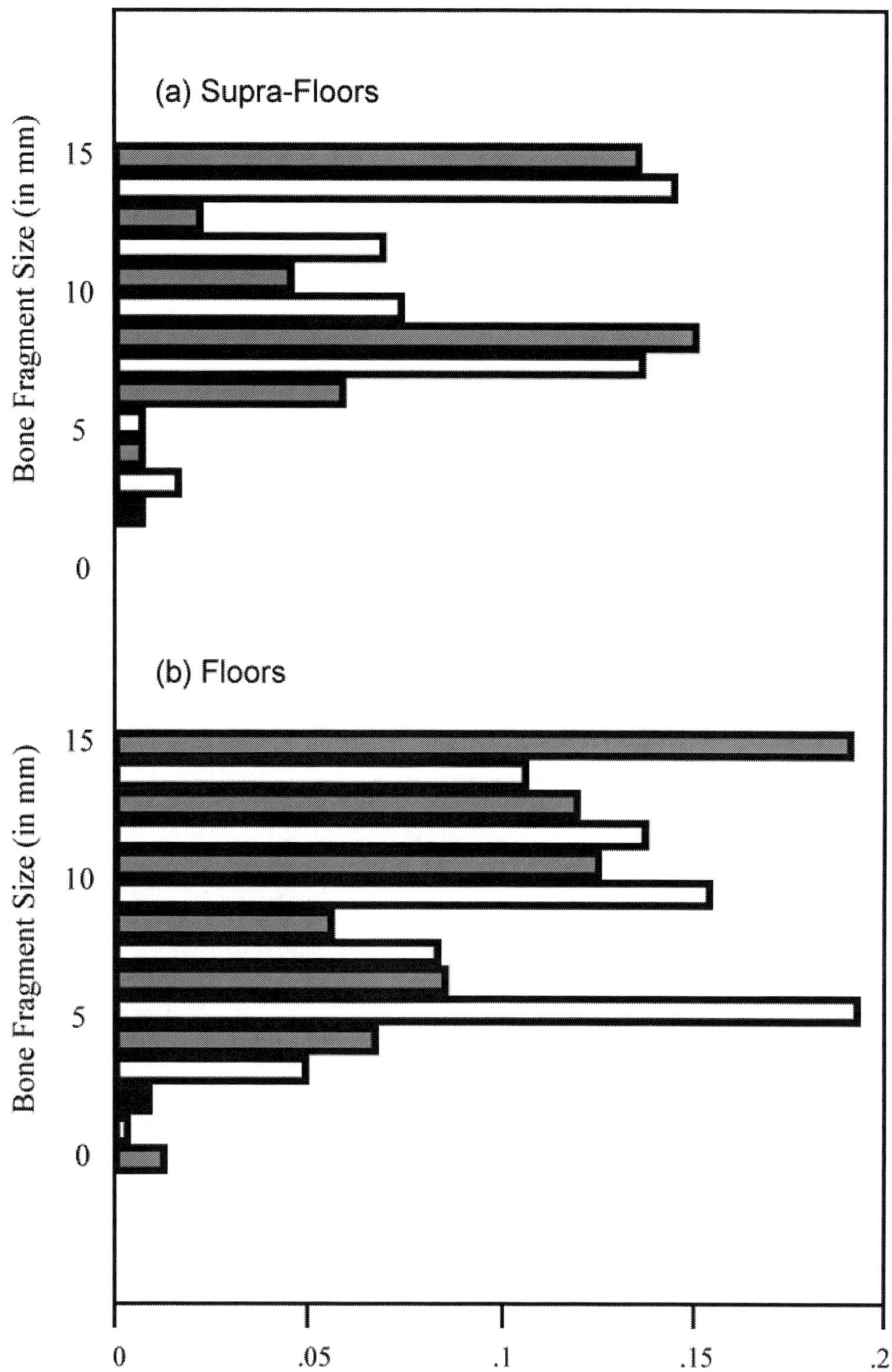

Figure 3.28. Degree of trampling on floors and supra-floors, as indicated by the size distribution of micro-bones. The horizontal axis indicates the density of micro-bone counts per liter.

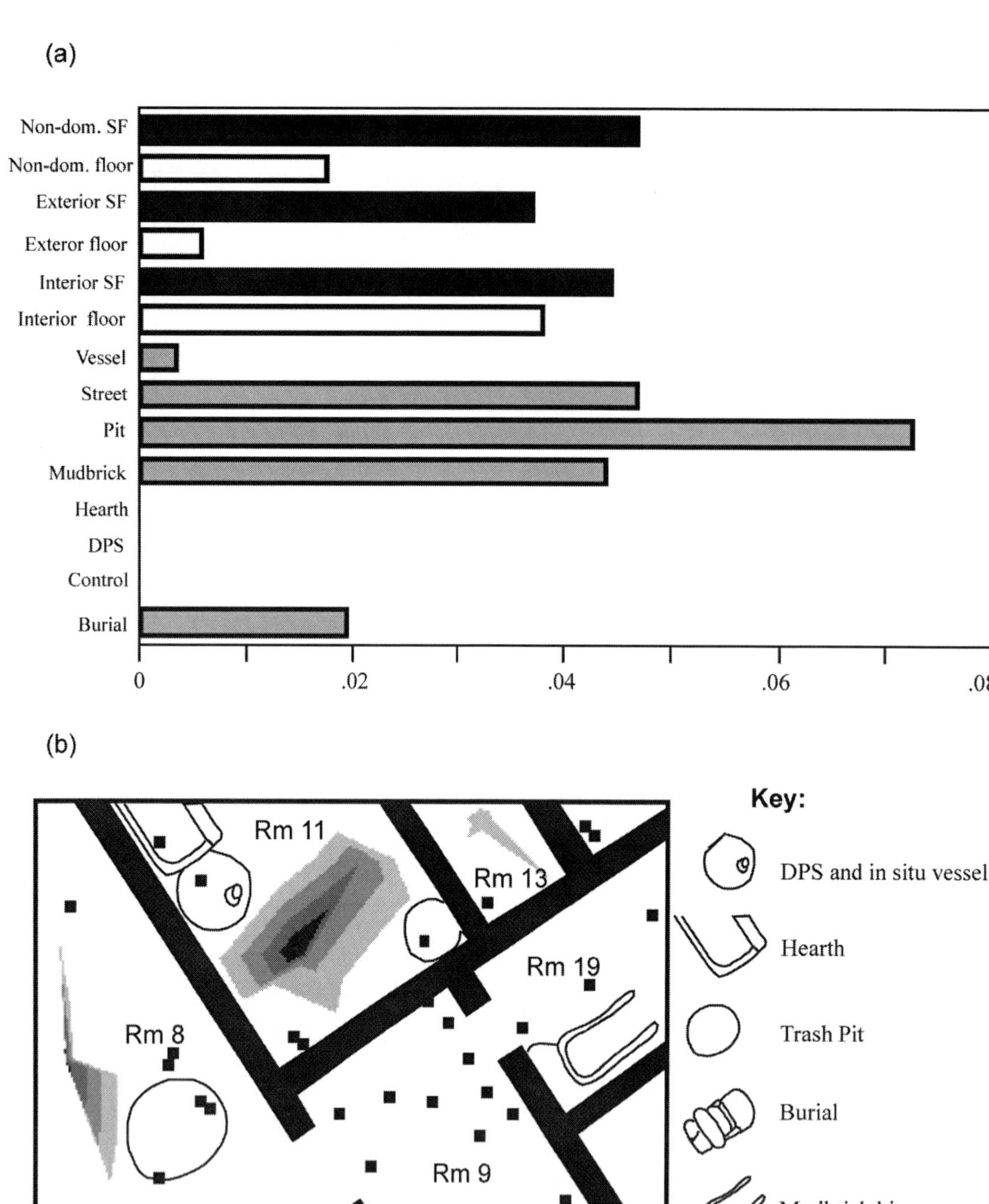

Figure 3.29. Rodent bones per locus type in Building Unit 4, Titriş. (a) The mean count density per locus type within Building Unit 4. The abbreviation "Non-dom" on the vertical axis stands for "non-domestic." The horizontal axis indicates the density of micro-artifact counts per liter. (b) The distribution of rodent bone count densities within Trench 80/87.

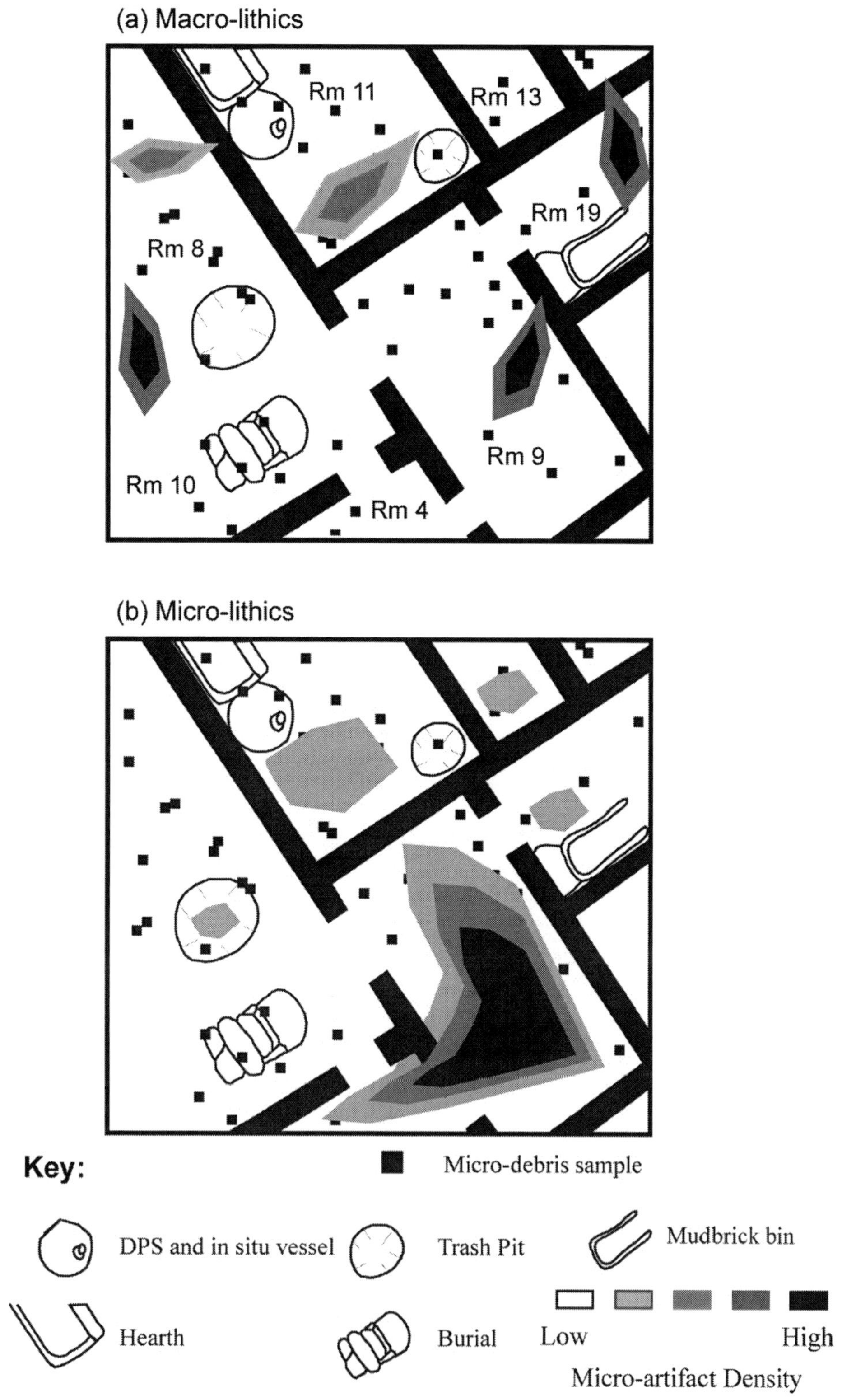

Figure 3.30. Distribution of macro- and micro-lithics in Trench 80/87, Titriş.

Figure 3.31. Micro-chipped stone distribution, Building Unit 4, Titriş. The gray arrow indicates the entrance into a later phase room (Room 10).

Figure 3.32. Micro-ceramic distribution, Building Unit 4, Titriş. The gray arrow indicates the entrance into a later phase room (Room 10).

Figure 3.33. Micro-faunal distribution, Building Unit 4, Titriş. The gray arrow points to the entrance for a later phase room (Room 10).

discrete episode of a dropped vessel. High concentrations of ceramics occurred in the courtyard (Room 8), a location interpreted through ethnographic parallels as the site of goods and food storage and of food consumption that may not have been kept as clean as interiors. In these modern examples, food and supplies are often stored in wooden chests, but in ancient times they may have been stored in ceramic vessels. Areas of moderate micro-ceramic densities included the kitchen and its storage room (Rooms 11 and 13), two other possible kitchens (Rooms 23 and 24), the area of grave goods in the burial (Room 10), and the room adjacent to the possible byre (Room 16b). In each of these rooms, ceramic vessels may have been used for preparing food, serving meals, or storing edibles or supplies.

Next, I graphed the micro-bone distributions (Figure 3.33). The highest concentration of faunal remains occurred in the kitchen (Room 11), possibly the remains of ancient meals or the remains of small scavengers (such as rats) that were attracted to an area of food consumption and storage. The living quarters in Room 9 also contained samples high and moderate in micro-bones, suggesting that food was regularly consumed in this room (supported by a high concentration of fine wares and an absence of cooking wares in this room). Samples from the burial in Room 10 also contained large quantities of micro-bone, in this case probably crushed human ones (the macro-skeletal remains were fragmentary and suggested at least one jar burial. And finally, a courtyard (Room 8) and two possible kitchens (Rooms 23 and 24) contained samples with moderate to high quantities of bone. A future project would be to sort, as far as possible, the bones by species. This would resolve many questions: what types of meat the family consumed; whether the high bone concentrations in kitchens represented scavenging rodents or ancient meals; what percent, if any, of the bones were human; and, possibly, what cuts of meat the family preferred (or were economically restricted to).

One final question concerning activity areas is the use of exterior as opposed to interior workspaces. Ethnographers have long realized that not all cultures conduct activities indoors (Kramer 1979c, Horne 1994). The micro-remains at Titriş supported this observation: higher amounts of debris were recovered from exterior surfaces (Figure 3.34). Moreover, chipped stone debris exhibited the largest discrepancy between outdoor and indoor surfaces. As discussed earlier, the hazard posed by the sharp lithic debitage probably resulted in a greater effort to keep interior surfaces clean of this type of debris.

In sum, micro-debris clearly helped identify activity areas within rooms. In the next chapter, the results from activity area analysis will be combined with features, architecture, and macro-artifacts to classify room types and structure functions throughout the three sites.

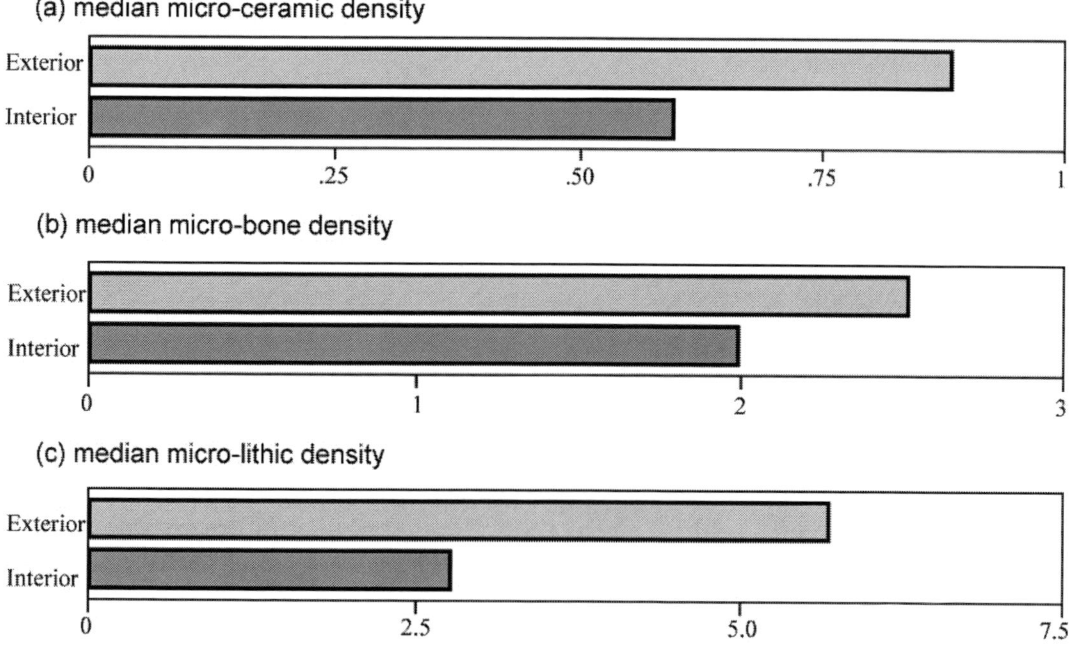

Figure 3.34. A comparison of micro-densities from exterior and interior surfaces. The horizontal axis indicates the density of micro-artifact counts per liter.

Chapter 4: Near Eastern Houses: ancient and modern

Because it is a growing field, household archaeology does not have clear topical parameters. Moreover, domestic life has been studied at several scales, from that of the distribution of settlements across the landscape to activity areas within rooms. These studies have ranged from studies of settlement patterns (often surveys of the distribution of villages and cities across the landscape and their relation to the natural environs — e.g., Willey 1956, Adams 1981), urban neighborhoods (Stone 1987, Stone and Zimansky 2004, Keith 1999), domestic architecture (Rapaport 1969, Bermann 1990), room functions (Ciolek-Torrello 1984, Roaf 1989), and activity areas within rooms (Flannery 1976, Kent 1984, Binford 1987). Traditionally, the narrowest unit of analysis is the study of the distribution of artifacts (e.g., vessels and tools) and features (e.g., hearths, storage pits, and burials) within domestic rooms. A more detailed level of analysis is provided by the study of micro-artifacts (between 1 and 10 mm) found in floors and features (Rainville 2001), the microscopic traces (under 1 mm) of chemical residues (Middleton 1998), and geological remains (J. Stein 1987, Davidson et al. 1992). These approaches clearly complement each other and, ideally, should be used together to answer questions concerning "archaeological formation processes, prehistoric sociopolitical and economic organization, prehistoric value systems and worldview, and processes of cultural evolution" (Bermann 1994: 19).

In the Near East, after decades of research on palaces and temples, some archaeologists have turned their attention to the excavation of domestic houses (e.g., Stone 1987, Gnivecki 1987, Banning and Byrd 1987, Roaf 1989, Veenhof 1996, Keith 1999, Stone and Zimansky 2004). As outlined in Chapter 1, a complete understanding of "households" includes more than simply analyzing the architecture that comprises the physical "house." Additionally, social and economic variables such as household membership, the relative status of family members, and the extent of craft production within the household are relevant. Despite this important distinction, most Near Eastern archaeologists have often limited their studies of domestic structures to architectural elements such as the layout of walls, location of doorways, and presence of roofed rooms (e.g., Henrickson 1982). These features have been used to assess household wealth and activities. To this I add an additional type of data: small artifactual remains.

Methods for Understanding the Built Environment

In this chapter, I summarize approaches to household archaeology to better examine the role of households in ancient states. In addition, a new method is presented to recover domestic data: micro-debris analysis. I studied households in order to understand those areas of ancient Near Eastern socio-economic organization that may have been beyond the control of large public institutions such as the temple and palace. Previous studies of Near Eastern households have focused on the houses of the elites, including priests and temples, kings and palaces, and wealthy individuals and vast estates (e.g., Delougaz et al. 1967, McCown and Haines 1967, Oates 1987, Forest 1999). Among these elite households, temple households (including priests and a large number of "impoverished classes" as workers) have received the most attention due to surviving architectural plans (e.g., Delougaz et al. 1967) and an abundance of economic texts (e.g., Gelb 1979). The results from these prolific studies (mostly in the realm of chronology and political history) will be discussed in Chapter 5, where domestic structures are compared to non-domestic structures within ancient neighborhoods.

My research revolves around the roles of households in an early civilization: the Upper Mesopotamian Early Bronze Age, "EBA," (ca. 3100-2100 B.C.E.). Data were collected from three sites in the Euphrates and Balikh River Basins in southeastern Turkey (ancient Upper Mesopotamia). I analyzed the patterning of structures, features, and artifacts to determine the economic and social organization of activities within EBA cities and villages. The variable distribution of these remains was used to answer questions about life in early cities and the role of households in these urban environments.

In order to answer these questions, I consider multiple lines of evidence from third-millennium sites: archaeological (e.g., architecture, features, and artifacts), settlement patterns (e.g., an analysis of the extent of urban planning), textual (e.g., third and second millennium economic documents), ethnographic (e.g., studies done on contemporary Middle Eastern villages and cities in Iran, Iraq, Syria, and Turkey), and micro-debris analysis (e.g., the study of small, under 1 cm, artifactual and ecofactual remains and their distribution in space). These types of evidence are analyzed to answer a variety of questions about Near Eastern households and their role in the burgeoning urban society of the EBA. Specifically, I investigate intra-room activity areas (including the locations of flint knapping, cooking, sleeping, eating, and socializing areas), room types (including kitchen, courtyard, storage, animal pens, and reception rooms), house types (including wealthy and poor households, lithic and craft workshops, and defensive structures), neighborhood types, and site types (including rural and urban settlements).

Approaches to Analyzing Structure Form

One approach to studying households is to analyze architectural configurations (e.g., Frankfort 1954, Crawford 1977, Heinrich 1982, Margueron 1982, Kubba 1987). Doorways, fundamental structural divisions, or wall thickness may indicate circulation patterns, segregated areas (based on gender, age, or status within the household), or the presence of a second story. For example, in his analysis of the tripartite plan of 'Ubaid houses, Margueron (1989) investigated the form and function of *contreforts* (buttresses) and *pilastres* (pilaster or pillar/bastion). Although such studies contribute to the inventory of ancient architectural plans, these approaches are often purely descriptive and without additional analysis, do not further our understanding of domestic activities, the use of space among various communities, or the possible socio-economic differentiation among domestic structures.

A purely architectural approach to structural form is made difficult by rebuilding and renovations. Technological and preservational factors influence structure use, re-use, and abandonment. In addition, inheritance patterns, the growth of a settlement, concerns for privacy, and the time available for moving influence construction and abandonment patterns (Horne 1994: 188). Goody (1971) identified these factors as part of a "domestic cycle." An interesting example of the impact of the domestic cycle on house plans comes from Old Babylonian Nippur, ca. 1750-1600 B.C.E. The houses at Nippur contained architectural modifications such as the blocking of doorways, the cutting of new doors, and the removal of walls to enlarge rooms (Stone 1981: 19). These modifications reflected changing inheritance and selling patterns (connected to the economic downturns that occurred during the reign of Samsuiluna, 1741-38 B.C.E.). Interestingly, in Turkish the house plan is called *karniyarik*, which translates as "split womb" referring to the tradition whereby the brothers divided the house (Delaney 1991: 233).

A second traditional approach to studying households is to document the recovery of macro-artifacts. If applied thoroughly, this approach should include the measurement of macro-artifact densities per room and the recording of the exact context and location of the macro-remains. For example, Roaf (1989) measured the distribution of pottery, clay artifacts, bones, and seeds in a burned 'Ubaid house at Tell Madhhur. Even in this case, Roaf recognized (after witnessing a contemporary fire in the same village) that objects might be removed from a burning house. Because of the possible removal of macro-artifacts, I also utilize *in situ* micro-artifacts to recover evidence for daily activities.

A third popular approach to analyzing domestic structures is to use them as the basis for population estimates which, in turn, are used to understand the types of settlement systems within an ancient civilization. Ethnoarchaeological research suggests that house area, specifically the area of certain rooms, may correlate with the number of people residing in the structure. Using data from contemporary villages in Iran, Kramer (1980: 321) proposed that each individual required an average of 10 square meters of space (excluding infants). Using this figure, we can estimate the number of individuals per household at Titriş (Table 4.1). It is very difficult to accurately apply this estimate to ancient populations. The possible limitations to this model include variability in the use of space among cultures, the nature and extent of indoor activities (and the resulting space needs), space requirements among different socio-economic groups within a culture, and cultural attitudes toward the use of space (Kamp 1982: 283). Furthermore, Çevik (1995: 50) cautioned that the number of rooms, and hence area, may correlate with social status, not the size of a family.

My interest in households is neither in population estimates nor a lifeless reconstruction of architectural form; rather, I summarize differences in household activities among domestic structures. Data obtained from micro-archaeology are well suited to achieve this goal. Because of the weakness in singular approaches to analyzing households, I suggest a combined approach that analyzes macro-artifacts, features, architectural modifications, and *in situ* micro-debris.

Functions of Built Habitats

Determining the daily activities performed by the residents of the various households proved a difficult task. At Kazane and Tilbes, trenches exposed only parts of structures, and even at Titriş, with extensive horizontal exposure (up to 1,723 contiguous square meters in the 80s neighborhood), the size and composition of the families or administrators who inhabited the structures is unknown. By comparing architectural, artifactual, and

Structure	Est. m^2	Estimated Family Size	Number of Nuclear Families	Hearth/ Oven	Number of Rooms
BU-1	289	29	7	1+ / 0	15
BU-2	266	27	7	1+ / 0	15
BU-3	122+	12	2	1+ / 0	9
BU-4	434	43	10	5+ / 0	27
BU-8	61+	6	1	1+ / 0	5+
BU-5	320	32	8	4+ / 2	17
BU-9	152+	15	4	2+/ 0	13+
BU-14	129+	13	3	+ / ?	10+
BU-12	~274+	27	7	0 / 1	~16

Table 4.1. Family and structure size from complete EBA houses at Titriş. The "+" indicates that the complete extent of the boundaries of the structure were not located. The abbreviation "BU" stands for "building unit."

micro-debris data, I devised a broad typology of structures: larger (and possibly wealthier) houses, smaller (and possibly poorer) houses, public structures, defensive units, and workshops (Table 4.2). Micro-debris supports this division. Among the 18 structures/discrete areas sampled in this study, the highest concentration of fine wares occurred in the samples taken from Kazane Areas E (defensive wall) and C (an area that included a very large, possibly public structure), Titriş Building Unit 4 (discussed previously, a house owned by a wealthy family), and the Titriş Terrace (a house in the same neighborhood as Unit 4 (Figure 4.1). The variability in micro-ceramic wares revealed areas where fine-ware bowls or cups were regularly used, suggesting that guests or prominent family members ate or drank in these rooms. In contrast, sandy wares may be associated with more commonplace or daily food/drink consumption. Sandy wares were recovered in the largest quantities from Area E (defensive wall), Area F (an area of possible manufacturing), Unit 4, Unit 8 (rooms in the defensive wall, possibly used for storing foodstuffs or goods in sandy vessels), and the Terrace. Cooking wares, associated with food preparation, were highest among Area F, Area H (a domestic area with craft activities), Unit 4, and the Terrace. In contrast to the urban settlements, the two areas excavated at Tilbes contained the highest amounts of sandy wares, fewer cooking wares, and very little fine wares (see further Appendix C).

Urban and Rural Households in the Archaeological Record

Insights gained from contemporary Middle Eastern villages and cities, when supported by macro and micro-archaeological evidence, are applied to better understand the use of rooms at three ancient sites: Kazane, Titriş, and Tilbes. In total, I sampled over 90 rooms from 22 structures. In each room, the median count densities of ceramics, bones, and lithics from floor surfaces were calculated. As mentioned earlier, combining micro-data from the three sites masked certain patterns unique to each. Thus, Figure 4.2 graphs only the micro-profiles from Titriş room types. The "craft" rooms, located within a lithic workshop, contained the highest amount, by far, of micro-lithics. Similarly, within the private rooms, the high quantity of lithics, while not equal to that of the workshop at Titriş, suggests that some tool production occurred at the household level. After streets, private rooms, and burials, kitchens contained the fourth highest amount of micro-bones and large quantities of micro-ceramics. Proportionally, courtyards shared a similar profile with kitchens, suggesting that food preparation (meat) and serving (sherds) occurred in both rooms. Storerooms tended to contain a lower density of micro-debris than courtyards, kitchens, or other frequently used rooms. This suggested that the items in the storage room were used or moved less often and thus less likely than objects used daily to break or chip.

The distribution of ceramic wares among room types adds to our understanding of activities within the rooms. As illustrated in Figure 4.3, the highest concentrations of fine-ware micro-ceramics occurred in private rooms and craft rooms, supporting the conclusion that people were consuming foods in these rooms and that, possibly, the lithic workers had an enhanced status. Conversely, kitchen and craft rooms contained the highest density of cooking wares (Figure 4.3c).

Micro-debris patterns alone are not sufficient to categorize rooms. Instead, architecture, features, and macro-artifacts must be analyzed in conjunction with micro-debris. Illustrating this technique, two case examples will be discussed from the Outer Town at Titriş: the 25 rooms in Building Unit 4 and the 15 rooms in the Terrace (Figure 4.4). Data for all analyzed structures are presented in Appendix B through D.

	Non-elite Domestic	Elite Domestic	Public	Craft / Workshop	Defense
Kazane	Area D	Area C	Area C	Area F	Area E
		Area F		Area H	
Titriş	Outer Town BU-1	Outer Town BU-4	40-34	Lithic Core	Outer Town 8
	Outer Town BU-2	Lower Town BU-5			
	Lower Town BU-3	Outer Town BU-6			
	Lower Town BU-9	Terrace			
	Lower Town BU-12				
	Lower Town BU-13				
	Lower Town BU-14				
Tilbes	Structure E	Structure A			

Table 4.2. Sampled structures at three sites. The abbreviation "BU" stands for "Building Unit."

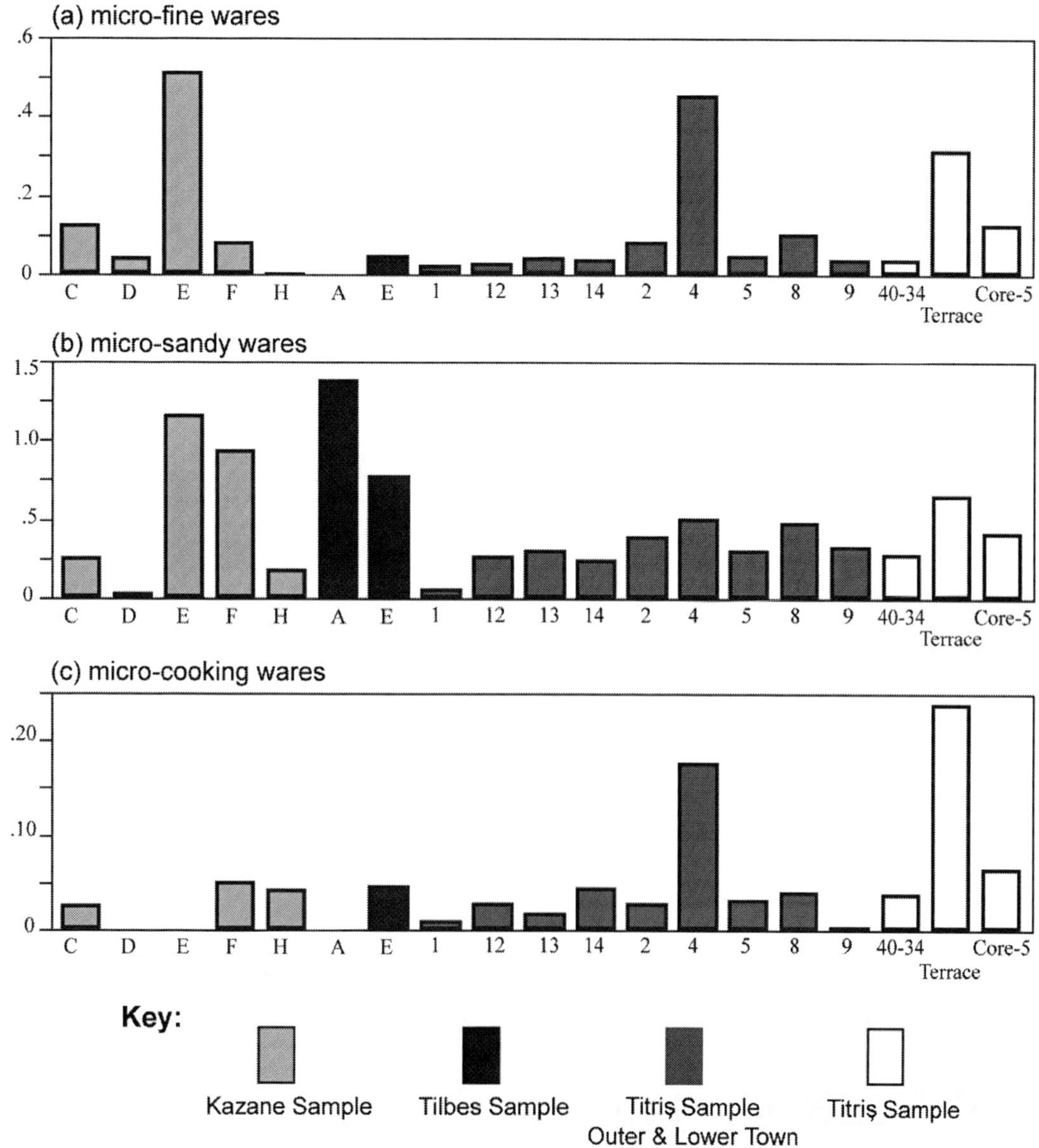

Figure 4.1. Distribution of ceramic wares among sampled structures. The vertical axis indicates the density of micro-ceramic counts per liter.

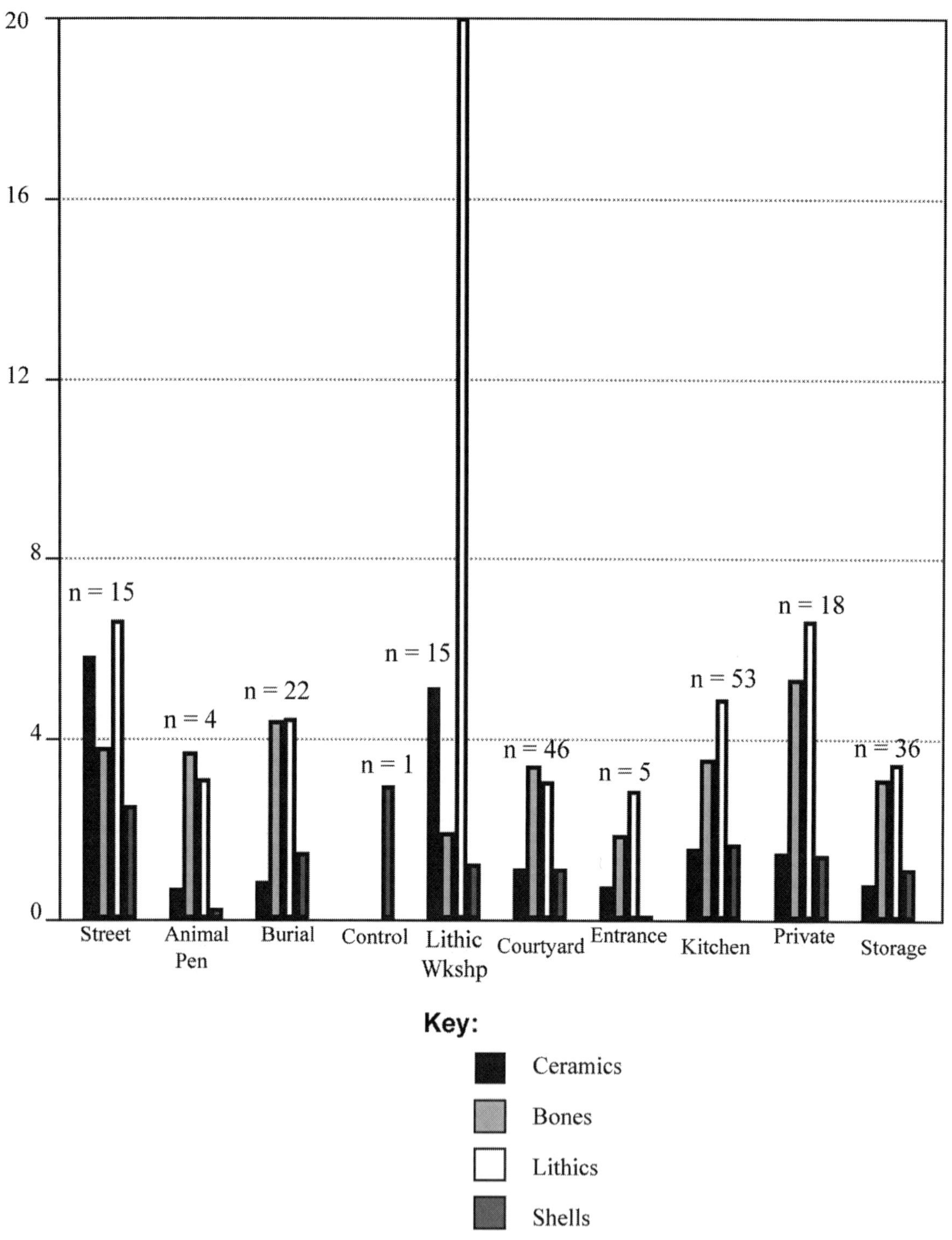

Figure 4.2. Micro-debris profiles per room type at Titriş. The "n" is the number of samples taken from each room type. The vertical axis indicates the density of micro-artifact counts per liter.

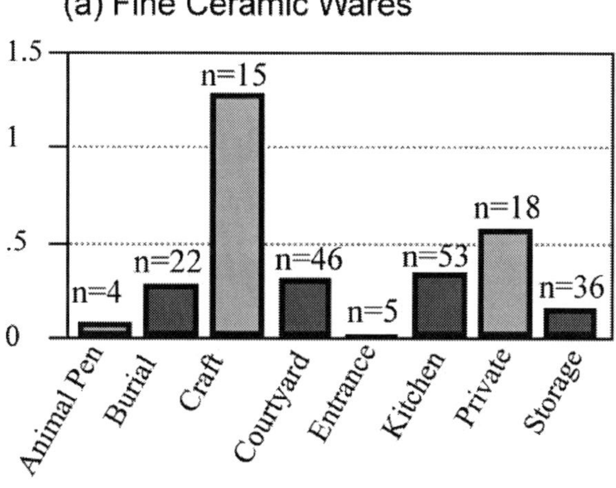

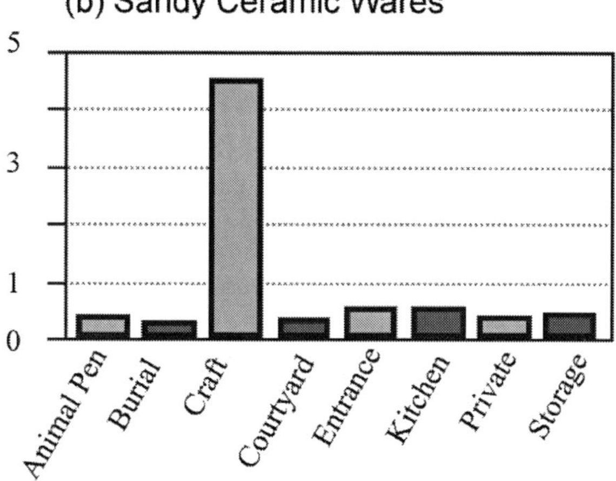

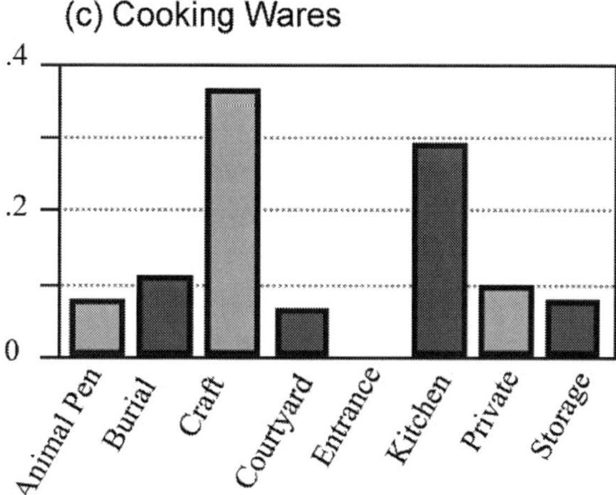

Figure 4.3. Variability in ceramic ware densities among room types at Titriş. The vertical axis indicates the density of micro-ceramic counts per liter.

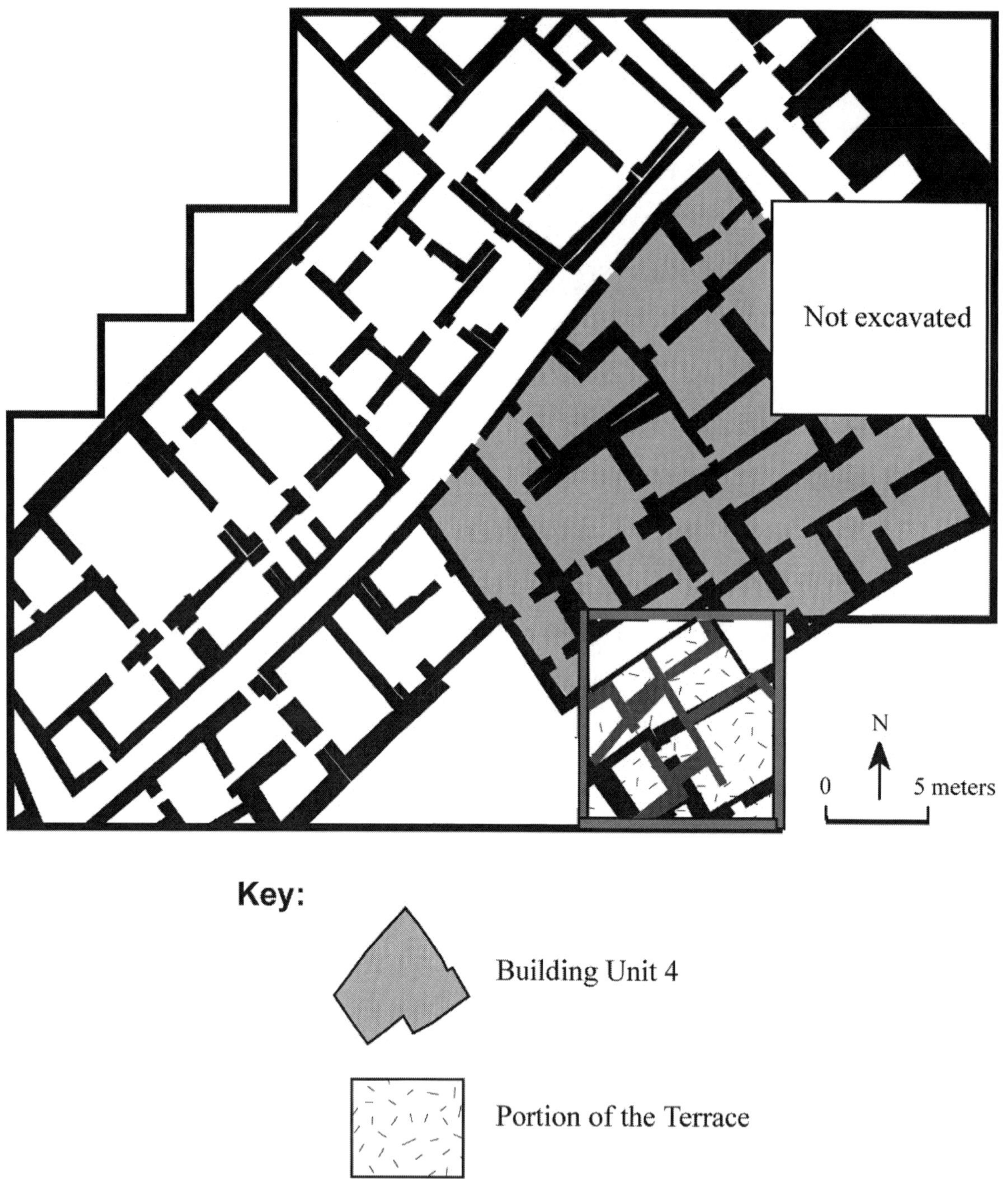

Figure 4.4. Location of Building Unit 4 and Terrace, Outer Town, Titriş. The gray box around the Terrace (Trench 79/87) contains earlier layers than the rest of the architecture depicted on the map.

Houses

Together, loci, activity areas, and rooms (surrounded by walls) make up individual houses. The resulting discrete physical structure and its exterior environs serves as the setting for household activities, family interactions, and social and economic exchanges. Rapoport (1969) discussed that there is a close relationship between the built environment and the lives of the inhabitants. Although acknowledging that there is no single or direct link between architecture and society, Rapoport argued that the "folk tradition" of building houses (structures built by non-specialists for ordinary people) expresses values and symbols important and specific to the culture that built the structure: "Building a house is a cultural phenomenon; its form and organization are greatly influenced by the cultural milieu to which it belongs" (Rapoport 1969: 46). Thus house design does not simply reflect responses to natural conditions (e.g., protection from wind, rain, or temperature) or to practical considerations (e.g., the availability of technological expertise or the availability of building materials); instead, once these factors are taken into consideration, design elements vary widely. Such elements can include the amount of privacy afforded, the presence/absence of doors, the allocation of space among family members, and their daily activities. Before analyzing the influence of cultural traditions on building forms, we must decide whether a structure is domestic (such as a residential house), non-domestic (such as a workshop or guardhouse), religious (such as a temple), or public (such as a palace or administrative structure).

In the sites considered in this study, no temples or palaces were excavated, but houses, workshops, and administrative structures are represented. In contrast to grandiose or professionally planned temples or palaces, domestic houses represent vernacular architecture. David and Kramer (2001: 284) distinguish between the two styles and define vernacular architecture as (a) not usually standardized, (b) reflecting the needs of the inhabitants who built the structure, and (c) typically built by construction workers who have no plan to occupy their handiwork. In the remainder of the chapter, I investigate the form and function of these domestic structures.

Room Functions

In this chapter, I classify rooms according to sets of daily activities that were recognized by the micro-signatures found among locus types and activity areas. Room types were identified by several attributes: (1) spatial location within the structure, (2) excavated features and macro-artifacts, and (3) micro-debris densities from surfaces and features. Primary room types include kitchens, living rooms, courtyards, animal pens, craft, storage rooms (for both goods and food), reception rooms or entrances, and burials.

By classifying the rooms into types, I only intend to suggest the primary use for a room, not to place a limit on the possible activities conducted within them. I recognize that room use may vary according to daily and seasonal needs and can change from generation to generation. In addition, most rooms can be the site of multiple activities and one activity may have been distributed across several rooms. For example, a room used to sleep in during the winter may be used for dining, entertaining, and small-scale craft production (such as spinning, chipped-stone retouching, or bead making) during the day. In addition, a family might build new rooms to accommodate newly arrived relatives (such as newly married children), to create additional storage space, or to improve the house as resources increased.

In archaeological excavations at Eshnunna (Tell Asmar), Hill (1967: 150) suggested that only two rooms contained unique and archaeologically recognizable activities:

> The two rooms which can be recognized from distinctive features are the bath or toilet room and the kitchen. The "kitchen" is so called for convenience and would be better defined as the place where bread was baked. There is no evidence that all food was prepared in this room; in some cases...even baking was not confined to a single room. It must be supposed that the preparation of food, like other phases of daily life within the house, may have taken place anywhere because of the flexibility of the use of rooms.

Although difficult to identify in the archaeological record, several other types of rooms may be recognized: kitchens, storerooms, reception rooms, stables, and private rooms. The term "private room" is used instead of "living room" to contrast these areas with the more public courtyards. Moreover, the term "living room" is an anachronism that originated in 19th Century Britain to distinguish the "parlor" (where bodies were laid out during wakes) from the room for living. In modern Middle Eastern villages and some cities, and at many urban fourth and third millennium sites (including Tell Asmar, Habuba Kabira, and Jebel Aruda), rooms were organized around central courtyards. Ethnographers have recognized similar patterns among contemporary Middle Eastern houses (Table 4.3). Archaeologists often utilize these ethnographic studies to interpret the patterning of archaeological remains, even though most of these studies were conducted in villages and may not be appropriate for comparison with ancient Near Eastern cities or, for that matter, ancient villages. Figure 4.5 illustrates the distinct layout of a house in a Turkish city (4.5a) compared to a compound in an Iranian village (4.5b). Whereas the village compound contains one row of rooms surrounding a courtyard, the city house is limited in size and form by densely packed structures to either side, and thus contains only one row of rooms arranged in a line.

Ethnographer:	**Kamp**	**Sweet**	**Kramer**	**Horne**	**Watson**	**Rainville**	**Rainville**
Location of fieldwork:	Syrian village	Syrian village	Iranian village	Iranian village	Zagros village	Turkish village	Turkish city
Kitchen	X	X	X	X	X	X	X
Storage (food & goods)	X	X	X	X	X	X	X
Animal pen or stable	X	X	X	X		X	
Entrance foyer		X			*aywan*	X	X
Oven		X		X	*tanur*	X	
"Living room"	X	X	X	X	X	X	X
Toilet			X	X			X
Other	Hay storage	Sleeping platform		Guest room		Craft work	Rooftop
Other	"Sitting"					Family tomb	

Table 4.3. Room types as observed by ethnographers working in the Middle East. The complete references are: Kamp 1982: 100-102; Sweet 1974: 110-112; Kramer 1982a: 94; Horne 1994: 148-9; Watson 1978: 135; Rainville 2001a: 154-167.

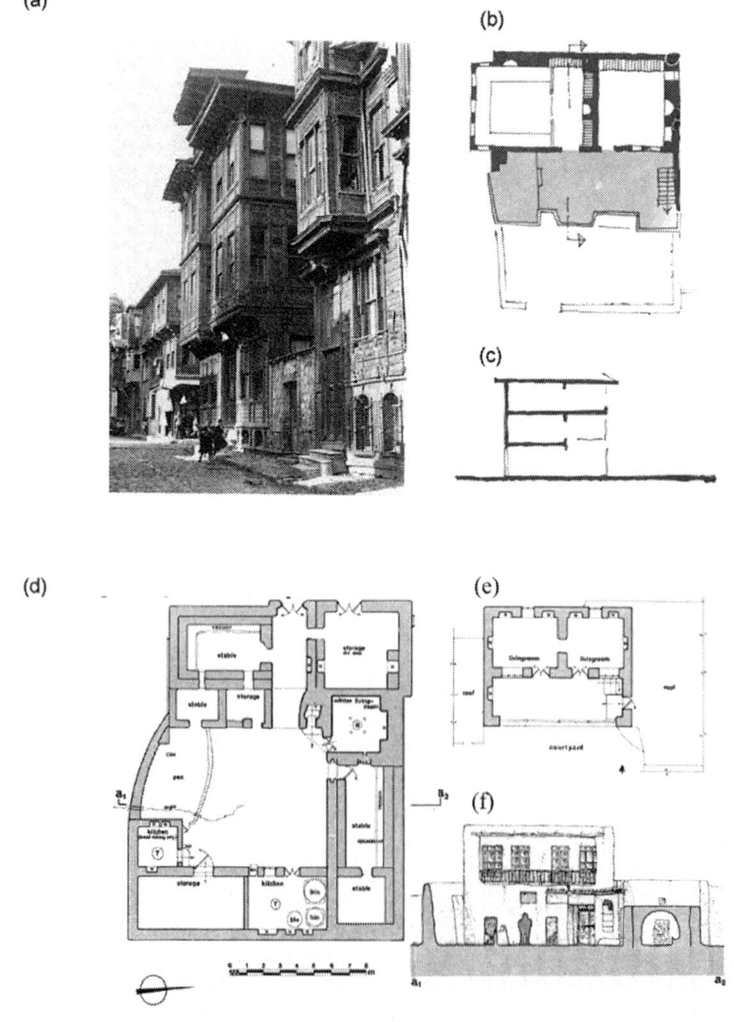

Figure 4.5. Contemporary urban and rural house forms. (a) An apartment house in a Turkish city, C.E. 1960. (b) The ground floor plan. (c) A schematic of the footprint. (a) – (c) are modified from Küçükerman 1992: 188. (d) A village compound in Aliabad, Iran, ca. CE 1975 (the ground floor plan). (e) The second floor plan. (f) A profile view of the front of the house. (d) – (f) are modified from Kramer 1982: 118.

Case Example: Building Unit 4, Titriş Höyük

Building Unit 4 provided evidence for two main architectural periods; both fall within the mid- to late-EBA, ca. 2600-2100. The earlier period contained 24 rooms (Figure 4.6a), while the later period contained 25 rooms (Figure 4.6b). A third (and latest) architectural phase was directly underneath the plow zone and was only recognized in the northern corner of the house. It will not be discussed here. Overall, the structure measured 24 meters to the northwest and northeast, 22 meters to the southeast, and 13 meters to the southwest, covering a total area of approximately 434 square meters (Algaze et al. 2001: 27). The walls ranged from entirely mudbrick, to limestone-footed walls with mudbrick superstructures. Their preserved height was estimated at over a meter, while their width varied from 35 to 65 cm. The individual rectangular mudbricks measured approximately 45 x 35 x 10 centimeters. One of the northern rooms contained a set of stairs. Whether this led to a second floor with usable rooms or simply accessed a flat roof cannot be determined (Algaze et al. 2001: 25-28).

Using architectural placement and design, the 25 rooms can be partially classified by type (Figure 4.7). For example, Rooms 8, 12, 15, and 20/21 were probably courtyards, based on their larger size, central placement, and accessibility to other rooms (each with a minimum of three doorways). Using similar logic, the 25 rooms were separated into different types. Table 4.4 summarizes the different room types based on architectural configurations.

In the following section, the results from micro-debris analysis are combined with macro-artifacts and features to test the architectural results and better classify the rooms by their primary activity.

Within Building Unit 4, 86 micro-debris samples were taken from floor surfaces and features, and an additional nine samples were taken from contiguous streets (see Figure 4.6a). Floor surfaces ranged from hardened surfaces composed of cobbles to relatively clean packed earth. Rarely, a floor was covered with a thin white plaster. Floor samples from the various room types indicated different sets of activities per room (Figure 4.8). For example, courtyards, kitchens, and private rooms contained the largest amounts of micro-ceramics, while only the private rooms contained large amounts of micro-chipped stone. The median micro-debris density of ceramics, bones, and lithics within each room was ranked into quartiles: high, moderate, low, and mostly or entirely absent (only rarely did a room completely lack micro-debris). These patterns were mapped onto the rooms and visually inspected for reoccurring patterns of high and low densities (Figure 4.9).

Although difficult to interpret, certain rooms had distinct profiles, such as Room 9. Two of the three kitchens shared a profile: high ceramics and bones, with moderate chipped-stone densities. And two of the three courtyards shared a profile: high chipped stone density, while only moderate ceramic and bone densities. This pattern mirrors the observations of ethnographers who note that outdoor courtyards were often preferred for flint knapping due to natural light conditions (Healan 1993).

Finally, hierarchical cluster analysis (using Spearman's coefficient) was applied to the individual samples within the rooms (which would be too difficult to analyze by visual inspection). Using the count densities of micro-ceramics, bones, and lithics as dependent variables, the cluster analysis identified five distinct clusters. After the statistical computer program, SPSS, placed each of the 65 early period samples into a cluster, I recorded the number and type of clusters per room (Figure 4.10). Although there is no single direct link between clusters and certain activities, it is highly suggestive that the main courtyard, Room 8, contained a large diversity of clusters. This result matches the observations from the modern village of Pamuklu, where the largest variety of daily activities occurred in the courtyard. The next highest diversity of cluster-signatures occurred in the street samples, the main kitchen, the main living room, and in an attached storage room. These rooms, minus the street samples, formed the core of the house and probably received the most use from the inhabitants. Conversely, fewer clusters occurred in peripheral rooms, suggesting fewer distinct activities. In sum, the clusters served as a rough estimate of the set of activity signatures per room.

In the following sections, each room type will be analyzed separately and in greater detail, using a combination of archaeological (both macro and micro), historical, and anthropological sources.

Building Unit 4: Courtyards

For millennia, Mesopotamian builders designed their houses around a central room, usually referred to by researchers as a courtyard. In order to provide lighting to adjacent rooms, courtyards were probably unroofed. Additional evidence that these rooms were exposed to the elements comes from the use of cobbled floors; this allowed the winter rain to drain better.

The Unit 4 courtyards varied in size (Table 4.5). Courtyards have been interpreted as serving a variety of purposes: ventilation for other rooms, as a source of light (see Woolley 1965: 156, discussing house plans at Ur), for meal preparation and consumption, for socializing, and possibly, in warmer and drier seasons, sleeping. Moreover, the courtyard is usually surrounded by rooms on all sides, affording the resident privacy in an otherwise tightly packed urban setting. As discussed earlier, houses in modern Urfa exhibited this same pattern, revealing that a majority of daily activities occurred in the courtyards. In Unit 4, the courtyards commonly included trash pits and multiple entrances into attached rooms. In addition, the three courtyards shared micro-debris signatures (the courtyard samples are highlighted in gray, Figure 4.11): high concentrations of

Figure 4.6. Location of micro-debris samples in Building Unit 4, Titriş. The small gray circles indicate the location of micro-debris samples. The white walls indicate the location of baulks or highly eroded areas that were reconstructed. In subsequent figures the plans will be drawn uniformly with the interpreted walls in black.

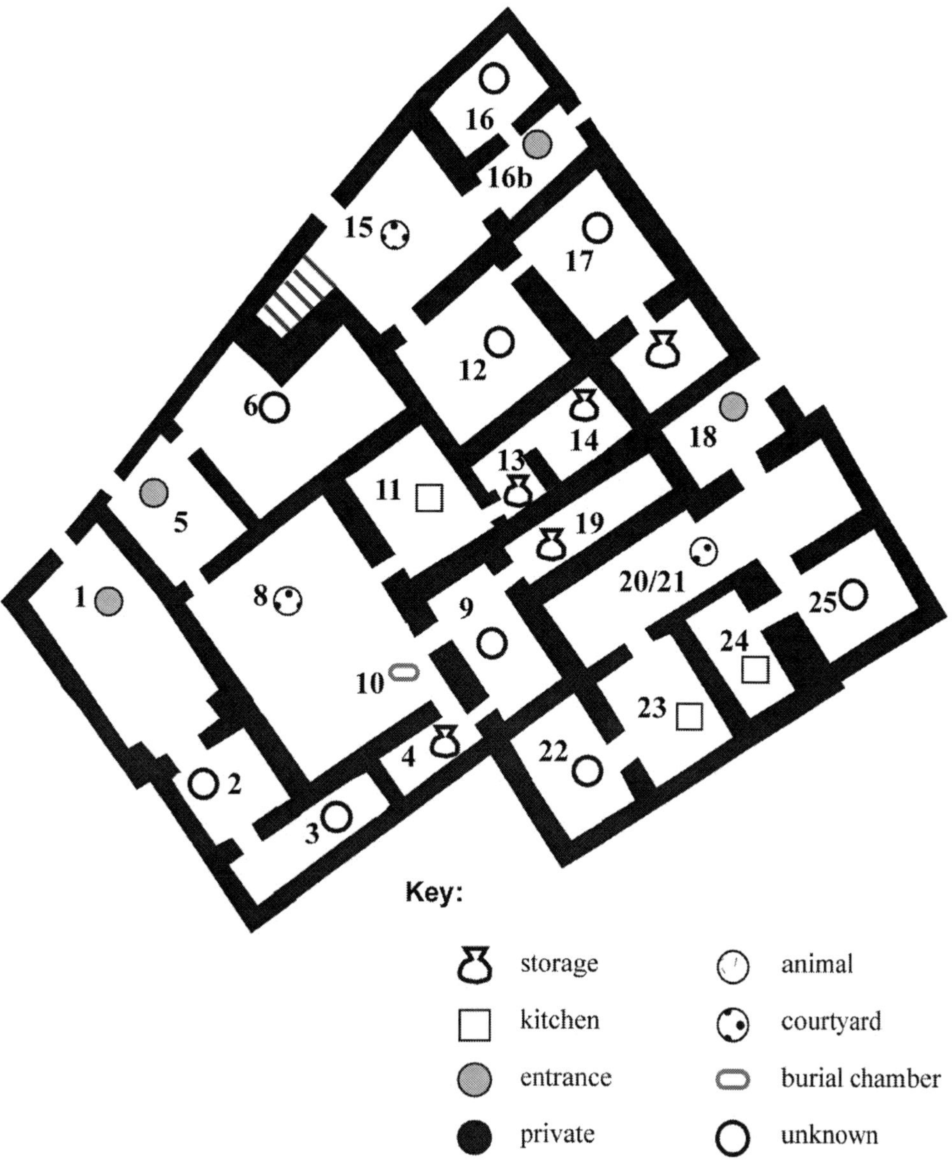

Figure 4.7. Classification of room types based on architectural attributes, Building Unit 4, Titriş. Quantity of room functions identified by architectural attributes: storage rooms (5), kitchens (3), entrances (4), private (0), animal pens (0), courtyards (3), burial chambers (1), and unidentifiable rooms (9).

Room Type	Room Numbers
Entrance	1, 5, 15, 16b, 18
Courtyard	8, 15, 20/21
Kitchen	none identified based on architecture based on hearths: 9, 23, 24
Private	none identified based on architecture
Storage	4, 13, 14, 19
Animal Pen	none identified based on architecture

Table 4.4. Building Unit 4 room types (based on architectural evidence).

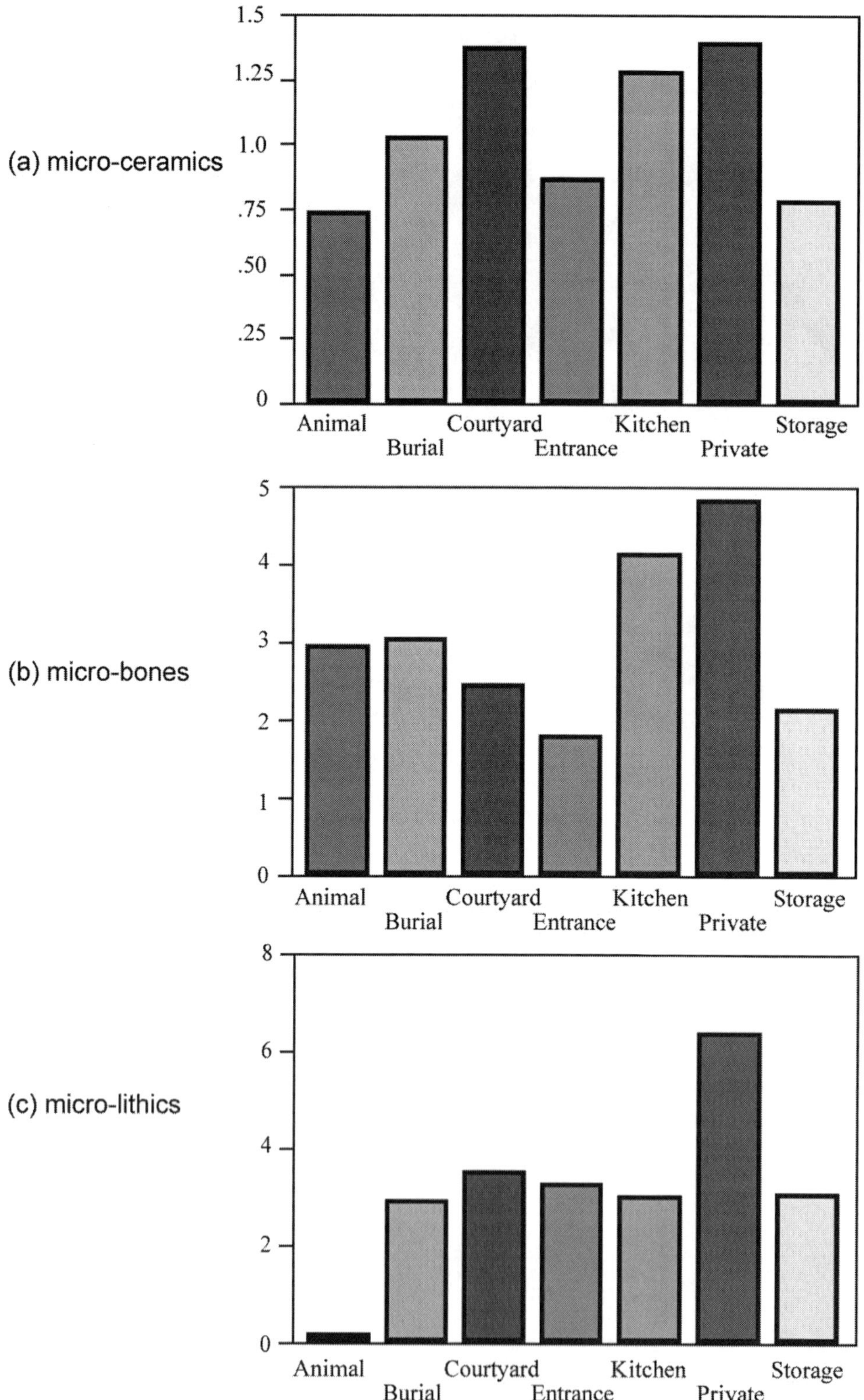

Figure 4.8. Micro-debris densities per room type in Building Unit 4, Titriş. The vertical axis indicates the density of micro-artifact counts per liter.

Figure 4.9. Micro-signatures per room type, Building Unit 4, Titriş. The three-letter acronym in each room represents the high, moderate, and low density of pottery (P/m/p), bone (B/m/b), and lithic debris (L/m/l).

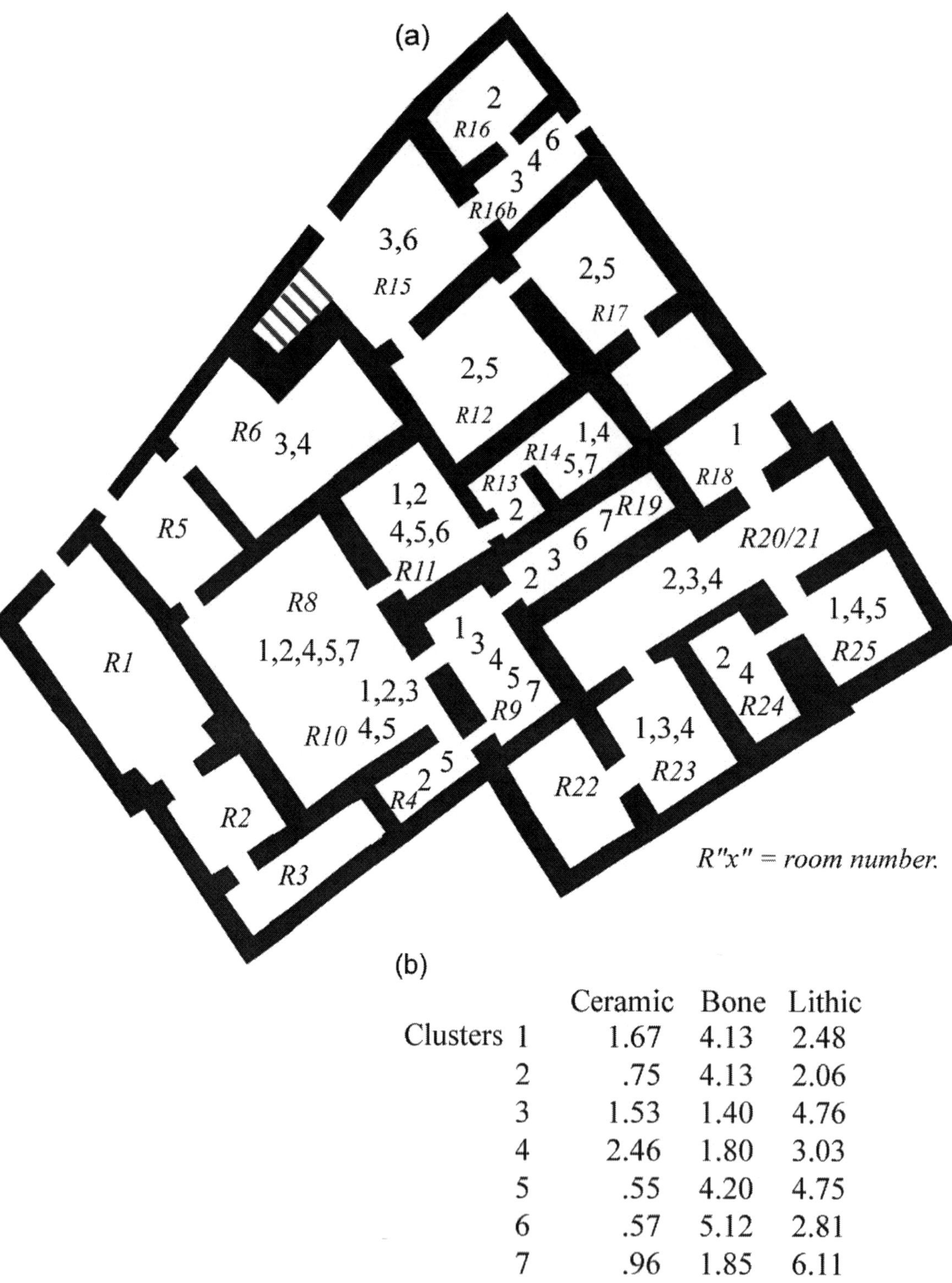

	Ceramic	Bone	Lithic
Clusters 1	1.67	4.13	2.48
2	.75	4.13	2.06
3	1.53	1.40	4.76
4	2.46	1.80	3.03
5	.55	4.20	4.75
6	.57	5.12	2.81
7	.96	1.85	6.11

Figure 4.10. Building Unit 4 cases: analyzed by hierarchical cluster analysis. (b) A chart with the mean per cluster for each micro-artifact type. (a) A map of the distribution of the six cluster types per room within Building Unit 4.

Courtyard	Dimensions	Square Meters	Number of Samples
8 (early)	6 x 7 m	42	6
8 (late)	6 x 4.4 m	26.4	6
20 / 21	8 x 3 m	22.65	4
15	4.3 x 3.85 m	16.55	2

Table 4.5. The size of courtyards in Building Unit 4, Titriş.

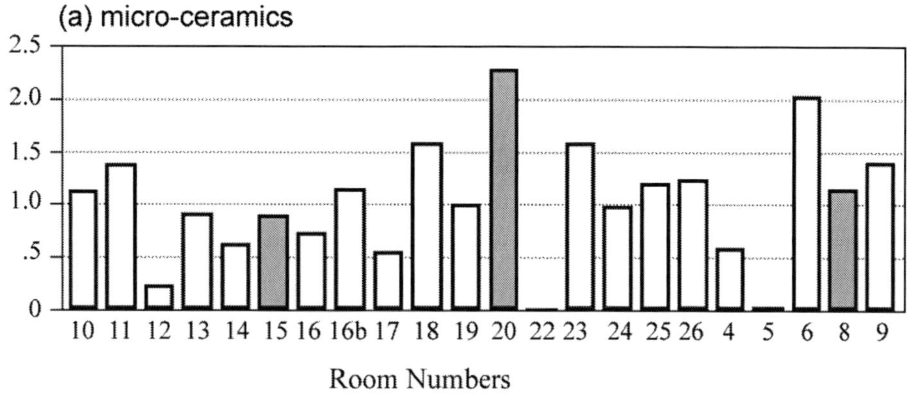

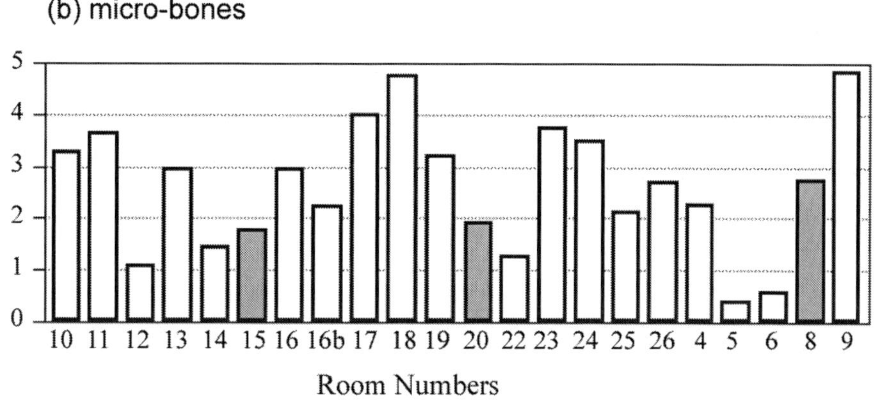

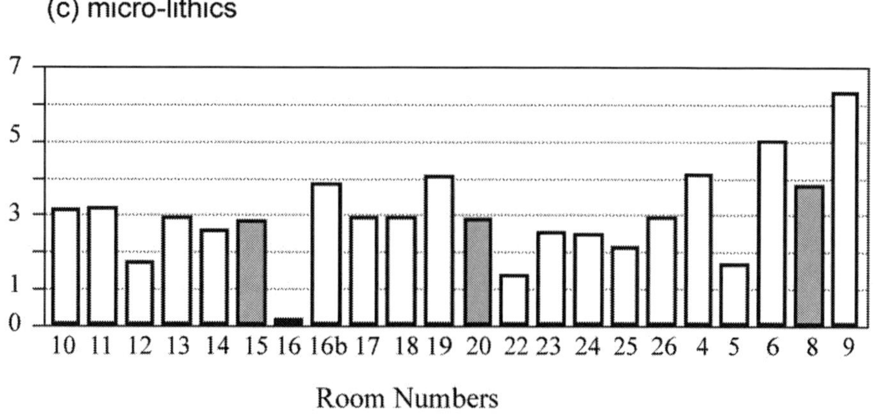

Figure 4.11. Building Unit 4: median density of micro-artifacts on surfaces. The vertical axis indicates the density of micro-artifact counts per liter.

micro-lithics and moderate to high amounts of micro-ceramics and bones. The improved outdoor light may explain the preference for flint knapping in courtyards, and ethnoarchaeological observations support the finding that a variety of other activities took place in courtyards.

Interestingly, the courtyards did not share ceramic-ware profiles (Figure 4.12). Rather, courtyard 8 contained a high amount of fine wares, sandy wares predominated in Courtyard 15, and Courtyard 20/21 contained only a moderate amount of fine and sandy wares. Courtyard 8 also contained the highest amount of mudbrick; these bricks were slightly burned, which enabled them to remain intact after the flotation process. And, finally, the early phase of Courtyard 8 was, by far, the largest among the three courtyards. These lines of evidence suggest that Courtyard 8 was preferred for receiving or serving special guests. Or, each courtyard may have been used by a different family or different age groups within an extended family (for example, a newly married son and daughter-in-law who utilized courtyard 20/21, as opposed to the head patriarch and his wife who used Courtyard 8 and the associated fine ware vessels). An accurate measurement of macro-artifact and macro-ceramic ware density per courtyard would confirm this hypothesis.

Building Unit 4: Kitchens

Based on the presence of hearths, plastered work surfaces (DPSs), and high concentrations of macro-sherds, three kitchens were identified: Rooms 11, 23, and 24 (see Figure 4.7). Interestingly, modern villagers in Turkey emphasize the importance of food in defining an *ev* or *hane* ("house"), which they define as "a group of people whose food is cooked in common" (Stirling 1965: 35). Due to its large size, a very high concentration of micro-burned bone (Figure 4.13), and both a hearth and a DPS (with an *in situ* vessel), I concluded that Room 11 was the main kitchen for the house. This room also contained a trash pit in its southeast corner. The contents of the vessel found on the DPS contained a very high concentration of micro-animal bone and a large number of burned wood charcoal and seeds, suggesting food storage or perhaps the remains of a meal. Among the 25 rooms, Room 11 contained a very high density of micro-cooking wares, as did an associated storage room to the northeast (Room 13) (see Figure 4.12).

Although difficult to prove, one or more of these hearths may have been used as a furnace for heating the room rather than simply cooking. In the modern Kurdish Village, House 2 contained such a device in Room 3 (in this case, a modern kerosene heater). Among the hearths, the one in room 11 is the most likely candidate for multiple uses — for example cooking and heating — due to its large size, formal construction (baked brick sides, approximately 60 cm high), and its location within a fairly large room.

The highest frequency of sandy wares occurred in peripheral rooms (see Figure 4.12). These micro-sherds may be pieces from storage jars or from vessels used for everyday use instead of entertaining. For example, the northeast rooms (Rooms 15, 16, and 16b) may be associated with animal penning, not social activities that required fine serving wares. In contrast, the concentration of fine wares occurred in the main courtyard, two of the living rooms (Rooms 6 and 9), and one of the kitchens (Room 11). The rooms with an overall low quantity of ceramic wares (labeled "fsc" in Figure 4.12) contained a small amount of all micro-ceramics. Thus the assemblages in Rooms 1, 5, 12, 14, and 22 suggest activities that did not involve the frequent use and breakage of ceramic vessels.

Building Unit 4: Entrances from Street

Access or reception rooms are much more difficult to identify in the archaeological record. These rooms may have served as "audience rooms" where visitors were received. Architecturally and spatially they may appear obvious (for example, the first room one enters in a house), but this does not mean that the ancient inhabitants used these areas in the same manner as front doors and hallways are used today. Instead, I divided access rooms into two categories: (1) from public streets into private rooms, and, (2) from small rooms into larger rooms (discussed in the next section). Accordingly, Room 5 may have served as a passageway from the main street into Unit 4's main courtyard (Room 8). In Ur III levels at Ur, Woolley (1965: 156) observed that occasionally a "lobby" containing a water jar and a drain for feet washing, was attached to a courtyard. Although no such feature was discovered in Room 5 or Room 10, both may have been constructed to prevent a direct entrance into the courtyard or to provide space and the necessary items for daily ablutions. Rooms 15, 16b, and 18 also provided access into the house. Each room probably served more than one function. Thus 16b may have been used for straw storage (discussed below) and Room 18 for food storage (suggested by the high amount of sandy and cooking wares, combined with the overall high quantity of micro-ceramics and bones).

Building Unit 4: Entrances into Other Rooms

Many of the interior passageways were created as part of remodeling efforts. For example, Room 10 was created during the late phase of the building after Courtyard 8 was sub-divided. This room may have been cordoned off to reinforce the sacred space connected with the burial (found in the early phase floor). Or the presence of ancestral skeletons may have been of secondary consideration to the need for extra privacy or screening before entering Room 9, the site of lithic production and food consumption. Room 2 may have served a similar function for Room 3 (spatially located in a very private and thus potentially important corner of this house). Once remodeled, these reception rooms afforded additional privacy and formality to the room entered next. Miglus (1996) found this type of room in Old Babylonian

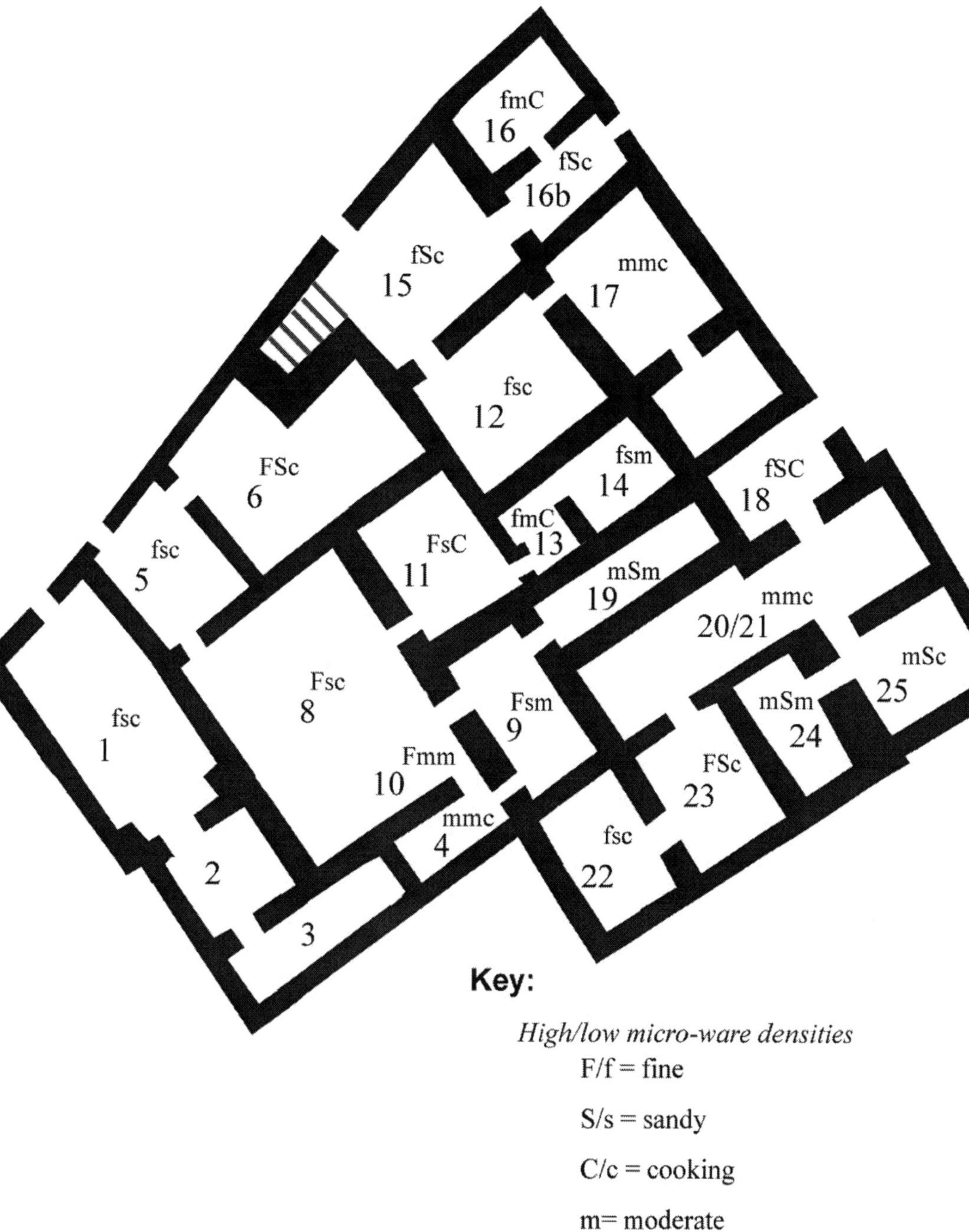

Figure 4.12. Distribution of ceramic wares, Building Unit 4, Titriş.

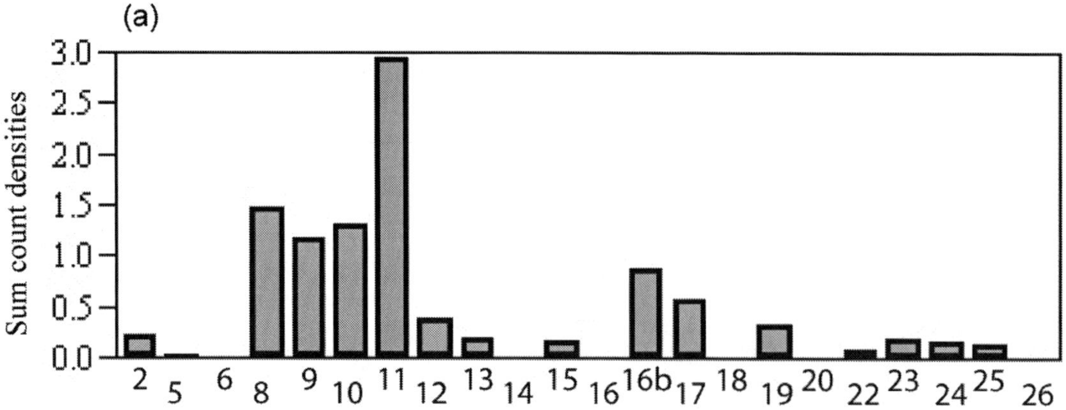

Figure 4.13. Distribution of burned bone, Building Unit 4, Titriş. (a) A histogram with the average count density of burned bone per room (the horizontal axis indicates the room numbers). (b) A map of the the location of the rooms with the highest burned bone densities.

houses. The reception room was usually the second-largest room in the house and often attached to the courtyard with well-built walls and, occasionally, an associated lavatory and a centrally located doorway (Keith 1999: 258). A modern parallel to this private room may be the Turkish *sofa*, or "central room," used for greeting, sitting, and circulating through.

Building Unit 4: Tomb

Room 10, segregated during the late phase in the corner of the courtyard, contained a burial which was cut into the early floors (Figure 4.14). The tomb, roofed with stone slabs, contained the disarticulated remains of two juveniles; a vessel buried in the tomb possibly contained the remains of at least one other individual (Laneri 1999). Burials under house floors are often interpreted as a symbol of ownership or ancestral ties. The practice of human burials within domestic rooms occurred in at least five separate structures at Titriş. The practice of sub-floor burials within domestic houses is commonly found through the ancient Near East (Potts 1997: 230-33). In one example, Woolley (1965: 160-1) discovered this pattern in Ur III private houses.

> There, under the nave of a chapel (if the house had one), was the family tomb. In most cases this was a brick vault which was opened and reused for each member of the house that died. The dead man, wrapped in matting and wearing his clothes and personal trinkets, was laid in the vault on his side (the bones of the last occupant being unceremoniously bundled away into a corner) with a cup of water held to his lips; the door of the tomb was bricked up, two or three clay vessels containing food were leant against the blocking....Children are often buried in clay jars.

This last comment about child burial practices may explain the presence of vessel burials at Titriş. Brick tombs and even well-built, vaulted ones were also common in the Jemdet Nasr through Early Dynastic III periods (e.g., at Ur, Postgate 1990: 234). Texts from these periods refer to burial rooms. For example, an Akkadian exorcistic ritual referred to a wing of a building as the "wing of the family spirits" (*šiddi eṭem kimti*; Bottéro 1995: 280). And Postgate (1992: 99) explained that when a family member who was to be buried under the floor died, a priest was brought to the house to administer the last rites. House floor burials are fairly common in the early historic period. Unfortunately, reasons for the choice of whose corpse was buried there remains elusive. The room may have been replastered for these rites, which would account for the large amount of micro-plaster in Room 10 in Unit 4. This room may have also served as a domestic chapel for the worship of family gods and goddesses or a cult of the ancestors. In the Old Babylonian period, letters frequently contained requests to familial gods. For example, one father asked that his cattle pen be expanded and his fold become wide (van der Toorn 1996a: 103).

Building Unit 4: Animal Pen

Several lines of evidence point to the use of rooms 16 and 16b as animal pens and for straw storage. Rooms 16, 16b, and 15 contained irregular, poorly constructed surfaces. In a micro-morphological study, Matthews et al. (1996a: 323) discovered that stable floors were characterized by dung pellets, digested plant remains, spherulites (small, usually spheroidal bodies consisting of radiating crystals), organic staining, and salts. In future studies, the application of micro-morphological analysis could confirm the use of a room as a stable. In the meantime, micro-archaeological samples from the floor in Room 16b contained large quantities of micro-lithics. The description in Chapter 3 of animal activity areas revealed that a high concentration of micro-chipped stone may indicate straw storage, presumably next to the stable where the animal(s) was housed. Another line of evidence for the use of Rooms 16 and 16b as animal pens are the rooms' spatial location within the house. Horne (1994) observed that straw and animal pens tended to be in the corners of structures. This arrangement had several advantages: less noise and smells (the room located furthest from the living rooms), easy access to the outside (16b, for example, opened directly onto the street), and little or no traffic through the room (which would not be the case in a more centrally located room). Flat-lying sherds and small lime-lined pits may also indicate that a room contained animals. In a Syrian village, Kamp (1982: 241) observed that broken pieces of pottery were occasionally embedded into courtyard floors to hold food or water for chickens. Alternatively, a small depression may be plastered with lime for this purpose.

The distribution of flint debitage colors is another line of evidence that suggests Rooms 16 and 17 were used for working on tools used for agricultural activities. The floors in both Rooms 16 and 17 were highest in tan-colored chipped stone (Figure 4.15). The tan colored tools may have been used to butcher animals or to thresh straw. Rooms 4, 9, and 19 also contained high levels of tan chipped stone. These micro-flakes may be debitage from using the agricultural tools to cut meat or from sharpening the tools (and subsequently storing them in Rooms 4 and 19). Conversely, two of the courtyards and a southern kitchen contained the highest amount of gray chipped stone, suggesting this stone type was preferred for domestic implements.

Finally, ethnographic observations reveal that rural and urban household rooms may be used to house domesticated animals. For example, in modern-day Urfa, some recent urbanites (Kurds from the surrounding countryside) brought cattle and chickens into their houses, much to the chagrin of their neighbors. And, in an Iranian village, English (1966: 131) observed:

> Cattle and donkeys are stabled in small adobe rooms or pens inside the household compounds. They are kept indoors to escape the summer sun,

Figure 4.14. Domestic tomb in Room 10, Building Unit 4, Titriş. Photograph taken by the author. Room 10 also contained two stone-lined thresholds and an *in situ* door socket (in the upper right-hand corner of the room).

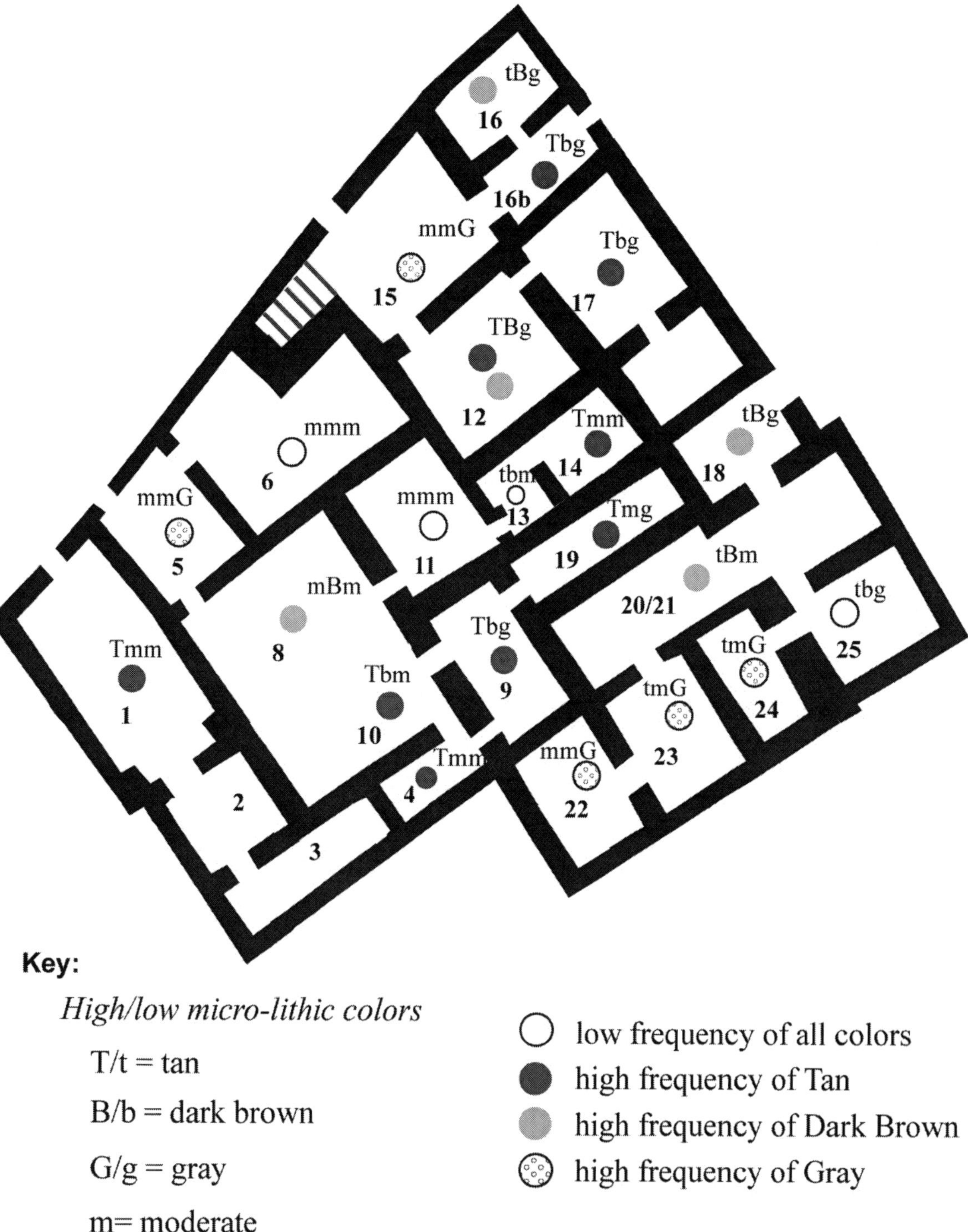

Figure 4.15. Distribution of micro-chipped stone colors, Building Unit 4, Titriş.

the winter cold, and the ever present possibility of theft.

I observed this pattern, for goats, at the modern village of Pamuklu in House 2 (see Figure 3.3). As one might expect, the surfaces in these rooms were usually not as well constructed as other rooms; they often contained mud-packed floors without any plaster, instead covered with dung and plant remains, including straw.

Building Unit 4: Private Living Room

Room 9 was a 2.62 x 5.14-meter rectangle. Under the lightly plastered surface, the floor contained irregularly spaced cobbles, possibly to help drain water from the floor. An *in situ* door socket, found near the southwest entrance, suggested a desire for privacy (and possibly kept out non-human house residents) and limited access to the room. No features were preserved within the room, making any functional assignment difficult. Moreover, the macro-artifacts were not significantly distinct from nearby rooms, but rather contained a typical assemblage of sherds, bones, and the occasional lithic tool.

I present several lines of evidence that suggest Room 9 was a "private room" used by men and their guests for socializing, food consumption, and flint knapping. Ethnoarchaeologists propose that wealthy households with sufficient resources may construct an extra living room to serve as a guestroom (Watson 1978: 132, Stirling 1965: 21). Kamp (1982: 102) argued "this structure theoretically reflects both their greater responsibility for hospitality and their greater ability to pay construction costs." To test whether Room 9 served a similar function, nine floor samples were randomly selected from the surface of the room. Among all of the rooms in Unit 4, this one contained the highest amount of micro-chipped stone. Specifically, four of the floor samples contained very high densities of tiny flakes (see Figure 3.30). In conjunction with the analysis of the finds from a flint workshop at Titriş, future analysis should determine whether the patterns of flint types and sizes resulted from lithic tool production or from tool use and recycling. Furthermore, research into tool types and possible standardization may resolve whether individual households engaged in tool production or if this craft was supervised and/or limited to workshops, such as the lithic one at Titriş.

Regardless of the tool type, the micro-debitage in Room 9 was concentrated around the edges of the room and in an entranceway to the southwest, which led into Room 4. This pattern suggested that Room 4 was a storage annex, possibly where the raw material worked on in Room 9 was kept. Furthermore, Room 9 contained a high density of fine ceramic wares, suggesting an area where socializing and eating occurred that was primarily used for the consumption of liquids in fine-ware cups or food in fine-ware bowls. This food may have been consumed by the craftspeople who made or repaired the lithic tools.

High densities of baked brick and/or plaster may indicate other rooms that were afforded greater attention. Figure 4.16 illustrates that the two potential private rooms, Rooms 9 and 6, contained high amounts of plaster and baked brick, respectively. In general, the rooms in the center of Building Unit 4 contained higher densities of this debris than the outlying rooms.

Building Unit 4: Storage – Goods and Food

The structure contained several possible storage rooms. Features within storage rooms may have included wooden chests, wall niches, window ledges, mudbrick or wooden shelves, pegs, reed baskets, or large ceramic jars. Textual evidence suggests that some of these items, particularly trunks filled with clothes or silver or jars filled with oil may have been included in a woman's dowry (Dalley 1980: 53-56). Thus the amount and quality of goods in storage containers might correlate with familial wealth (although the bride may have married above or below her own family status). Since these artifacts and features, if present, were most likely removed before the residents abandoned the site, we must turn to other lines of evidence to identify goods or food storage rooms in the archaeological record.

Architecturally, we expect that storage rooms were usually the smallest ones within a domestic structure. Furthermore, windows, light, and even the ability to stand upright were unimportant. Within any given house, several rooms may have been set aside for food or water storage (e.g., House 2, Room 2 in the modern village, see Figure 3.3; or the subterranean rooms in the Alman Evi, see Figure 3.4). Horne (1994: 94) observed that 40% of the rooms within an Iranian village were used for agricultural or pastoral storage and stabling. These rooms often opened onto courtyards (Horne 1994: 189, Kramer 1982a: 106). In Unit 4, this would suggest that Rooms 4, 18, 25, and 12 were used for storage. Inaccessible corner rooms (such as Room 22) may have also been preferred for storage. Conversely, these rooms may have been used for animal penning (if they opened directly onto a street) or for a private chapel (especially common during the Ur III period; Crawford 1991: 101).

At the micro-archaeological level, the micro-debris profiles of storerooms often resembled that of larger, contiguous rooms. Accordingly, cluster analysis associated the "Goods Storage" (identified by the author) Rooms 4 and 19 with the micro-profile in Room 9 (see Figure 5.12). Similarly, "Food Storage" (identified by the author) Rooms 13 and 14 shared a profile with the kitchen (Room 11). Although these rooms shared micro-profiles, the actual density of debris tended to be less in the storage room, as opposed to the room where the activity originally occurred.

Building Unit 4: Facilities/Water Installations

Although no water-related facilities were excavated in Building Unit 4, Building Unit 2 at Titriş included a drainage system that directed water from the courtyard out to the street. Unit 4, Room 6, located adjacent to the

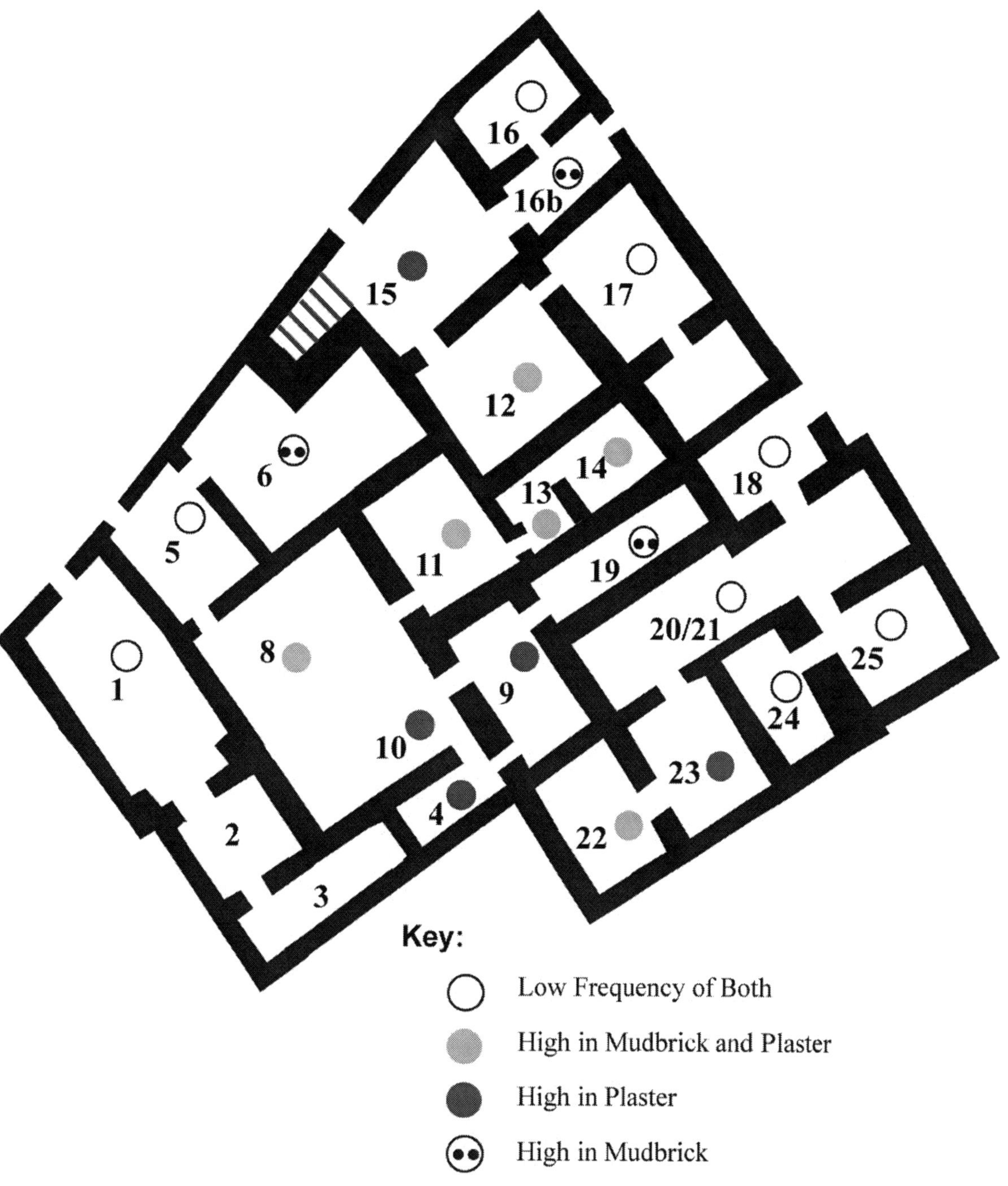

Figure 4.16. Quantity of mudbrick and plaster per room, Building Unit 4, Titriş.

staircase, may have contained a bathing area. Similarly, at Ur, during the late EBA, Woolley (1965: 159) discovered a "lavatory with a drain in its paved floor" underneath the staircase. Drains may have been associated with households of people with higher status (Henrickson 1981: 69).

Conclusion: Building Unit 4 Room Functions

In sum, micro-artifacts helped identify room functions within Unit 4. Moreover, micro-archaeology revealed activity areas and, subsequently, preferred rooms for conducting certain activities within the house. Compared to the results obtained from architecture alone, micro-archaeology provided evidence for a more detailed classification of room types (compare Figure 4.17 to Figure 4.7, where no private or animal rooms were identified). Comprehensive sampling from the remaining three domestic structures in this neighborhood would enable the micro-archaeologist to suggest differences in economic and social status, household production and craft specialization, and the types and distribution of daily activities among the households. An example of this approach will be presented later in this chapter when Building Unit 4 is compared to Building Unit 5 (see Figure 4.35).

Case Example: Terrace, Titriş Höyük

The "Terrace" was a partially excavated structure, slightly earlier in date than Building Unit 4. This structure lies below the numbered units in this neighborhood and was referred to by the site supervisor as "the terrace." In the absence of an assigned number, that designation will be used here. The Terrace contained three main architectural phases, but samples were only taken from two earliest phases (Figure 4.18). After the structure was abandoned, the area was probably used for trash disposal. By then the building was situated between three later structures: Building Units 4, 6, and 7. The Terrace contained a set of rooms similar to Building Unit 4: courtyard, kitchens, storage chambers, and a room for the burial of an ancestor. Based on double walls and the orientation of the rooms, Rooms L, M, and K are probably associated with a later structure (Building Unit 7).

The median densities of micro-debris on floor surfaces suggested different activities within the rooms (Figure 4.19). For example, the trash pits in Rooms C and V and the DPS in the early-phase courtyard contained the highest density of micro-ceramics, while the pits in Rooms B and V contained the largest quantity of micro-bones. The sections below examine each room individually, combining data from micro-debris, macro-artifacts, and features.

Terrace Courtyard

The Terrace's courtyard (Room A) was the largest excavated room within the structure with multiple entrances (similar to Building Unit 4). In the early phase, the room was divided into two sections (Az and A), but later the wall was removed to create one large room. In the late phase, Room A contained trash pits with large amounts of micro-bones and ceramics and a plastered preparation area. These two lines of evidence suggest that food preparation occurred here (Figure 4.20).

Applying hierarchical cluster analysis (using the same micro-profile criteria as in Building Unit 4), I graphed the distribution of clusters per room (Figure 4.21). Again, the main courtyard, Room A, contained the largest number of individual clusters, suggesting a multitude of activities: food preparation, food consumption, flintknapping, and possibly socializing among family members.

Terrace Kitchen

Rooms C, U, and V were tentatively identified as kitchens based on the presence of a hearth or a DPS. Rooms C, U, V, and X contained one or more of these features. As demonstrated in Building Unit 4, the co-occurrence of high amounts of micro-ceramics and burned bones is one signature of kitchens. This co-occurrence was noted in Rooms C, V, and in the pits in Courtyard A. In addition, the distribution of micro-cooking wares supports the conclusion that Rooms C, U, V, and X were kitchens where food was prepared in thick-walled vessels (Figure 4.22). The highest density of cooking wares occurred in sample 172 (a pit in Room C), sample 251 (a floor in Room X), 250 (a pit in Room V), and sample 358 (a hearth in Room U). Adjacent samples to the ones mentioned above contained high amounts of burned bone, suggesting meat roasting and, possibly, a cremation (Figure 4.23). Sample 355 was taken from the burial fill in Room Y, 108 from a floor in the courtyard, 171 from a pit in the courtyard, and the samples next highest in micro-burned bone (in the upper 95% of the mean) were from a hearth in Room V and floors in Rooms X and A. Among the areas where cooking occurred, cluster analysis suggested that Rooms D/V and C/U contained similar activities, represented by clusters 4 and 1 respectively (see Figure 4.21).

Entrance Room to the Terrace Building

We cannot conclusively locate the entrances into this building unit without further horizontal excavations. But based on the other house plans at Titriş, we would not expect an entrance directly from the street into the courtyard. Furthermore, we would expect a row of rooms around the courtyard and an entrance from the street into a second tier of rooms. Of the excavated rooms, possible entrances include Room E, Room J, or Room Z. Another possibility is that the entrance has not yet been excavated and lies to the west or to the south of the trench.

Terrace Burial Chamber

The earlier phase of Room B (Room Y) contained a burial. The samples taken from the burial fill and adjacent surfaces contained a high concentration of micro-bones and lithics, most likely associated with

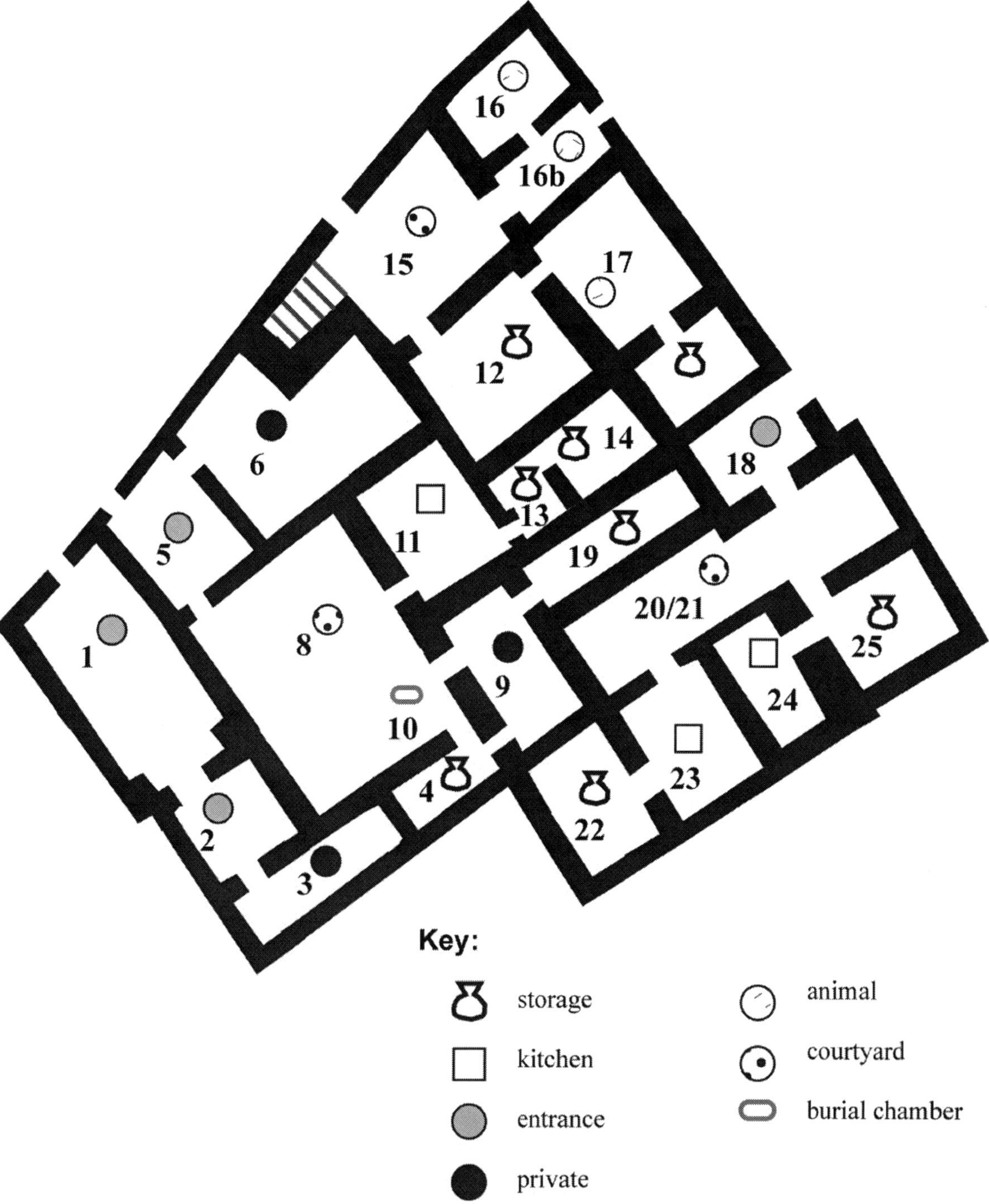

Figure 4.17 Classification of room types based on multiple lines of evidence, Building Unit 4, Titriş. Quantity of room functions identified by several lines of evidence: storage rooms (8), kitchens (3), entrances (4), private (3), animal pens (3), courtyards (3), and burial chambers (1). Compare these results with the results in Figure 4.7 (using only architectural elements).

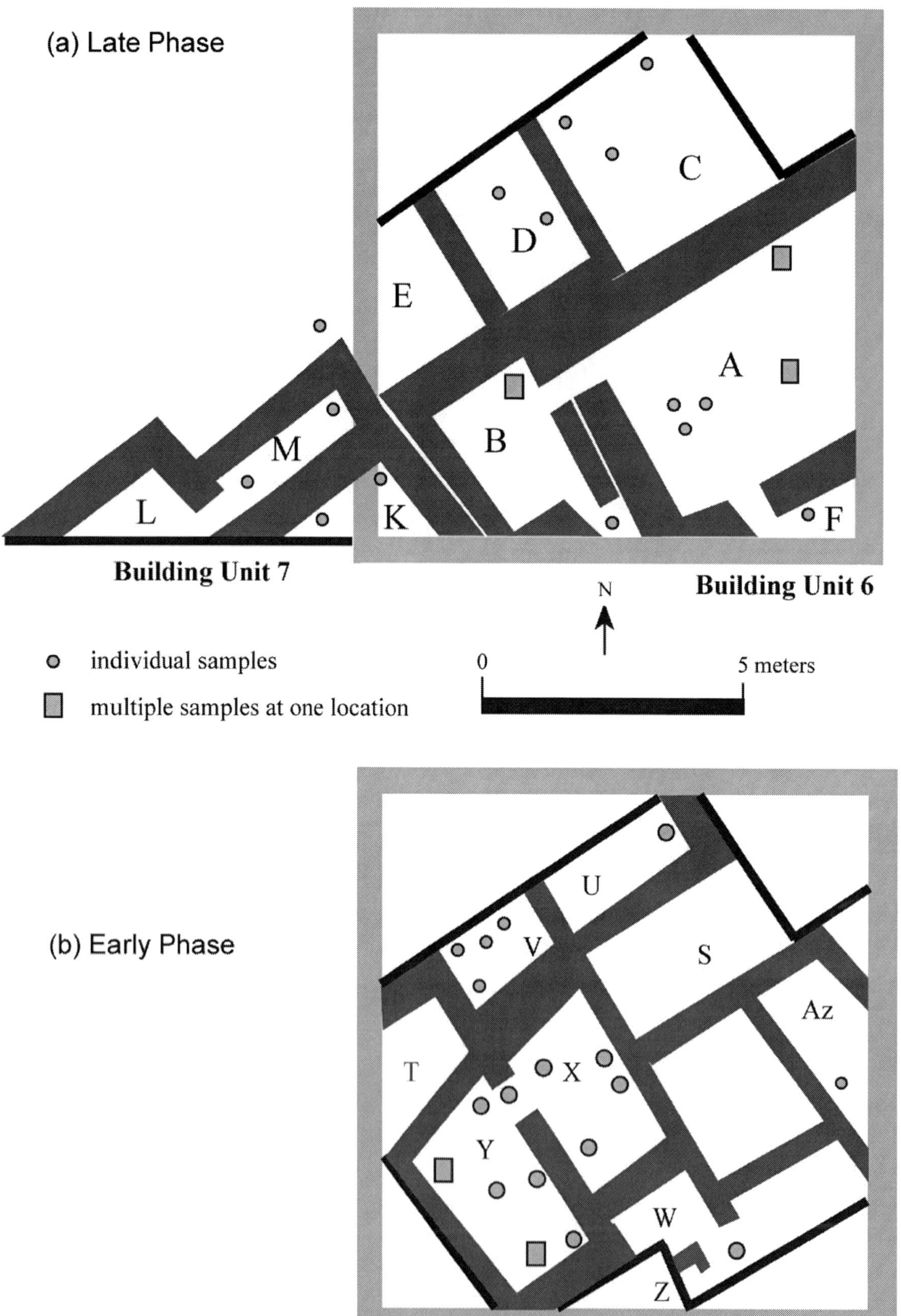

Figure 4.18. Location of micro-debris samples in the Terrace, Titriş. The trench is surrounded by a 50cm baulk (indicated by a gray square). Building Unit 7 (shown in the Late Phase) is in an adjacent trench.

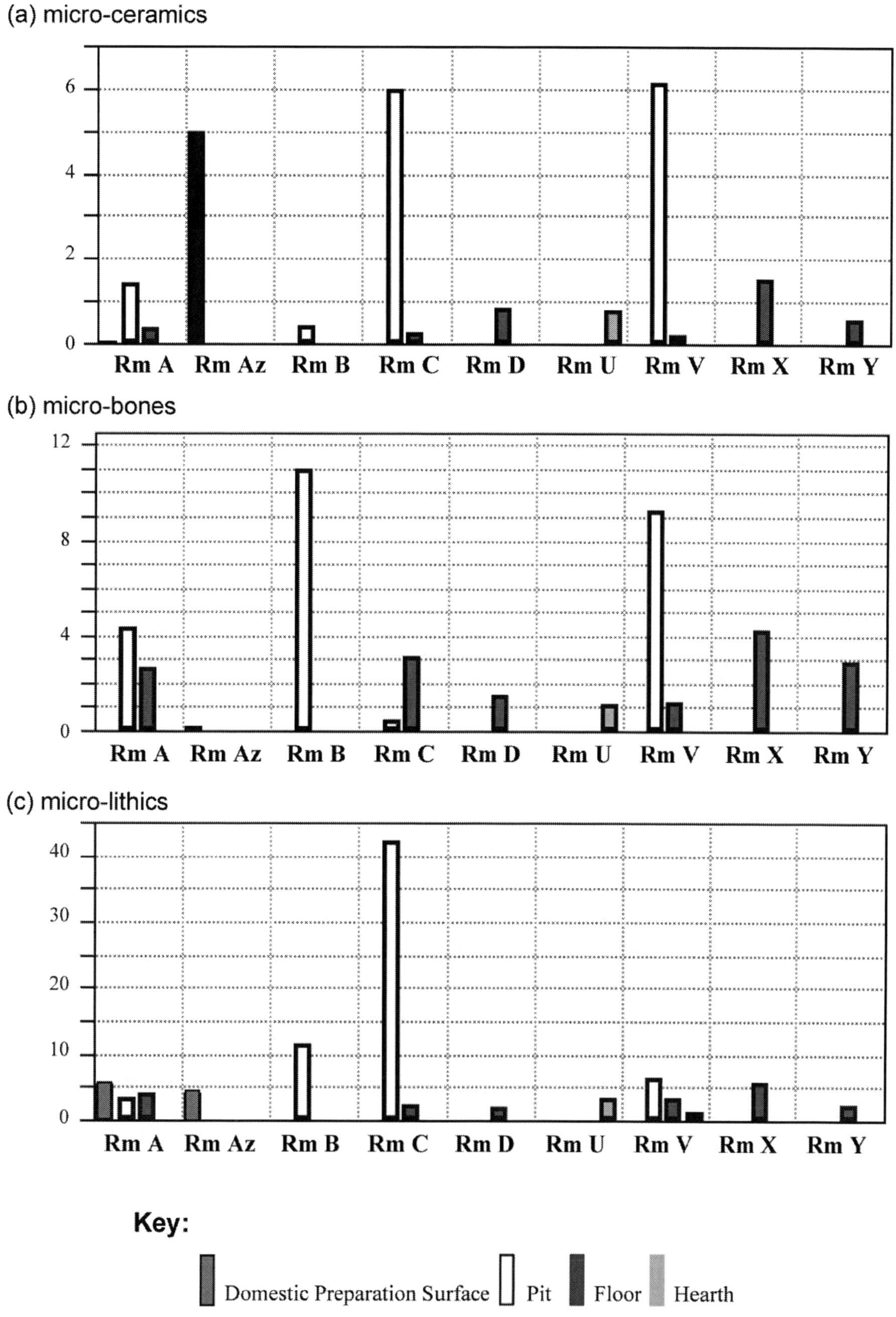

(a) micro-ceramics

0 2 4 6

Rm A Rm Az Rm B Rm C Rm D Rm U Rm V Rm X Rm Y

(b) micro-bones

0 4 8 12

Rm A Rm Az Rm B Rm C Rm D Rm U Rm V Rm X Rm Y

(c) micro-lithics

0 10 20 30 40

Rm A Rm Az Rm B Rm C Rm D Rm U Rm V Rm X Rm Y

Key:

Domestic Preparation Surface Pit Floor Hearth

Figure 4.19. Distribution of micro-debris densities per locus within each room of the Terrace, Titriş. The vertical axis indicates the micro-artifact count density per liter.

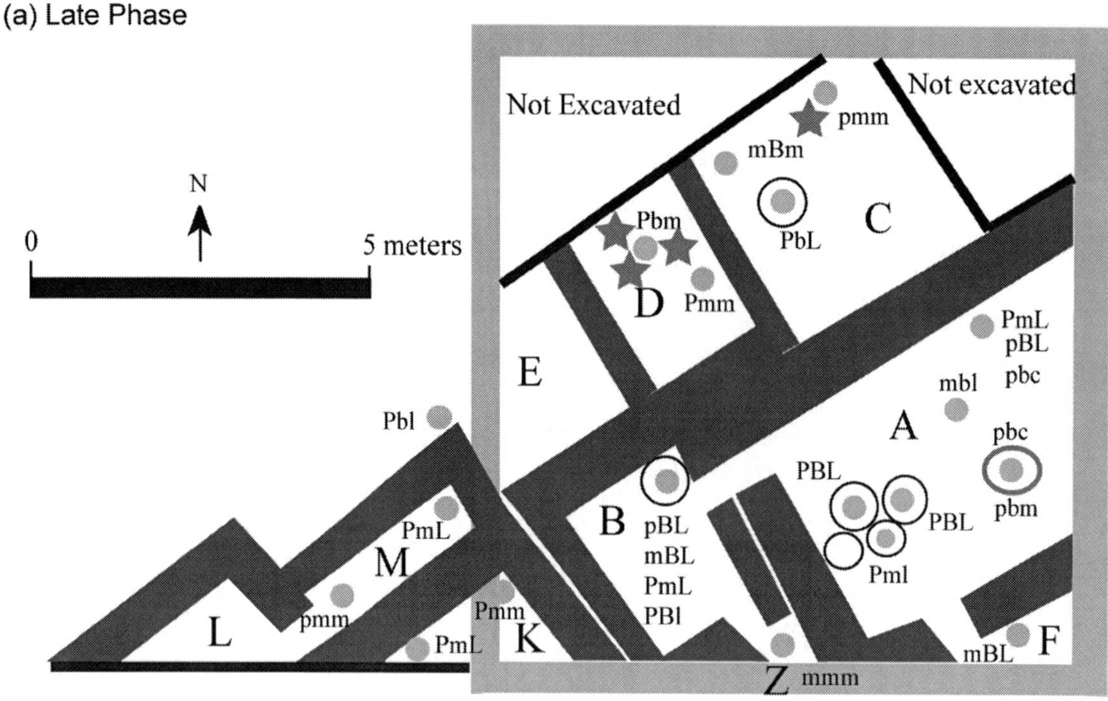

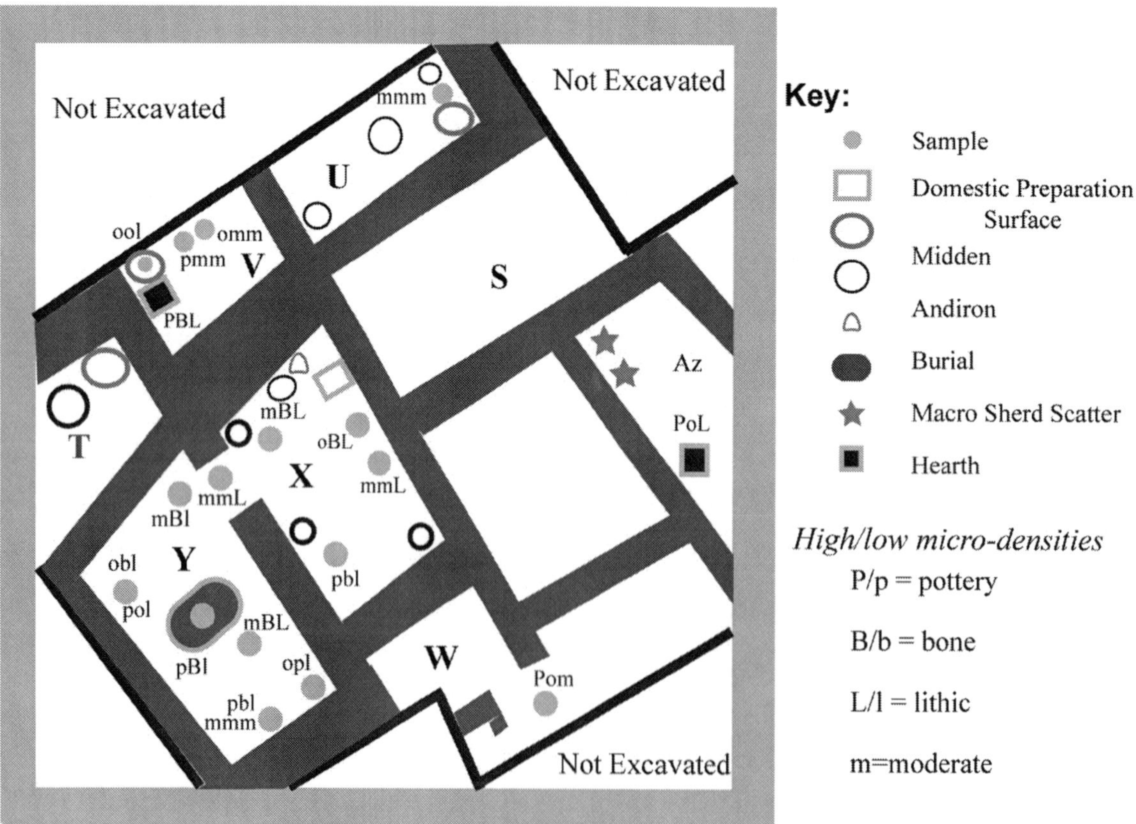

Figure 4.20. Micro-profile of ceramics, bones, and lithics per individual sample, Terrace, Titriş. The trench is surrounded by a 50cm baulk (highlighted by a gray square).

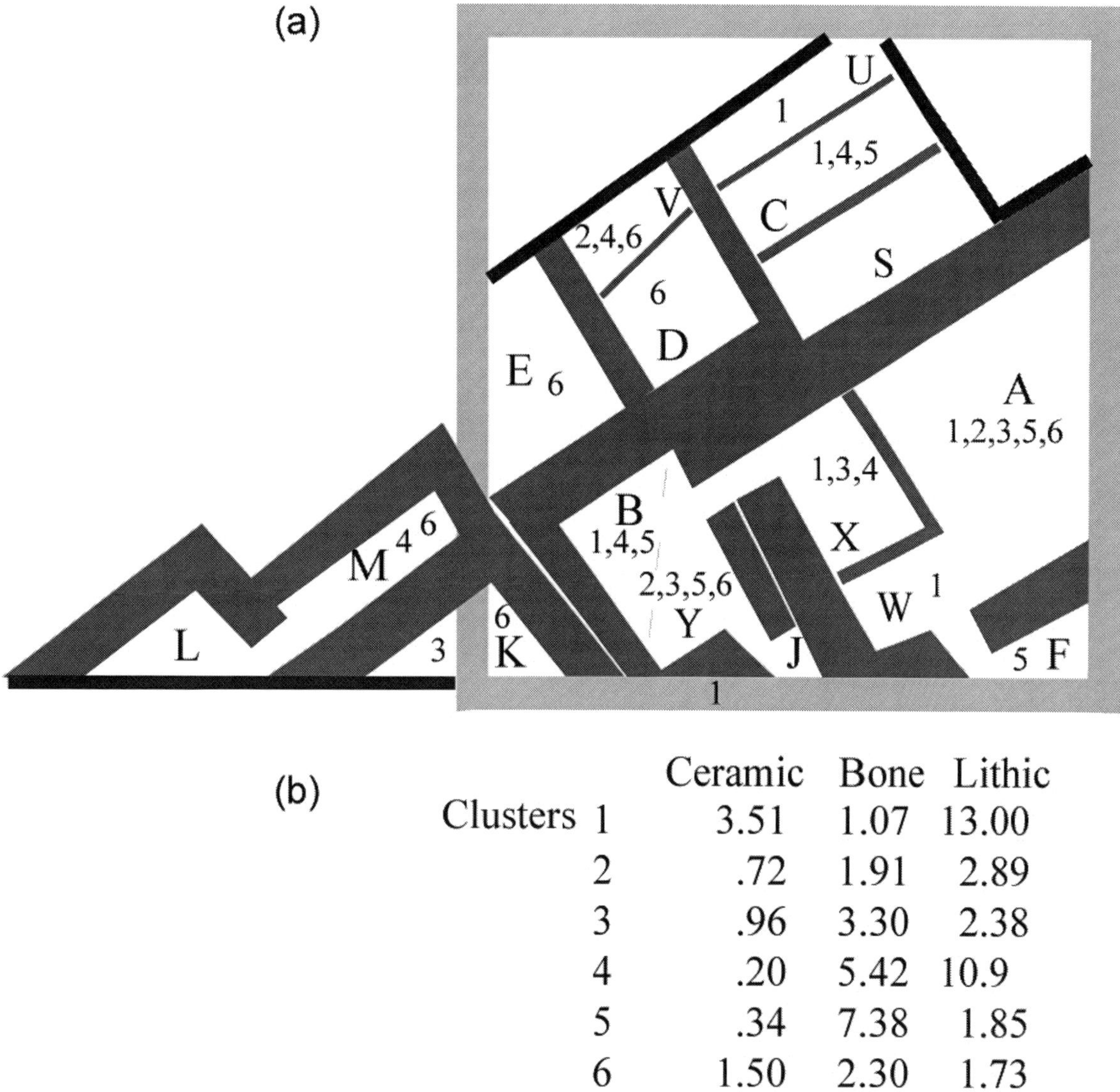

		Ceramic	Bone	Lithic
Clusters	1	3.51	1.07	13.00
	2	.72	1.91	2.89
	3	.96	3.30	2.38
	4	.20	5.42	10.9
	5	.34	7.38	1.85
	6	1.50	2.30	1.73

Figure 4.21. Terrace cases: analyzed by hierarchical cluster analysis. (b) A chart with the mean per cluster for each micro-artifact type. (a) A map of the distribution of the six cluster types per room within the Terrace.

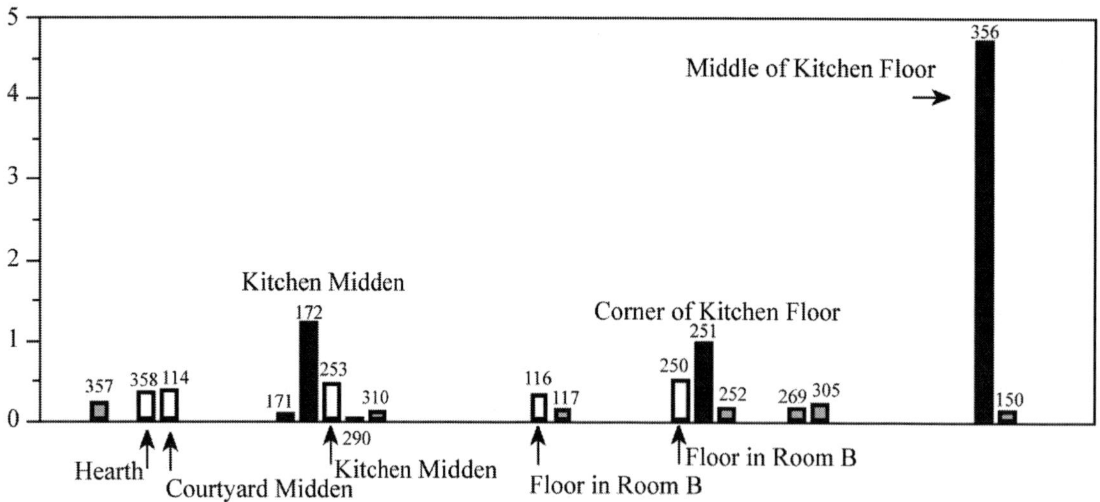

Figure 4.22. Distribution of cooking wares among individual Terrace samples, Titriş.

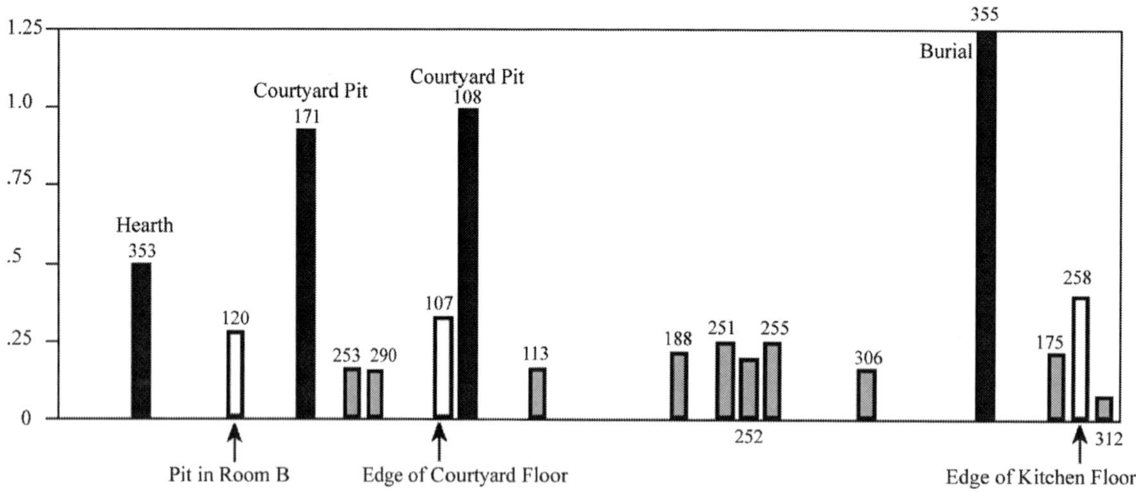

Figure 4.23. Distribution of burned bone among individual Terrace samples, Titriş.

human skeletal remains and crushed grave goods. When compared to other rooms, the floor samples in Room Y ranked moderate to low in all types of micro-debris, suggesting that few activities occurred in this room or that greater attention was paid to keeping this room clean. Either explanation would be understandable given the reverence and/or attention expected to be paid to the room containing ancestors.

When all of the samples in the Terrace were sorted into clusters, the samples in Rooms B and Y contained a very similar combination of clusters: 2, 4, and 5. The earlier Room Y contained one further cluster: 3. These similar profiles suggested that the room use did not substantially alter from the early to the late period.

Terrace Storage

In Building Unit 4, I identified several storage rooms. In the Terrace, the incomplete horizontal exposure made interpretation difficult. Turning to micro-debris profiles to identify storage rooms, we expect either (a) a micro-signature high in one or two types of debris which correspond to a contiguous room's highest debris densities or, (b) a room located in a corner or otherwise less accessible than other rooms. If Room A was indeed a courtyard, Room E may have been such a less accessible room, while the broken vessels in Rooms D and C point to the possibility that they were used to store foods.

Case Example: Building Unit 3, Titriş Höyük

In contrast to the two large structures discussed above, Building Unit 3 at Titriş contained less than 10 rooms. Depending on how the plan is interpreted, there may be as few as four rooms (with a second house containing an additional four or five rooms; see Figure 5.17). A widow and her children may have lived in smaller houses, such as Building Unit 3. One of the texts (ca. 2400 B.C.E.) from the Lagash (a city-state located in southeastern Iraq) archives lists household members, an unusual subject for the otherwise mostly economic nature of the archives. The "Person List" (from the Hermitage, #14019) mentions 12 families. Four of the families consist of widows and children, and an additional family included a mother and daughter, but no husband (Selz 1989: 135) (Thanks are due to Scott Beld for bringing this text to my attention). A smaller family such as "Mrs. Urshapada" and her five children may have been forced by economic necessity to move into a smaller house after the death of the husband/father.

In conclusion, micro-debris analysis provides an invaluable window into the distribution of activities within rooms. Coupled with more traditional lines of evidence, such as macro-artifacts, features, and architectural plans, micro-archaeology is a useful technique for interpreting house plans. In the next section, the analysis of these lines of evidence will be broadened to other sites, notably Kazane and Tilbes, and used to sort structures into domestic versus non-domestic and wealthy versus commoner structures. Before turning to the three sites analyzed for this research, I provide a very brief overview of select Near Eastern house forms to demonstrate that contrary to common assumptions, domestic architecture is not static.

Overview of Early Bronze Age Domestic Structures at Upper Mesopotamian Sites

It is difficult to develop a diachronic perspective on Near Eastern houses because domestic areas are often underreported in monographs or not excavated at all. Most theoretical discussions of domestic organization only consider prehistoric periods. When considering historic periods, these discussions turn to political and economic themes, neglecting houses (e.g., Meyers 1997). Those few studies of domestic structures that exist have focused on substantial residences such as temples, palaces, and large estates (e.g., Henrickson 1982, Delougaz et al. 1967; for exceptions see Woolley 1954, Stone 1987, Veenhof 1996, Keith 1999).

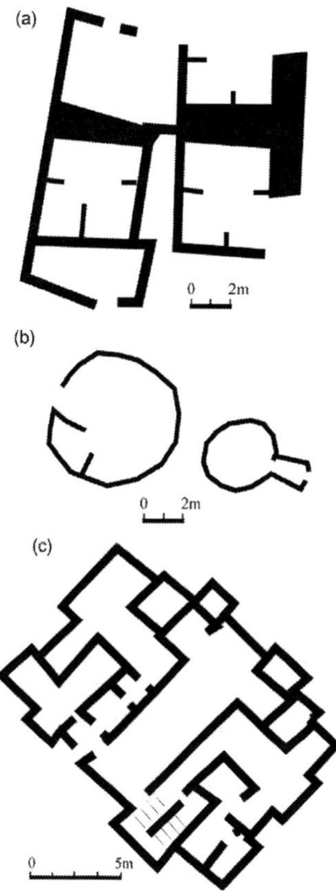

Figure 4.24. Select examples of prehistoric house forms. (a) A 7th mill. house from Hacilar, Level II, Block B. Modified from Eslick 1988: 22. (b) A 6th mill. house from Tell Halaf. Modified from Aurenche 1981: 446. (c) A 5th mill. house from Tell Abada, Level II. Modified from Jasim 1983: 174.

It is often assumed that there was a single, unchanging Middle Eastern household form or "type," the courtyard house. A brief overview of domestic forms indicates that ancient Near Eastern houses include a much greater diversity of architectural plans. These include unicellular structures with limited partitions (Figure 4.24a), circular forms (Figure 4.24b), "cruciform" or "T-shaped plans," (Figure 4.24c), "fully flanked main rooms," (Figure 4.25a), courtyard forms (Figure 4.25b), and rectangular "apartments" (Figure 4.25c).

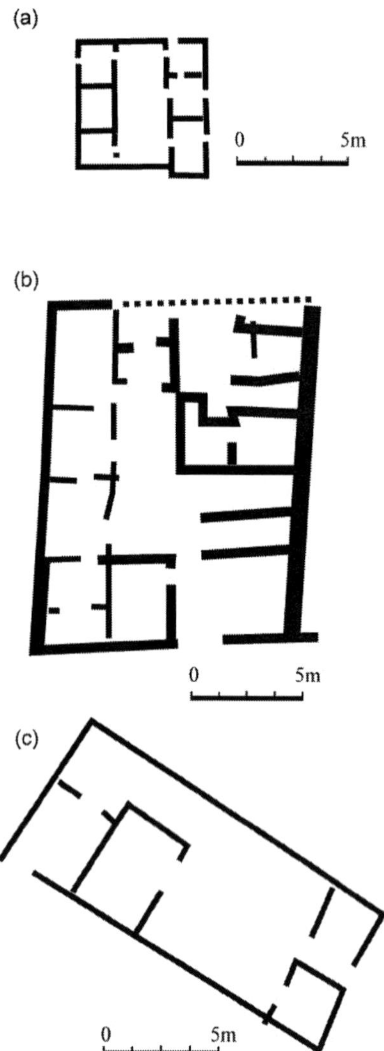

Figure 4.25. Select examples of historic house forms. (a) A 4th mill. "courtyard style with flanked rooms" house from Habuba Kabira. Modified from Vallet 1997:50. (b) A 3rd mill. "modified courtyard / rectangular style" house from Tell Taya. Modified from Reade 1971: 97. (c) A 2nd mill. "rectangular style" house from Ur. Modified from Woolley 1954: 176.

Later Islamic style houses are yet an additional variant on the theme of inner courtyards (Figure 4.26). The privacy offered by inner courtyards combined with the natural lighting provided by the open court were reasons for this architectural preference. A comprehensive diachronic study of elite and non-elite residences in the Near East remains to be written. For now I will simply note that a significant difference of modern compared to earlier "courtyard forms" is the increased use of stronger building materials, such as lime mortar and baked brick. These new materials enabled builders to construct three- and four-story houses, substantially increasing the available floor space within otherwise crowded urban environs and improving the climactic environment. In contrast, third millennium houses tended to be one or two stories.

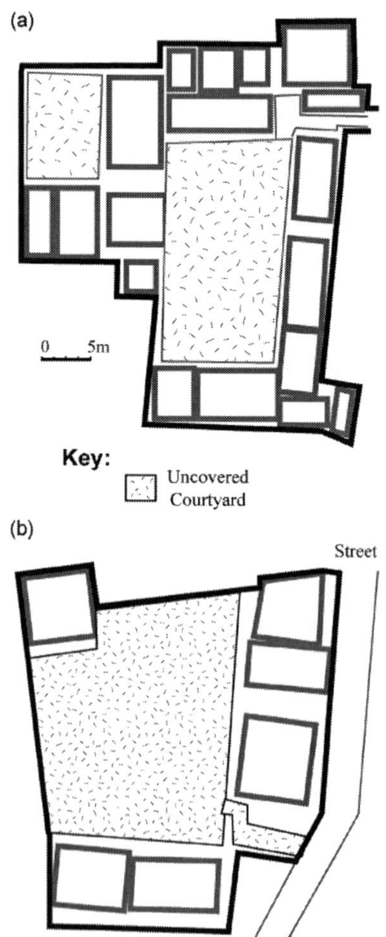

Figure 4.26. Select examples of Islamic house forms. (a) A 17th Century house from Aleppo, Syria. Modified from Raymond 1984: 77. (b) A 20th Century house from Urfa, Turkey. Modified from Oren 1997.

In the following three sections I present a brief overview of the diversity of domestic forms in the third millennium with emphasis on Upper Mesopotamia. This is to try to counteract the trend in most site reports that describes ideal domestic "types" rather than investigating the "on the ground" variability of ancient houses. House form is a significant variable in interpreting ancient society because architecture structures activities and mediates social interactions (Rapoport 1982). The following discussion follows the chronological categories suggested by Ehrich 1992. There is not room here to discuss the difficulties in determining precise dates for these periods using dendrochronology and carbon 14 methods (see further Wright 1980: 95-7, Wright and Rupley 2003).

The Early EBA (ca. 3000-2650 B.C.E.)

In the south, the Early Dynastic sequence, I, II, and III, was established by Henri Frankfort (1934) for sites in the Diyala Region. The first two-thirds of the Early Dynastic period fall into the time period of this section: Early Dynastic I (ca. 3000-2750) and Early Dynastic II (ca. 2750-2650). In the north, this corresponded approximately to the Ninevite 5 Period in the eastern part of Upper Mesopotamia (Schwartz 1987) and Early Bronze I in the west (Algaze 1990: 297). During this period many southern settlements grew in size, resulting in high population densities in urban settings (Adams 1981). Densely settled cities affected the design of domestic units, creating ad hoc structures formed when small parcels of land (often left over from the construction of two larger structures) were built upon. An example of a southern site with early third-millennium domestic architecture is Shuruppak (Fara; Martin 1988). In the Diyala (in Iraq), Eshnunna (Tell Asmar; Delougaz 1967) and Tutub (Tell Khafaje; Delougaz 1967) contained limited domestic remains.

Houses at these sites were often large, well planned, and built around a central courtyard. In some households, we can identify different room types: reception rooms, kitchens, courtyards, and water installations. The rural counterpart to these urban forms was the farmstead, such as Sakheri Sughir (Wright 1969: 43-56).

The Middle-EBA (ca. 2650-2350 B.C.E.)

In the south, this period corresponds, roughly, to the Early Dynastic III, ca. 2650-2350. Southern sites with large horizontal exposures of domestic architecture include Shuruppak, Eshnunna, Lagash, and Abu Salabikh. The limited domestic exposure from these sites revealed a "courtyard-style house" composed of a large, often square, room surrounded on all sides by smaller ones (Figure 4.27c). Although often conflated with the 'Ubaid style, Uruk houses also included linear forms that lacked clear courtyards (Figure 4.27a and 4.27b). This rectangular style may reflect a cultural preference, urban compactness, and/or family size. These houses contained a series of rooms along one side, a central hall, and other smaller rooms.

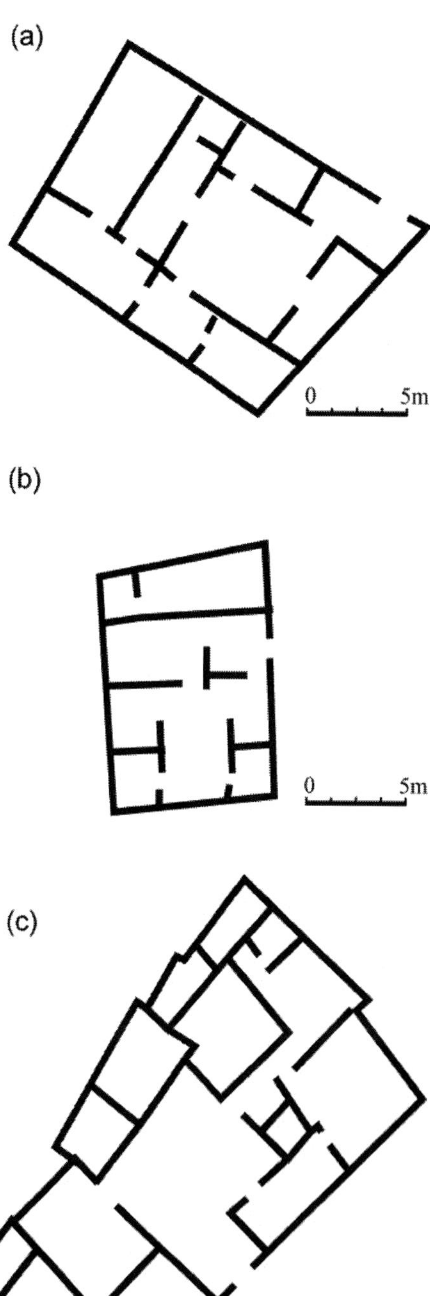

Figure 4.27. Select examples of second millennium house forms. (a) A house from Ur in southern Iraq. Modified from Woolley 1954: 176. (b) A house from Shaduppûm in the Diyala. Modified from Keith 1999:209, after Baqir 1946. (c) A house from Hattusa in northern Turkey, Level IV.

(a)

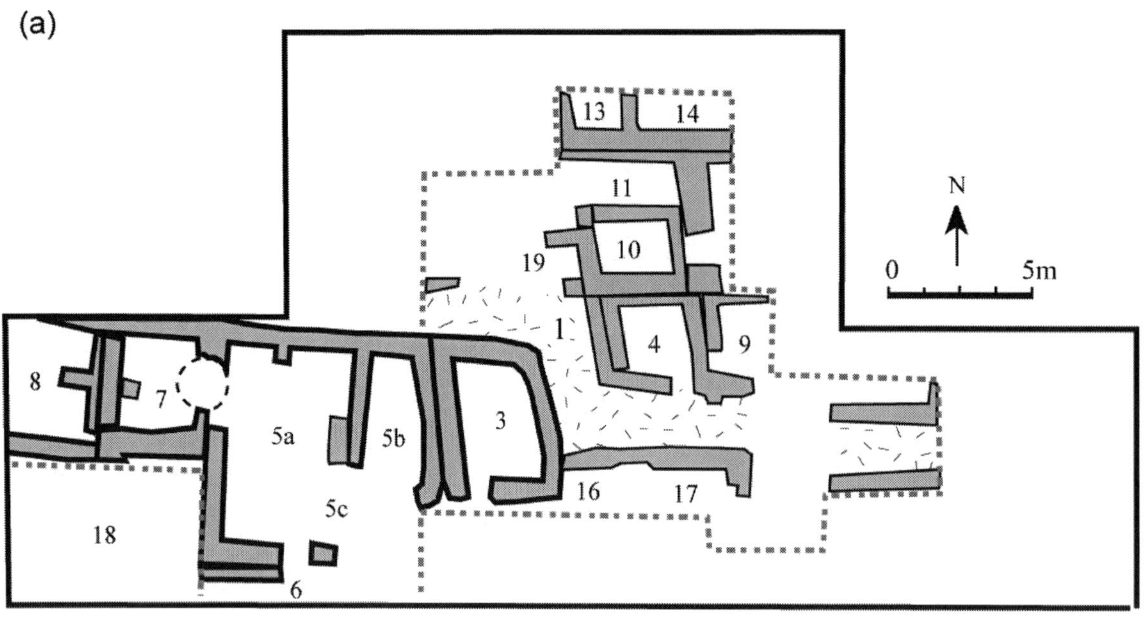

(b)

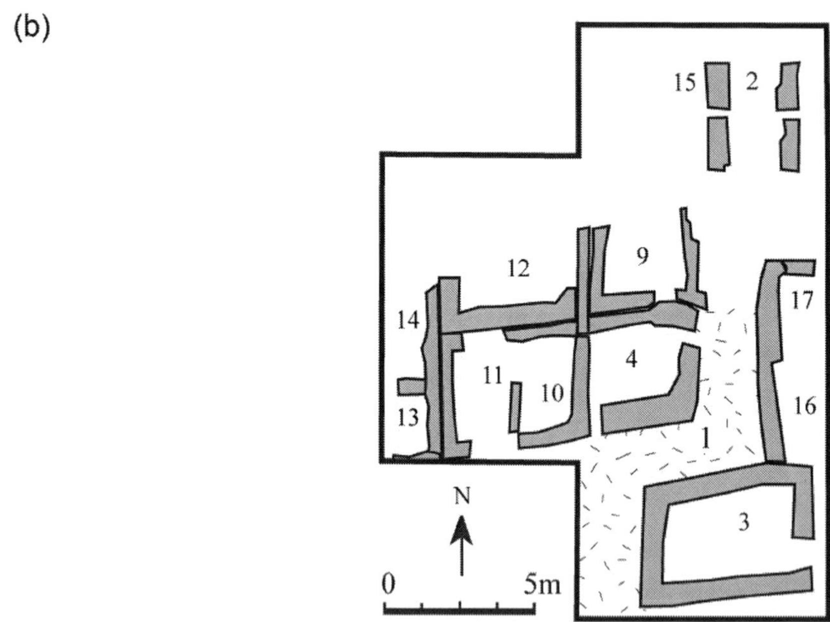

Figure 4.28. Domestic architecture at Kurban Höyük, ca. 2100 – 2500 B.C.E. (a) Area B, Periods III and IV. (b) Area B, Period IV. The walls are fragmentary in this level. Modified from Wattenmaker 1998a: 112-113; Figures 29 and 30.

In the north, archaeologists have evidence of only a limited amount of coherent domestic remains from this period. One site with relevant materials is Tell Taya; unfortunately, little was excavated. The citadel was surrounded by a roughly circular, defensive wall over 5 meters high (3 meters of stone footing, and 2 of mudbrick), monumental buildings (one of which was most likely a temple, with a bent-axis temple plan and faience beads characteristic of temples), and a dense concentration of residences spread over a kilometer (Reade 1982: 72-3, Reade 1968: 239). Domestic remains dating to ca. 2300 B.C.E. reveal a mixture of courtyard-style and rectilinear plans (see Figure 6.6). The diversity of house forms may have resulted from the exigencies of road construction and household expansion.

Another roughly contemporaneous set of domestic remains was excavated at the second tier center of Kurban Höyük. Over 1,000 square meters of domestic architecture was excavated, but unfortunately most contiguous exposures are only 25 to approximately 200 square meters apiece. Moreover, the absence of excavated doorways makes any determination of the property boundaries impossible (Wattenmaker 1998a: 112-13). The larger exposures reveal contiguous structures built along cobbled streets (Figure 4.28). Wattenmaker (1991: 110) determined that some houses were more substantial than others, suggesting a degree of socioeconomic variability within the settlement. From the limited horizontal exposures, it appears as if these houses do not follow the "courtyard style" plan found at the urban site of Titriş, but rather contain less well-planned clusters of individual rooms. The different domestic forms between the two sites may indicate different degrees of city planning, site-specific construction specializations, differences between more or less urban architectural forms, or a changed domestic form from the mid to the late EBA (the structures at Titriş are later than those at Kurban).

The Late-EBA to Early-MBA (ca. 2350-1900 B.C.E.)

Archaeological surveys suggest that agricultural production intensified during this period. In Upper Mesopotamia at least two distinct settlement patterns have been proposed. The first, in the Ataturk area, was characterized by urban collapse, ruralization, and a decline in population densities. The second, in the area of modern-day Birecik and Carchemish, witnessed an increase in population (Algaze, Breuninger, and Knudstad 1994: 17). During this period, the site of Titriş was abandoned, either for environmental reasons or for reasons of social conflict. During this period, Titriş contained courtyard-style houses, narrow, possibly two-storey "apartments," and small, one- to three-room workshops and storage units. The house types dating to this period will be discussed in further detail later in this chapter.

Structures: Domestic Residences and Public Buildings

I collected micro-debris samples from 18 structures at the three archaeological sites (excavation uncovered a total of 22 structures; 14 of these are houses, Figure 4.29). My goal in this section is to determine who used the 22 structures and for what purpose. The next step is to develop a model of typical Early Bronze Age Upper Mesopotamian domestic architecture. In order to do this, we must first identify the boundaries of the 22 units and sort the structures by function. This chapter deals primarily with domestic houses, but public structures and workshops are contrasted to houses in order to highlight the design and use of residential units.

Structure Forms at Three Upper Mesopotamian Sites

Variability in the physical form of a structure often correlates with function. Many design elements influence the form of a structure: building materials, overall scale, patterns of circulation, and the layout of the rooms. Identifying the boundaries of a domestic unit is the often difficult first step. Although the boundaries of administrative or religious structures were often clearly delineated to set these non-domestic units apart for practical and symbolic reasons, domestic structures were often constructed next to each other, making it difficult to identify the beginning and end of each structure. This is especially difficult at Titriş when not all doorways can be identified. Occasionally only a double wall, or two single walls with a small space between them, defined the boundary between two domestic units. In other cases, the only indication of structure boundaries was repeated clusters of room types that corresponded to specific household activities and requirements. For example, the components of a modern house in a Turkish village include: "three rooms for living quarters, stables, a storage room for fuel and hay, a hearth room for baking bread, a courtyard, and low stone-built constructions for storing dung cakes" (Çevik 1995: 44). I will examine whether such groupings existed at the ancient sites of Titriş, Kazane, or Tilbes.

Form of Structures at Titriş

Among the three sites, Titriş had the most extensive horizontal exposure and thus the most complete architectural plans. There are four broad categories of architectural forms (Figure 4.30): (1) Courtyard: rooms arranged around an open square (in the 30s and 80s neighborhood); (2) Rectangle: 1 room wide, 2- to 3-room-deep "apartments" (in the 30s neighborhood); (3) Open: exterior work areas with the occasional enclosed room (lithic workshop); (4) Wall: small to medium rooms secondarily built up against the city wall (in the 80s neighborhood)

In the domestic neighborhoods there is evidence that additional streets were laid out within neighborhoods as

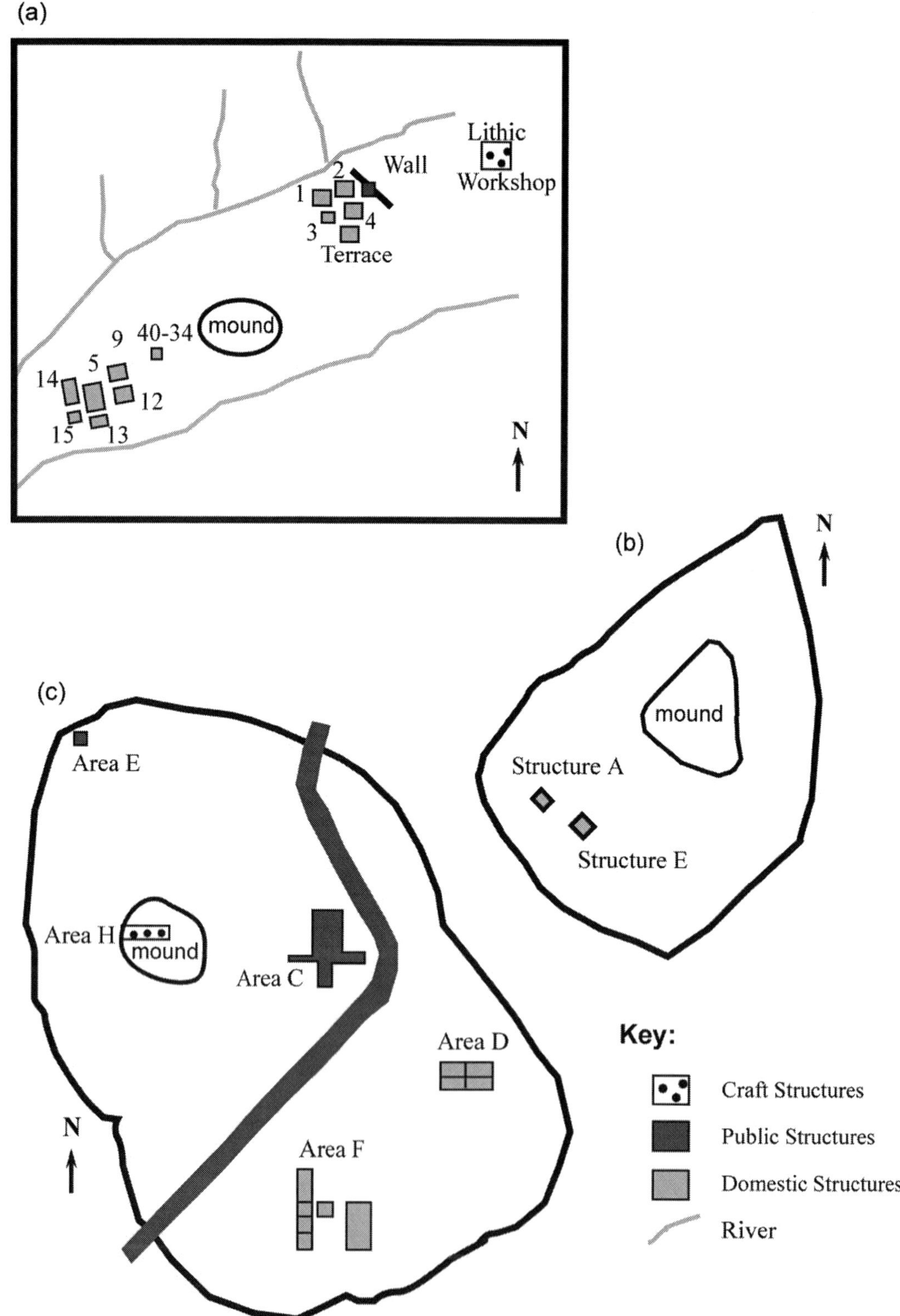

Figure 4.29. Structures types at the three sites. (a) Titriş, (b) Kazane, and (c) Tilbes. The location of each site can be found on Figure 1.1.

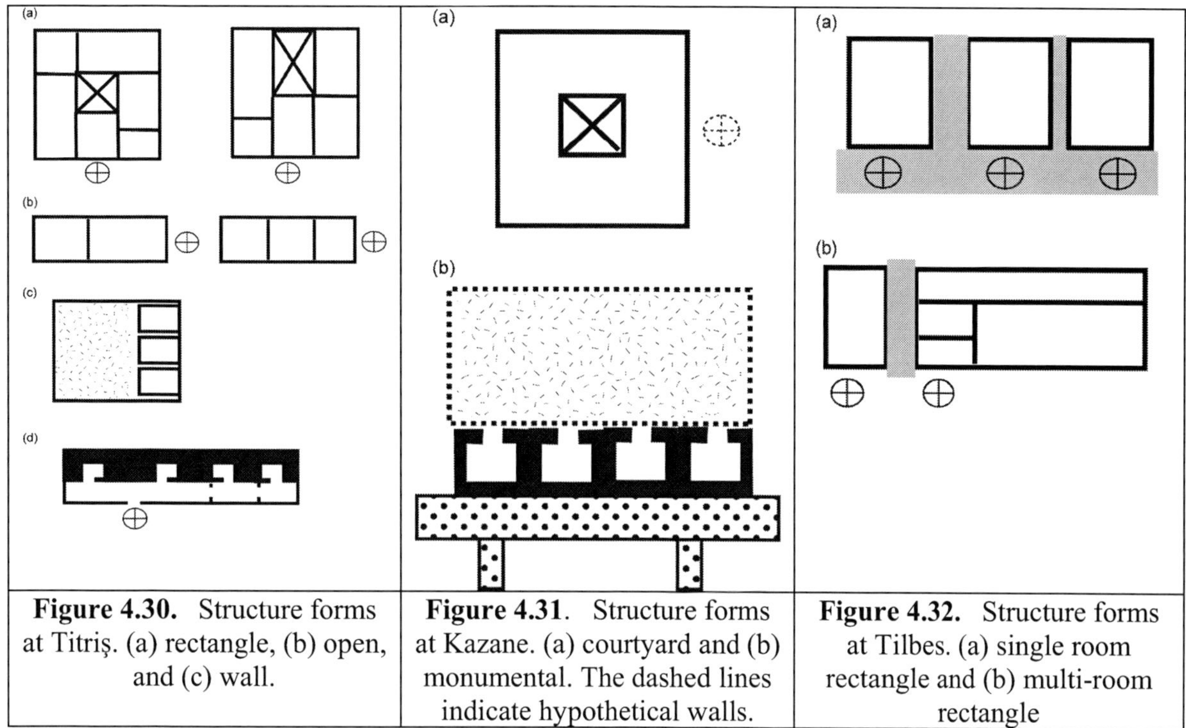

Figure 4.30. Structure forms at Titriş. (a) rectangle, (b) open, and (c) wall.

Figure 4.31. Structure forms at Kazane. (a) courtyard and (b) monumental. The dashed lines indicate hypothetical walls.

Figure 4.32. Structure forms at Tilbes. (a) single room rectangle and (b) multi-room rectangle

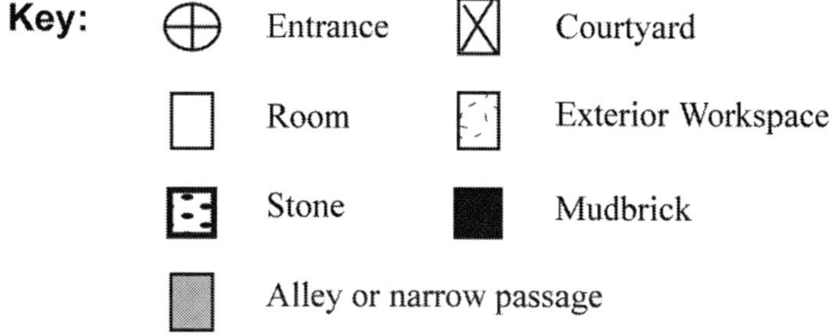

needed — e.g., in the 80s trenches the four rooms in BU-4 in the southeast corner were probably originally part of a wide street between BU-3/BU-4 and BU-6/BU-7. Similarly, in the 30s trenches a former street was filled in by small rooms (see Figure 4.36).

Form of Third Millennium Structures at Kazane

To date, only a handful of complete plans have been excavated at Kazane; the published material includes only partial plans. Beginning in 2003, magnetometric work has begun to outline large expanses of town planning and, within these broad horizontal plans, identify house forms (Wattenmaker and Creekmore, personal communication). The forms discussed here are limited to the patterns excavated in Areas C and F (Figure 4.31):

•Courtyard: only fragmentary walls preserved (possibly Area F)

•Monumental: large rooms situated within very thick walls (Area C and F)

Form of Structures at Tilbes

The nature of the EBA trenches at Tilbes did not allow for the recovery of complete plans. But the excavated walls do suggest at least two possible house plans (Figure 4.32):

•Single Rectangle

•Multi-room Rectangle

Examples of these different forms will be discussed below using architectural and micro-debris data.

Case Example: Surfaces

At Titriş, I sampled 12 structures: nine houses, one set of rooms in a defensive wall, one lithic workshop, and one possible administrative structure. Due to limited horizontal exposure in the non-domestic areas, only the defensive structure was architecturally coherent: a series of small to medium rooms arranged in a row, two rooms wide, built up against the six-meter-wide city wall. The possible administrative structure in Trench 40-34 appeared, in its limited horizontal exposure, larger than other domestic units at the site, suggesting it was a very wealthy household or that it was used for non-domestic purposes. In the lithic workshop, several rooms were excavated.

The comparison of average densities from floor surfaces suggests differential activities among the 12 structures (Figure 4.33). Although the sample size was small, re-occurring sets of micro-profiles emerged that could be associated with different types of structures.

Surfaces: Ceramics

Among the 12 structures at Titriş, Unit 4 and the Terrace contained the highest amount of micro-ceramics, but contained fewer, relative to other structures, micro-bones and lithics (Figure 4.34). The excavators classified both these structures as houses and, as a result, we expect that the ceramic debris is from food preparation and consumption. In contrast, the floors in Trench 40-34, the administrative structure, contained only a moderate amount of micro-ceramics. Specifically, the 40-34 floors contained very few pieces of micro-cooking ware (see Figure 4.1). This suggests that the ceramics in 40-34 were used primarily for consumption, perhaps consumed during official gatherings. Or, alternatively, we have yet to excavate the food preparation area at 40-34.

Table 4.6 demonstrates that while micro-fine wares were highest in Titriş Unit 4 floors, the Terrace had a higher density of cooking wares, suggesting a greater amount of cooking occurred there. This, in turn, suggests either a larger family or more frequent social gatherings. In addition, the Terrace contained more micro-sandy wares than Unit 4. This data, combined with the micro-fine ware densities, suggested that Unit 4 served family members or guests in fine bowls or cups more frequently than other sampled houses. In the 80s neighborhood, both the Terrace and Unit 4 contained a higher amount of fine wares than either Unit 1 or 2, suggesting these families were socially or economically more prestigious. A comparable situation was found in the 30s neighborhood, where Unit 5 was high in fine wares, as opposed to a high density of sandy wares in Units 9 and 12.

Surfaces: Bones

Units 2 and 8 contained the largest number of micro-bones and only moderate amounts of ceramics and lithics (see Figure 4.33). Unit 2 is a domestic structure in the 80s neighborhood with 15 or more rooms. Unit 8 includes the rooms in the defensive wall. The high quantity of bones from these floors suggests that animals were butchered there, or the occupants consumed a large quantity of meat, or that bones were dumped there later. Alternatively, the house floors may have been kept cleaner of food debris than an area used for soldiers' quarters or food storage. The high amount of rodent bones in the Unit 8 floors (the highest for any floor surface in the 80s neighborhood) presents further evidence for lower cleanliness standards in Unit 8. The lowest density of micro-bones occurred on floors from Units 12, 14, 9, and 1. There are several explanations for this: lower economic status prevented the regular consumption of meat products, the structure was used less frequently for food preparation and consumption, the floors were kept cleaner than other structures, or a combination of these explanations. To test whether the pattern resulted from more efficient housekeeping, I compared micro-bones from trash pits, which partially eliminates the bias of more effective cleaning (Table 4.7).

While the workshop pits and floors contained a high amount of micro-lithic debitage, the Terrace floors ranked very low in micro-bone, while the Terrace pits ranked highest in bone. This may indicate more efficient sweeping in the Terrace, which cleared a commonly produced type of debris —in this case, bone— from the

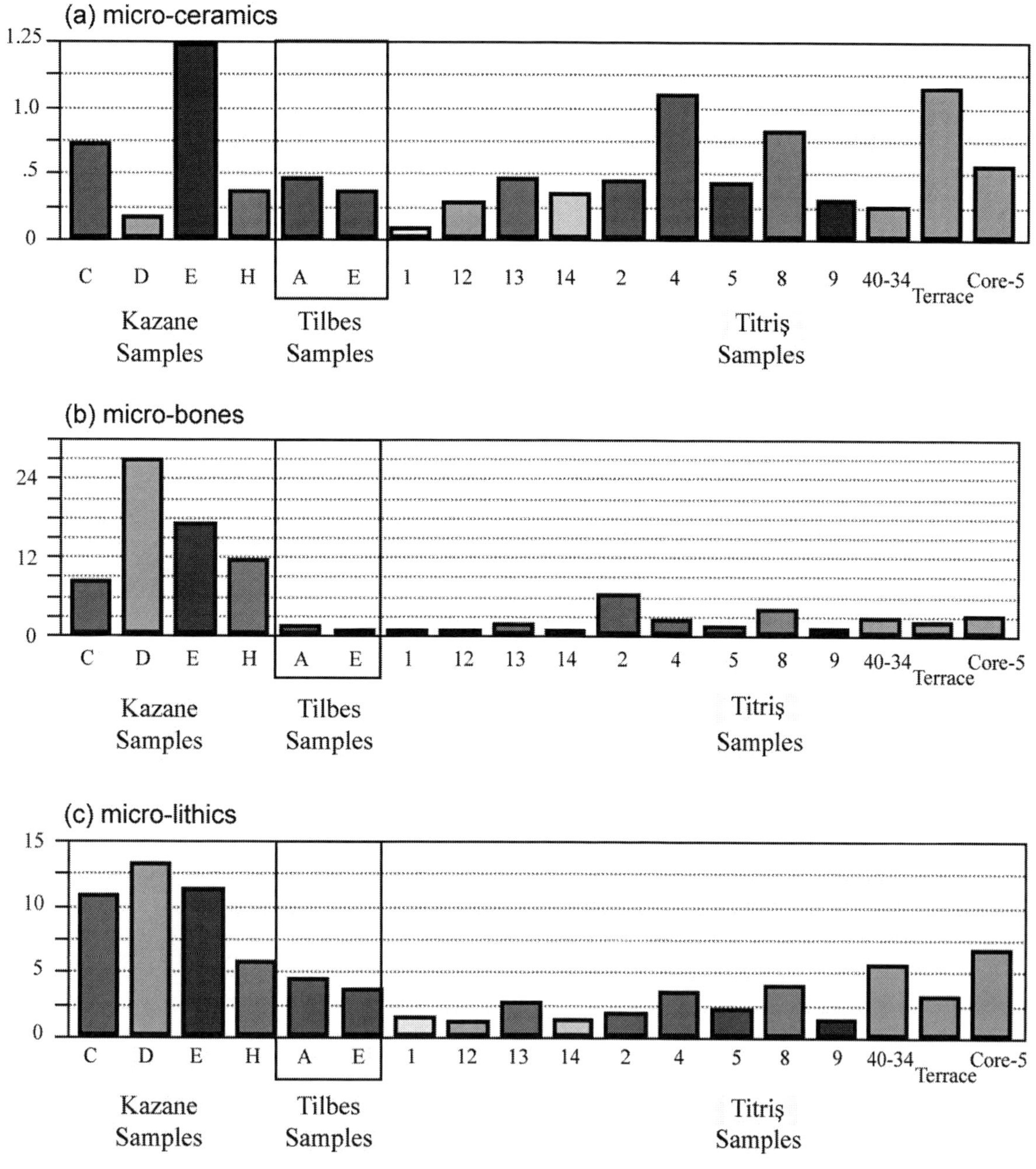

(a) micro-ceramics
1.25
1.0
.5
0
C D E H A E 1 12 13 14 2 4 5 8 9 40-34 Terrace Core-5
Kazane Samples
Tilbes Samples
Titriş Samples
(b) micro-bones
24
12
0
C D E H A E 1 12 13 14 2 4 5 8 9 40-34 Terrace Core-5
Kazane Samples
Tilbes Samples
Titriş Samples
(c) micro-lithics
15
10
5
0
C D E H A E 1 12 13 14 2 4 5 8 9 40-34 Terrace Core-5
Kazane Samples
Tilbes Samples
Titriş Samples

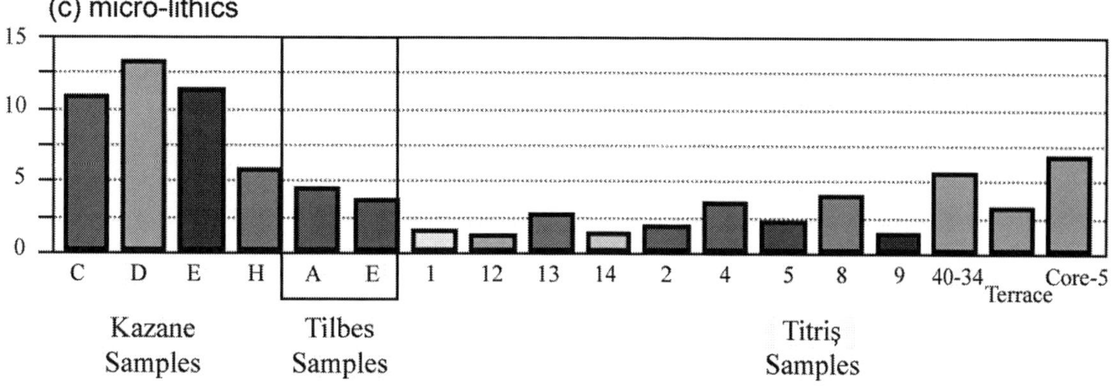

Figure 4.33. Density of micro-debris from floors at three sites. Structures at Kazane include Area C (no. 1 in Fig. 4.34), Area D (no. 2 in Fig. 4.34), Area E (no. 3 in Fig. 4.34), Area F (no. 4 in Fig. 4.34), Area H (no. 5 in Fig. 4.34.). Structures at Tilbes include Trench A (no. 6 in Fig. 4.34) and Trench E (no. 7 in Fig. 4.34). Structures at Titriş include the nine structures in the Outer and Lower Town (no. 1, 2, 4, 5, 8, 9, 12, 13, and 14 in Fig. 4.33) and three additional structures (in Trench 40-34, the earlier Terrace structure, and the lithic workshop in Core-5).

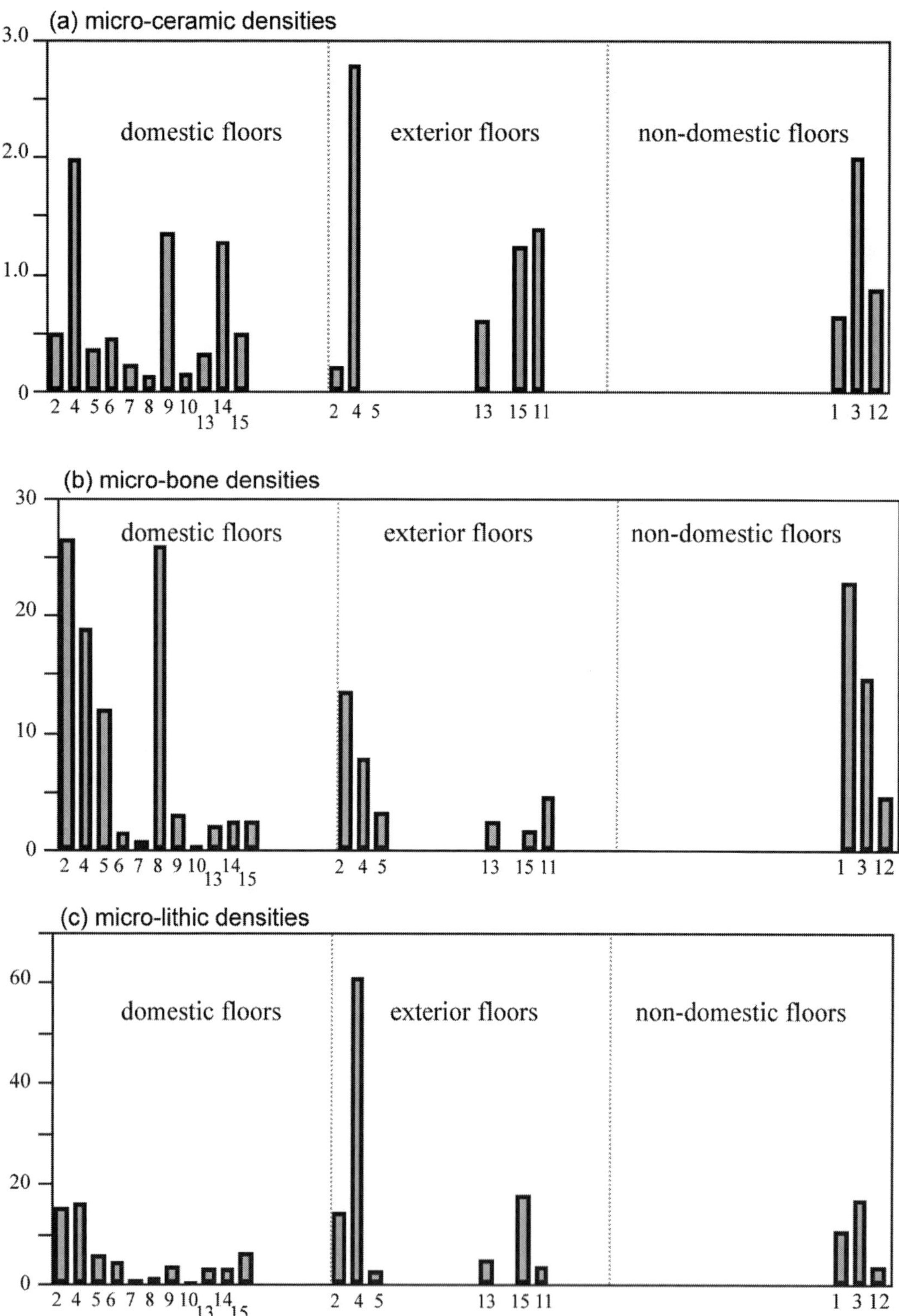

Figure 4.34 Micro-debris densities from three types of surfaces at 15 structures. The numerical abbreviations used for structures at Titriş in include Unit 2 (no. 8), Unit 4 (no. 9), Unit 5 (no. 10), Unit 9 (no. 11), Unit 8 (no. 12), Trench 40-34 (no. 13), the Terrace (no. 14), and the Lithic Workshop (no. 15). See Fig. 4.33 for the abbreviations for Kazane and Tilbes.

80s Surfaces	Highest Rank					Lowest Rank
Fine	4	terrace	8	core	2	1
Sandy	terrace	8	4	core	2	1
Cooking	terrace	4	2	8	1	core
30s Surfaces	**Highest Rank**					**Lowest Rank**
Fine	13	5	40-34	12	9	14
Sandy	5	13	9	12	40-34	14
Cooking	14	5	12	13	40-34	9

Table 4.6. Building Units at Titriş ranked by count density of ceramic wares.

	Pits with the highest density of micro-bones	Pits with the lowest density of micro-bones
Pottery	Terrace	Workshop
Bone	Terrace	40-43
Lithic	Workshop	Unit 4 and 14

Table 4.7. Ranked micro-bone density from pits at Titriş. Samples were taken from pits in Units 14, 4, 40-34, Terrace, and the lithic workshop. Samples were not taken from Units 8, 9, or 1.

Site	Structure	*n*	Tan	Brown/ Gray	White	Pink	Clear
Kazane	C	22	4.97	0.89	0.32	0.75	**1.05**
Kazane	D	12	6.47	1.26	0.21	0.85	**1.25**
Kazane	E	2	**9.73**	**2.58**	0.33	**1.58**	**1.42**
Kazane	F	10	**9.44**	1.19	0.33	**1.52**	**1.46**
Kazane	H	5	2.67	0.65	0.36	0.39	.045
Kazane	Street	22	5.18	1.17	0.61	0.41	0.34
Tilbes	A	3	2.08	1.01	**0.92**	**1.95**	**2.03**
Tilbes	E	25	1.01	0.52	0.47	0.80	0.60
Titriş	BU–1	5	0.88	0.23	0.05	0.10	0.04
Titriş	BU–2	9	1.04	0.25	0.16	0.10	0.06
Titriş	BU–4	86	1.82	0.59	0.55	0.19	0.08
Titriş	BU–12	8	0.72	0.29	0.05	0.12	0.04
Titriş	BU–13	3	0.39	0.41	0.23	0.29	0.03
Titriş	BU–14	6	1.18	0.48	0.03	0.23	0.10
Titriş	BU–5	16	1.22	0.50	0.05	0.15	0.10
Titriş	BU–8	25	1.81	0.48	0.27	0.29	0.59
Titriş	BU–9	6	0.84	0.31	0.06	0.14	0.01
Titriş	40–34	24	2.79	0.46	0.42	0.41	0.44
Titriş	Terrace	45	2.83	0.57	0.42	0.17	0.60
Titriş	Workshop	18	**22.89**	**1.53**	**1.32**	0.95	0.34

Table 4.8. Distribution of lithic colors among sampled structures. Structures with the highest chipped stone densities per color are highlighted in bold.

floors' surfaces and deposited it in pits. The highest and lowest densities of supra-floors were entirely different than either the floor or pit patterning, suggesting, as one might expect, that supra-floor remains might not be connected with the original room activity.

Surfaces: Lithics

The highest amount of micro-lithics occurred, as expected, in the lithic workshop samples. This pattern was most dramatic on the exterior surfaces of the workshop, with densities that far exceeded any other type of surface or location at any of the three sites. After the workshop surfaces, trench 40-34 contained the highest amount of micro-lithics, suggesting it was used as an informal workshop or that flintknappers congregated here to retouch damaged or dull tools. Among lithic color-types, the workshop and 40-34 shared a similar count density of tan lithics, but the workshop contained many more pieces of dark brown and gray micro-debitage (Table 4.8). This suggests the core workers had access to a wider range of lithic materials, while the 40-34 knappers were more restricted in the range of raw materials used. For example, the tan flint may have been favored for agricultural tools such as clay sickles (with flint teeth), while the brown and gray materials were used for kitchen knives. The inability to own land and harvest crops may explain the low quantity of tan-colored lithics at Unit 13 and Unit 1. Conversely, the wealthy houses (Units 4 and 40-34), the workshop, and the guardhouse (Unit 8) contained large quantities of this color.

Variability in Daily Activities

In this section, five case examples from different structure types illustrate differences in the distribution and kind of daily activities conducted in private households, public structures, and craft workshops.

Case Example: Two Domestic Residences, Building Units 4 and 5, Titriş Höyük

Architecturally, Houses 4 and 5 are similar, consisting of rooms grouped around a central courtyard (Figure 4.35). In this section I will refer to these two buildings as "houses" due to their clear domestic nature. Moreover, each structure contained several kitchens (Rooms 11, 23, and 24 in House 4; Rooms 2, 11, 16, and 17 in House 5). Several small rooms served as either entrances or reception rooms that led into larger ones (Rooms 10, 18, 5 in House 4; Rooms 1 and 3, and possibly 4, in House 5). Both houses contained living rooms, large rooms situated far from the main entrance, possibly used for entertaining guests (Room 9 in House 4; Room 6 or 7 in House 5). In total, House 4 contained as many as 28 rooms and House 5 contained 17 rooms.

It is not possible to determine the chronological relationship between the phases from the two houses, but each structure has at least two main building phases. In House 4, rooms clustered into three sectors: a western wing (Rooms 1, 2, and 3), center (Rooms 4, 5, 6, 8-11, 13, and 14), and an eastern wing (Rooms 12, 15-25). Over the years, these rooms were subdivided. For example, the main courtyard, Room 8, was divided to create Room 10. In contrast, House 5 contained one central unit (rooms grouped around a courtyard, Room 5). Originally a street was located to the north of the structure, indicated by a series of double walls (possibly the exterior walls to two distinct buildings; Figure 4.36). In a subsequent building phase, the area of the street was filled with small rooms and House 5 was extended to the north. Another interpretation is that the series of small rooms running east to west (Rooms 10, 11, 13, and 14) were the rear rooms to four different rectangular "apartments." Without excavations in the northern trench, it is unclear whether there were northern doorways to each of the larger rooms (Rooms 12, 17, 16, and 15).

Assuming for the moment that House 5 is one complete domestic house, as indicated in Figure 4.36c, how does its circulation pattern differ from House 4? Superficially, they are similar: entrances from the street that eventually lead into interior courtyards and the occasional "dead-end room" located in a corner of the structure. But in terms of accessibility, House 5 is organized around a central corridor, while House 4 contained a greater number of access "nodes." Hillier and Hansen (1984: 97) computed a "complexity" measurement designed to measure the various circulation paths within structures and to determine the ease of accessibility among rooms. Using this measurement, House 5 had an average of .3 doorways separating one node from another (Table 4.9). In contrast, House 4 yielded a lower average of .22. This suggests that there were fewer doorways to limit movement within the house. Each house, however, placed the most accessible rooms (in terms of entrances in and out) in the interior of the structure. Although easily accessible via doorways, access into this interior core was nonetheless restricted because at least one room separated these private rooms from public thoroughfares.

The least accessible rooms were located along the edges of the structures. In House 4, the small rooms in the northeast corner, possibly used as kitchens and for storage, were the least accessible. In House 5, a large room in the northwest corner (Room 15) and two smaller ones in the northeast (Rooms 2 and 9) were the least accessible. Room 9 contained a basin for processing grapes and Room 2 was a kitchen. Several pieces of evidence suggest that Room 15 was a private living area (comparable to Room 9 in House 4): a cobbled floor to assist in drainage, its large size, and its inaccessibility.

Both houses contained central courtyards that ranged between 42 and 44 square meters in area. But House 4 contained two additional courtyards, each about half the size of the central one (Table 4.10). This points to multiple kin groupings, such as family groups, within the structure or to different sets of activities, such as craft specialization or animal husbandry that necessitated

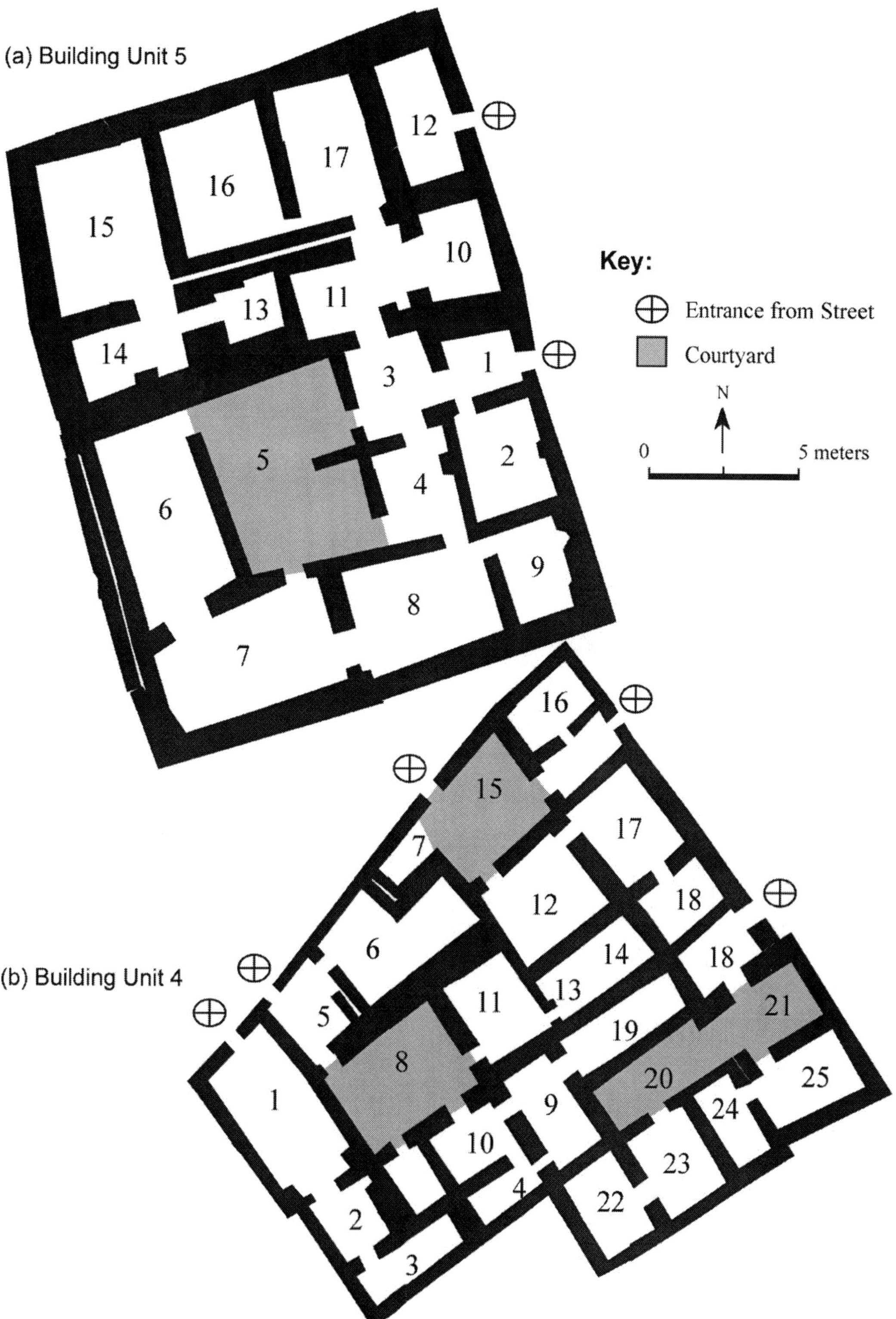

Figure 4.35. Building Unit 5 compared to Building Unit 4. The plan for Building Unit 4 illustrates the Late Phase architecture.

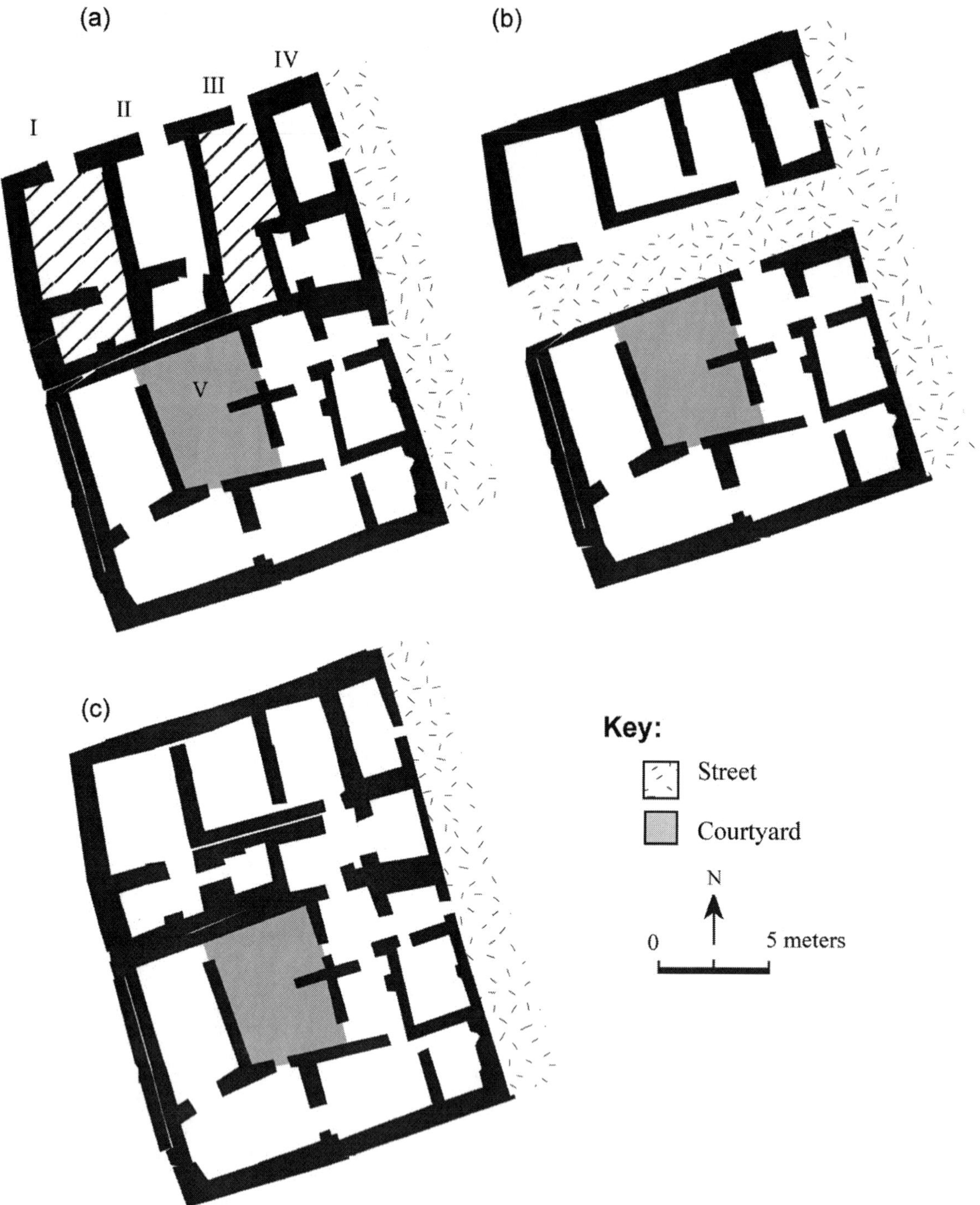

Figure 4.36. Models of Building Unit 5's room arrangement. (a) Five urban "apartments," each apartment is labeled with a Roman numeral. (b) An earlier phase with two separate structures. (c) A central courtyard plan.

(A) Building Unit 4 – Number of Interior Doorways

	x	4	5	6	8	9	10	11	12	13	14	15	16	17	18	19	20	22	23	24	25	26	To.	Rank
x	0	4	1	2	2	4	3	3	2	4	5	1	2	3	1	3	2	4	3	4	5	6	64	1
4	4	0	1	2	2	4	3	3	2	4	5	1	2	3	1	3	2	4	3	4	5	6	88	7
5	1	3	0	1	1	3	2	2	3	3	4	4	5	4	6	4	5	7	6	7	6	7	84	6
6	2	4	1	0	2	4	3	3	4	4	5	5	6	5	7	5	6	8	7	8	7	8	104	12
8	2	2	1	2	0	2	1	1	2	2	3	3	4	3	5	3	4	6	5	6	5	6	68	2
9	4	2	3	4	2	0	1	3	4	4	5	6	5	5	3	1	2	4	3	4	3	4	72	3
10	3	1	2	3	1	1	0	2	3	3	4	4	5	4	4	2	3	5	4	5	4	5	68	2
11	3	3	2	3	1	3	2	0	1	1	2	2	3	2	6	4	5	7	6	7	6	7	76	4
12	4	4	3	4	2	4	3	1	0	2	1	2	1	7	5	6	7	8	7	8	7	8	94	9
13	4	4	3	4	2	4	3	1	2	0	1	3	4	3	7	5	6	8	7	8	7	8	94	9
14	5	5	4	5	3	5	4	2	3	1	0	4	5	4	8	6	7	9	8	9	8	9	114	15
15	1	5	4	5	3	5	4	2	3	3	4	0	1	2	8	6	7	9	8	9	8	9	106	13
16	2	6	5	6	4	6	5	3	2	4	5	1	0	1	9	7	8	8	9	10	9	10	122	18
17	3	5	4	5	3	5	4	2	1	3	4	2	3	0	8	6	7	9	8	9	8	9	108	14
18	1	5	6	7	5	3	4	6	7	7	8	8	9	8	0	2	1	3	2	3	2	3	100	11
19	3	3	4	5	3	1	2	4	5	5	6	6	7	6	2	0	1	3	2	3	2	3	76	4
20	2	4	5	6	4	2	3	5	6	6	7	7	8	7	1	1	0	2	1	2	1	2	82	5
22	4	6	7	8	6	4	5	7	8	8	9	9	10	9	3	3	2	0	1	2	3	4	120	17
23	3	5	6	7	5	3	4	5	6	6	7	7	8	7	2	2	1	1	0	1	2	3	91	8
24	3	6	7	8	6	4	5	7	8	8	9	9	10	9	3	3	2	3	2	0	2	3	117	16
25	3	5	6	7	5	3	4	6	7	7	8	8	9	8	2	2	1	3	2	1	0	1	98	10

(B) Building Unit 5 – Number of Interior Doorways

	x	1	2	3	4	5	6	7	8	9	10	11	12	13	14	15	16	17	Total	Rank
x	0	1	2	2	3	3	4	4	4	5	4	3	5	4	5	6	5	4	64	10
1	1	0	1	1	2	2	3	3	3	4	3	2	4	3	4	5	4	4	48	5
2	2	1	0	1	3	3	4	4	4	5	4	3	5	4	5	6	5	4	69	12
3	2	1	2	0	1	1	2	2	2	3	2	1	3	2	3	4	3	2	36	1
4	3	2	3	1	0	1	2	2	1	3	3	2	4	3	4	5	4	3	46	4
5	3	2	3	1	1	0	1	1	2	3	3	2	4	3	4	5	4	3	45	3
6	4	3	4	2	2	1	0	1	2	3	4	3	5	4	5	6	5	4	58	9
7	4	3	4	2	2	1	1	0	1	2	4	3	5	4	5	6	5	4	56	8
8	4	3	4	2	1	2	2	1	0	1	4	3	5	4	5	6	5	4	56	8
9	5	4	5	3	2	3	3	2	1	0	5	4	6	5	6	7	6	5	72	13
10	4	3	4	2	3	3	4	4	4	5	0	1	3	2	3	4	3	2	54	7
11	3	2	3	1	2	2	3	3	3	4	1	0	2	1	2	3	2	1	40	2
12	4	4	5	3	4	4	5	5	5	6	3	2	0	3	4	5	2	1	66	11
13	4	3	4	2	3	3	4	4	4	5	2	1	3	0	1	2	3	2	50	6
14	5	4	5	3	4	4	5	5	5	6	3	2	4	1	0	1	4	3	64	10
15	6	5	6	4	5	5	6	6	6	7	4	3	5	2	1	0	5	4	80	14
16	5	4	5	3	4	4	5	5	5	6	3	2	2	3	4	5	0	1	66	11
17	4	3	4	2	3	3	4	4	4	5	2	1	1	2	3	4	1	0	50	6

Table 4.9. Circulation patterns in Building Units 4 and 5, Titriş. A "0" indicates no access from one node to another; "1" signifies a connection between nodes; "2"+ signifies multiple connections. Adapted from Blanton 1994: 34, following his "Path Matrix" method.

	Building Unit 4		Building Unit 5	
Number of rooms	26		15	
Square Meters	434		285	
Average room size	16.69		19.0	
Number of courtyards	3		1	
Courtyard sizes	6 x 7: 42 m^2		7.3 x 6: 43.8 m^2	
	8 x 3: 24 m^2			
	4.3 x 3.85: 16.55 m^2			
Number of...				
Kitchens	3		1	
Entrances	3 or 4		2 or 3	
Burials	1		none	
Storage Rooms	6, or more		3, or more	
	Mean BU-4	Mean BU-5	Median BU-4	Median BU-5
Ceramic Density	1.22	0.45	1	0.29
Bone Density	3.07	1.73	2.54	1.12
Lithic Density	3.61	2.31	3	1.73
Ceramic ware: fine	0.46	0.05	0.38	0.02
Ceramic ware: sandy	0.51	0.32	0.33	0.26
Ceramic ware: cooking	0.18	0.03	0	0
Lithic: tan	1.82	1.22	1.57	1.03
Lithic: dark brown	0.59	0.50	0.50	0.29
Lithic: gray	0.59	0.50	0.50	0.29
Lithic: white	0.55	0.05	0.41	0.04
Lithic: pink	0.19	0.15	0.06	0.10
Lithic: clear	0.08	0.10	0	0.03

Table 4.10. A comparison of Building Unit 4 to Building Unit 5, Titriş.

additional space within the house. Another possibility is the division of the house into "public" male-dominated space and more "private" family areas where women could enjoy complete privacy. The average size of rooms in House 5 was larger (19 square meters) than in House 4 (16.69 square meters). There are at least two explanations: more resources were put into constructing House 5 and building larger rooms, or House 4 was a slightly later house which contained more remodelling (most likely sub-divided rooms) than House 5. This latter scenario would be particularly likely in the case of an extended family with multiple sons/daughters living with their families within the ancestral homestead. In sum, it is difficult to distinguish between the domestic cycle of a family and differential access to resources.

The macro-finds from House 5 included Canaanean blades (possibly used as sickle elements), stone loom weights (suggesting domestic production of textiles), and a stone mold for lead trinkets in the courtyard. There were also two interesting features: a plastered surface in Room 9 that drained into the street and may have been used for processing wool or fleece and a prepared surface in Room 10 that may have been used to process grapes. In one of the courtyard floor samples from House 5, a 10-mm-long mother of pearl shell was found, along with a small flake of green paint or copper.

The macro-finds from House 4 have not been fully processed. But the excavators reported uncovering similar domestic artifacts.

Analyzing the micro-ceramic densities sheds some light on the comparison between the two houses. Overall, House 4 contained a higher density of micro-ceramics, which suggests either a larger family size or a longer occupation of the structure. A very tentative suggestion of greater agricultural activity comes from the higher density of tan chipped stone in House 4 since, as discussed in Chapter 3, tan chipped stone may be associated with agricultural tools (versus the gray and dark brown colors possibly used for domestic implements). If this were the case, the data suggests the residents of House 4 retouched or produced more agricultural implements than House 5, suggesting that House 4 farmed more land than House 5. The use of Room 16 as an animal pen in House 4 further suggests that the household owned animals and possibly owned or worked on pasture land. The number and kind of animals owned by a household correlates, among contemporary Middle Eastern villages, with household wealth (Kamp 1982: 121), and it is not unreasonable to assume a similar pattern in past villages and cities.

Case Example: A Wealthy House or Administrative Structure in Trench 40-34

Of the structures excavated to date at Titriş, the one located in trench 40-34 is the closest to the höyük (see Figure 1.3). Although the höyük is not yet excavated (due to a couple dozen meters of later Hellenistic and Islamic levels), based on analogy with contemporaneous site plans, the palace and/or temple was probably located on this central mound. Matney and Algaze (1995) proposed that the neighborhoods closest to the höyük had the higher status. If so, we would expect that trench 40-34 contained high-status dwellings. Support for this contention comes from the walls of the structures, which are approximately one meter thick. Unfortunately, the trench is badly disturbed by later, Hellenistic pits (Algaze et al. 1995: 24). The mid-EBA levels of the trench contained two poorly preserved large mudbrick structures with a paved street running between them (Figure 4.37; Matney and Algaze 1995: 44). The two pits in the center of the trench date to a late EBA phase, and one of the two pits was used to store acorns. Similar to the houses in the 30s neighborhood, Trench 40-34 contained a burial (along the northern edge of the trench). The fire installation in this room supports the contention that this was a domestic residence. But the large mudbrick walls (four or more courses thick) suggest more resources were used in constructing this building than the domestic residences in the 30s and 80s neighborhoods. These large walls and a lack of domestic macro-artifacts led the excavators to propose that the structure was used for administrative purposes.

At the micro-level, the density of micro-ceramics in the hearths and pits resembled the quantities found in a domestic residence (Building Unit 4). But the floor surfaces in Trench 40-34 contained a lower density of micro-ceramics, suggesting that the structure was swept more frequently or fewer vessels were dropped and broken. The interior floors and exterior surfaces in the trench contained a rather high density of micro-chipped stones (greater than the domestic residences, such as Building Units 4 and 5, but still substantially less than the lithic workshop). Despite the grandiose architecture, 40-34 contained fewer pieces, on average, of micro-fine wares than other domestic units. Instead, the hearths in the trench contained a higher than average amount of sandy wares. Although there is no direct correlation between fine wares and high social status, in this case the relative paucity of fine wares suggests that the serving of goods and beverages in sandy wares to the residents or guests in 40-34 was acceptable. The other, opposite conclusion one could draw is that the occupants of 40-34 used metal vessels.

Case Example: A Lithic Workshop, Titriş Höyük

The lithic workshop at Titriş was distinguished by the occurrence of more than 1,500 lithic cores and by storage pits that contained a variety of flint types. The borders of one room, at least two perpendicular streets, several isolated walls, and storage pits were uncovered in the "Core" Trenches (named after lithic cores, not because they are centrally located). Unlike the domestic houses, the workshop rooms were most often only one room deep

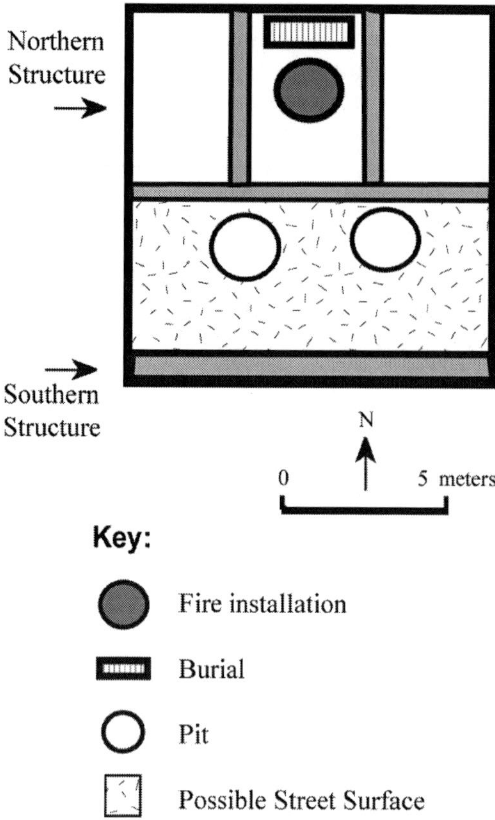

Figure 4.37 Schematic plan of Trench 40-34, Titriş.

(i.e., directly abutting the street) and most of the working space was exterior surfaces containing storage pits. The presence of two grinding stones and broken vessels suggested that the workshop was used for domestic activities and probably housed the lithic workers and possibly their families.

The micro-debris provided a more detailed picture of the distribution of activities within the workshop. The room in the eastern part of the trench contained the highest density of micro-ceramics and bone, while the pits contained the highest amount of micro-debitage, probably broken during storage. The streets were also very high in micro-ceramics, but moderate to low in micro-bones. Cluster analysis, using count densities of micro-ceramics, bones, and lithics as the dependent variables, revealed an interesting spatial distinction between the western and the eastern halves of the trench, clusters 1 and 3 respectively (Figure 4.38). The clusters mirrored the distributions of micro-bone concentrations (cluster 3) and the micro-lithic concentrations (cluster 1). Analyzing each sample separately demonstrated further that the only high density of ceramics occurred in the street samples, while the micro-lithics were carefully cleaned from floor surfaces and found in pits. This corresponded to features at the macro level. The western half of the trench contained storage pits and fragmentary walls, while the eastern half contained a room, a grinding stone, and a burial. Each storage pit contained Canaanean blade cores, usually mixed in with the flakes. The great majority of macro-flakes and all of the cores from these pits were made from the fine-grained gray or tan/pink tabular and nodular flint used for Canaanean blade production.

Case Example: An Administrative Structure in Area C, Kazane Höyük

Area C at Kazane contained a very large structure. During excavation, this structure was tentatively labeled the *Merkez*, Turkish for "the center." The structure contained several architectural phases. The latest one, probably modified after the original building fell out of use, suggested a "squatter" occupation with less substantial walls. In contrast, the earlier stone-footed walls, approximately 1.5 meters wide (but as thick as 5 meters), enclosed small, but well constructed rooms. Features such as ovens and ash layers suggested a domestic use, or perhaps that food was cooked for large numbers of employees or workers. Until the final architectural and artifactual analyses are completed, this area remains enigmatic. In the meantime, micro-debris evidence revealed several patterns.

Compared to other structures at Kazane, the floors in this structure were moderately high in micro-ceramics, very high in micro-bones, and low in micro-lithics

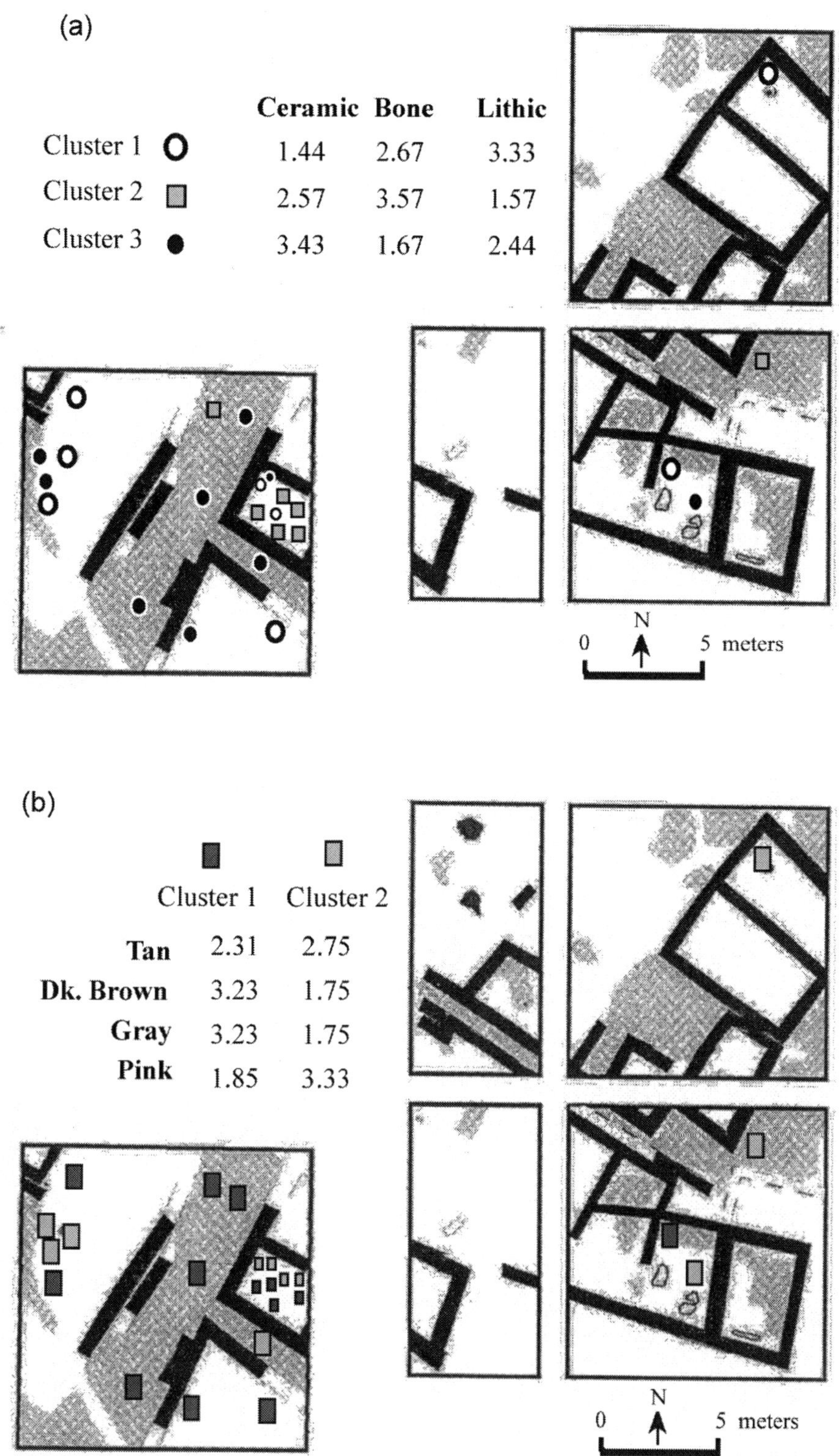

Figure 4.38. Lithic manufacturing area (the "Core") at Titriş: analyzed by hierarchical cluster analysis. (a) Cluster analysis based on the mean count density of micro-ceramics, bones, and lithics. (b) Cluster analysis based on the mean count density of lithic raw materials per sample (based on the color of the debitage: tan, dark brown, gray, and pink). Plans modified from Hartenberger 2003: 147, Figure 5.27.

(Figure 4.39). Among its four rooms, Room 1 contained the highest density of micro-ceramics (specifically, sandy wares) and bones. The co-occurrence of ceramics and bones suggested that food preparation and consumption took place in this room. Because of the high density of sandy wares, as opposed to fine wares, I suggest that this room was used for less socially significant meals than Room 4, which (among all other rooms at Kazane) contained a high amount of micro-fine wares. This same pattern occurred in Room 9 in Building Unit 4 at Titriş where food was served to guests or family members in fine-ware bowls (or cups). Relative to other rooms at the site, Room 4 in Area C contained a high amount of micro-lithics and ceramics, suggesting that meat was cut or animals butchered here. The cooking wares were highest in Rooms 2 and 4, suggesting that a majority of the cooking occurred in these rooms. Although it lacked a high density of cooking wares, Room 3 contained an oven, indicating a further distribution of cooking activities within Area C.

Case Example: City Wall and Associated Rooms, Titriş Höyük

Over 10 meters of the city wall have been excavated at Titriş. Running roughly northwest to southeast, the wall runs from river to river, creating an effective barrier on the eastern edge of the site (see Figure 1.3). The excavated stone footings of the wall were massive, over 6 meters in width, with a mudbrick superstructure (Algaze et al. 1995: 21). Small rooms were regularly distributed along the wall, built up against it (see Figure 3.22). These rooms may have stored valuable objects or simply food reserves. In addition, guards or soldiers may have spent time in these rooms during their guard duty shifts. A parallel feature is found at Tal-i Malyan in Iran, where a proto-Elamite wall, constructed during the Late Banesh period, spanned 5 meters and rose about 2.5 meters in height, enclosing around 200 hectares (Sumner 1985: 153, 159). A test trench revealed two rooms built against the wall. Again, the precise function of these rooms is unclear.

Another northern site that contained a large citadel wall was Tell Taya, roughly contemporaneous with Titriş and located in northern Iraq. Similar to Titriş, the wall at Taya contained rooms (Reade 1968: 243). An estimate of the ruined building material at Taya suggests that the wall once rose 5 meters in height (3 meters of stone footing, and 2 of mudbrick) and spanned 1.6 meters (Reade 1982: 73). If this were the case, stairs would have been necessary to reach the top of the wall for a view of the surrounding countryside (and presumably watch for approaching visitors, whether hostile or friendly). At Taya, stairs were preserved inbetween the rooms for access to the top of the wall. To date, no stairs have been excavated at Titriş.

Gatherings of people may have occurred at city walls. In later, Old Babylonian times, gates served as social gathering places, markets, and possibly the location of "city council" meetings. The presence of multiple gates at an Upper Mesopotamian site might correlate with such events (Stone and Zimansky 1992).

Early Bronze Age Household Members

Determining who lived in these domestic structures is a much more difficult task than identifying architectural forms. The study of family types and domestic activities are important because relations among family members provided the basis for economic and social relations within Ancient Near Eastern communities. The family played an active role in decisions concerning labor requirements, economic matters such as consumption, and demographic changes. According to Hareven (cited in Friedman 1984: 39): "The family appears as a process over time, rather than as a static unit within certain time periods." In particular, we must investigate the potential contributions of the domestic economy to broader economic trends.

One strategy for estimating household size and family type is to combine archaeological, textual, and ethnographic sources. For example, we learn from texts that the concept of "household" is fundamental to Mesopotamian society. Both kings and gods were envisioned as heads of households, albeit special ones (Oates 1978: 476). Moreover, some researchers suggest that large households composed of related kin and non-kin dependents, or *oikos* (taken from the Greek for "household," as in the domestic economy), laid the foundation for the eventual specialization of temple and palace institutions (Jacobsen 1970, Maisels 1990, Lamberg-Karlovsky 1999, Pollock 1999). Poorer people served as attached specialists in these wealthy households. In other cases, individuals who owed agricultural, military, or manufacturing services worked in royal or religious households in return for payment in rations, such as oil, wool, and barley. In poorer households, the men tended the fields and animals and occasionally manufactured pottery, while the women cooked, cleaned, cared for children, wove, spun, ground grain, and looked after pigs (Oates 1978: 477).

In Southern Mesopotamia, during the later Isin-Larsa period, texts reveal that at the time of a father's death, two or three sons were usually living, suggesting that a total of five or more children often survived into adulthood within individual families (Van De Mieroop 1992: 213). Texts also revealed the existence of domestic slaves, monogamous marriages, and cohabitation of houses by several brothers and their families — i.e., extended families (Van De Mieroop 1992: 214-15). In the Old Babylonian period we learn that some women had an amount of financial independence: they could invest in overseas trade, sue in court, and receive loans (Van De Mieroop 1992: 216). Children were expected to take care of their parents until the latters' death. If children pre-deceased the parents or did not exist, arrangements were

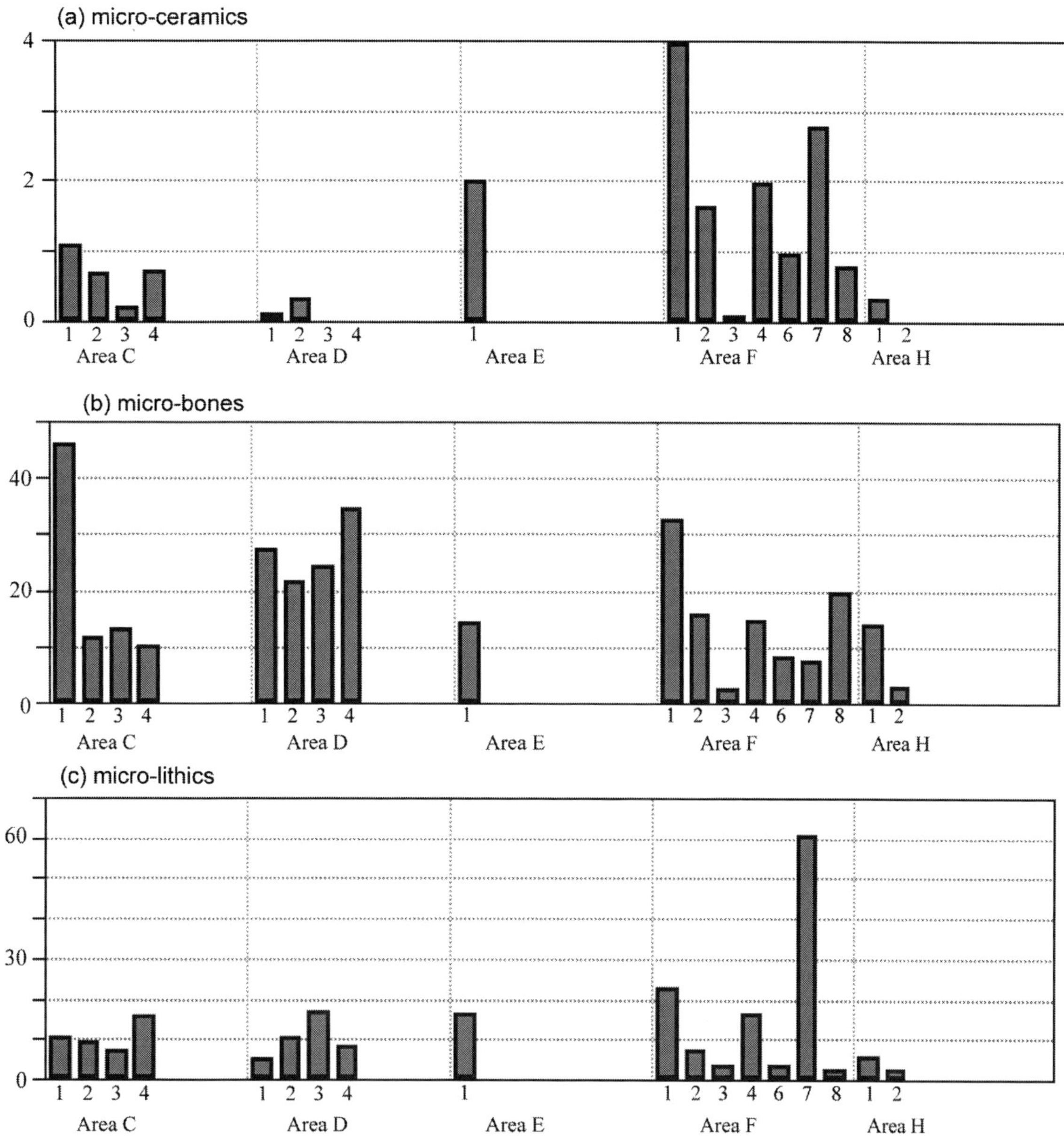

Figure 4.39. Distribution of micro-debris among rooms within structures, Kazane. The vertical axis indicates the micro-artifact count density per liter.

made for a substitute caretaker (Van De Mieroop 1992: 217). Craft or business specialities were often passed from father to son (e.g., at Ur in Area AH among priestly families and in Area EM and EH among moneylenders and shepherds, Van De Mieroop 1992: 219).

Cuneiform texts provide us with emic categories of kinship relations, including terms that translate as "family," "extended family," and "house of brothers" (see further Glassner 1996: 104, Sjöberg 1967, Potts 1997: 209). Unfortunately, few of these texts date to the third millennium and none are from Upper Mesopotamian contexts. However, recent excavations at Beydar have uncovered over 165 tablets that date to c. 2400. Most of the tablets were found within a house located near the palace, and record royal bookkeeping, rations for people and animals, and administrative decisions (Ismail 1996).

Due to the lack of in-situ texts and careful, room-by-room excavations, we are rarely able to identify "individuals" in the Upper Mesopotamian archaeological record. However, this should not prevent us from considering social categories such as "mothers" or "children." These social categories are created from more than simply kinship bonds. Instead, age, gender, class, and ethnicity have a bearing on social roles, both in terms of choices and options. For example, age may correlate with differing levels of prestige within the household. The senior household members may have controlled when to expand the house, whom their children could marry, and / or possessed specialized knowledge about craft production techniques.

An important component of understanding social relations is a study of relations between genders. Because of the focus on institutions and "great men" (i.e., kings named in texts), Near Eastern historians and archaeologists have often ignored relations between individual men and women. When these gendered interactions are studied, they are often only analyzed from the perspective of elite women and men (certainly more written records exist for these individuals than for a farmer and his wife — e.g., Pollock 1991). Another limitation is that historical documents, such as law codes and myths, often present idealized relations between men and women, rather than the realities of day-to-day interactions. A more accurate picture of the realities of interactions come from studying accounts, contracts, and letters, as well as the archaeological record.

Whether a male head of household had obligatory military duty or simply long days in the fields, many day-to-day household decisions were likely under the control of the senior female. Among the Maya, Hendon (1999: 266) suggests women's weaving and spinning served as a symbolic counterpart to men's participation in warfare (as both, in the Mesoamerican tradition, involve metaphors of creation, reproduction, and war). Thus, household activities, such as cloth production or perhaps figurine or bead production, may have enhanced women's prestige within kin groups or broader social spheres. Ideally, any study of households would investigate the possibility of gendered tasks or activity areas within houses. Because of the difficulties in associating material culture with individuals, few Near Eastern archaeologists have attempted this (for a notable exception, see Pollock 1992 and Wright 1998). In the final section, below, I synthesize the results of activity area analysis and possible gendered room use within one house at Titriş.

Conclusion

Micro-debris analysis cannot stand alone as a technique. It must be combined with data from macro-artifacts, features, and architecture to answer questions about domestic socio-economic practices. When combined with other lines of evidence, micro-archaeology provides a window on daily activities that are missed by traditional methods. With additional data from other specialists—botanists, faunal analysts, and ceramic specialists—at the various sites, we should be able to produce a much richer model of daily life in ancient Anatolia. Figure 4.40 represents a preliminary attempt to model the location of daily activities and the nature of social and economic relations among household members in Building Unit 4 at Titriş Höyük. This two-dimensional drawing can in no way substitute for or completely convey the complexity of household dynamics. The recreation, based on several lines of evidence, including micro-debris, features, architecture, and ethnographic data. I include it here to provoke questions, some provisionally answered above. Although micro-debris cannot answer all of these questions, it allows us to pose additional ones based on the patterns observed at the micro-level.

• Did this large dwelling unit contain a large household, a wealthy nuclear family, or co-residing nuclear families?

• Was the house divided into three sections that corresponded to different families? did these families constitute an extended family? was this social organization commonplace for the EBA? if not, did the ability to have an extended family housed under one roof correlate with economic wealth? did various neighborhoods contain both extended and nuclear families? if not, does this indicate neighborhood differences based on socio-economic levels or occupational types?

• Were animals stabled within houses in cities? (this is a common practice within village compounds, but few archaeologists have tested this suggestion for ancient cities)

• Does this drawing over-emphasize the lower stories? i.e., did many of the daily activities such as drying, preparing, and cutting foods occur on the roof? (if so, the collapse within the building may contain the material evidence for these activities)

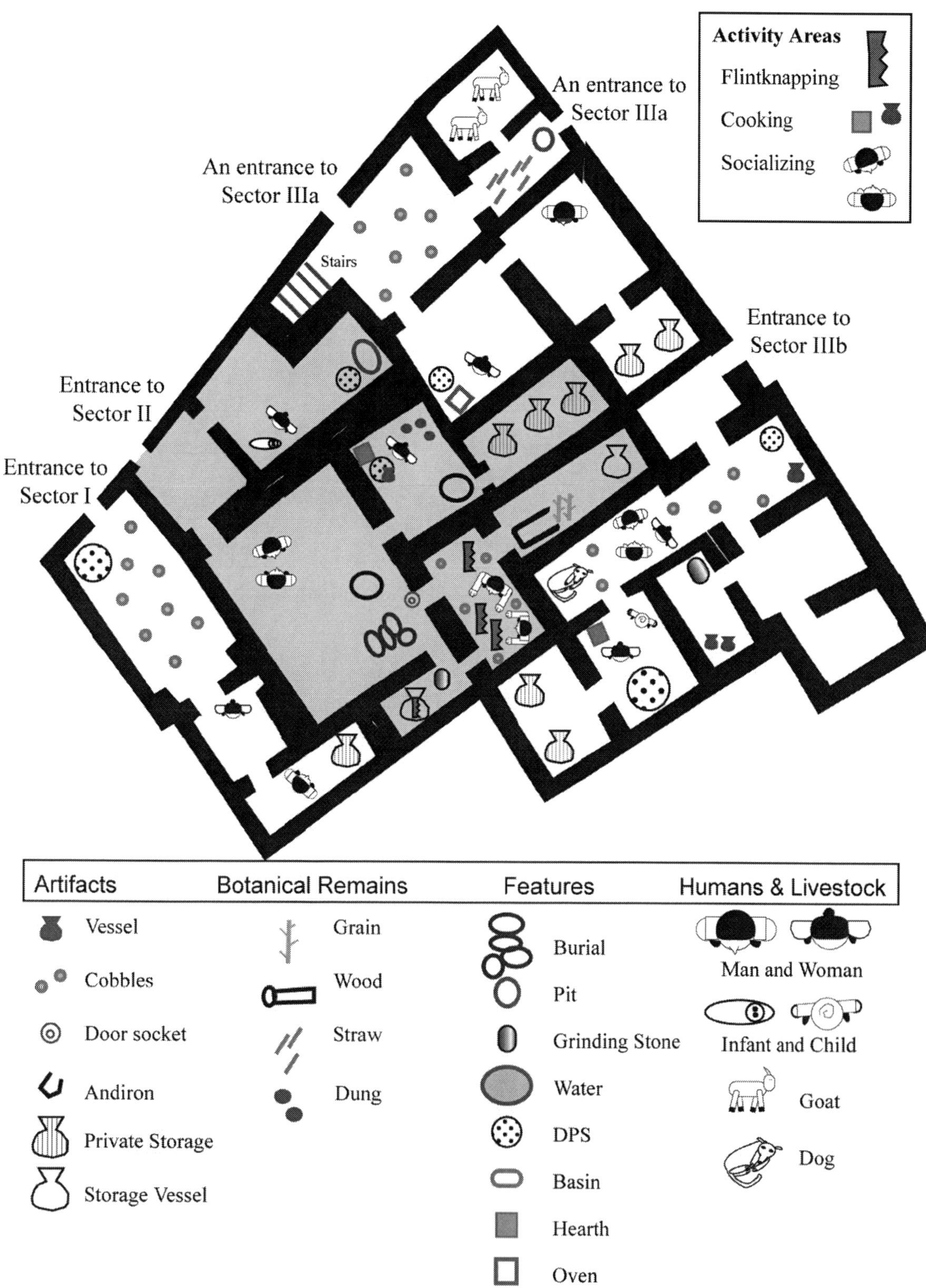

Figure 4.40. A model of the daily activities conducted in Building Unit 4, Titriş.

• Were any of the rooms gender specific? e.g., was Room 9 used exclusively or primarily by flintknappers? or were Rooms 22-25 segregated to provide women with privacy from the rest of the household?

• Did households produce surplus products? if so, did they barter them with relatives/friends/neighbors, or were professional traders or state representatives involved?

Answers to some of these questions will be discussed in the next chapter. In Figure 4.40 the distribution of these activities suggests broader socio-economic patterns including gendered spaces, household economy, and social differentiation between families. These socio-economic patterns, in turn, allow us to understand the composition of neighborhoods. This level of analysis — neighborhood organization — is the focus of the next chapter.

Chapter 5: Locating Ancient Neighborhoods

In this chapter I attempt to answer the question: were Early Bronze Age Upper Mesopotamian cities organized into coherent neighborhoods? If so, what attributes (social, economic, political, religious), if any, determined which families lived where? Archaeologists rarely ask these questions explicitly and answer them even more infrequently (for rare exceptions, see Stone 1987, 1991, 1996; Keith 1999, 2003). Ancient neighborhoods are not commonly investigated for two main reasons: the analysis of neighborhoods is only possible when large horizontal exposures are excavated, and even then, most archaeologists focus on either macro-settlement patterns (such as the hierarchy of site sizes within environmental or political space) or micro-settlement patterns (such as the distribution of individual houses within sites). The "mid-range" settlement pattern, the neighborhood (clusters of houses within cities), is rarely studied. For example, the index for a recent book devoted to Mesopotamian cities contained only two references to neighborhood-level organization (Van De Mieroop 1999: 112, 183). To rectify this lacuna, I situate houses within their local community and investigate what shared traits, if any, linked households into neighborhoods within ancient Mesopotamian cities.

In this chapter, I build upon the results of the micro-debris analysis presented in Chapters 3 and 4 to locate activity areas and houses of different socio-economic status within two EBA residential neighborhoods at Titriş Höyük. This chapter proposes methods by which neighborhoods may be investigated. By raising the question of how to investigate neighborhood composition, we increase the likelihood that future projects will be interested in these questions and that excavation strategies will be planned accordingly.

Locating Neighborhood Boundaries and Identifying Neighborhood Attributes

Using data from face-to-face interviews and questionnaires, sociologists emphasize personal interactions in their definitions of neighborhoods: "The sociological conception of neighborhood emphasizes the notion of shared activities, experiences, values, common loyalties and perspectives, and human networks that give to an area a sense of continuity and persistence over time" (Keller 1968: 91). A fundamental social relation within neighborhoods is the interactions among neighbors. Although it is difficult to establish unique "neighbor" attributes, Keller (1968: 27) defined the term as "any unrelated person living in the same street or block, with whom there was a customary or prearranged contact at least once a month on the average." The temporal contact is not very useful archaeologically, but the interactions among spatially proximal neighbors may result in shared artifact assemblages (most likely where a nearby store or market stocks similar products) or, casually distinct, but producing the same result, neighbors that share beliefs or traditions (such as an ethnic enclave) that results in similar material culture.

Social scientists recognize that these small-scale community interactions are often an individual's first taste of non-family traditions and rules. Mann (1970: 572) specified that "neighborhood" social relations were very important in the life of children whose first non-familial social contacts were likely to be with other neighborhood children. Sociologists also observe that neighbors provide assistance in child rearing and, subsequently, the physical neighborhood might include areas where children congregate to play (Hester 1975). Urban anthropologists suggest that secondary streets often fulfill this function; areas for children to play tend to be in close proximity to their parents. Neighbors are also sources of local gossip and, occasionally, the origins of "popular" or "grass roots" protest, activism, or dissent from the authorities. And, finally, neighbors may conform to informal standards and/or rules, such as agreed-upon amounts of night-time noise levels (Keller 1968). A modern American analogy would include neighborhood watch groups (to keep an eye on young children playing) or agreed-upon quantities of front-lawn clutter among residents (often enforced by district-level zoning ordinances). Ethnographic observations suggest that these social interactions had important ramifications for the success or failure of state-level directives (e.g., community groups in a 20th-Century Turkish village, Kandiyoti 1974). As a result, these supra-familial interactions are relevant to our complete understanding of ancient cities.

Neighborhoods in the Archaeological Record

The previous section discussed "neighborhoods" in terms of social interactions; here I treat neighborhoods as physically bounded entities, realizing that in some cases these boundaries may overlap or be nested. I define the term "neighborhood" as small groups of houses whose inhabitants, due to their proximity, interacted on a daily basis. Although these social interactions may not always leave material residues, residents in ancient communities probably had daily encounters with their neighbors. Based on sociological studies of neighborhoods, I would expect that residents in ancient cities knew each other by name and, most likely, interacted socially, be it children playing (see Stevenson 1985: 26), neighbors sharing household tasks, arranging marriages, or houseowners discussing land sales. Neighbors may have also shared craft specialization skills, bread-making tasks, informal tool production and/or repair, and, perhaps, animal husbandry chores (including butchering). This level of cooperation is often assumed in "simple" societies but rarely investigated in "complex societies." This assumption results in a simplistic view of ancient cities, where researchers posit a dichotomy between household and state level administrative activities instead of investigating the potential diversity of urban life among households and neighborhoods.

In the archaeological record, neighborhoods may be spatially distinguished based on craft specialization, social status, religion, ethnicity, or aggregation over time that creates older and newer sections. The comparable signaling in a modern city might include named streets, a change in architectural design and/or the spacing of structures, or the more intangible change in the volume of noise, smells, or activity in the streets. In the archaeological record, these markers are often poorly preserved or hard to interpret. To make neighborhoods even more difficult to identify, neighborhood boundaries (whether physical or symbolic) have often moved or disappeared altogether over time.

Although it may be clear that many social interactions were conducted within the neighborhood, who were the social actors? The social interactions discussed above can take place within homogeneous or heterogeneous neighborhoods. Neighborhood diversity, or in some cases uniformity, may be based on particular socio-economic, ethnic, or religious attributes and be visible in house size, design, or features. These attributes can be deliberately or unintentionally chosen over generations. Different neighborhoods might be separated physically (by gates, walls, or, less drastically, narrowed access lanes) or symbolically (by street signs or differences in house design). For example, neighborhoods within contemporary Muslim cities are often linked by ethnic identity, religion, or occupation and contain separate sets of the most basic institutions, such as bread bakeries and mosques (Stone 1987: 4). In a Moroccan town, Eickelman (1974: 283) uncovered the existence of networks of personal interaction which, he argued, resulted in a sense of "closeness" among neighbors. Of course, these groupings are unlikely to be determined by the same attributes that were valued 5,000 years ago. A case in point: the impetus for forming contemporary neighborhoods varies considerably. Greenshields (1980: 134) cataloged a diversity of processes that formed discrete Middle Eastern neighborhoods: immigrations of homogeneous migratory groups, mass regrouping within cities, and population movements on an individual basis related to socio-economic status, religious preference (including proximity to religious sites), or family establishment patterns. The complexity behind the formation of modern neighborhood formation cautions the archaeologist against making facile interpretations about the creation, growth, and dissolution of ancient neighborhoods.

I define neighborhoods broadly as a grouping of structures, streets, and/or empty lots that were recognized by their inhabitants as separate from other areas of the city. Accordingly, I first investigate any possible emic references to neighborhoods. As archaeologists, we may not be able to conclusively locate neighborhood boundaries, but this should not prevent us from exploring the possibility that residents of ancient cities lived (whether by choice or force) in certain neighborhoods.

Toward the goal of provoking questions to be answered with archaeological data, I have incorporated ethnographic and historical data from medieval Arab cities and contemporary Islamic ones. Although this is not an ideal analogy — even 1000-year-old medieval Islamic cities were founded several centuries after the collapse of Mesopotamian society — some of the patterns visible in contemporary Middle Eastern cities have archaeological correlates at ancient sites. Another challenge in using this data is the difficulty of distinguishing among Hellenistic, Roman, Sassanian, and Islamic urban plans when they are superimposed, often at the same location, as an ancient Mesopotamian city. With these caveats in mind I review emic (or insider perspective on cultural traditions) and etic (an outsider point of view) terms and conceptions of Mesopotamian neighborhoods.

Emic Visibility for Neighborhoods

An Akkadian word, *babtum*, provides one of the first suggestions that the ancient Mesopotamians recognized discrete areas within their cities. The word *babu(m)* means "gate" in both Akkadian and Arabic. In 18th-Century C.E. Tripoli, four neighborhoods contained the word *bab* in their names (Gulick 1967: 153). The Akkadian term *babtum* is translated as "a quarter of a city, neighborhood, or ward (as a subdivision of a city's population)" (Chicago Assyrian Dictionary, CAD, volume B: 10a). This translation conflates several possible scales of residential organization. In attested cases the term refers to both individuals (e.g., *babtuu,* "neighbor woman in the ward") and to groups of individuals within a specified area (e.g., *babtuu,* "wives and daughters who live in the same ward cannot sleep on account of you") (CAD volume B: 10a). In her study of second-millennium neighborhoods, Keith (1999: 80) preferred the former definition, defining *babtum* as a group of people. In contrast, Van De Mieroop (1997: 112) suggested that the term referred to areas of the settlement, each of which had its own governmental structure and responsibilities. Although the precise referent remains unclear (or perhaps varied in usage), it is clear that the Mesopotamians used a vocabulary that could specify a level of supra-household organization.

Another suggestion for emically recognized neighborhoods is found in references to "the gates of the city." These gates were placed within wide city walls that enclosed cities (at least the original part of the city). The Akkadian word is *bābu,* translated by the CAD (as a primary definition) as: "opening, doorway, door, gate, or entrance (to a house, a building or a part thereof, to a palace, temple or part thereof, to a city, to a cosmic locality)" (CAD volume B: 14). In addition, both residential and agricultural districts were named the "gate of x" (Keith 1999: 83, 101). In Sumerian, the word for gate is KA_2, and the city gate is referred to as the KA_2.GAL (*abullum* in Akkadian) or "great gate." Clear archaeological examples of city-wall gates can be found in all four historic millennia — e.g., at Habuba Kabira, Ebla, Eshnunna, Babylon, and Nineveh (Figure 5.1). At Tell Beydar, a mid-third millennium town in Syria, texts from an on-site archive reveal that the town was divided into districts, called "gates" (Ismail, et al. 1996: 32).

Even more relevant to the discussion of neighborhoods, texts refer to a *bāb mahīrim* "gate of the market" or "commercial district." The text is a letter, provenience unknown; the writer requests Nunnatum to buy goods at the "market gate" (cited in Keith 1999: 76). And a second text, from Babylon, refers to a *suq šimatim,* or "shopping street." The text is an extispicy record asking whether "the large gem which he bought and which lies here be sold in the 'shopping streets' for profit?" (cited in Keith 1999: 76). These terms suggest that the ancient Mesopotamians recognized and labeled discrete spaces for commerce within cities. Unfortunately, both these terms are only attested in second, as opposed to third, millennium texts. Moreover, many of the cities cited above are located in southern Mesopotamia, not Upper Mesopotamia. As a result, we cannot rely solely on texts to come to a conclusion. Instead, we must investigate the archaeological existence of wards within northern Mesopotamian cities.

One archaeological example of neighborhood boundaries is street layouts that either hindered or enabled access to clusters of houses. In order for neighbors to interact with each other, they needed access to their neighbors, even if it was only a chance meeting in the street. While we might expect straight, broad avenues to characterize the "main street" of an ancient city, narrow and twisting alleys tended to be characteristic of individual neighborhoods. The streets in Area AH at Ur provide a good example of this patterning. On one hand, wide streets allowed convenient, visible, and easy access (including a breadth wide enough for draft animals and carts) among houses. Conversely, narrow, and often dead-end, alleys linked individual houses into neighborhoods. Using these criteria, it appears that at Ur anywhere from seven to ten houses comprised separate neighborhoods (Figure 5.2). Without better control of the "small finds," this figure is necessarily preliminary and very difficult to apply to other sites. But clearly the inhabitants of ancient Middle Eastern cities recognized the difference between a large open street and a narrow alley. Moreover, these narrow alleys were not considered fully public; rather, one entered them only if you were visiting or had business to conduct, all the while recognizable as a "stranger." At the other end of the urban planning spectrum is the site of Haradum, located about 90 km southeast of Mari on the Euphrates (see Figure 1.2). Founded some time after the fall of Mari, c. 18th Century B.C.E., the town was well planned and contained straight streets with courtyard-plan houses (Kepinski-Lecomte 1992).

In 'Amran, a modern Arabian town, Stevenson (1985: 12) observed that many families preferred to live in the traditional part of the town, the *madina,* because men viewed its "narrow winding streets, where only friends and neighbors enter, as a safe place for their women." Although we cannot definitively attribute this reasoning to the ancient urbanites, narrow streets, in contrast to broad "main streets," clearly signal some degree of restriction.

Ancient urbanites probably recognized countless other types of neighborhood boundaries. For example, changes in noise levels and smells may have been associated with different neighborhoods. Abu-Lughod (1987: 161) commented on the higher volume of noise in Muslim, rather than Hindu quarters in 20th-Century Indian cities. These intangible and often unconsciously recognized features contribute to an individual's sense of place within their own neighborhood.

Etic Visibility for Neighborhoods

Unfortunately, many of the attributes discussed above are impossible to see in the archaeological record. Even a foreign visitor to an ancient city might have had similar problems recognizing emic boundaries. As a result, both archaeologists and strangers need more obvious, and physical, signals. One such signal, discussed above, is the layout of streets. A more drastic boundary is a complete physical segregation of areas, into upper towns versus lower ones or outer versus inner towns. Excavators have identified this pattern in Syro-Anatolia, but it may represent artificial boundaries created by archaeological

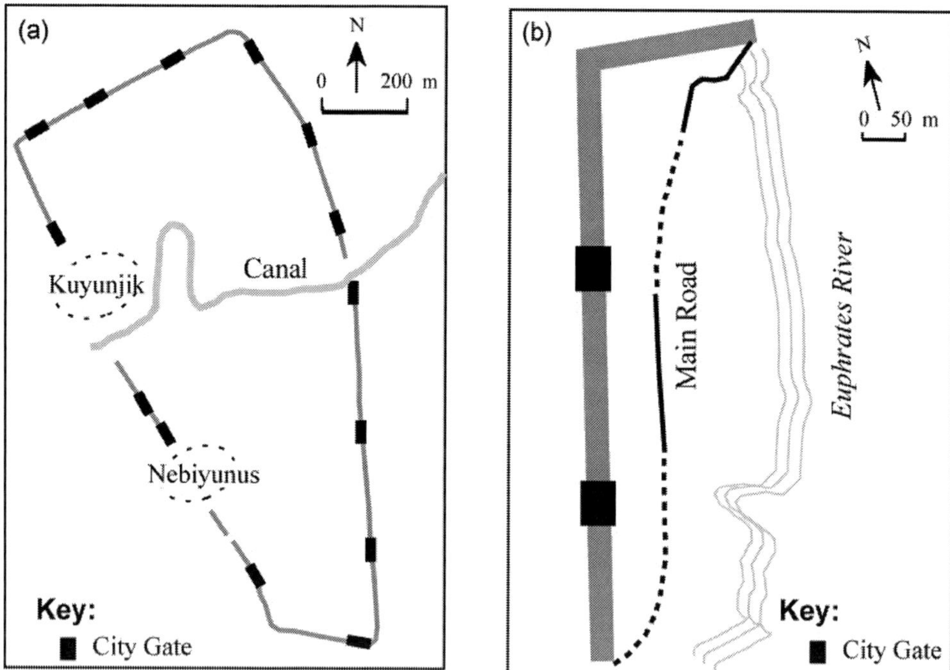

Figure 5.1. "The Gates of the City" at two northern Mesopotamian cities. (a) Nineveh, 1st mill. B.C.E. in northern Iraq. (b) Habuba Kabira, 4th mill. B.C.E. in Syria.

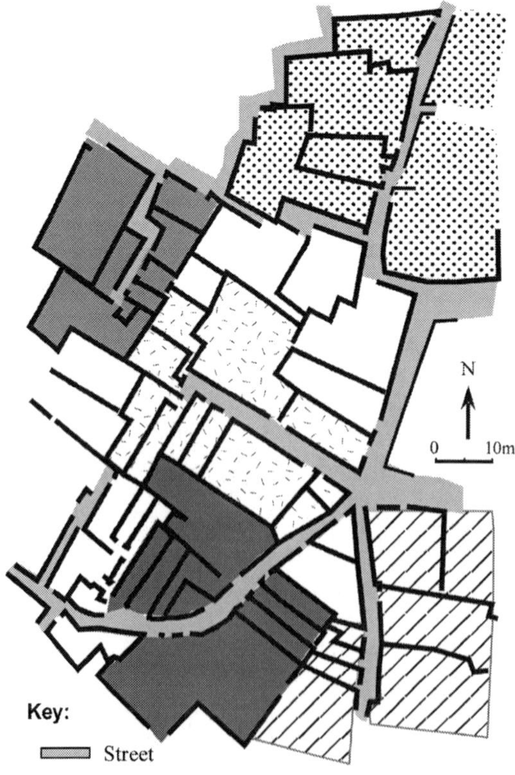

Figure 5.2. Ur neighborhoods as determined by doorways and street patterns. The differential shading indicates clusters of houses that may correspond to ancient neighborhoods. Modified from Van De Mieroop 1999: 80.

sampling techniques. Another physical difference among neighborhoods may be the design or layout of homes. For example, an older section of a city might contain tightly packed structures, while a newer section might still contain open spaces. Another signal might be the presence of a neighborhood shrine (in modern times, probably a mosque) or other public meeting spaces such as open plazas. In his study of the old city of Herat, Afghanistan, English (1973: 82-3) demonstrated that neighborhood activity focused around small mosques and shrines. Perhaps this held true for the ancient city of Ur. Chapels containing small shrines are clearly distributed throughout the excavated area at Ur and may be linked to different neighborhoods (see Figure 5.5).

In the following discussion, I apply emic and etic categories of observation to try to identify the composition of neighborhoods in two areas at Titriş Höyük.

Ancient Neighborhoods at Titriş Höyük

In this section I evaluate whether we can identify the complex of attributes, if any, that characterized different residential neighborhoods at Titriş Höyük. If neighborhoods did exist, what was membership based upon? This question cannot be answered conclusively without further horizontal excavation, but based on the extant discoveries, several models can be suggested and provisionally tested.

The main categories of structures investigated at Titriş were houses (including the small-scale production that may have occurred in some of them), workshops, stores, and guardrooms within defensive walls. Texts found on excavations in southern Mesopotamian cities reveal other types of structures: chapels, bakeries, and taverns (Moorey 1982: 202-04). To date, none of these structures have been conclusively identified at Syro-Anatolian sites (most likely due to the lack of texts which, at other sites, such as Ur, enabled researchers to definitively identify these structures). In addition, much of the work in Syro-Anatolia has focused on public and religious structures, rather than uncovering large expanses of neighborhood planning.

In the following analysis, I try to "split" rather than "lump" household variability. This approach produces new models, rather than simply confirming existing ones. Accordingly, I analyze evidence for neighborhoods in three stages. First, I attempt to identify the boundaries of ancient neighborhoods. Second, I evaluate quantitative and qualitative differences in the types of daily activities that were conducted in various neighborhoods. Third, I try to determine whether neighborhood residents shared cultural, economic, or religious backgrounds.

Identifying Neighborhood Boundaries at Titriş Höyük

Because the location of artifacts and features are not always readily available in preliminary site reports, often only architectural plans are available to work from. Given this limitation, I suggest three strategies, based on architectural plans alone, for identifying neighborhoods.

Street Placement

The placement of streets within an urban setting can demarcate bounded areas. Depending on their width, the quantity and nature of turns, and duration (or length), streets can unite or divide sections of a city. For example, the diversity of street-widths at Habuba Kabira, a late Uruk site, suggests several neighborhoods (Figure 5.3). In Mesopotamian cities the width and course of streets varied from broad, fairly straight thoroughfares to narrow, winding alleys (Table 5.1). Scanlon (1970: 186) reported that in Fustat, 7th Century C.E. Cairo, two meters provided "just sufficient [room] for the passage of two horsemen abreast." We have no evidence that the inhabitants of Titriş used horses, but donkey carcasses were found in burials. It is not clear if these donkeys were used to pull carts, saddlebags, or drag plows, but if they were used as beasts of burden, the main streets at Titriş would have been sufficiently wide to permit carts, pulled by two donkeys, to pass. If draft animals pulling carts did not, in part, determine the width of the streets, what did? Possible influences on the street width include herding goats to pasture from their winter living quarters, creating places for children to play, enabling privacy between opposite neighbors, accommodating pedestrians; or, perhaps, socializing among neighbors.

Given that streets can be strategically planned so as to hinder or allow for movements of animals and people, who, if anyone, determined their route? Unfortunately, we have no direct evidence from documents that civic authorities controlled the planning of streets in Mesopotamia. But we learn from an omen text that, at least in an idealized civic order, residents were interested in keeping the thoroughfares free of obstructions:

> If a house blocks the main street in its building, the owner of the house will die; if a house overshadows (overhangs) or obstructs the side of the main street, the heart of the dweller in that house will not be glad (Frankfort 1950: 111).

Other evidence for planned streets comes from the presence of long, mostly straight streets that were clearly laid out before the construction of the buildings (Matney and Algaze 1995: 37). In several EBA sites, the patterning of streets divided structures up into blocks that contained anywhere from three to twenty structures each. Eshnunna (modern Tell Asmar), Mashkan-shapir (modern Tell Abu Duwari), and Titriş Höyük (ancient name unknown) all contained a combination of wide and narrow streets and alleys (Delougaz and Lloyd 1967, Stone 1991, Algaze et al. 1996). Although not fully

Figure 5.3. Neighborhoods at Habuba Kabira (West Sector). Individual structures are numbered. The differential shading indicates clusters of houses that may correspond to ancient neighborhoods. Modified from Vallet 1997: 115, Figure 3.

Site	Locale within the site	Main Roads	Alleys
Titriş	80s Neighborhood	1.5 to 2 m	n/a
	30s Neighborhood	2 to 2.5 m	n/a
Eshnunna (Tell Asmar)	Level IVa (middle road)	3.1 m	0.96 to 2 m
	Level Va (middle road)	2.5 m	1.5 m
Habuba Kabira	West Sector	5 to 6 m	1 to 3m
	North Sector	2.5 to 3.3 m	1.1 m
	South Sector	n/a	1 m
	East Sector	1 m	0.5 m
Jebel Aruda	South Quarter	5 m	2 m
	North Quarter	1 m	3 m
Abu Salabikh	Sector A	2.2 m	0.8 m
	Sector E	5 m	1.3 m
Mashkan-shapir (Tell Abu Dawari)	Building A – E	1.5 to 4+ m	n/a

Table 5.1. Street widths in Upper and Southern Mesopotamian cities. Most of these measurements were calculated from published plans and thus are approximate. The estimates only include streets and alley-ways.

excavated, magnetometric plans from the Lower Town at Titriş show the outline of at least five main north/south streets and two east/west streets (Figure 5.4b; the plan depicts stone-footings from architectural remains as a negative image; Matney and Algaze 1995: 44). The Outer Town at Titriş contained a similar combination of major north/south and east/west streets (Figure 5.4a). At Mashkan-shapir, Stone noted that the blocks, situated inbetween the main streets, covered about one hectare. One hectare corresponds to the average size of small villages in ancient Mesopotamia (Stone 1995: 240). Stone suggested that this may not be a coincidence, but rather indicative of the similar "building blocks" that created Mesopotamian communities. This proposition will be tested in Chapter 7, where a rural community, Tilbes Höyük, is compared to an urban one, Kazane Höyük.

Variable street widths determine, in part, boundaries between neighborhoods. Within these neighborhoods we find a diversity of structures. At Ur, for example, shops, chapels, large elite residences, smaller urban "apartments," and an area that contained kilns ("Baker's Square") were all found within the perimeter of two wide streets (Figure 5.5). The functions of some of these structures were identified by texts found within the structures. Lacking texts, we cannot positively identify shops at Titriş, but we can search for repeated clusters of room types. Chapter 3 laid the groundwork for the types of rooms we expect within urban houses. In short, there are two main house styles in third millennium Upper Mesopotamian cities: elongated rectangles and courtyards (Figure 5.6). Each house-type contained smaller storage rooms, larger courtyards, private rear rooms, and an area for cooking. Identifying these clusters of rooms within the 30s and 80s neighborhoods suggests a distribution of larger, possibly elite, structures and smaller structures (Figure 5.7).

At Titriş the layout of streets suggests a slightly different arrangement between two different areas of the site: 30s trenches and 80s trenches. The excavated streets in the 80s neighborhood suggest one-structure wide "blocks" separated by narrow and wide streets. Each of these blocks abuts the city wall, separated by a very narrow street. In contrast, the 30s neighborhood appears to contain two-structure (or more) wide "blocks." In both neighborhoods the streets seem fairly well planned (as evidenced by mostly straight courses). But the 80s neighborhood street layout provides more privacy (in terms of access in and out of the structure) than the more tightly congregated structures in the 30s. It is impossible to make a final verdict without interpreting the rest of the magnetometric image, but we can observe that distinct areas of habitation may be visible in the archaeological record based on variable street patterns. These areas may correlate with different types of activities. For example, at Mashkan-shapir, Stone (1995: 239) identified different sectors (in this case, separated by canals that ran between distinct mounds): religious, administrative, or residential-artisanal residences (Figure 5.8). In the north, we have no evidence that watercourses flowed through the city.

Circulation Patterns

Earlier, in Chapter 4, I analyzed circulation patterns within houses; in this chapter I turn to the possibility of access between households. I assume that houses with relatively easy access to each other most likely represent neighborhoods. Streets and narrow alleys provided access in and out of houses and routes to other houses. To safeguard privacy, many of the entrances from the streets opened into small passageways with the next entrance

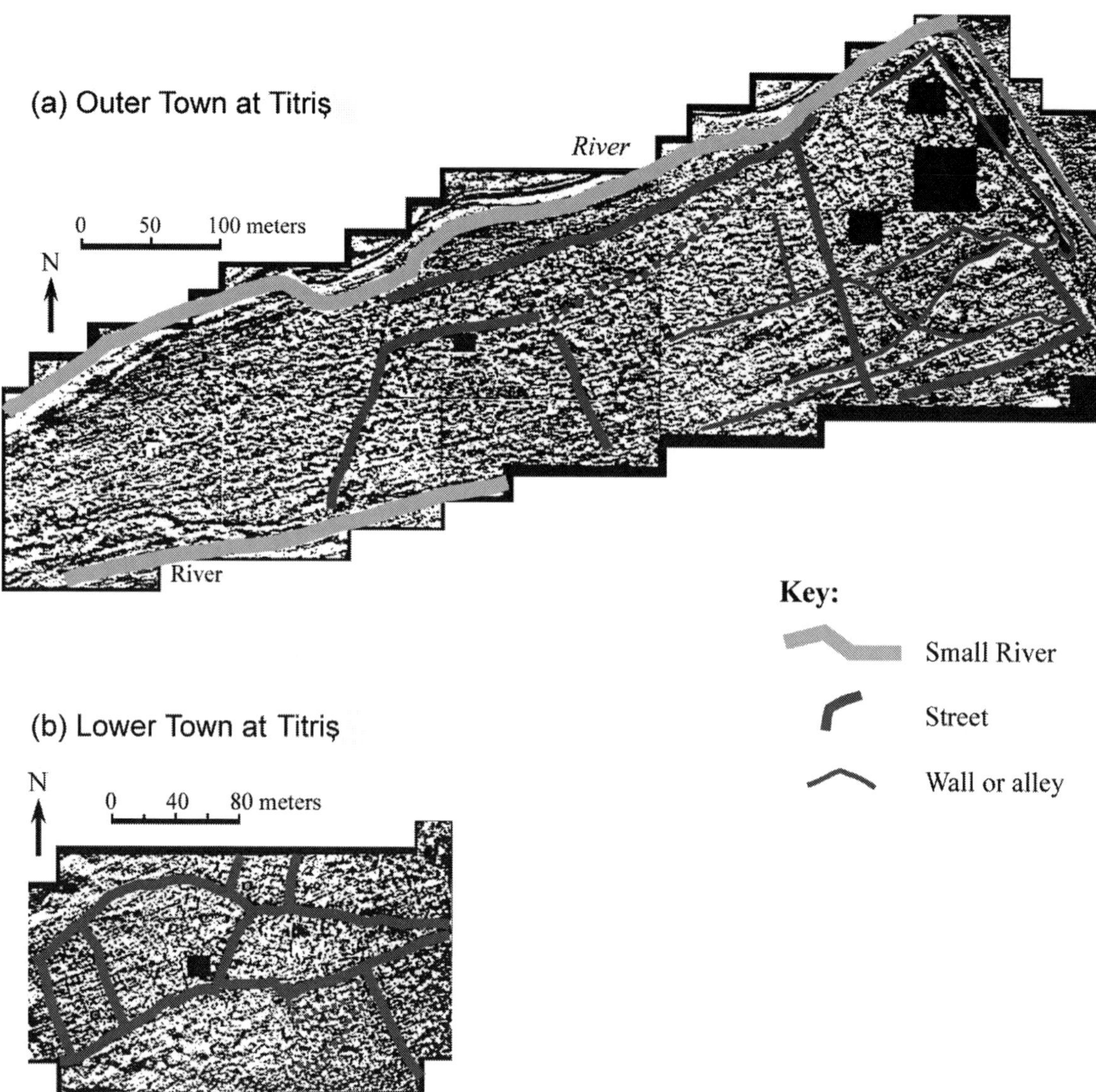

Figure 5.4. Outer and Lower Town magnetometry, Titriş. The "streets" and "walls" or "alleys" indicated on the plan are those interpreted by the author based on copies of the magnetometry, not based on the original data. Thus, these maps do not represent a comprehensive interpretation of the data. Modified from Figure 3 (p. 37) and Figure 13 (p. 45) in Matney and Algaze 1995; the maps were prepared by L. Somers, Geoscan (USA), Inc.

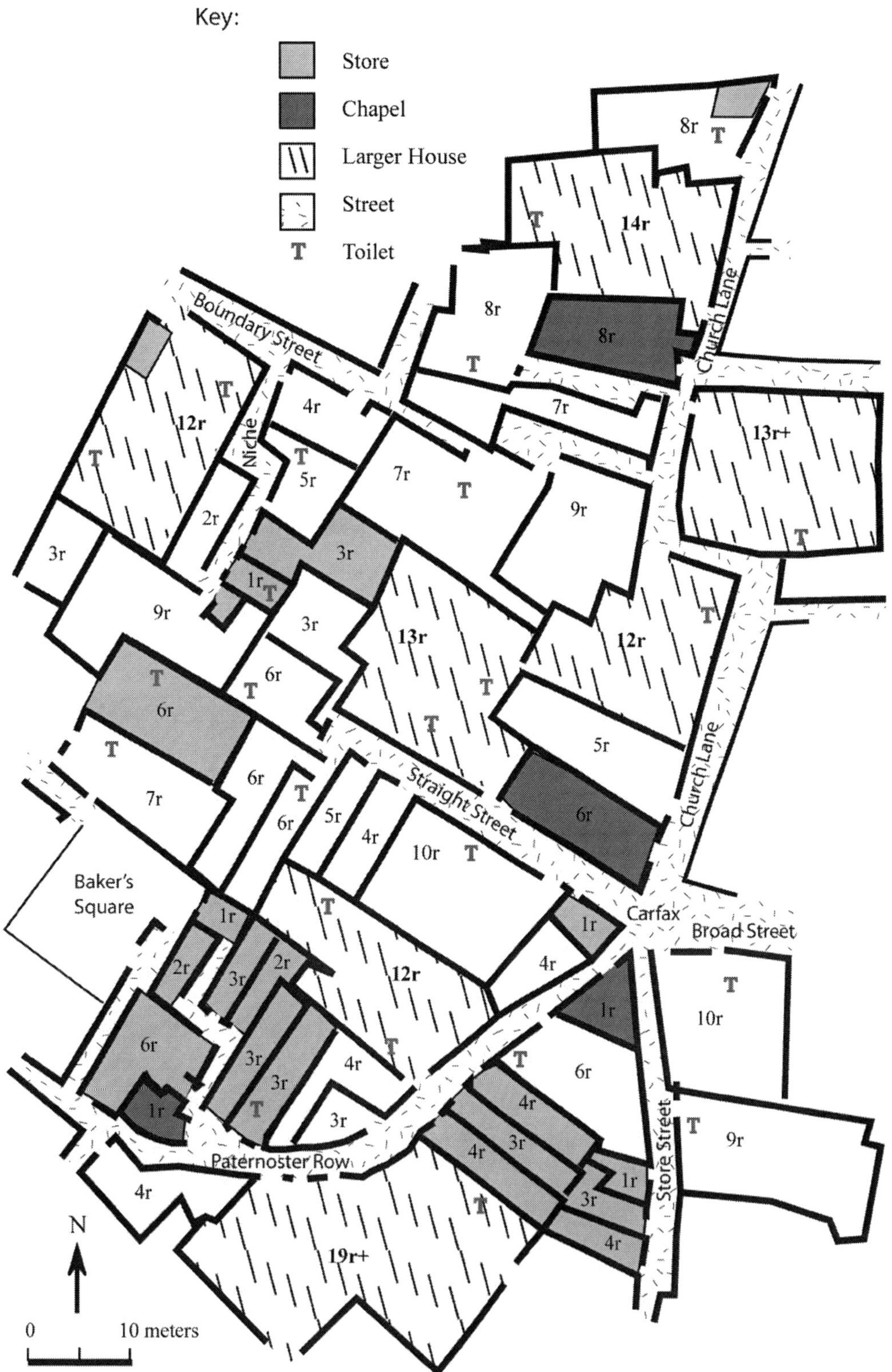

Figure 5.5. Distribution of residences, stores, and chapels in Area AH, Ur. The level indicated corresponds to the Larsa Period (ca. 2,000 – 1,750 BCE). The map is modified from Woolley 1976: Plate 124. The stores were identified by Battini-Villard (1999: Figure 182) and the calculation of room numbers (indicated by the numbers accompanied by "r") was taken from Woolley 1954: 176, Figure 12.

Figure 5.6. House forms in the 80s neighborhood, Titriş.

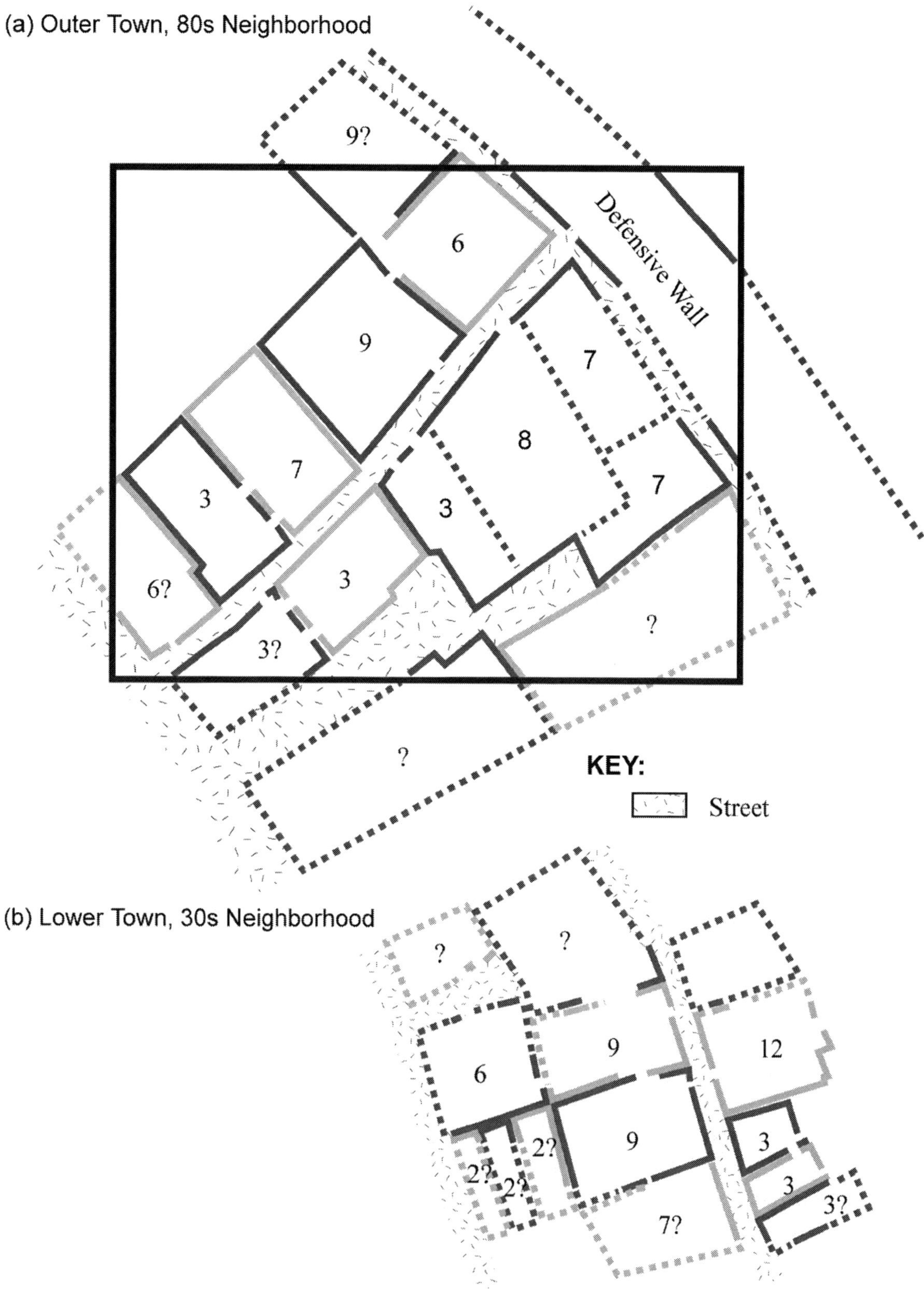

Figure 5.7. Variable house size within two neighborhoods, Titriş. The numbers indicate the quantity of rooms per structures and the question marks indicate incomplete house plans and thus an estimate of the number of rooms within the structure.

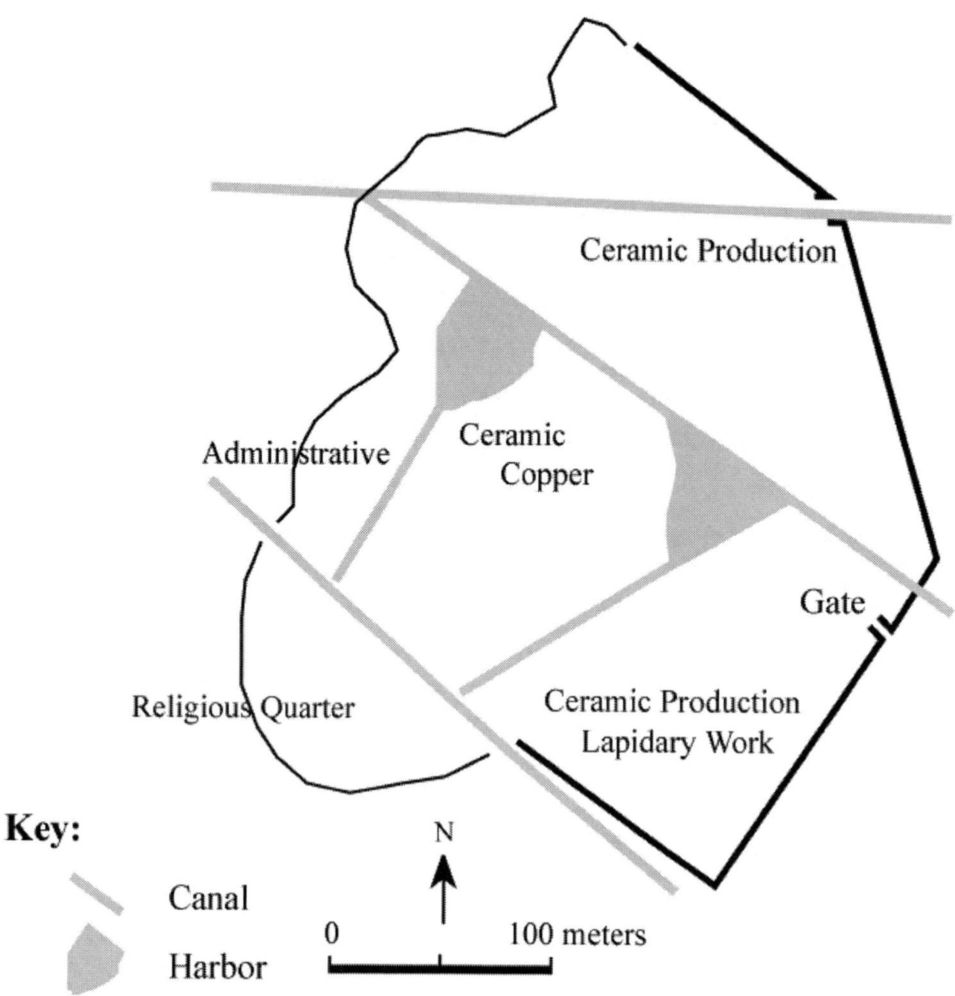

Figure 5.8. Neighborhoods at Mashkan-shapir. Modified from Stone 1995: 122.

(into the rest of the house) offset from the street-entrance to prohibit curious eyes from seeing further into the house. Despite certain barriers designed to protect the household's privacy, several houses contained passages that linked one household to another. It is tempting to assign the connected households a kinship affiliation, but this may also be as a result of street and structure modifications which necessitated the sharing of a communal entrance by two unrelated families.

A second circulation pattern was the placement of doors on opposite sides of main thoroughfares (Figure 5.9). I suggest that houses that faced each other (as determined by entrances opposite each other) were more likely to interact on a daily basis with each other than their near, but less accessible "rear" neighbors. For example, it seems clear that although the Outer Town (80s neighborhood) is only partially excavated, BU-1, BU-2, BU-3, and BU-4 were more likely to interact on a daily basis with each other than with BU-6 or BU-7. Similarly, in the Lower Town (30s neighborhood), there was an increased possibility that the residents in BU-5, BU-13, and BU-9 interacted with each other than with BU-15 or BU-14 (which, based on the current plan, were probably accessible only after walking "around the block"). An interesting difference between the circulation patterns in the 30s and 80s neighborhoods was the placement of these street-facing doors. In the 30s neighborhood, the doors were offset from another, while the 80s neighborhood contained parallel entrances. Unfortunately, this small sample does not permit a definitive interpretation. But the difference in placement suggests a different level of privacy between the two neighborhoods. This may be due to fewer kinship or social ties between neighbors in the 30s, or simply because of changed urban plans from the time that the 30s houses were constructed.

Daily Activities within Neighborhoods: Who did what where?

I next turn to an analysis of what activities occurred in these neighborhoods. To answer this query, I return to the interpretation of micro-debris distributions within the two residential neighborhoods at Titriş. Variations in micro-debris (e.g., between fine and sandy wares) may have

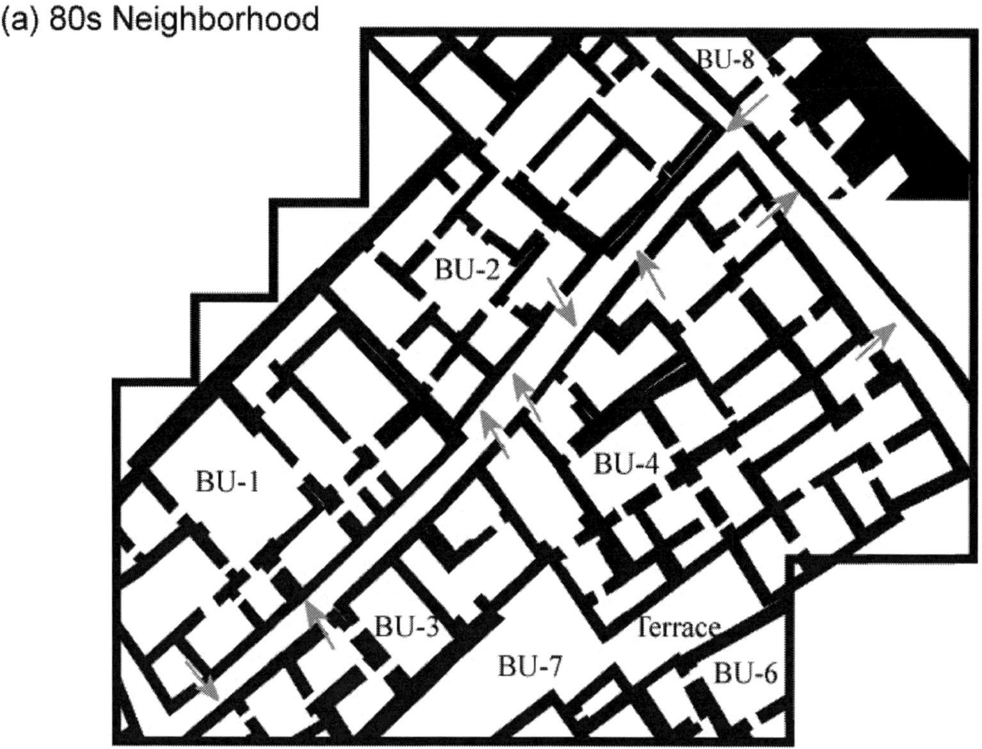

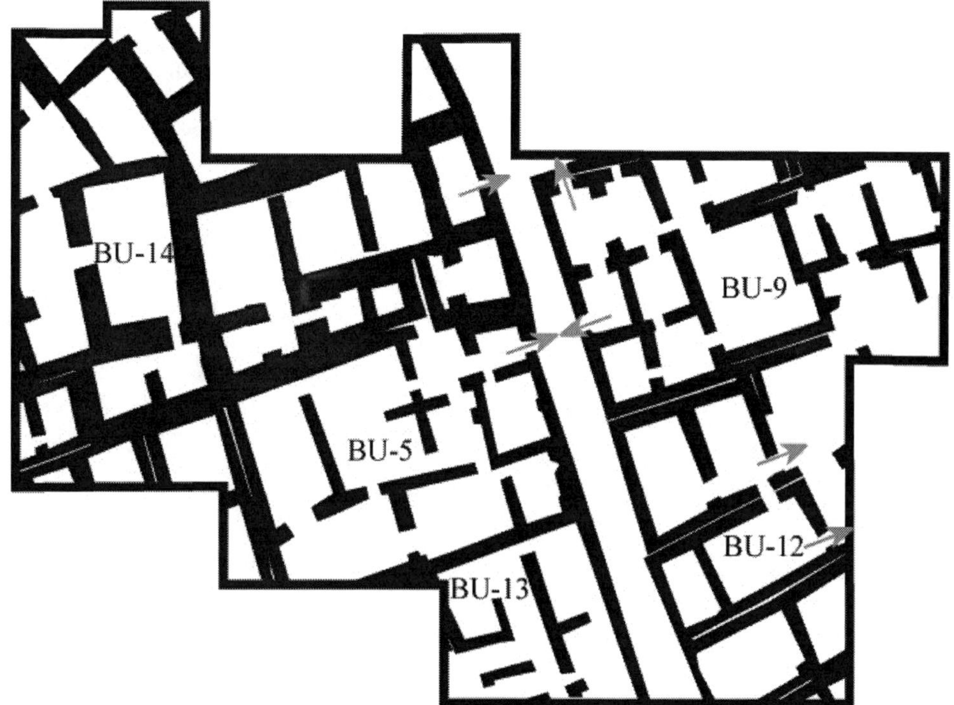

Figure 5.9. Access among houses within two neighborhoods, Titriş. The gray arrows indicate a possible egress from the structures. The plans are modified from (a) Algaze et al. 2001: 83 (Figure 2) and (b) Matney et al. 1997: 74 (Figure 2).

implications for household social obligations, such as the number of visitors entertained or the socio-economic class of the visitors.

Table 5.2 illustrates the variability in micro-debris medians among houses. The largest densities of micro-ceramics were located in Unit 4 and the Terrace (within the 80s neighborhood) and in Unit 14 (in the 30s neighborhood). In other cultures, increased feasting, necessitating ceramic cups and bowls, accompanied the imposition of governmental demands. For example, after the Inca conquest (in ancient Peru), women spent more time making corn beer to serve at state-sponsored feasts that were hosted to repay subjects for their labor (Hastorf 1991). The change in serving practices was evidenced by increased sherds from beer cups and supported by ethnohistorical observations. At Titriş, micro-bones were recovered in the highest densities from Unit 2, followed by the rooms in the defensive wall and Unit 14. The high quantity of bones from these floors suggests that either animals were butchered there or that the occupants consumed large quantities of meat. Or, from a different perspective, these two structures may not have been cleaned as regularly as others. The lithics, not surprisingly, were found in the highest concentration in the samples from the flint workshop. In fact, the overall density of micro-lithics in the workshop trenches is up to 18 times higher than samples from residential floors. Note, the samples from the street are exceptionally high in micro-ceramics and also high in micro-lithics.

In the next section I turn to an analysis of the macro-artifact and feature distribution in order to interpret the micro-patterns discussed here.

Macro-Artifacts and Features

Although the macro-artifacts from Titriş are not yet fully analyzed — this will be available with the publication of the final report — the distribution of ovens, grave goods, and features is known. The distribution of these features has several repercussions for the distribution of craft activities in the two neighborhoods (Figure 5.10 and 5.11). First, no kilns were excavated in the two neighborhoods, suggesting that ceramic vessels were obtained from kilns located in other neighborhoods or, possibly, from another site. For example, EBA levels at the nearby site of Lidar Höyük (see Figure 6.1), contained an area devoted to pottery production, evidenced by nine kilns containing vessels and rejects, often with potter's marks (Hauptmann 1982: 18). At Titriş, we do not know if the source of ceramic vessels was an independent shopkeeper, an "attached specialist," a traveling trader from another city or village, or whether there was a separate neighborhood, as yet unexcavated, dedicated to ceramic production. Second, tombs containing more than one individual were distributed among the houses. The practice of intramural tombs is widespread in Syro-Anatolia in the second half of the third millennium B.C.E. (Laneri 1999: 222-3; e.g., at Tell Ahmar and Titriş). We do not know if each household constructed and maintained a family crypt. The existence of an extramural cemetery proves that not all residents were buried in their houses, but it is unclear what factors determined who was buried where.

Many third millennium sites contain domestic interments below house floors. Of the sites in this study, seven of the houses at Titriş contained family crypts (see Figure 5.10 and Figure 5.11). In the later Ur III dynasty in the south these burials were often located in a separate room, or chapel (Woolley 1954: 188, Plates a and b). Many of these burials contained vessels for food and drink offerings leaning against the door to the vault (Woolley 1954: 188). These graves may have helped establish family ties to specific houses, suggesting that families made every effort to pass house ownership to their children. Small clay models of houses, found in a variety of ancient Near Eastern contexts, including the Upper Mesopotamian site of Kurban Höyük (Algaze et. al 1990: 400) may have helped assuage the family members who were not able to remain in the ancestral house (see van der Toorn 1996a and 1996b).

At Titriş, eleven burials have been excavated within houses. In general, the tombs are distributed among individual houses, suggesting that each tomb represents the remains of household occupants. Most of the tombs are rectangular, constructed of stone, with a semi-circular entryway into the funerary chamber, often referred to as a *dromos*. Offerings in the form of animals and vessels were often left in these entryways. The bodies are rarely complete, suggesting secondary burials and, possibly, the accumulation of bones from different individuals (Laneri 1999: 230). The sex, age, or quantity of individuals per burial does not appear to correlate with house size, nor do they exhibit any other clear patterns. It is clear, however, that only a minority of the deceased were buried under house floors, with the remainder of the population buried in an extramural cemetery (located to the west of the Titriş settlement and excavated by a German expedition; see Hauptmann 1993). The presence of burials under house floors may have increased the connection between house and "home," in other words, between the physical structure and family ownership and memories of the house. This may have had implications for the permanency of neighborhood boundaries and/or it suggests that kinship ties were highly valued in establishing familial claims to land and structures.

Chipped stone debris and finished products vary considerably in their distribution across the site. Although work on this is ongoing, excavations in the "core" trenches revealed a clear area of lithic specialization (Hartenberger 2003). In contrast to the thousands of cores and Canaanean blades found in this workshop, only two cores were found in the Lower or Outer Towns (Hartenberger, Rosen, and Matney 2000: 53). Interestingly, other than the overwhelming presence of cores and blades, the workshop architecture is similar to domestic areas and contains a multitude of typically

Structure	*n*	Ceramics	Bones	Lithics
30s Neighborhood				
BU–5	16	0.45	1.73	2.31
BU–9	6	0.47	1.41	1.63
BU–12	8	0.38	1.12	1.45
BU–13	3	0.48	2.15	**2.79**
BU–14	6	**0.50**	**2.48**	2.30
80s Neighborhood				
BU–1	5	0.14	1.50	1.54
BU–2	9	0.53	**7.14**	1.91
BU–4	86	**1.22**	3.07	3.61
Wall	25	0.80	**3.92**	3.70
Terrace	45	**1.34**	3.34	**5.13**
Other Areas of the Site				
40-34	24	0.45	2.95	**5.07**
Lithic Core	18	0.63	**3.23**	**27.44**
Streets	20	**6.42**	3.16	**8.60**

Table 5.2. Mean densities of micro-debris among neighborhoods at Titriş. The highest micro-artifact densities per neighborhood are highlighted in bold.

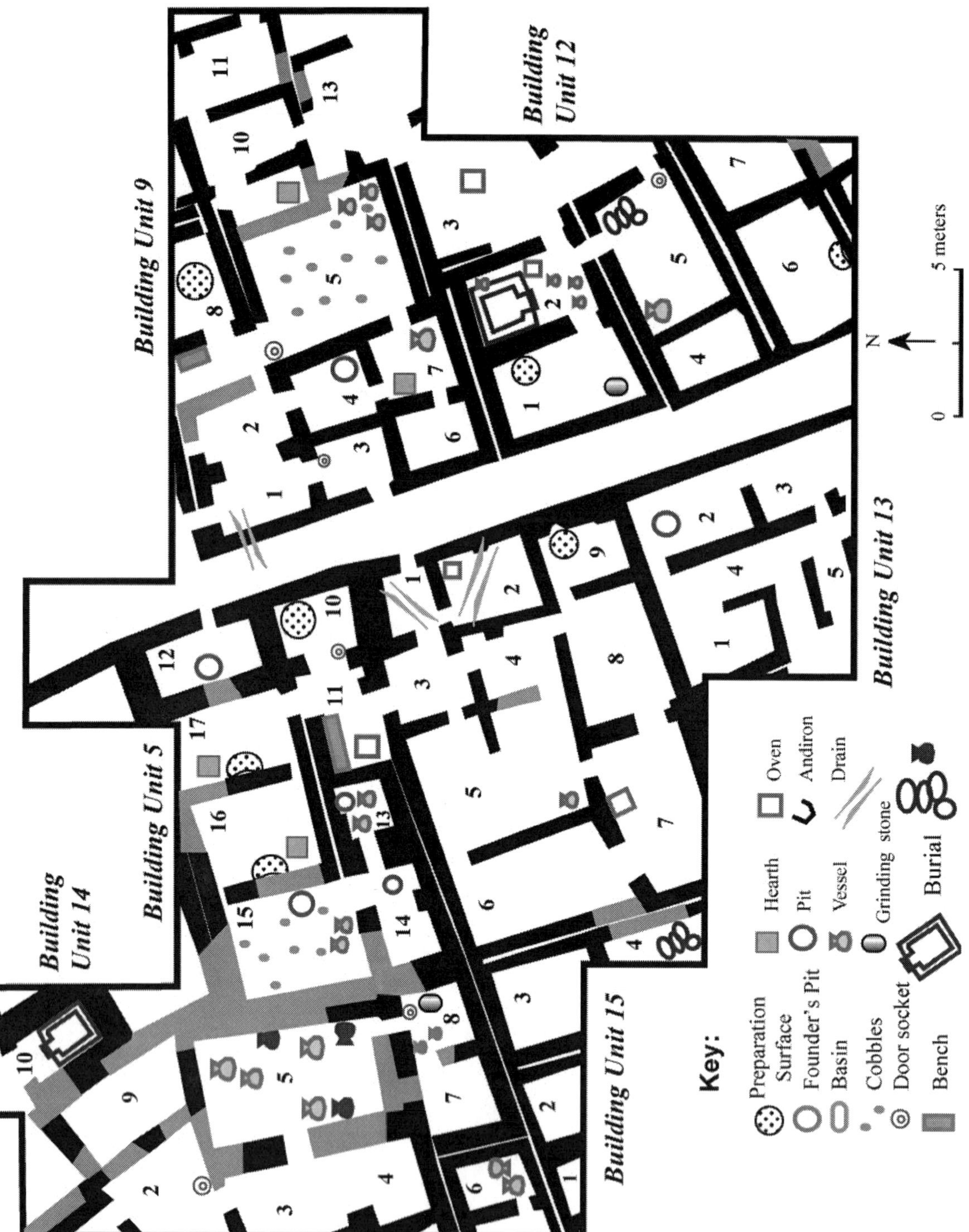

Figure 5.10. 30s Neighborhood at Titriş: distribution of features and architecture. The plan is modified from Matney et al. 1997: 74 (Figure 2). The light gray walls are reconstructed.

Figure 5.11. 80s Neighborhood at Titriş: distribution of features and architecture. The plan is modified from Algaze et al. 2001: 83 (Figure 2).

domestic artifacts (including three basalt grinding stones and a mortar and pestle). Although no hearth was excavated, it appears that this was not simply a workshop, but also a domestic area lived in by lithic specialists. Although lithic debitage is found in the residential neighborhoods (in the form of non-standardized flakes and simple blades), Canaanean blade production is restricted to the workshop (Hartenberger, Rosen, and Matney 2000: 55).

Once the lithic analysis is complete for both the workshop and domestic areas, we should be able to determine whether the knappers were attached to a palace or temple or if they worked independently. The presence of ceramic vessels and small rooms suggested to the excavators that the "workshop" was located within a domestic structure. The location of the workshop far from the central höyük (presumably where a palace and/or temple was located) and, moreover, beyond the city wall, suggests that the knappers were not under direct royal or religious control (Hartenberger, Rosen, and Matney 2000: 56). Moreover, the tools produced in the workshop were not high-quality pieces, but rather blades used by farmers for harvesting grain or as blades for threshing sledges. In other words, lithic production at Titriş was specialized, but not managed by elites. From the perspective of neighborhood organization, it is interesting that these specialists lived in the "suburbs" outside the main city wall. It would be interesting to examine the macro-ceramics and paleobotanical remains in order to investigate whether these individuals were of a different background than the residents within the city wall.

Other types of artifacts are only occasionally preserved. For example, very few spindle whorls or loom weights were excavated. It is impossible to determine who did the weaving and whether surplus textiles were produced for barter or private consumption. Although several pieces of lead, silver, and bronze were excavated in the 30s neighborhood, we lack both textile and wooden remains because of acidic soil and a rainy climate. Rooms probably contained rugs, cloth bags, wooden chairs or stools, and/or beds or cushions (as one might expect, based on the furnishings within Islamic houses; e.g., Küçükerman 1992).

Micro-Debris Medians

Mean count densities of micro-ceramics, fauna, and chipped stone were calculated from five roughly contemporaneous structures in each neighborhood at Titriş (Figure 5.12). This only provides a rough guide to the activities that occurred in each structure because it conflates a variety of loci and activity areas. Nevertheless, certain patterns emerged that correspond to other lines of evidence. For example, the lithic workshop, compared to any other structure at the site, contained the highest density of micro-lithics.

In the 80s neighborhood, Units 8 and 2 contained similar micro-profiles. The sediments taken from these structures contained a very large amount of bones, but relatively few ceramics and lithics. One explanation is that larger numbers of animals (eventually butchered for cuts of meat) were kept in these structures. In the case of the city wall, these animals may have been held communally, reserved for severe food shortages and, in the meantime kept under "lock and key" to protect them from raids by other communities. Or the bones may represent meals consumed by individuals (such as soldiers) with less-than-desirable housekeeping habits. The profiles of Unit 4 and the Terrace point to a more balanced distribution of activities. The different amounts of faunal remains suggest that some families may not have been able to afford animals, either for consumption or as draft animals. A more detailed study of the type of faunal remains per household may reveal differences in the quantity, cut, or quality of meat.

In the 30s neighborhood, all the structures contained a skewed profile, with micro-bones dominating each of the assemblages. Among these houses the interesting distinction is the distribution of micro-lithics: highest in Units 5, 13, and the street samples. Unit 5, the largest house in the neighborhood, may have paralleled Unit 4 (in the 80s neighborhood) as a household engaged in particularly prolific chipped-stone tool production and/or retouching. The Terrace samples also contained a large amount of micro-lithics.

The distribution of ceramic wares per structure provides a second line of micro-evidence to support the above conclusions (Figure 5.13). Structures 4 and 5 (in the 80s and 30s neighborhood, respectively) each contained the highest amount of fine ceramic wares in their areas, suggesting a higher social status or more feasting. This corresponds to the architectural evidence that suggests that each of these houses was the largest within its neighborhood. This will be discussed further below in the "dominant household model."

The two neighborhoods contained very different ceramic ware profiles among the houses. Each of the structures in the 80s neighborhood contained a profile dominated by sandy wares (i.e., the debris from everyday serving bowls and cups), followed by fine wares (although Building Unit 4 and the Terrace contained the highest ratio), and trailed by cooking wares quantities (to be expected because serving vessels most likely outnumbered cooking pots). In contrast, the samples from the 30s neighborhood contained a very large amount of sandy wares and significantly fewer fine and cooking wares. An interesting exception is Building Unit 14, which contained slightly more cooking ware than fine ware fragments. One explanation is that the cook who prepared meals for individuals then consumed the food elsewhere.

The count density of micro-debris per room can also be analyzed by cluster analysis. Repeated, distinct clusters within certain structures provides an additional window into household activities and, in the end, neighborhood variability. I conducted the cluster analysis using the

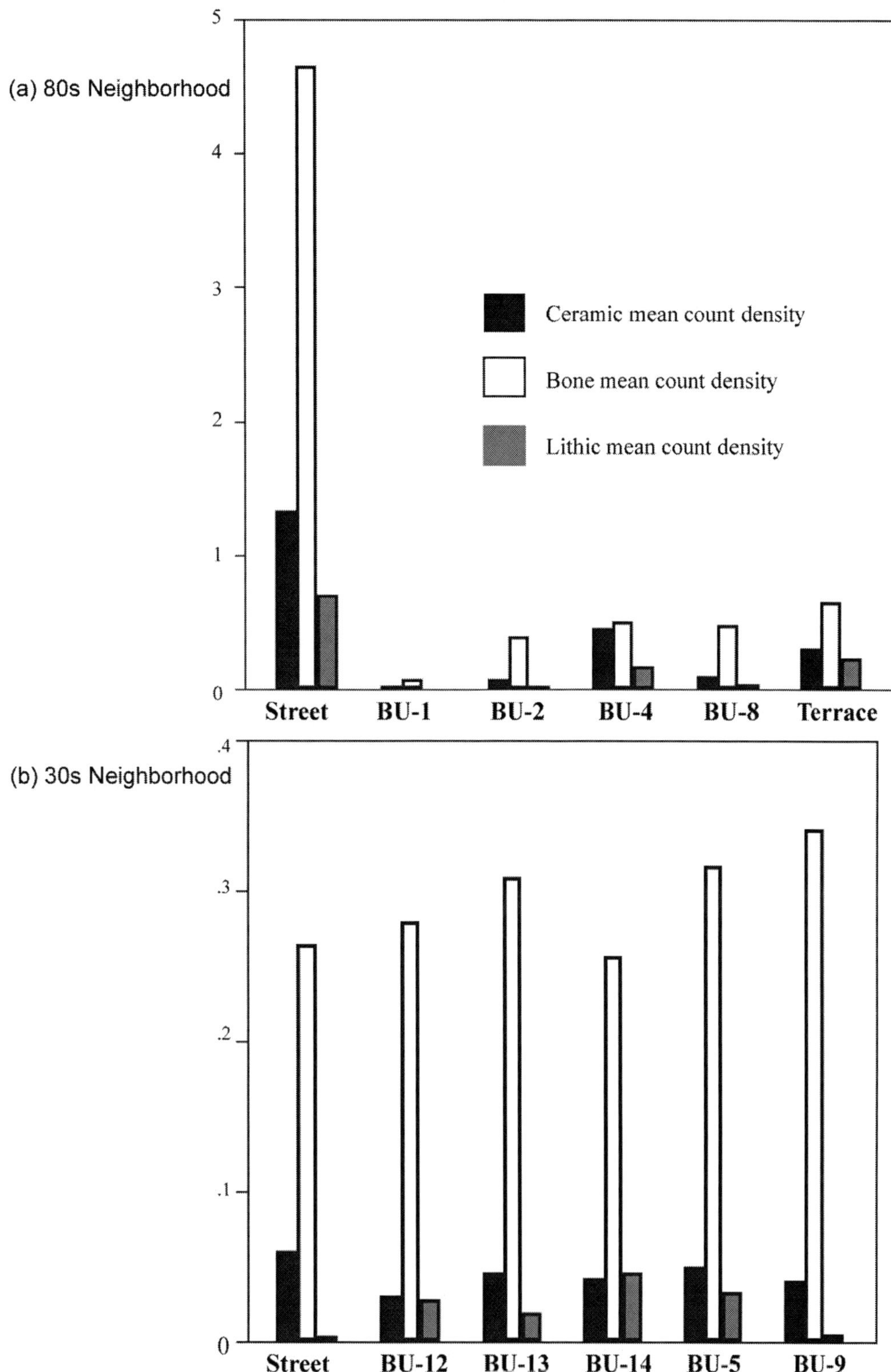

Figure 5.12. Distribution of micro-debris among houses in two neighborhoods at Titriş (a) and (b) have two very different scales because of different sampling strategies (described in Chapter 2 and labeled HF / LHF). The abbreviation "BU" stands for "Building Unit."

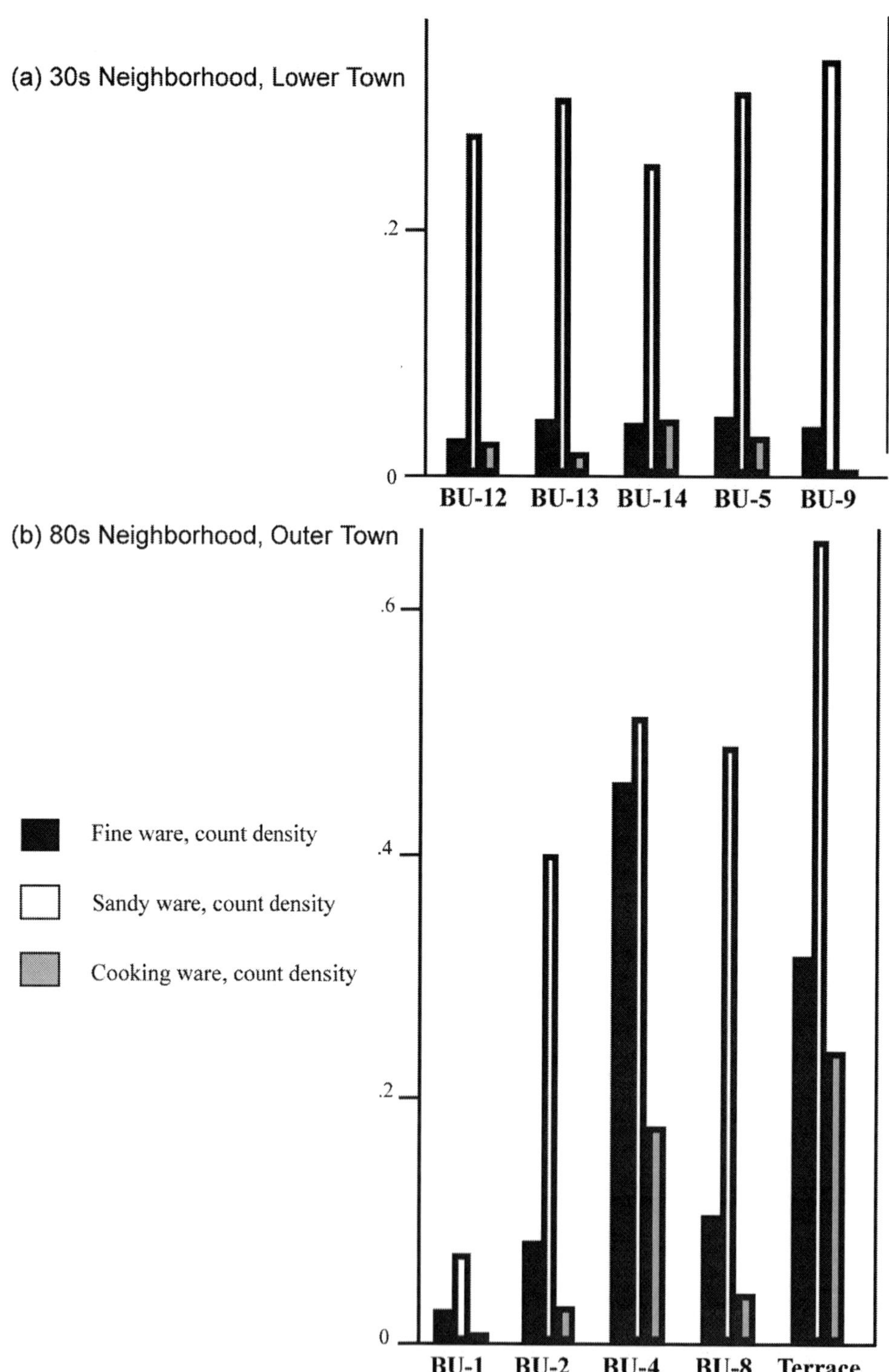

Figure 5.13. Distribution of ceramic wares among Building Units in two neighborhoods at Titriş. The abbreviation "BU" stands for "Building Unit."

SPSS statistical database program. Micro-densities of ceramics, bones, and lithics were calculated per room. These count densities were transformed to quartile ranks in order to reduce the bias from outliers. The resulting profile per sample was slightly "jittered" (a statistical transformation whereby I added a small amount, .01, to one column of variables). This calculation avoided the problem of equivalent profiles (that would have had repercussions for the subsequent application of correlation analysis). Hierarchical Cluster Analysis was applied using between-group-linkages and Spearman's correlation. I determined four clusters and mapped the clusters per room (Figure 5.14).

A majority of the rooms fell into Cluster 1 or 3. Both clusters contained moderate amounts, on average, of lithics, but Cluster 1 contained more bone and less ceramics, while Cluster 3 included the opposite quantity of micro-remains: high ceramics, low bones. The "ceramic cluster" was often found in kitchens (e.g., Rooms 23 and 11 in Building Unit 4). Courtyards in both neighborhoods were represented by Cluster 1 or 3, never Clusters 2 or 4. Cluster 2 is dominated by lithics and characterized by smaller rooms, possibly used for storage. The exception was Room A in the Terrace, a possible courtyard which, as discussed above, supports the conclusion that the knappers produced a larger-than-normal amount of tools in this structure. Cluster 4 contained high amounts of ceramics and bones and was found in a room associated with a kitchen (Room 24, BU-4), a room containing a tomb (Room 10, BU-4), two rooms associated with animals (Room 16 and 18, BU-4), and a large room with (during one phase) direct access to the street (Room 13, BU-2). In each of these, except the last example, a correspondence between ceramics and bones (be it human or animal) fits the profile of the room as determined by macro-artifacts, features, and architecture.

The clusters and micro-debris medians provide only very preliminary inferences. Tentatively, I suggest that the residents in Building Units 4 and 5 served people more frequently on fine ware dishes, knapped more tools, and, in the case of Building Unit 4, owned animals. Residents in many of the other houses ate off sandy ware vessels more frequently, possibly cooked for larger numbers of people, and knapped less frequently. In the future, a wider variety of samples should be taken from each structure to better explain the differences in densities. In the meantime, this section points to the potential of micro-signatures, taken with other lines of evidence, for distinguishing the quality and quantity of craft and social activities among houses.

Neighborhood Models: Who lived where?

Now that we have some understanding of what activities were conducted in the various households and neighborhood, we can ask the questions: Who did the acting? Did neighborhoods contain homogeneous households, all belonging the same social, economic, and religious group? I present five distinct models below, and synthesize my results in a sixth one. Most of the attributes discussed below are inseparable, such as kinship and social status. But I present each model separately to try to tease out the complexities behind social categories such as "kin" and "status."

Kinship and Ethnicity

Urban planners and anthropologists often identify kinship ties as a significant impetus in house choice and, subsequently, the composition of neighborhoods. "Ethnic groups" are often difficult to define within living communities and even harder to identify in the archaeological record. Broadly, they can be defined as groups which maintain a certain identity based on a shared religious, linguistic, cultural, or ancestral heritage (both familial and regional). A group's ethnic similarity may or may not be correlated with occupational, religious, or economic/social status. For example, Coptic populations in late 18th Century C.E. Cairo clustered in port and former port areas due to their preference for occupations as scribes, account-keepers, and customs officials (Abu-Lughod 1971: 59). And in 11th Century C.E. Jerusalem, the Christian groups were able to claim the wealthier western ridge of the town due to their comparative wealth, leaving the Jewish inhabitants with less desirable low-lying land inside the Dung Gate, albeit this was relatively close to the Wailing Wall (Greenshields 1980: 126). Ethnic quarters can be voluntary associations among groups of people who share something in common, or involuntary segregation—e.g., the formation of Jewish quarters in North Africa (*mellah* in Morocco, *hara* in Tunisia) by the Muslim authorities (Greenshields 1980: 123). Even though kinship ties may be an important factor in choosing a place to live, practicalities may make this goal difficult. For example, in tightly packed cities the third and fourth generations may not have had the space to live in close proximity (even factoring in the eventual death of the initial generation) to their parents or children. And, of course, upon marriage, daughters probably accompanied their husbands to different neighborhoods.

In the archaeological record, ethnic quarters or neighborhoods have been only rarely identified. But in one particularly rich example, Stein (1999: 93) identified typically Uruk assemblages (associated with a southern Mesopotamian cultural phenomenon) in an Upper Mesopotamian "enclave" or "trading colony": the site of Hacinebi. Stein identified the Uruk quarter at the site based on several types of material culture characteristic of southern Mesopotamian sites: ceramic wall cones, administrative technology (including cylinder seals, bullae, and jar sealings), and ceramics (especially the ubiquitous beveled-rim bowl; Stein 1999: 139-45). Physically, this material was concentrated in the northeast corner of the site, suggesting a separate ethnic

	ceramic rank mean	bone rank mean	lithic rank mean
Cluster 1	1.97	2.97	2.72
Cluster 2	1.80	1.60	3.20
Cluster 3	3.00	1.91	2.37
Cluster 4	2.99	3.22	1.78

Figure 5.14. Room level cluster analysis: micro-ceramics, bones, and lithics at Titriş. The plans are modified from (a) Algaze et al. 2001: 83 and (b) Matney et al. 1997: 74. The gray walls indicate areas that were reconstructed and dashed lines indicate unexcavated areas.

enclave. At Titriş we have no direct evidence for ethnic quarters, but the lithic workshop did contain distinct architectural forms. In the lithic workshop trenches, there appear to be more exterior courtyards, no central courtyard plan, and possibly a different burial tradition (which included the burial of an equid). In addition, these individuals were physically segregated beyond the confines and protection of the city wall. Each of these factors may correlate with either ethnic affiliations and/or occupational specialities.

Even if family ties are considered important in choosing where to live, family lands may be dispersed throughout urban and rural settlements (Keith 1999: 300, Antoun 1972, Horne 1994). This creates a difficult pattern for archaeologists to recognize: the distribution of one family's property, including land, rooms, or structures, throughout both city and countryside. As archaeologists, the lesson to take from this is that if we identify a one-room structure, such as a shop, it is possible that the shopkeeper lived in a non-contiguous structure. This, in turn, has important ramifications for the homogeneity or diversity of social and economic classes within various neighborhoods. The combination of small and large structures may indicate differences in family size, wealth, or simply non-contiguous land. Realizing that the owner or tenant may have lived elsewhere, one-room structures (such as the ones found at Ur and Titriş) may be animal stables, additional storage rooms, or shops. This same pattern was found in a modern Kurdish village where separate houses were used for stabling animals, storing items, and selling merchandise (Çevik 1995: 41). In contemporary villages, the walls of storage rooms and stables were usually built of unworked stone and not plastered. If a similar lack of attention were paid to ancient storerooms, we might be able to identify them in the archaeological record based on their inferior construction materials and decoration.

Status

An individual's or family's status is probably one of the most difficult attributes to identify, even in ethnographic contexts. Although this is not the place for a full discussion of the complexities of defining class or status distinctions, I review several models for the creation and display of social status. Stirling (1953) suggested that social rank is the combined outcome of "aspects of prestige and power, mediated through attributes such as age, wealth, piety, etc." As a result, no one type of material culture can accurately indicate the social or economic rank of an individual. Moreover, as amply discussed in historic archaeology, many individuals consciously manipulate material culture to mask or, conversely, accentuate status difference (McGuire 1991, Leone 1984). Matney (1995:49) suggested socio-economic status determined the placement of different neighborhoods within Upper Mesopotamian sites. Other archaeologists concur that the locations nearest to the central tell should be the most socially desirable due to their proximity to the (archaeologically predicted) palace and temple. For example, at Eshnunna the Early Dynastic layers contained clusters of poorer residences in large residential districts, while wealthier ones were located near the palaces and temples (Henrickson 1981: 54-6). In this model, the houses in the 30s neighborhood at Titriş and the structures in trench 40-34 should contain the wealthiest and/or socially important residences. More excavations would be necessary in 40-34 before we could conclusively prove or disprove this, but the residences in the 30s neighborhood do not appear to be more or less grandiose than those in the 80s.

Another strategy for correlating social status and residence is locating the presence of drains. In excavations at Ur, Khafaje, and Eshnunna, Frankfort (1950: 111) discovered that a wealthy individual might pave the street in front of his house or provide it with a drain. Schmidt (1964: 144) concurred that the owner of property directly in front of a stretch of road could maintain it as he wished. This often took the form of stretches paved with potsherds, others with stones, and others may not be paved at all (Keith 2003). If this were the case at Titriş, a close analysis of the quality of the streets may indicate which houses were owned by wealthier residents. To date, only a handful of drains have been found (see Figure 5.10 and Figure 5.11). If these drains correlate with wealthier residences, it would support the following argument that wealthy and poor individuals lived side by side.

In sum, I would suggest that archaeologists have not investigated the full extent of the diversity *within* urban neighborhoods and that if the variability were investigated, it would become clear that very often wealthy and poor residences occur within the same neighborhood. For example, Elizabeth Stone's work at Nippur (located in Iraq) and Mashkan-shapir (modern Tell Abu Duwari, located approximately 40 kilometers due north of Nippur) revealed that, at these sites, residential neighborhoods were not divided on the basis of class. Instead, texts and archaeological data demonstrate that "an important official could live beside a humble fisherman, and that large, well-appointed houses were nestled among small, poor structures" (Stone 1995: 241). In addition, artifacts that are usually associated with elite ownership, such as cylinder seals, stone bowls, and high densities of copper, were distributed throughout the site (Stone and Zimansky 1994: 442, 444, 454). And my interpretation of the plans from Eshnunna, based on an architectural search for urban forms, suggests that larger and smaller residences emerged side by side (Figure 5.15). Note that these findings contradict a popular model that suggests the wealthy lived closer to the center, while the poor lived further away. Larger horizontal exposures at Upper Mesopotamian sites may resolve this issue.

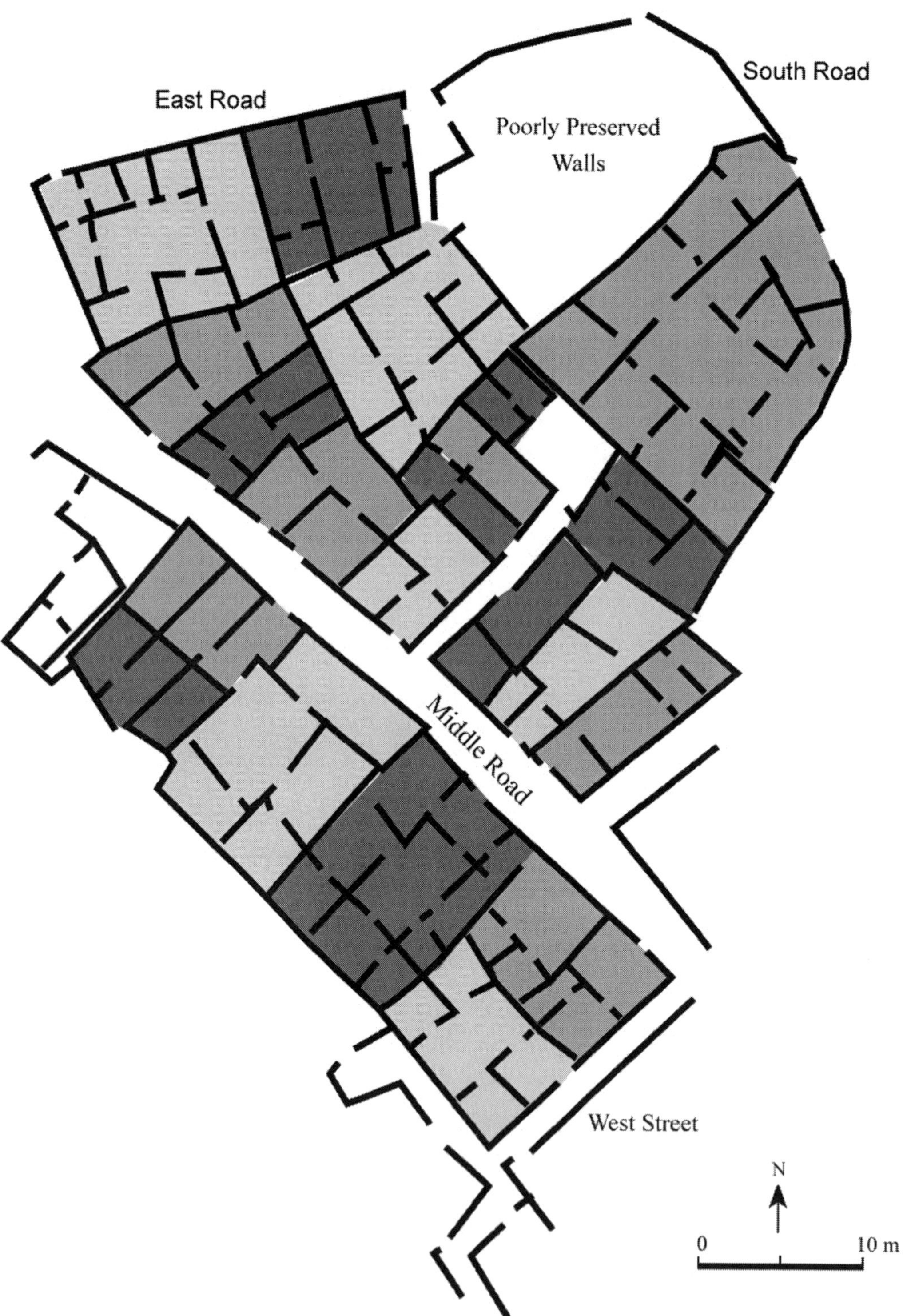

Figure 5.15. Small and large residences within neighborhoods, Eshnunna. Variable shading represents possible structure boundaries as determined by the author using the reasoning outlined in this chapter. The plan illustrates the Early Dynastic II and III layers. Modified from Matney 1993: 279.

Occupations / Craft Specializations

Akkadian and Sumerian texts record the existence of various specialized craftsmen (Table 5.3). Many archaeologists have presumed that these artisans were physically segregated within ancient cities, as has been observed in some modern Middle Eastern cities, where residential quarters are often characterized by craft specialization (one of the original proponents of this model was Georges Marçais (1945) who, in turn borrowed from W. Marçais (1928)). Superficially, this arrangement resembles the "concentric model" proposed by European urban planners (Burgess 1926, Hoyt 1933). In this model, specific intellectual, religious, and craft areas are segregated in various sectors or "rings" with the mosque at the intellectual center, surrounded by a market or a bazaar (which, in turn places the most offensive crafts—e.g., blacksmiths— at a further distance from the center). The city gates enclose these areas and residential quarters. Beyond the city walls live and work craftspeople with the most offensive odors, sounds, or connotations, including dyers, tanners, and potters (Abu-Lughod 1987: 157). Although originally formulated to describe North African cities, this model has been uncritically applied to describe all "Middle Eastern Cities."

The model also suggests that the religion of Islam required practitioners to live in cities. These cities must include a bazaar, mosque, and a bath. Although not uniquely a Middle Eastern phenomenon (if you substitute market for bazaar, church for mosque, and bar for bath), this model has been used extensively to explain the architectural and social composition of Middle Eastern neighborhoods. One of the many drawbacks to this model is that it implies and, in fact, is limited to, a degree of residential uniformity and homogeneity, where all neighbors share occupations, kinship, or class ties. Although archaeological evidence does exist for a certain degree of craft segregation, this model should not be uniformly applied to all areas of every city.

Leonard Woolley discovered archaeological evidence that is consistent with this model in the southern part of Paternoster Row at Ur (in Area AH), where many of the residents shared both occupations and kinship. Similarly, the first millennium city of Nineveh contained distinct neighborhoods of goldsmiths, leather workers, bleachers, and potters. And in Babylon, a street was named after a specialized ceramic form: *huburu* or "beer jar" (Van De Mieroop 1997: 183). Tracing these wards back in time is based on occupational specialities is difficult. Van De Mieroop (1997: 183) only traced craft quarters back to 13th-Century B.C.E. Assur, where a gate was named the "gate of the metalworkers."

Segregated craft neighborhoods may be created by institutions to provide a dependable supply of labor. This commonly occurred around temples in southern Mesopotamia, where residences in close proximity to the temple contained priests or temple dependents. Texts found in houses at Ur (from the Isin-Larsa Period) showed that the residents who lived to the south of the Nannar Temple complex (areas EH and EM) were associated with the cults in the temple and their entourage. Specifically, these residents were priests and prebendaries, people who held a share in a priestly office and engaged in other activities the rest of the time (Van De Mieroop 1992: 123). In Nippur, area TB was perhaps the residential quarter for landless employees of the state (Stone 1987: 76), while occupants of TA seem to have been small property owners (Stone 1987: 71).

It is important to remember that these patterns of segregated crafts are biased toward large institutions and their workshops. Thus the pattern may not hold within neighborhoods not connected to palaces or temples. In short, some residential areas probably had stronger institutional affiliations than others, but it is difficult to test without texts.

In contrast to the above model of craft segregation, Mari included neighborhoods that contained a *diversity* of craft specialities. According to Van De Mieroop (1997: 183):

> It may thus be best to conclude that all residential quarters had the facilities to generate craft products for the basic needs of the inhabitants, although certain crafts were primarily performed in a particular neighborhood. ...Perhaps only in the first millennium did all the craftsmen limit their activities to certain areas of the town.

Support for this view comes from Mashkan-shapir. Mashkan-shapir was the second capital of the kingdom of Larsa in the 19th and 18th Centuries B.C.E., located in modern-day Iraq. It was excavated by Elizabeth Stone and Paul Zimansky prior to the 1991 Gulf War. Residential areas in this Old Babylonian city contained a mixture of craft debris, suggesting that various small-scale craft producers lived within each neighborhood (Stone and Zimansky 1992: 217). Similarly, early Isin texts documented that carpenters, leatherworkers, reedworkers, and felters shared quarters because many of their products were later combined to produce finished products, such as felt-lined leather boots (Van De Mieroop 1986: 89-90). This analogy may not be entirely appropriate to the third millennium because the Isin texts follow after the highly bureaucratic Third Dynasty of Ur and thus the dynasty may have controlled and organized (possible) private enterprise and crafts to a greater extent than earlier periods.

In order to test the degree of segregation of craft specialists at Titriş we would have to correlate occupational specializations with domestic residences. Without the benefit of texts and due to the perishable nature of many products of craft specialization (such as textiles, reeds, and pieces of wood), we may never locate the full range of remains representing ancient craft specializations. There were, however, several tantalizing

Craft specialist	Sumerian term
potter	*báhar*
stone worker	*zadim*
goldsmith	*kug-dím*
leather worker	*asgab*
reed worker	*ad-KID*
felter	*túg-du$_8$*
carpenter	*nagar*
metal worker	*simug, tibira*
A selection of professions found in Akkadian documents	
builder	wood worker
copper worker	shoe maker
oil presser	boatman
scribe	priest
butcher	farmer
shepherd	dream interpreter
brewer	innkeeper

Table 5.3. A selection of common occupational terms found in cuneiform texts. See also Van De Mieroop 1987: chapter III. The "Sumerian" column is modified from the Larsa Texts (cited in Van De Mieroop 1987: 26-37). The "Akkadian" column is modified from Keith 1999: 282-4.

suggestions of shops. In the 30s neighborhood, there were several clusters of small rooms with entrances that opened directly onto the street. In Ur, isolated rooms were identified as shops by Woolley. Without the final analysis of macro-artifact distributions, we cannot test this hypothesis at Titriş beyond compiling the architectural evidence of small, isolated rooms that always opened onto a street. If these rooms were indeed shops, it would suggest a more commercial nature for the Lower Town (the Outer Town did not contain these isolated rooms).

Although the Outer Town lacked isolated rooms, it did contain a curious feature: two mudbrick walls placed in front of the east part of Building Unit 2 (Figure 5.16b). While this wall may simply have served as a retaining wall, there is at least one other explanation. Shops within later Islamic cities occasionally contained benches. Several 19th- and 20th-Century explorers and anthropologists observed these features (e.g., Roger Le Tourneau 1949, 1961, who studied early 20th-Century Fez, and Edward Lane 1836, who toured 19th-Century Cairo). As shown in Figure 5.16a, these benches, in Arabic *mastaba*s, allowed the shopkeeper to actively cajole passerbys into stopping and provided the customer with a place to sit and possibly take tea with the owner. If Unit 2 were indeed a shop, the Outer Town included both commercial and residential structures.

Rural/Urban Migrations

Each of the models discussed above presumes that the residents had a choice in where they lived—e.g., related individuals who owned adjacent property or wealthy individuals who purchased contiguous plots. This simplified model does not take into account subsequent residential exigencies. Survey evidence suggests that many rural residents moved into cities during the EBA. This presents an important question: As these rural families migrated into the cities, did they form homogeneous neighborhoods? Today this process occurs frequently, as many rural farmers lose their jobs to mechanized industry and falling crop prices (Karpat 1975: 16-23). For example, in contemporary Urfa, immigrants from the surrounding countryside have migrated to the city and occupied centuries' old houses in the "traditional" neighborhoods. Meanwhile, urban dwellers move into new high-rises equipped with technological conveniences and located closer to the modern supermarkets and a new shopping mall. Although the rural newcomers probably preferred to live near any extant relatives (Horne 1994: 105-7), this may not always be feasible in a crowded city. In ancient cities, Early Dynastic III texts excavated at Fara prove that at least some ancient neighborhoods contained related kin. In other words, some early cities contained kin-based residential groupings (Postgate 1992: 91). This scenario should be considered in interpreting the different building phases at Titriş. In the later phase of a house, immigrants might have moved in and made structural and other adjustments, such as the addition of animals to otherwise "urban" structures. This occurs occasionally in Urfa, when recent rural immigrants bring chickens and, in one instance, a cow, into their urban houses (much to the distress of their neighbors).

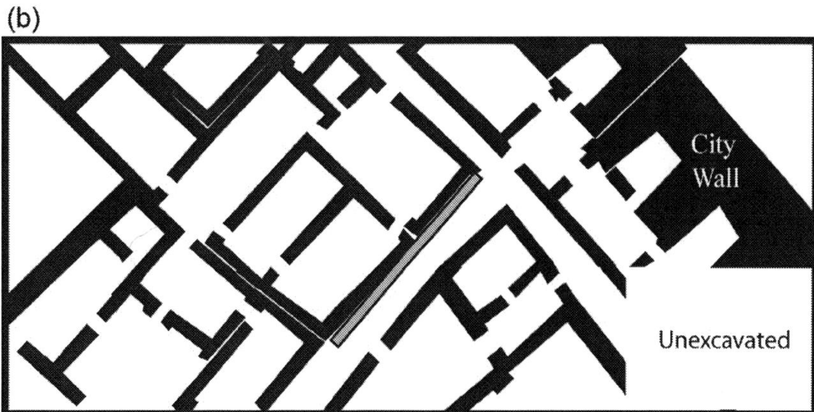

Figure 5.16. Shops within neighborhoods. (a) Shop with a mudbrick store front in a 19th Century C.E. Cairo neighborhood. Modified from Lane 1836: 8. (b) A similar feature excavated at Titriş Höyük. The mudbrick "bench," or, possibly, wall support is outlined in light gray. The plan is modified from Algaze et al. 2001: 83.

Synthesis: Dominant Household

Clearly the models presented above are not mutually exclusive. Related kin may share occupational specializations and try to live in close proximity to each other. Or a mixture of social classes may, due to the exigencies of migrations or other reasons, live side by side. From a different perspective, individual households may have served as a uniting force within neighborhoods. For example, Medieval Islamic cities contained neighborhoods based on other occupations or kinship ties (including family inheritance generation after generation), or, occasionally, religion (including Islam, Christian, Jewish, and Zoroastrian faiths).

Despite some researchers' expectations, neighborhoods were rarely segregated by economic class. Instead, a wealthy household often dominated neighborhoods that included both wealthy and commoners' houses. This model suggests one explanation for the role of the two largest houses found to date in each of the neighborhoods at Titriş: Building Units 4 (Figure 5.17) and 5 (Figure 5.18). These two structures were much larger than their neighbors. This pattern of increasing discrepancy in house size is found at other third-millennium sites — e.g., the Early Dynastic III level at Eshnunna that contained houses ranging from 44 to 268 square meters (Crawford 1991: 97). The wide range of house sizes suggests an increasingly stratified society, supported by the distribution of grave goods and a lack of manufacturing debris within individual houses. In the 80s neighborhood, Building Unit 3 most likely housed a smaller family unit than its neighbors', and possibly a less wealthy family.

Conclusion

This chapter demonstrated that wealthier houses were constructed adjacent to smaller ones within residential neighborhoods at Titriş. In other words, neighborhoods at Titriş most likely contained a combination of wealthy and poor families. This variability may indicate different family structures, classes, or levels of domestic production. This result cautions archaeologists and anthropologists about modeling ancient neighborhoods as socially homogenous. Instead, we need to design research projects that test for variability in form and function within and between households.

Figure 5.17. Possible house boundaries in the 80s neighborhood, Titriş. The house boundaries are suggested by the author based on published plans of the excavation (Algaze et al. 2001: 83).

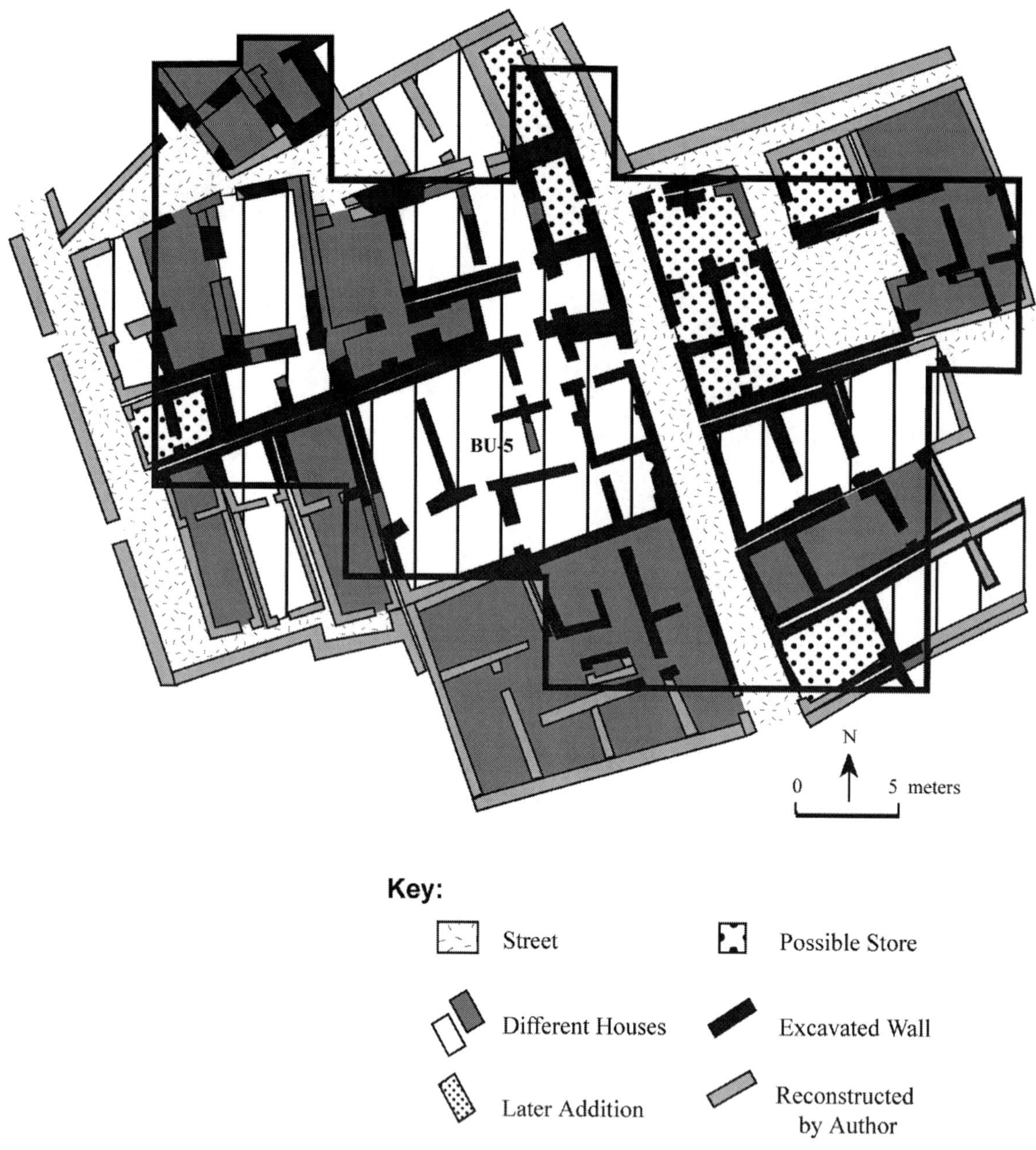

Figure 5.18. Possible house boundaries in the 30s neighborhood, Titriş. The house boundaries are suggested by the author based on published plans of the excavation (Matney et al. 1997: 74).

Chapter 6: Examining Upper Mesopotamian Urbanism

After analyzing activity areas within rooms and houses within neighborhoods, these domestic units should be contextualized within ancient cities. Just as households do not exist in isolation, neighborhoods must be understood within their cultural context: ancient cities. Accordingly, in this chapter I discuss forms of modern and ancient Middle Eastern cities. I include the modern examples because, very often they serve, explicitly or not, as the basis for models of ancient Near Eastern cities (e.g., Stone 1987, 1996). Both modern and ancient models will be reviewed in order to understand ancient Upper Mesopotamian city planning and organization.

The term "city" has been the subject of much discussion in anthropology, geography, sociology, and other fields. In his recent survey, Southall (1998:4) gave the following description of the city in history:

> [cities] ... have been the greatest point of concentration and of increasing density in their time and space: a concentration of women and men and their social relationships; of shelter, buildings and physical plant; of productive resources, goods and services, consumption and exchange activities; of wealth, power and energy; of information, communication and knowledge, intellectual training ...; of religion, ritual and ceremonial, of creative, aesthetic sensibility and innovative stimuli.

Such a description, however, may apply to villages as well. A fundamental difficulty in defining the city stems from conflicting views on which attribute(s) to prioritize: architectural, social, economic, political, technological, or structural features. Lapidus (1986: 258-9) highlighted various definitions for the concept of the city:

> Some writers attend to the physical fact of the city—its facilities and concentration of population—the commanding presence of a dense settlement standing like a monument in a landscape of animals, trees, and grain. Others attend to the economic or technological activities, the cultural qualities, or the political history of cities. Other writers use the word 'city' as a shorthand way of referring to the defensive functions, economic exchanges, patterns of specialization and differentiation of labor, forms of social stratification, organized politics, and sophistication of culture.

One of the more famous formulations, based on European cities, comes from Weber (1958: 88), who identified five distinguishing characteristics of cities: "fortifications, markets, a court, ... distinctively urban forms of association, and at least partially autonomous law." Unfortunately, many of these features are difficult to observe in the archaeological record. Instead, archaeologists recognize cities based on a large occupied area (especially when a dramatic increase from earlier periods occurs), monumental architecture, economic specialization among the residents, fortifications, heterogeneity in structures (including public, religious, and residential ones), or the top level of a three-level hierarchy of settlements. An agricultural surplus and concomitant specialists enable many of these features. In my view, villages may contain many, if not all, of these features, but on a smaller and/or limited scale.

Modern Middle Eastern Cities

Historians, geographers, and others have discussed whether unique features can be found in Islamic Cities and whether these cities were created by a unique set of environmental or political forces. Many historians have argued that Islamic law and religion have produced a distinctive set of urban features, including the mosque, citadel, and suq (Marçais 1945, LeTourneau 1949). These features are hardly unique. The corresponding "Christian" version of these features includes cathedrals, castles, and markets. Moreover, these features were found in most preindustrial cities (Sjoberg 1960). Abu-Lughod (1987: 161) concurred that the forces that created the traditional Islamic city—terrain/climate, technology of production, distribution and transportation, a system of social organization, and a legal/political system—were not unusual. Thus similar forces have created similar urban forms in both Islamic and non-Islamic cities. For example, the "harbor" found at many southern Mesopotamian sites is also found at Egyptian ones. In both cases, cities were located along waterways (due to ease of transport and communication), and areas were set aside for the docking and unloading of ships. In short, for each city we have to investigate historical circumstances and outside influences to evaluate the reasons for and nature of urban forms.

Although many of the features found in Islamic cities can be found in non-Islamic cities, the "Islamic neighborhood" may be one of the more consistent and somewhat unique attributes of Middle Eastern cities. Abu-Lughod (1987: 162) concurs that because the Islamic state took a laissez-faire attitude toward civil society, community-level organizations, such as groups of neighbors, filled a variety of functions, including social control and economic organization. Evidence for this statement comes from the existence of self-governed, individual districts within Middle Eastern cities, each with similar sets of institutions, shops, and religious structures. For example, 19th-Century Irbid, Jordan (population c. 1,000) was organized into nine neighborhoods, each relatively self-sufficient and organized by clan, country of origin, or the religion of the inhabitants (Shunnaq and Schwab 2000: 75). And 18th-Century Cairo had 53 quarters, each with an average population of about 4,500 people (Gulick 1967: 153). Ethnographic research suggests that these quarters were held together informally by religious or tribal leaders. For example, in Damascus, the enduring "institutional feature" of society was "men of learning" who acted as agents of authority within urban quarters (Lapidus 1973). Within these neighborhoods, gender segregation was prescribed by Islamic morals. These two features—residential quarters and gender segregation within domestic units—form the basis for traditional Islamic urban plans. The next step is to test whether these features existed in ancient Mesopotamian cities, and, if so, whether similar forces created them.

Ancient Mesopotamian Urbanism

Scholars have distinguished northern and southern variants of Mesopotamian urbanism. In the south, cities grew in size during the Uruk period. By 2600 B.C.E. cities contained "full urban characteristics" (Milano 1995: 1220). These characteristics included city walls, palaces, temples, and a large population, and texts. In the north, outside of the dry farming zone, cities developed around 3000 B.C.E. at Habuba Kabira North and Tell Qannes and possibly earlier at Tell Brak. Around 2500 B.C.E., the large city-sites of Mari and Ebla were founded. Palaces were excavated at both sites (Margueron 1977, Matthiae 1980). The excavations at both sites also uncovered temples, city ramparts and gates, and private homes. Adams (1966) suggested that the genesis (in the fourth millennium) for the southern urban centers occurred earlier than in the north, due to the effects resulting from cooperation among the different populations: farmers, herders, fishers. In this model, cities became centers of contact where these groups exchanged raw materials and finished products. Other scholars suggested that trade was the catalyst for the growth of cities because southern Mesopotamia lacked many important resources (Snell 1997: 24). And in a third model, the necessity of coordinated labor for irrigation systems is identified as a possible factor in southern urbanism (Nissen 1998: 60).

None of these models fit the circumstances of northern urbanism very well. First, the north controlled a more-than-adequate resource base that included, among other materials, wood, metal, and stone. Second, Upper Mesopotamian resources were not as centralized as in the south. Thus, the populations (and surrounding farmlands) were not restricted to irrigation canals or watercourses; instead, villages were scattered evenly over the arable land. For example, herding could take place in the relatively nearby anti-Taurus mountains, rather than, as in the south, the more distant Zagros Mountains (see Figure 1.2).

Another difference between Upper and Lower Mesopotamian urbanism is the size of the cities. In the former, urban settlements ranged from 15 to 100 hectares (Weiss 1983). In contrast, Lower Mesopotamian cities attained areas of 400 hectares or more during the third millennium (Wilkinson 1994: 483). In Upper Mesopotamia, settlements along the Euphrates can be sorted into a four-tier settlement hierarchy (Figure 6.1). The smallest were single tell sites, while the larger ones contained central tells, lower towns, and, in the case of Titriş and Sweyhat, extensive outer towns. Although we do not know the exact nature of economic or political relations among these settlements, Wilkinson's application of central-place theory to this region suggests that "feeder" dependent towns and villages supported the largest centers (Wilkinson 1994).

Unfortunately, it is difficult to estimate how many people lived in each of these cities. Despite efforts to create applicable cross-cultural models, estimates of ancient populations remains an inexact science. Archaeologists have utilized several models for estimating population (Kramer 1980: Table II, 35 persons per hectare; Wilkinson 1990: 97, 100 persons per hectare; Naroll 1962, 1 person per every 10 meters; Johnson 1973: 66, 1 person per every 9 to 10 meters). For a particularly sophisticated and detailed effort to estimate an urban population see Postgate 1994. Using a representative low and high estimate, Kazane (at around 100 hectares) might have had a population of approximately 3,500 to 10,000 people, and Titriş (at around 30 hectares) a population between 1,155 and 3,300. Based on agricultural productivity in rain-fed regions, Wilkinson (1994: 483) suggested that cities of 100 hectares and their surrounding farmland could support a maximum 20,000 people.

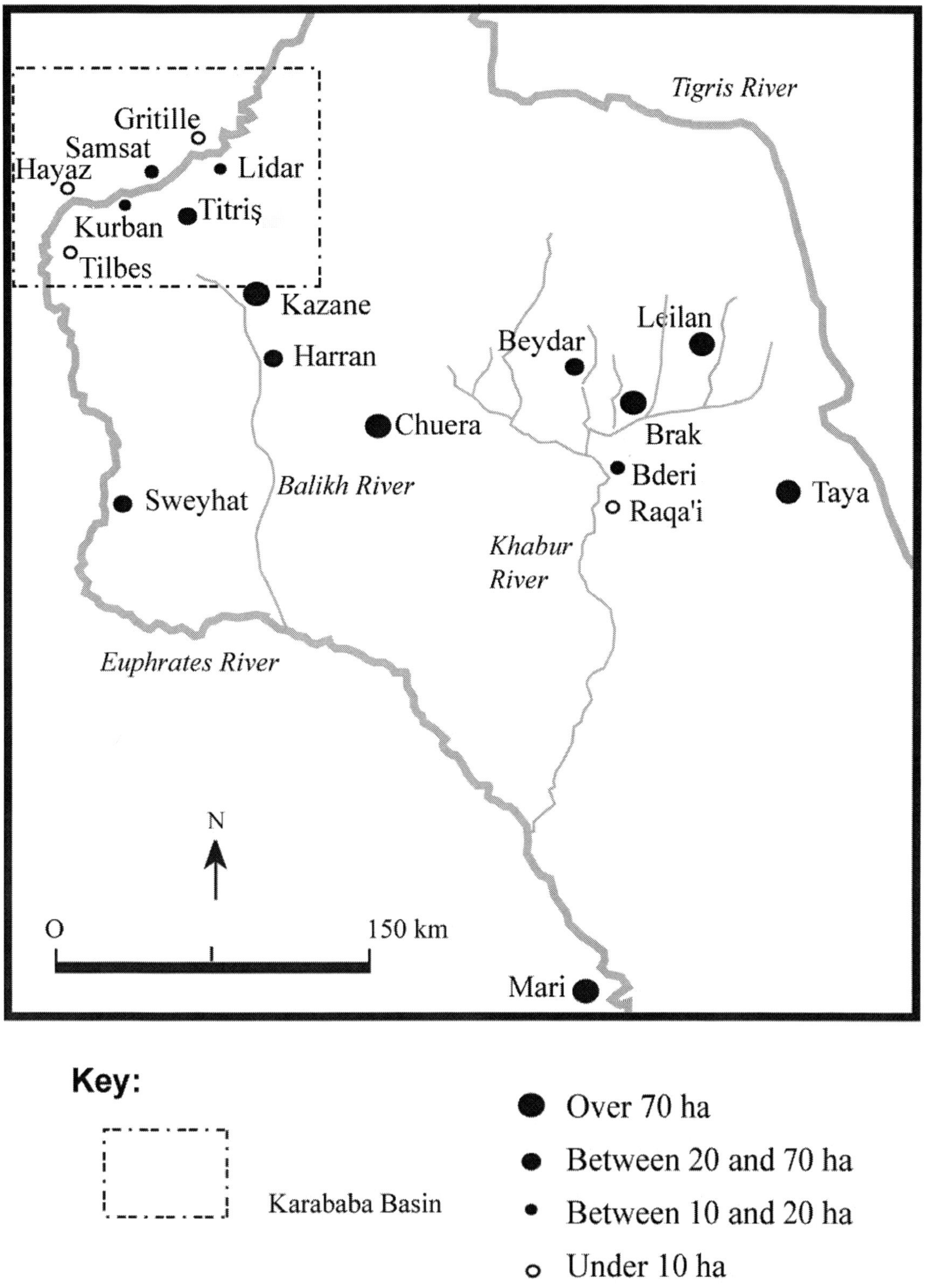

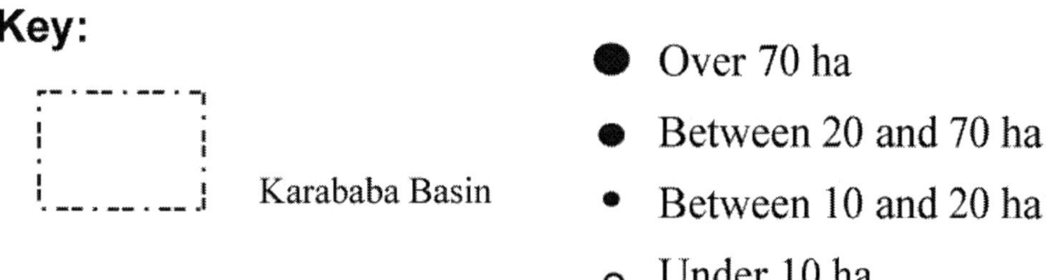

Figure 6.1. Third millennium Upper Mesopotamian settlement hierarchy. Compiled from information in Wilkinson 1994 and Wilkinson 1990: 98. The map only depicts excavated sites. The actual settlement hierarchy is much more complex.

Old Babylonian, Southern Mesopotamian Cities

Because cities are not static, I will limit my comments to southern Mesopotamian cities in the second millennium, a period with abundant evidence for urban design from sites such as Ur, Larsa, Eshnunna, Nippur, and Sippar (e.g., Stone 1987, Harris 1975, Keith 1999, Van De Mieroop 1999, Battini-Villard 1999). The prevailing interpretation is that southern Mesopotamian cities were highly segmented with distinct foci of administration, religion, manufacture, market, and residential districts (Stone 1997: 19).

Stone (1995: 235) argued that these cities served three functions: "They were political centers, sometimes only of their immediate hinterland, but occasionally capitals of great empires; they were centers of trade and commerce; and they were the seats of the gods of the Mesopotamian pantheon." Literary compositions from the Early Dynastic period support the view that to some observers the most important feature of the city was that it was a ceremonial center that housed the central shrine of the local deity (Postgate 1992: 73). In the south, walled cities contained temples, often located in a corner of the settlement near the wall (Stone 1995: 239). In other cases, the temple was located on the earlier "village" mound and the city wall incorporated the earlier mound in its circuit. Some of these settlements contained multi-leveled ziggurats. There are about 30 known ziggurats in Southern Mesopotamia; i.e., not all cities had one (Roaf 1990: 104-5).

Palaces were more difficult to locate. The palace occasionally contained small-scale workshops (Parrot 1958: 280-305). Other structures, with thick walls and a large, overall plan, may have been additional public structures. Southern cities also contained irrigation canals and waterways that fed into urban harbors. These canals divided the available building land into multiple mounds that became different urban sectors. Within these mounds Stone (1995: 240) identified several "quarters": religious, administrative, and craft (including separate sectors for ceramic and copper production and lapidary work). Scatters of manufacturing debris throughout the residential areas suggest that each district may have had its own potter, smith, and lapidary worker who supplied local needs (Stone 1997: 20). In sum, southern Mesopotamian cities "were physically divided into different sectors by these canals: religious, administrative (or religious-administrative in the case of Larsa), and residential-artisanal sections" (Stone 1995: 239). While there may have been a division between "people attached to large institutions and the more independent small landowners" (Stone 1997: 20), for the most part there was no spatial segregation based on class (Stone 1987: 125).

Third Millennium, Upper Mesopotamian Cities

With limited horizontal exposures at most EBA urban sites, the Southern Mesopotamian model is hard to test at Upper Mesopotamian cities. Based on site plans and the distribution of public and domestic structures, I suggest that Upper Mesopotamian cities contained economically and socially heterogeneous quarters. Akin to modern Middle Eastern neighbors, the residents of these residential quarters, or neighborhoods, may have participated in shared activities and beliefs (e.g., to instruct children in moral values, protest governmental policies, such as price increases, or enforce a group's social, religious, or ethnic identity).

There are four main urban patterns found at Upper Mesopotamian tell sites. The first type of settlement consisted of an upper area (situated on the tell) and a lower area (just above ground level) (Figure 6.2a). Although the physical segregation is clear, it is not clear whether this division was a conscious symbolic separation (such as the Greek model, see Nevett 1999), an unintended consequence of overcrowding on the tell, which, as the settlement grew, overflowed onto the lower plains, or a means of separating high- and low- status areas of the settlement. Stone (1995: 243) interpreted this pattern as symbolic, suggesting that "the old settlement mound took on the role served by the platforms and ziggurats found in the cities of the south."

Other Upper Mesopotamian cities were divided into lower and outer towns, surrounding a central tell (Figure 6.2b). For example, Tell Taya (in northern Iraq), inhabited ca. 2400-2100 B.C.E., contained a walled citadel and an unwalled outer town that covered over 155 hectares.

Ancient texts referred to the "heart of the city" by the Akkadian term *libbi āli* ("inner city") (CAD volume B: 11). This center included a palace, temple, and houses. In this urban plan, the structures and residences closest to the tell may have been owned by higher-status individuals or have served administrative functions. In Southern Mesopotamian settlements this inner, walled city was divided into several quarters, each associated with a gate in the city wall (Oppenheim 1969: 6). Gates were also found at some Upper Mesopotamian sites, such as Tell Taya and Bderi.

A third urban plan, found only in the largest of Upper Mesopotamian sites, was the presence of suburbs (Figure 6.2c). At Titriş, eight hectares of "suburbs" were located beyond the city wall. Akkadian texts refer to houses, fields, date groves, cattle folds, and fortified outposts beyond walled settlements (Van De Mieroop 1997, Potts 1997, Keith 1999). The Titriş settlement demonstrates this pattern with a central core protected by a wall and bounded by two streams and a non-fortified suburb located further out on the plain (Figure 6.3).

The fourth plan was marked by the absence of a lower town.

How were residences, temples, palaces, and public buildings distributed throughout these settlements? Based on analogy with contemporary sites in southern Mesopotamia, we would expect the central temple and

(a) Upper Town vs. Lower Town

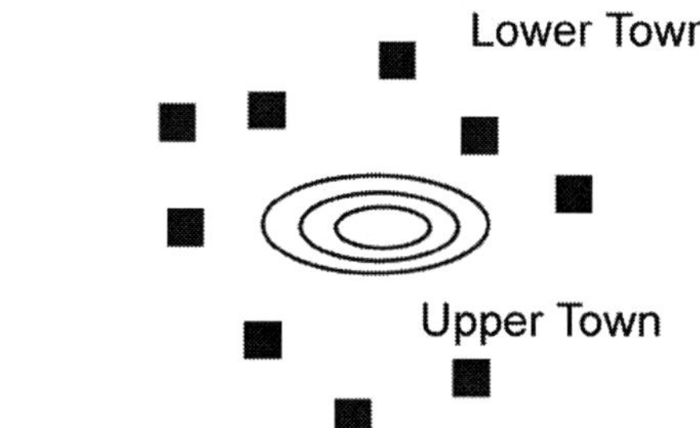

(b) Outer Town vs. Lower Town

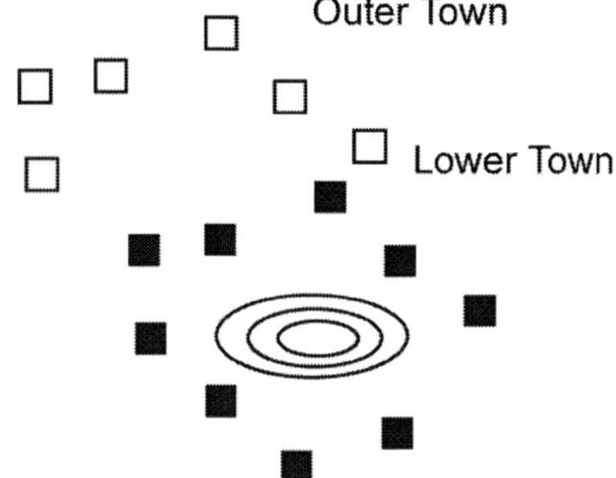

(c) Urban Center vs. Suburbs

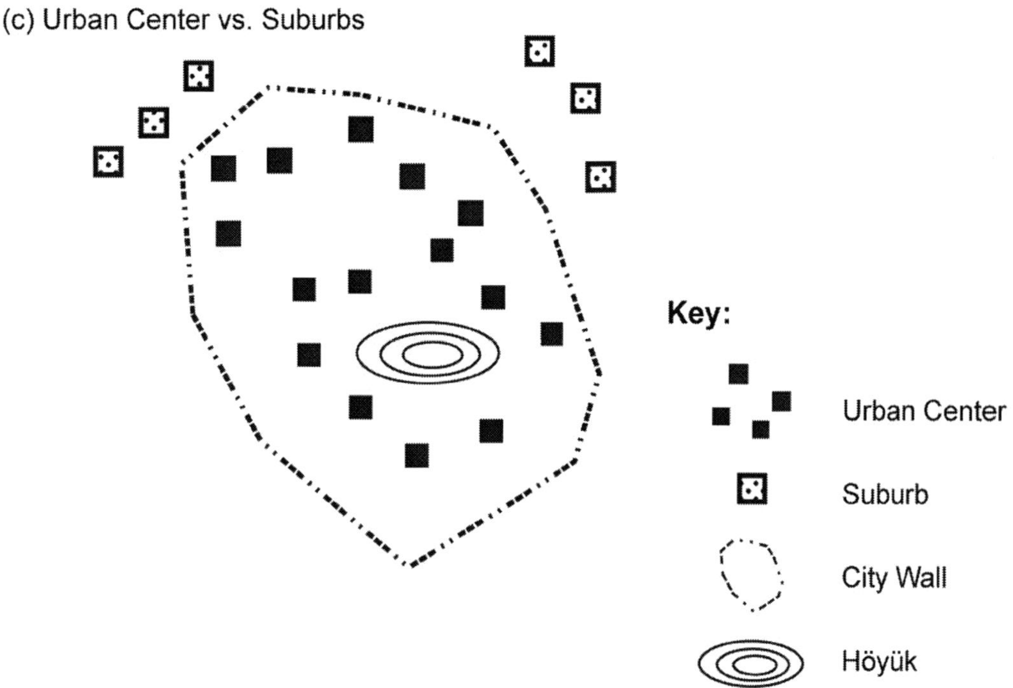

Figure 6.2. Upper Mesopotamian urban settlement patterns.

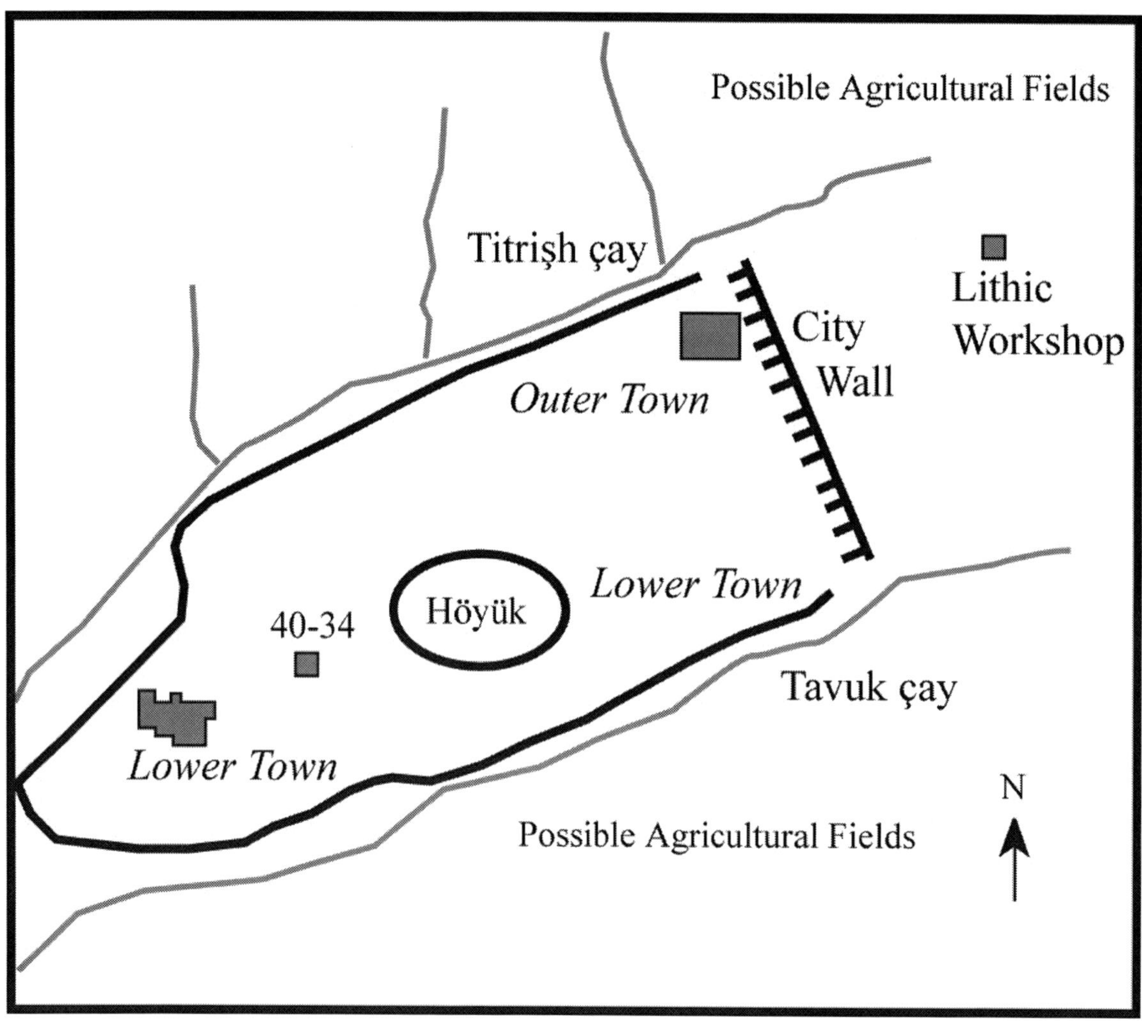

Figure 6.3. Titriş settlement and city wall. Modified from Algaze et al 2001: 82 (Figure 1).

perhaps the palace of the ruling family to be located on the höyük. This cannot be tested at Titriş until meters of Hellenistic and Islamic layers are removed from the surface of the mound. However, several public structures have been identified in the lower town (Figure 6.4). These structures were not concentrated in one area, but rather distributed around the höyük. At Kazane there is one large structure that may serve a public function, the "merkez" building (Figure 6.5). Public structures include palaces, temples, or administrative/official warehouses, storehouses, or accounting offices (e.g., the "wool office" mentioned in bureaucratic texts from Ur, ca. 2100 B.C.E). Note that these structures and personnel may be "private" in the sense that they are not directly under the control of the palace or temple. In addition to architectural features, large, circular threshing floors may have been located around the edges of the settlement (Wilkinson 2003: 57). Kazane also contains a large monumental structure that may have served a public function (Figure 6.5).

The houses at Tell Taya illustrate the diversity of structures within different neighborhoods. The extant site plan maps stone foundations (Figure 6.6). Although difficult to interpret without the results of feature and artifact distributions, it appears that a majority of the houses were large courtyard style houses, with an occasional "block" of smaller houses. These singular rooms or paired rooms may have been shops, the houses of smaller or poorer families, or a part of a larger house which was not organized around a central courtyard. The city plan included "major traffic arteries, open spaces, blind alleys, houses of various sizes, buildings that were probably small temples at some street junctions, industrial areas, notably potteries and a flint-knapping center" (Reade 1982: 77).

In sum, we need broader horizontal exposures at Upper Mesopotamian urban sites to determine how they were structured and whether they resemble Southern Mesopotamian (or modern Islamic) cities. The presence of suburbs in Upper Mesopotamian cities may be due to the increased availability of cultivable land. The next important question to ask is what impact these sprawling cities had on interactions among households, neighborhoods, and intra-site economic exchange.

Interpreting Ancient Urban Planning and Design

Decades of insightful research (Rapoport 1969, 1982, 1990a) suggest that the built environment provides signals for appropriate behavior in certain settings. Chapter 4 applied this theory to individual structures. Here I analyze city plans to determine if streets, alleys, and buildings were consciously designed to signal boundaries between neighborhoods. As discussed in Chapter 5, narrow alleyways almost certainly signaled less public thoroughfares, and doorways set slightly askew across a street imply a concern for privacy. Another piece of evidence that indicates concern for privacy is the absence of numbered or otherwise explicitly identified houses. Traditional Islamic cities do not contain numbered houses or individual mailboxes. Unlabelled and mostly identical building exteriors, such as stone and mudbrick houses set along narrow streets, would make a specific, but unfamiliar, person or house very difficult to locate without assistance. Gulick (1967: 150) explained the social consequences of this anonymity: "To find a Tripolitan in his house in the Old City, one must either know him personally or locate him through someone else who does. And the latter, if he chooses, can easily warn the person one seeks in advance of one's finding him." Although we may be missing some form of signaling in the archaeological record, if the ancient city did indeed lack 'addresses' for individual houses, it would have reinforced an intangible boundary between one's familiar neighborhood and unfamiliar environs. This emic perspective on known and unknown areas of the city may help reinforce one's sense of place within one's own neighborhood and result in tighter social bonds among neighbors.

The design of a house can also communicate information about a household's socio-economic prestige. Perhaps most clearly, the overall size and quality of construction may indicate greater wealth or resources. In addition, subtleties of exterior design may have been interpretable by ancient residents. For example, in America, these features might include the type of mailbox (e.g., does it include space for a daily newspaper), the presence of lawn ornaments, the frequency with which the lawn is cut, and exterior debris. The comparable signaling on ancient houses may have included the quality and quantity of daily trash (most likely disposed, in part, in the street. Ancient residents would probably have been aware of their neighbors' trash disposal habits (e.g., if they could afford to dispose of broken, but mendable, ceramic vessels), the presence of drains, additional wooden grillwork above or incorporated into the front door, the presence and/or quality of a wooden lock, or the presence of a second story.

Because of this awareness of neighborhood behavior, subtle changes in house design probably did not go unnoticed by neighbors. Moreover, much of it was probably intentional signaling of socio-economic prestige. The route of different streets may have also signaled a "wrong side" or, conversely, a "high status" area of the city. For example, streets that led directly to the central tell may have contained more elite residences or shops than narrow side streets. In short, the urban built environment is a potentially rich source of information about the lives of both rich and poor.

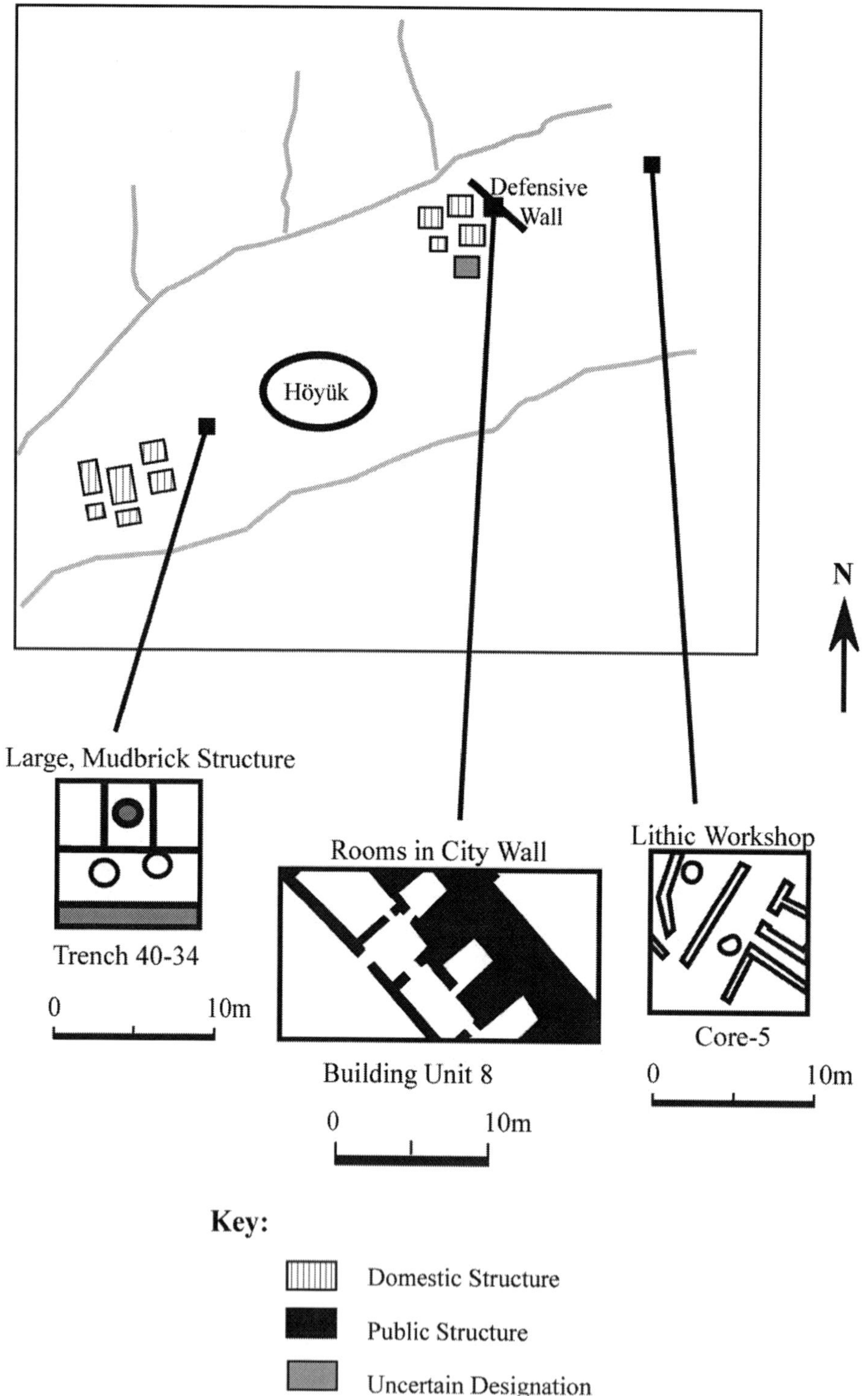

Figure 6.4 Public structures at Titriş.

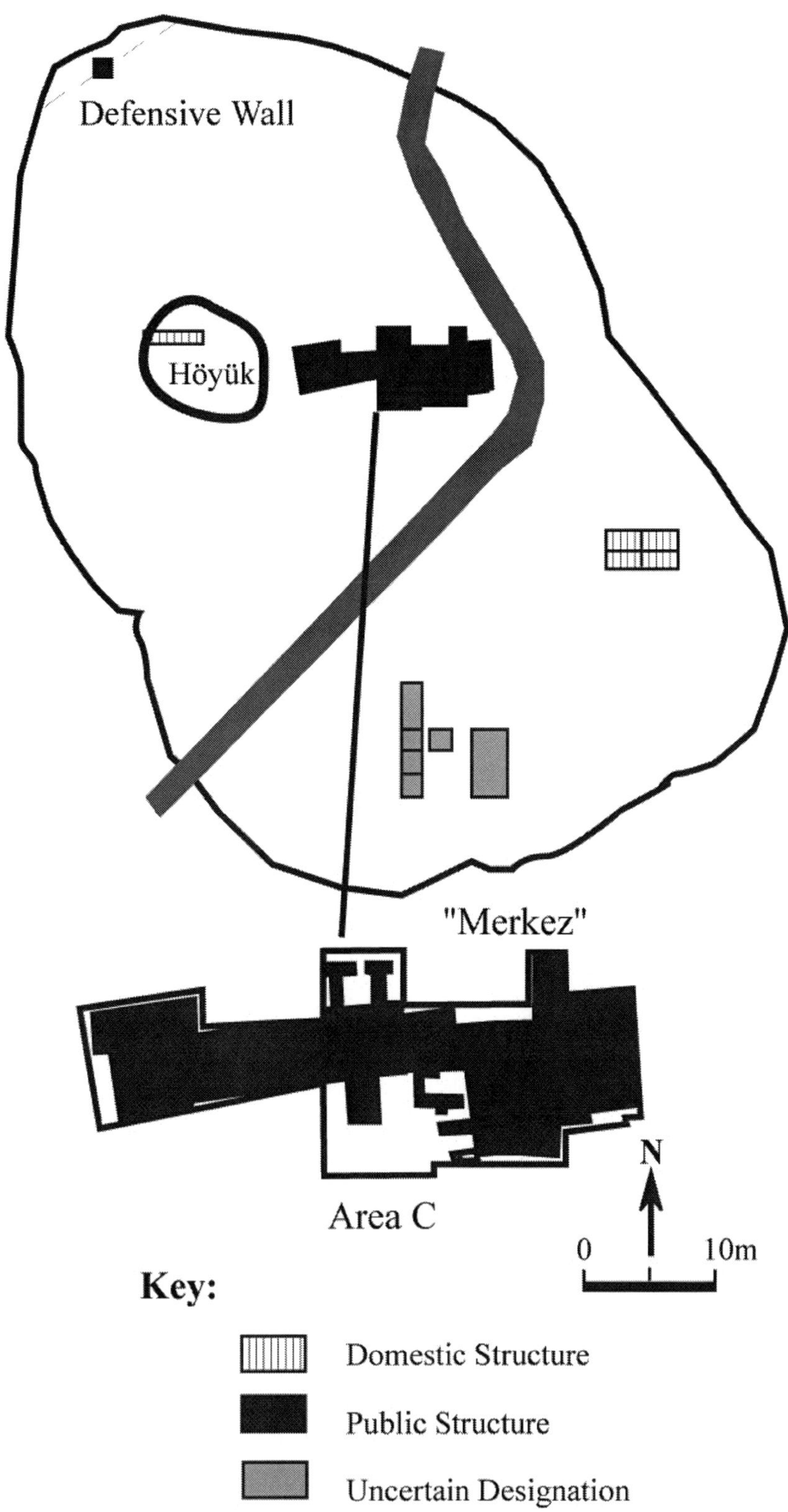

Figure 6.5. Public structures at Kazane.

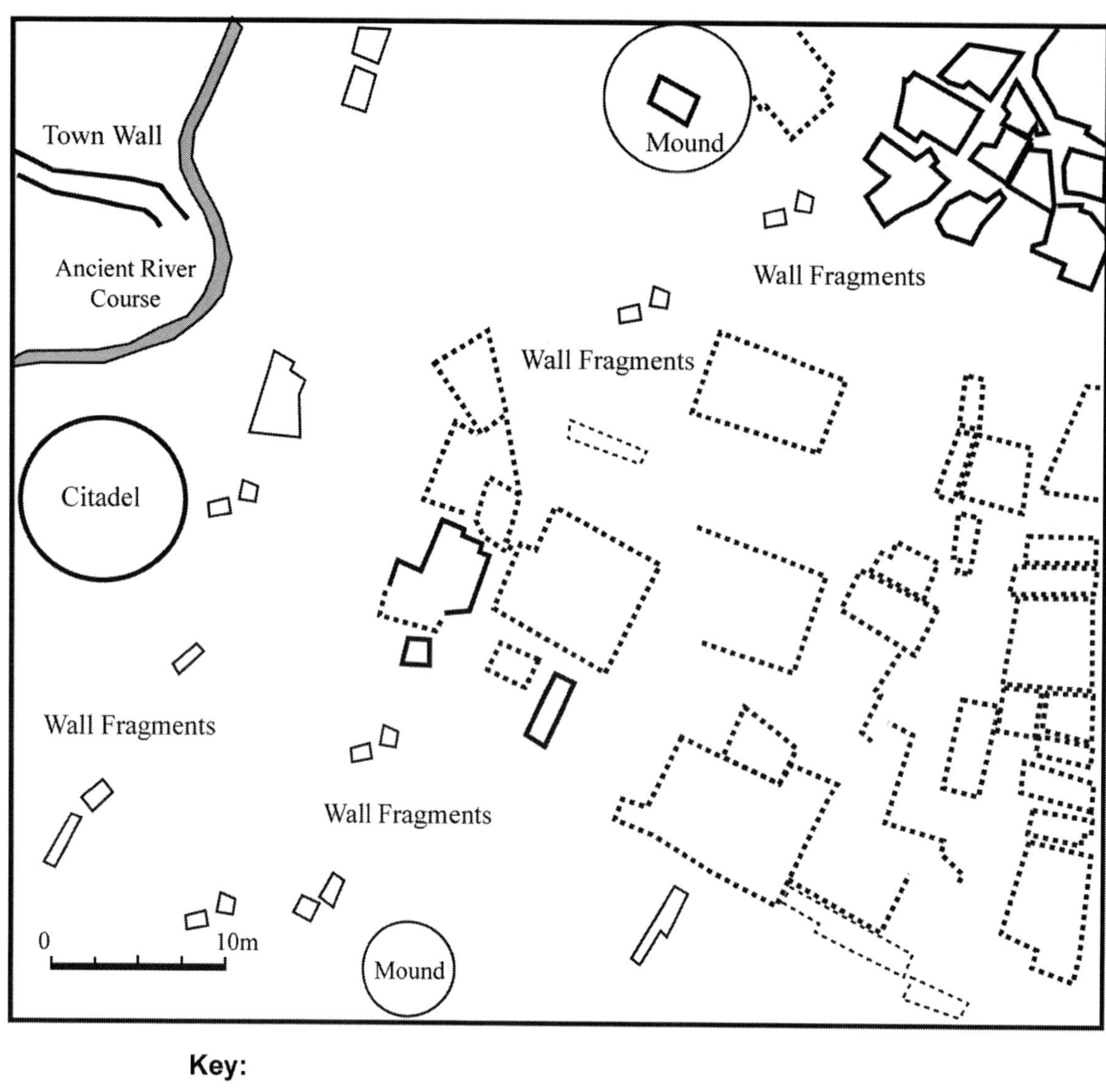

Key:

Outline of fully excavated structures

Structure boundaries, as reconstructed by the author

Figure 6.6. Plan of Tell Taya. Modified from Reade 1973: LVIII-LXIII.

An Upper Mesopotamian City: Kazane Höyük

To test the ideas presented in this chapter on the degree of urban homogeneity, I collected micro-debris samples from a large regional center: Kazane Höyük. As a large EBA site located in southeastern Turkey, Kazane was probably the center of a regional state dominating much of the rich upper Balikh valley. Kazane is strategically located "at the border between the Taurus foothills and lowland steppe region, at the entrance to the Urfa Plain" (Wattenmaker and Mısır 1994: 177). The site was surrounded by a fortification wall that enclosed an upper town and a lower town. Kazane was continuously occupied from the Halaf period (ca. sixth millennium B.C.E.) until its abandonment in the early second millennium B.C.E. (Wattenmaker and Mısır 1994: 177-178). Kazane's largest period of growth was in the mid third millennium B.C.E. (EB II-IV), when the site reached its maximum size of 100 hectares (Wattenmaker and Mısır 1994: 179). Excavated EBA layers at Kazane are slightly earlier than those at Titriş (located about 40 kilometers away). To date, excavations at Kazane have revealed at least two types of neighborhoods: Area C, which contained a large structure that was either an elaborate residence or a public building, and Area F, which was a possible area of manufacturing and small-scale domestic complexes, as well as a more substantial building. In addition, a test trench along the outskirts of the settlement revealed parts of the city wall (Area E). Earlier layers included an area of Halaf houses and outdoor areas (Area D) and chalcolithic workshops and houses (Area H).

Here I will focus on the two roughly contemporaneous mid-third millennium neighborhoods: Area C and Area F. At a gross level, means in micro-debris count densities can be summarized by neighborhood (Table 6.1). This unavoidably conflates a variety of loci, but certain patterns emerge that can be supported by other lines of evidence. In general, Area C contained the highest densities of pottery, chipped stone, plaster, and mudbrick. Area F contained samples low in bone, chipped stone, and shell, while high in pottery and mudbrick. An explanation for these differences is obtained by combining macro-artifactual and architectural data with micro-results.

Location	*n*	Ceramics	Bones	Lithics
		Kazane		
Area C	22	0.46	**17.68**	8.85
Area F	10	1.61	13.69	**14.89**
Area H	5	0.30	10.30	5.29
Wall	2	**2.02**	14.75	**16.95**
		Titriş		
30s	45	0.50	1.88	2.12
80s	154	1.52	3.38	2.98
40s	24	0.45	2.95	**5.07**
Wall	25	0.80	**3.92**	3.70
Workshop	25	**3.04**	3.09	**24.45**

Table 6.1. Micro-debris count density means per neighborhood. The highest density of micro-artifact type, per site, are highlighted in bold.

Area C contains two main architectural features, a 5 meter-wide stone foundation wall and mudbrick walls delineating small rooms adjacent to the stone wall (Figure 6.7). Only one of these rooms contained a clear set of features: Room 13, with three partial ovens. A narrow passage approximately 13 meters long between two stone walls suggests that there may be more than one stone structure. Several of the stone "extensions" may have served as buttresses or "tower bases" (Wattenmaker 1997: 84). The mudbrick rooms contained lime-plastered floors and interior walls. Although relatively clean in macro-artifacts, these rooms contained large amounts of seeds, charcoal, and phytoliths. These remains may be associated with the cooking conducted in Room 13 and/or storage of food items in Rooms 21 and 22. Additional plastered features on the floor of Room 21 suggest some sort of food preparation area. When the micro-artifact distribution was analyzed, the "cooking area" (Room 13) contained the highest concentration of micro-ceramics, bones, and lithics. Specifically, a plastered area in the southwestern corner contained a high association between burned bones and lithic debitage, reinforcing the conclusion that this room was used for food preparation (Figure 6.8). Surprisingly, the samples in room 13 did not contain a large amount of cooking wares, but they did contain high densities of micro-fine and sandy wares (Figure 6.9). The combination of fine and sandy wares suggests that the vessels stored and/or used in this room served a variety of social functions, from elite serving ware to everyday sandy wares. The high density of micro-fine and sandy wares is equaled in the samples from Room 22, suggesting that the food and drink prepared in Room 13 was consumed here. Clearly, further samples from a wider horizontal area are necessary before final conclusions can be made.

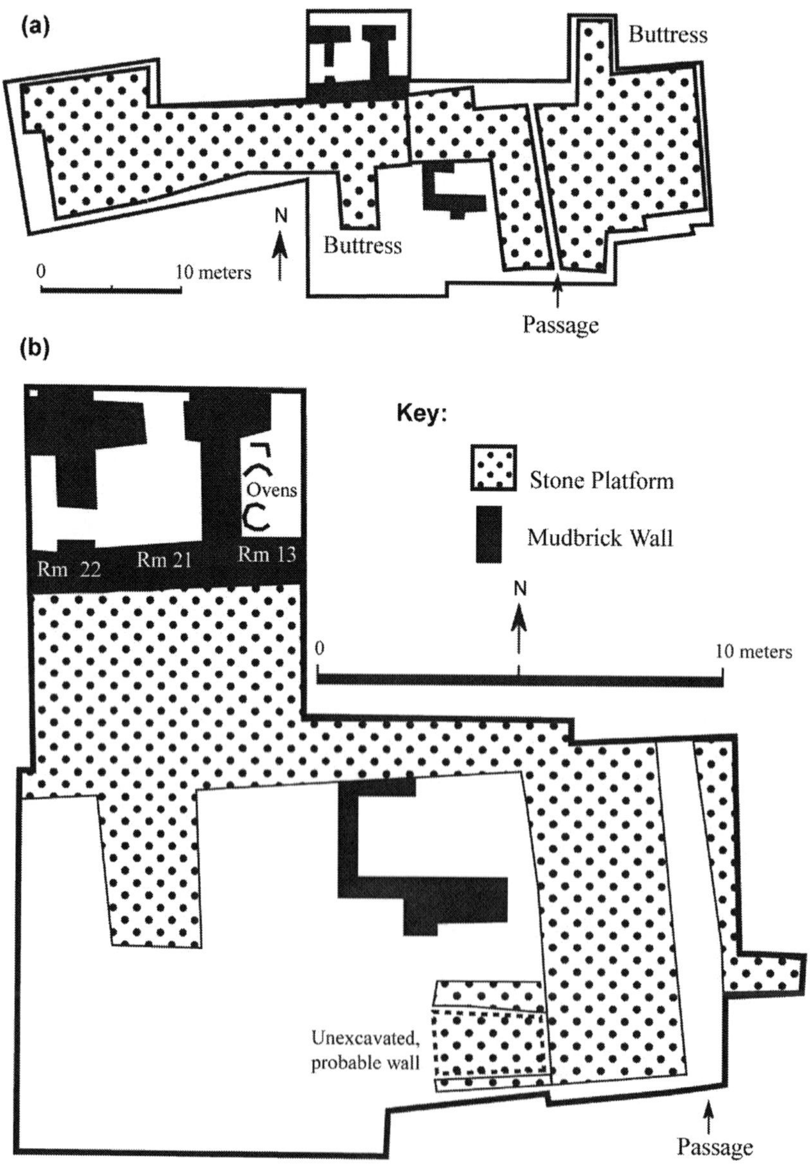

Figure 6.7. Area C architecture, Kazane. (a) Overview of the structure. (b) Close-up of the center of the excavated area. Modified from Wattenmaker 1996: 90 (Figure 5).

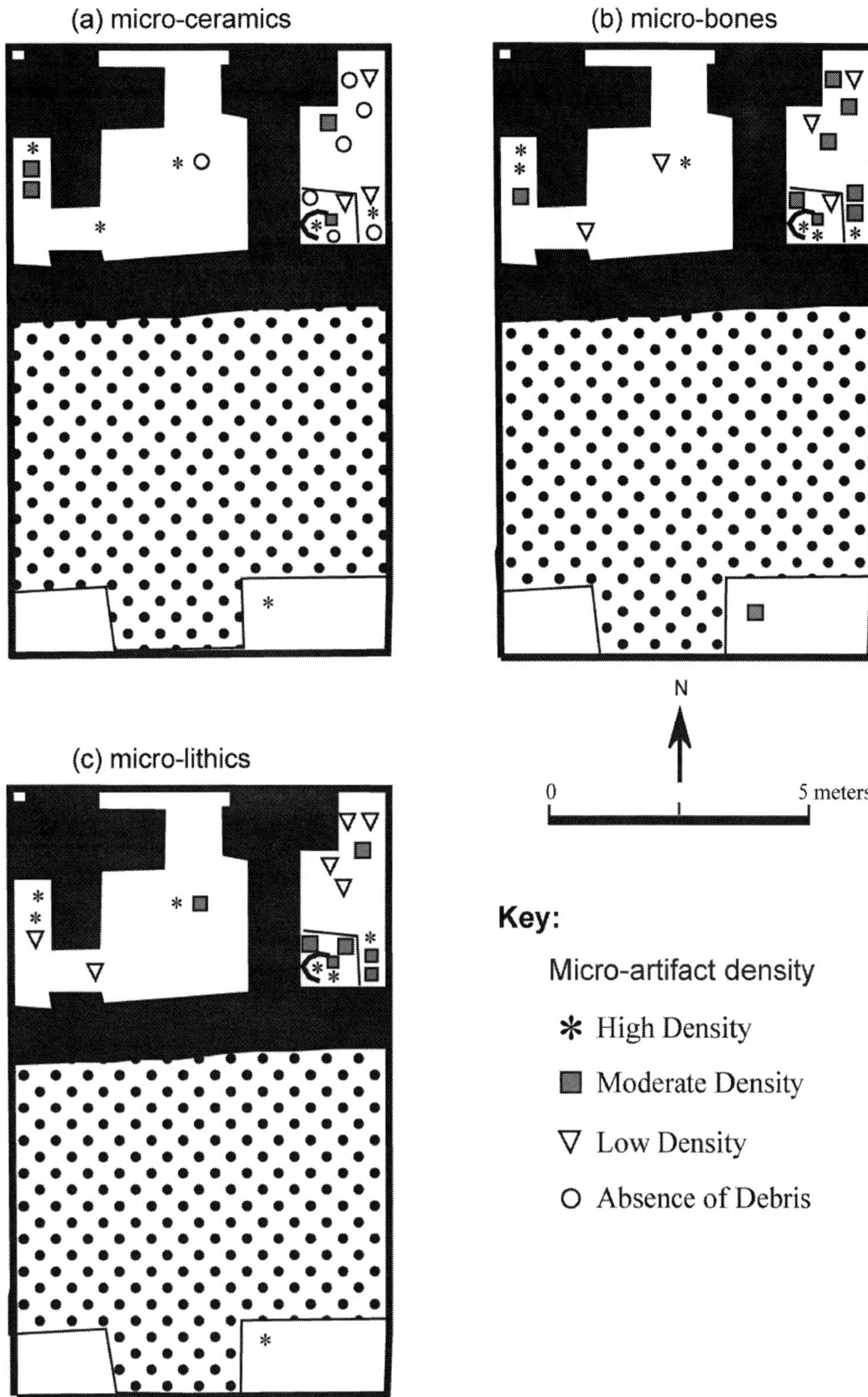

Figure 6.8. Distribution of micro-debris in Area C samples, Kazane.

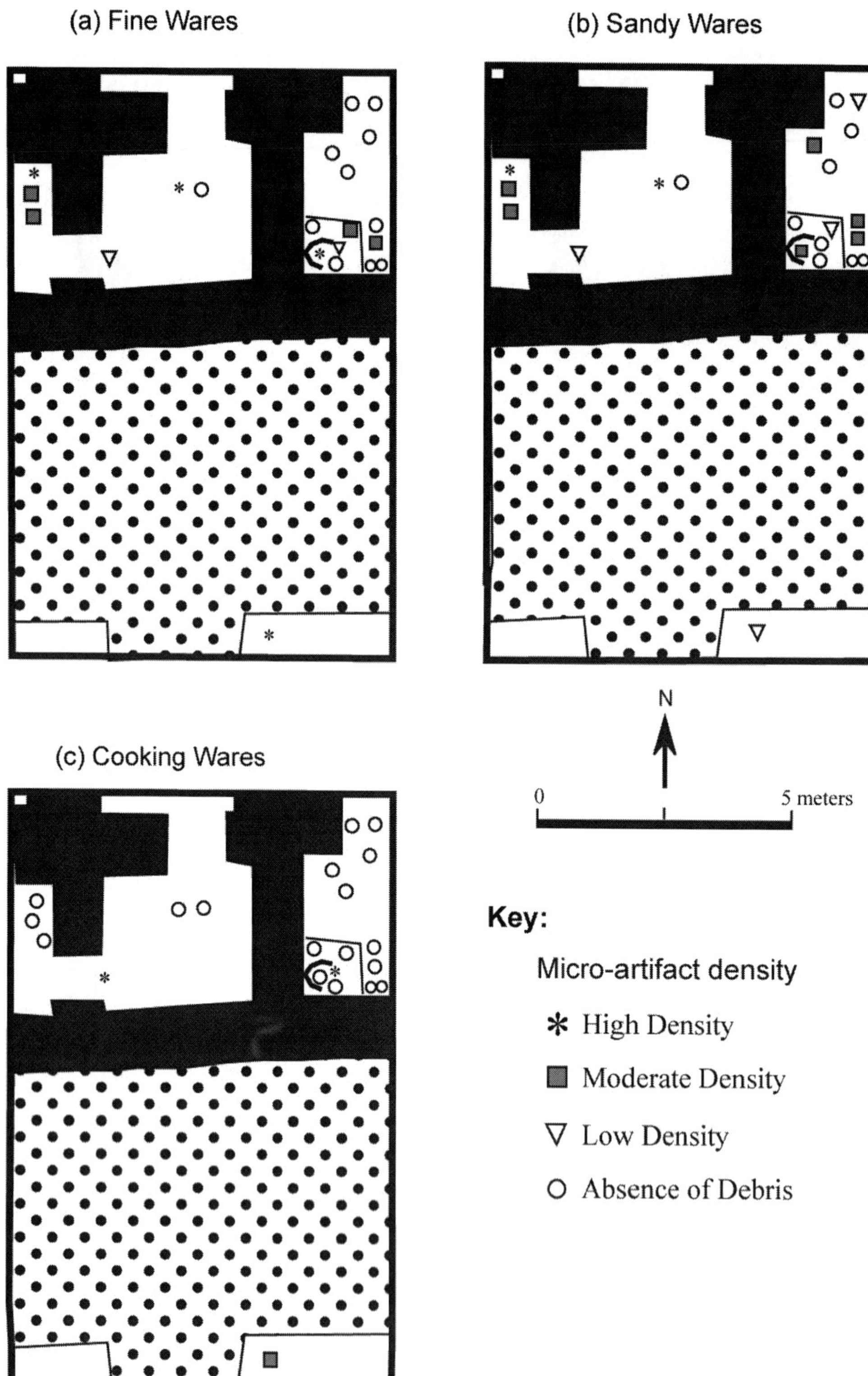

Figure 6.9. Distribution of micro-ceramic wares in Area C samples, Kazane.

In Area F, a series of four small, 2.5 square meter, trenches and one, 2.5 x 10 meter trench yielded an outdoor cobbled work area with ovens (Wattenmaker 1997: 86). The recovery of two large spindle whorls and a bronze needle, in addition to other weaving artifacts, suggests that textiles may have been manufactured here. To the east of these five trenches, a larger sounding revealed thick stone-wall footings, suggesting either a wealthy residence or a large public building. The presence of large quantities of macro-ceramics, sealing clay, and two clay jar stoppers suggests that this building may have been a storage area controlled by an urban bureaucracy (Wattenmaker 1997: 87). In contrast to the lithic workshop at Titriş (located outside the city wall and, apparently, not under direct supervision), this possible textile workshop appears to have been under the supervision of a nearby administrative office.

At the micro-level, the hearths in the workshop area were low in micro-bones, suggesting they were more often used to provide warmth during the cool Turkish winters than to regularly cook food. The micro-ceramics were abundant, paralleling the macro-results. In particular, sandy-wares dominated the micro-assemblages. These medium-width ceramics were probably pieces of larger storage vessels or jars, rather than fine-ware cups and bowls that were used for serving food. In sum, the micro-artifacts supported the conclusion that the area was used for working and storage, rather than daily food consumption. It would be interesting to explore the surrounding space around Area F to see whether this part of the site was a specialized craft area, or whether the residential areas were interspersed within the workshops and public buildings.

When the micro-artifact densities were summarized by locus type for the five excavated areas at Kazane, Area C floors contained the least amount of micro-debris. In contrast, the floors from rooms in the wall (Area E) and Area F floors were very high in micro-ceramics and lithics (Figure 6.10). This reinforces the conclusion that Areas E and F were, in part, used to store goods. In contrast, Area C may have been a large, elite residence where a variety of social activities occurred: drinking out of fine-ware cups, cooking in multiple hearths, and plastering floors for aesthetic and/or prestigious reasons.

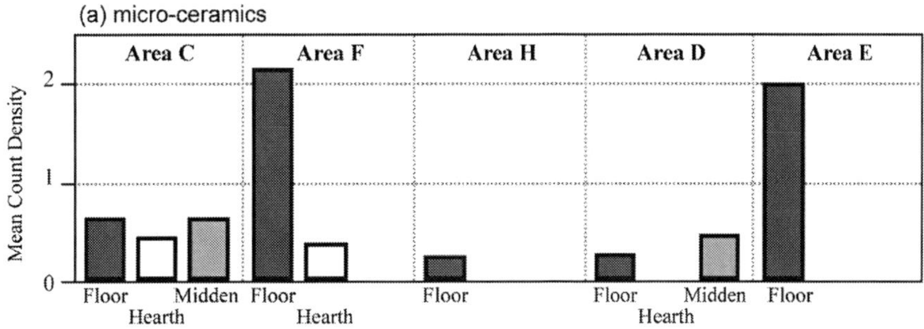

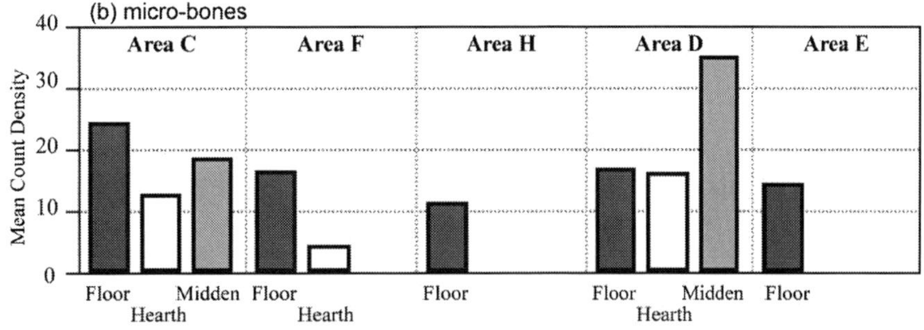

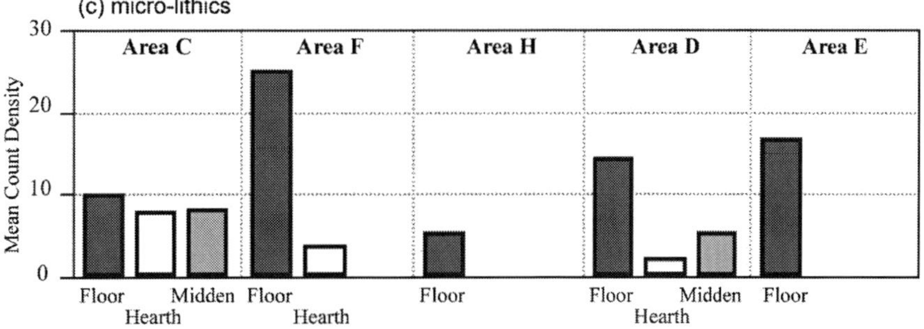

Figure 6.10. Micro-artifact densities per neighborhood, Kazane.

Conclusion

In conclusion, with the current exposure, Kazane's urban plan appears to be more segmented than at Titriş. For example, excavations have not, to date, revealed modest domestic residences at Area F. Instead, Area F was an area of specialized craft production, possibly textiles, with an administrative storehouse or administrator's office located nearby. In contrast, the lithic workshop at Titriş contained evidence for domestic habitation alongside debris from lithic production. In sum, no one model describes the distribution of domestic and public structures within ancient Upper Mesopotamian cities. We do not understand the reasons for this urban variability yet, but this variability should at least be noted. In sum, craftspeople worked in a wide variety of settings from specialized workshops (such as Area F at Kazane), to workshops within households (such as the Lithic Workshop at Titriş), to private households (such as Building Unit 4 at Titriş).

In order to build a better model of Upper Mesopotamian urbanism, we must sample a wider range of urban sites and integrate micro-archaeological techniques into excavation strategies. The accurate mapping of macro and micro-artifacts, features, and architectural remains enables us to examine variability, not simply uniformity, in ancient cities. This, in turn, provides a much richer understanding of the "faceless blobs" that inhabited ancient cities and their role in socio-economic activities. The term "faceless blobs" was used by Ruth Tringham to describe the sterile and abstract reconstructions of ancient society that characterize much of archaeological research. Tringham concluded, "until you can engender prehistory, you cannot *think* of your prehistoric constructions as really human entities with a social, political, ideological, and economic life" (Tringham 1991: 94, original emphasis).

Chapter 7: Insights from a Rural Village

To fully understand ancient Mesopotamian cities we must consider their relationship with villages and farmsteads in their hinterlands. Although there is a rich anthropological and ethnoarchaeological literature on modern and ancient village life (Makal 1954, Erdentug 1959, Antoun 1972, Kramer 1982a, Horne 1994, Aurenche et al. 1997), here I address only a few propositions about rural settlements: that there was little or no craft specialization, that there were no economic elites, and that kinship ties permeated all socio-economic relations to an extent not found in cities. In this chapter I present data from modern Turkish villages. This information cannot be uncritically applied to understand ancient behaviors, rather it must be tested with archaeological evidence. The flow of materials and people between villages and cities seems to be one of the enduring characteristics of urban life in the Middle East that dates as far back as the first cities (Rowton 1976:18).

Many archaeologists argue that in addition to raising families, a substantial amount of village activity revolved around agricultural pursuits. This view is encapsulated by Pierce's observation about a 20th-Century Turkish village: "Such things as births, marriages, circumcisions, deaths, tilling the soil, and harvesting the crops were of greatest importance" (Pierce 1964: 58). Most likely, the majority of individuals in *both* cities and villages were concerned, on a day-to-day basis, with similar events. This model also assumes that villages lack specialized structures and workers—e.g., temples and craft specialists. Moreover, this model suggests that city dwellers were free from any and all agricultural chores. To the contrary, textual studies reveal that urbanites owned gardens, orchards, and fields (Keith 1999: 68-69, 80). In this chapter I investigate a handful of Upper Mesopotamian villages to investigate the accuracy of modeling a dichotomy between agriculturally-based villages and occupationally specialized cities.

Craft Specialization

At the heart of economic models for rural-urban interactions is the assumption that ancient cities contained a concentration of craft specialists (such as potters, weavers, metal workers, or knappers), whereas villages contained few, if any, specialists. In addition, researchers presume that farmers only lived in villages. To the contrary, Ur III texts reveal that, at least in Southern Mesopotamia, a significant number of city dwellers tilled fields as part of their institutional obligations (Maekewa 1996: 177). And evidence from at least one ancient Syrian village suggests that craft specialization was not entirely absent from rural communities (Schwartz 1987: 418-19, Klucas 1996). For example, using data from neutron activation analysis, Falconer (1991: 128) proved that villages in the Jordan Valley produced specialized pottery in Early Bronze IV and Middle Bronze II periods. Many of Falconer's results are based on excavations he conducted at Tell el-Hayyat, Jordan. The farming hamlet was .5 ha, with approximately 100 to 150 inhabitants; it was occupied between ca. 2100-1500 B.C.E. He concluded that villages contained "an unexpected degree of social and economic diversity and potential independence in such diminutive communities." This occupational diversity continues to this day in modern Islamic villages (see Antoun 1972: 27, Table 6, which lists occupations of Jordanian villagers). In sum, it appears that instead of a presence or absence, the extent of craft specialization within ancient villages varied.

> Bronze Age villages … were not necessarily dependent on large central places for manufactured commodities. Rather, in some economic capacities, the countryside of the southern Levant was marked by surprisingly self-sufficient and important *small* places that actually contributed these commodities to much more imposing towns and cities." (Falconer 1991: 138-9)

Because of this variability, the extent of craft specialization within villages must be explored rather than presumed. Moreover, we need to determine whether this economic specialization was controlled by regional centers.

Social or Economic Elites

Another prevailing assumption in models of village life is that rural society is primarily egalitarian, even within state-level systems. These models often contrast urban elites to rural commoners. Again, this model is overly simplistic and neat. The reality is much more complex. Not only did villages probably contain leaders — the occupational diversity discussed above most likely translated into different levels of social, if not economic, prestige. For example, some villages contained temples (e.g., the Middle Bronze Age Syro-Palestinian sites of Tell el-Hayyat, Kfar Rupin, and Tell Kittan). This probably formed part of the social hierarchy: priests and temple workers versus farmers. Meanwhile, cities contained a diverse mixture of elites and commoners (including slaves, people without land, landed individuals, elites, and royalty). Today, the villages themselves are often owned by tribal or urban elites. Thus it is probably more accurate to describe the difference between rural and urban socio-economic elites as one of degree, not of quality.

Kinship Ties

One of the most prevalent models for rural communities is that villagers rely on kinship to organize relations among individuals. In its most extreme form, researchers suggest that kinship ties cease to be an important social factor in cities, but remain significant in villages. For example, Knapp (1988: 62) suggested that family relations became less important in cities: "Urban life necessitated changes in social organization: loyalties were redirected from kin to kings." To the contrary, textual evidence demonstrates that kinship relations were important in both urban and rural communities. For example, land-sale documents from the Old Babylonian period reveal that families jointly owned land (Postgate 1992: 94). In addition to shared property rights and economic ties, ancestral tombs under house floors and textual references to regular graveside ceremonies and mortuary offerings demonstrate the importance of kinship obligations toward both living and deceased relations (for detailed references to domestic funerary rituals see Postgate1992: 99-101 and his notes, numbers 140 to 148 on pages 311-12). This is not to say that kinship ties were not important in villages, but rather that these ties do not become irrelevant in an urban context.

Interactions between Cities and Villages

A weakness in some "urban studies" is the implicit assumption that urban adaptations are diametrically opposite to rural ones, implying an animosity or separation between the two communities. The rural-urban dichotomy obscures the fact that a majority of city dwellers were engaged, on a daily basis, in socio-economic pursuits similar to those of their rural counterparts. While a small percentage of city dwellers engaged in inter-city trade, most of the urban population was concerned with obtaining food stuffs and raw materials from the rural hinterlands or urban gardens. A parallel overlap in urban/rural activities can be seen in contemporary Middle Eastern settlements where urban features, such as markets, mosques, and even baths, are also found in villages. This serves as an important reminder that in distinguishing the urban from the rural we are often looking at a difference in kind or degree not presence or absence. A richer model of ancient society considers cities and villages as sharing a need for labor, goods (both exotic and local), and control over resources.

Exchange of Goods

Social, economic, and political interactions between ancient cities and their rural hinterlands are still not fully understood. Some authors suggest that urban elites controlled trade in exotic raw materials, such as obsidian (Santley 1983: 70, citing the example of Teotihuacan, in Mexico). Other researchers argue that the exchange of staple commodities, such as grain and animal products, dominated the exchanges (D'Altroy and Hastorf 1984: 347, citing an example from the Andes). Clearly, the population densities of third-millennium cities required substantial imports of food products in exchange for services and manufactured goods (Zeder 1991). But it is not clear to what extent these transactions were supervised or controlled by state authorities.

In these exchanges, villages received military protection and access to regional exchange networks. In some cases the rural communities may have owed service or taxes, in addition to agricultural surplus, to regional centers. For example, the 200+ villages that surrounded the second-millennium city of Ugarit owed collective tax, military, and labor obligations to the crown (Falconer 1995: 401). Although the specifics of urban/rural interactions in Upper Mesopotamia are not yet known, goods and, most likely, ideas were exchanged between urban centers and their rural hinterlands. Because of this interdependence, we cannot understand Mesopotamian urbanism without studying those rural communities.

Exchange of People

Urbanites and villagers exchanged much more than goods and foods; there was also a large degree of population fluidity in the third millennium. From archaeological surveys we know that many Mesopotamian cities grew in size during this period (Adams 1981). Presumably, the new urban inhabitants arrived from surrounding villages (borne out by a concomitant decrease in rural populations during this same period). Furthermore, villages may have owed military service (such as the *ilku* service required in the south during the Old Babylonian Period) or temple duty to urban centers, necessitating temporary resettlement for at least the men. The cities did not simply absorb rural immigrants. Rather, the fabric of urban society changed as citizens left their villages in search of greater opportunities; conversely, city populations shifted as some residents abandoned city lifestyles after jobs and/or income dried up. They returned to family lands in the country. Similarly, in times of epidemics, violence, or famine, city dwellers may have fled to villages. Without land documents, lists of personal names or extensive work in tracking the movement of individuals to and from the countryside, we can only observe this population movement at a gross level (through the use of survey data and settlement pattern analysis). I am interested in the impact that these new immigrants have on the nature of urban life.

A well-documented example of the flight from rural communities to cities is found in Adams and Nissen's (1972: 18-19) survey work around the southern city of Uruk. They studied artifact concentrations on site surfaces and concluded that between the late Uruk (ca. 3200-3100 B.C.E.) and the end of the third millennium, Uruk and its environs experienced an increase in urban settlements, while the number of small villages decreased. Using a different approach (a Monte Carlo simulation of rank-site size), Falconer and Savage (1995: 47) similarly concluded that in the Early Dynastic I, "society became highly urbanized by relocating and reducing its rural population." Yoffee (1986) referred to this process of urban growth and concomitant rural reduction as "ruralization." Earlier Hourani (1970: 22) used this term to refer to the migration of people to cities from villages and the establishment, by these people, of separate quarters. The resulting settlement pattern contained sets of villages clustered around urban centers.

A parallel situation exists in modern Turkey in a rural area 200+ kilometers east of Ankara (near the archaeological sites of Cadir Höyük and Kerkenes Dag). Villages, comprising 25 to 200 homes, are located within 40 kilometers of each other but grouped into distinct areas, separated by foothills (Snyder 2000: 174). Although we do not yet have complete survey data for southeastern Turkey, initial work (Algaze 1986, Algaze et al. 1994) suggests that Kurban Höyük and surrounding villages may resemble this contemporary Turkish model. Along the Anatolian section of the Euphrates there were several urban centers surrounded by satellite communities (Figure 7.1).

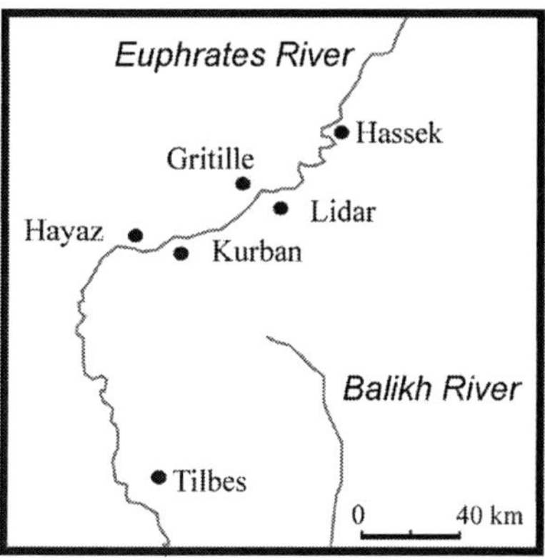

Figure 7.1. Villages along the Euphrates River in southeastern Turkey.

For example, Titriş may have demanded tribute from nearby Lidar or Tatar Höyük (Algaze et al. 1992: 42). A similar situation occurred to the southwest, in Syria, where Ebla demanded resources from its neighboring rural communities.

> Ebla's power ... depended on its political hegemony over a territory dotted with autonomous minor urban centers that were nevertheless forced to cede to the main center [Ebla] grazing rights for its flocks and free circulation of its goods. (Milano 1995: 1221)

Moreover, research from the "hinterland" of the Diyala and Levantine sites suggests a form of urbanism distinct, rather than identical, to that of the heartland of Mesopotamia (see Falconer and Savage 1995).

Exchange of Food

Using evidence from southern Mesopotamian sites and the logical necessity of feeding a city, we know that Syro-Anatolian cities must have relied on a rural hinterland for their daily subsistence. A minimum of .5 hectares of land was needed per person in order to provide 3,100 calories a day to each individual (Lupton 1996: 11). Other ethnographic research suggests as many as 1.5 hectares of land per person was necessary (Falconer 1991: 122). If we conservatively estimate the population of Kazane at 10,000 people, the city would have required an additional 5,000 to 15,000 hectares of farm land to support their citizens. Titriş, with a population of at least 3,000 people, would have needed approximately 1,500 to 4,500 additional hectares of agricultural land. In other words, these cities were, in part, dependent on either forced, tributary, or reciprocal exchanges with their rural hinterlands.

A Turkish Village: Tilbes Höyük

In the remainder of this chapter I analyze the micro-archaeological evidence collected from a rural site, Tilbes Höyük, to determine what activities were conducted on a regular basis in this small village. Tilbes was a rural settlement, located along the Euphrates, that covered perhaps as many as six hectares (Figure 7.2). To date, a series of EBA buildings have been excavated, but there is evidence for extensive Chalcolithic levels as well (Rothman 2000, Tilbes website at http://muse.widener.edu/~msr0001/tilbesnew.html). Two trenches have yielded horizontal exposures with domestic architecture, Trench A/E 1-5 (shortened to "Trench A" in the following discussion) and Trench E4aE3E8 (shortened to "Trench E"). Trench A dates to the Early Bronze II period, while Trench E contained Early Bronze I, IV a, IV b, and possibly III, layers (see Table 1.2). Both these trenches contained fragments of mudbrick walls, plastered and bricked surfaces, stone walls, and burials. Taken together with the macro-artifacts, ceramic vessels, fertility figurines, animal bones (especially

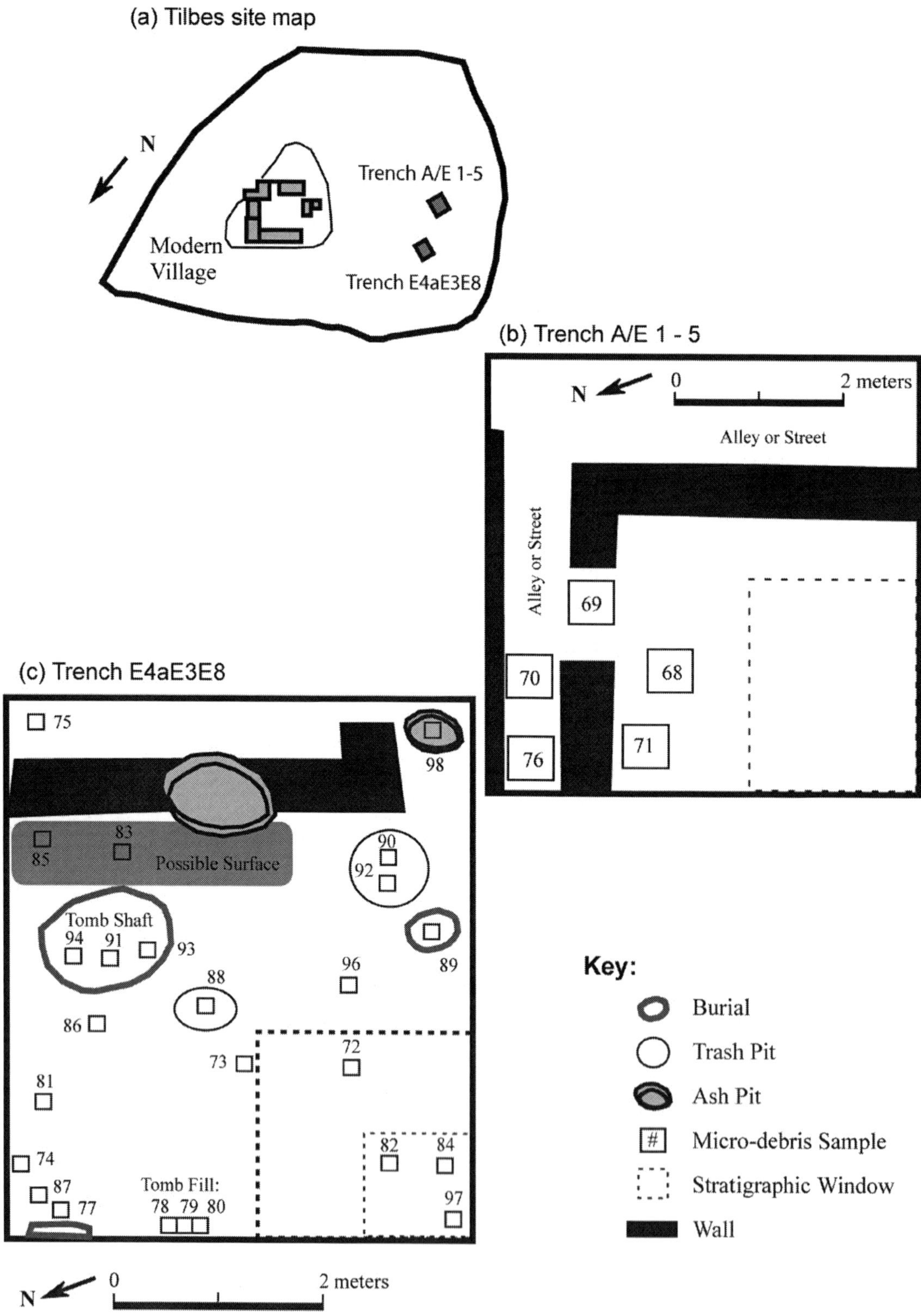

Figure 7.2. Tilbes Site Map. Modified from (a) Fuensanta et al. 1999: 213, Figure 1, (b) Trench notebook, and (c) Trench notebook.

caprids), and two tokens (Fuensanta, Rothman, and Bucak 1999: 211), the architecture appears to be domestic in nature.

Because up to 40% of modern Near Eastern villages are made up of non-residential open spaces (Kramer 1980: 320), we would expect that, with further excavations, threshing floors, animal stables, and possibly bread ovens would be exposed on and, perhaps, below the tell. Beyond the tell we would expect agricultural lands, grazing areas, and possibly mudbrick sources (if the dirt for the bricks was removed from the tell itself, it would have left large, open pits that would have created a hazard).

Tilbes would have needed additional land to support itself. Ethnographic research suggests that between 100 and 250 people live per hectare in traditional southwestern Asian villages (Antoun 1972, Sumner 1972, Kramer 1980). Falconer (1991: 122) compiled data from ethnographic and ancient Mesopotamian texts to derive a figure that estimates the ancient productivity of wheat and barley (using rainfall farming) at 1.5 hectare per person. Using these data, Tilbes, at six hectares, with a population of approximately 200 people, would have required between 100 and 300 hectares of cropland to feed the village.

Micro-Archaeology at Tilbes

In 1999, I collected 24 sediment samples from the Early Bronze I layers in Trench E at Tilbes. The Early Bronze I levels in Trench E included an outdoor work area, the exterior wall of a structure in the northeast corner, three tombs (possibly within a larger structure and thus under the floor), two ash pits, and two trash pits. The tomb in the northwest corner dated to the Early Bronze I period and, at the macro-level, contained fruit stands, other reserved slip pots, four bronze pins, and some beads (Rothman 2000, Tilbes website). Unfortunately, the architectural plans remain incomplete, so the patterning of micro-debris densities was difficult to interpret. But at least some of the micro-signatures per feature resembled those found at Titriş, such as burials with high quantities of micro-bones and micro-ceramics. Interestingly, at the rural site, the burial fill contained exclusively sandy wares, not fine wares (the opposite pattern occurred in the burial in Building Unit 4 at Titriş).

When the micro-artifact densities were graphed onto the trench plans, a concentration of micro-ceramics, lithics, and the occasional bone occurred on a possible preparation surface (a bricky surface) in the northeastern corner (along the outside of a wall) (Figure 7.3). The ceramics were primarily sandy wares, suggesting that this area was used to consume, rather than cook, food (Figure 7.4). A nearby ash pit may have provided warmth for flintknappers working outdoors. The trash pits contained high amounts of ceramics and lithics, while only moderate amounts of micro-bones. The overall low quantity of micro-bones in the trench suggested that the inhabitants consumed meat less frequently than some of their counterparts at Titriş or that scavengers (perhaps dogs or rats) routinely carried away any scraps of meat. In general, the highest densities of ceramics occurred in the northwest and northeast corners (Figure 7.5). The bricky surface may have continued throughout this area, suggesting a preparation surface or a locale that was regularly used for food consumption (this area also contained the highest concentration of cooking wares). High quantities of bone, in this case possibly crushed human remains, were found in the burial fill from the northwest tomb and in a few samples on the bricky surface.

When the quantities of micro-debris from Trench A were compared to the chronologically later Trench E, several patterns emerged (Figure 7.6). The first result was that most of the samples from Trench A (except a street sample) contained high quantities of micro-lithics. Trench A samples also contained a more regular distribution of micro-bones, although in no case was any single sample particularly rich in fauna. Among the samples in Trench E only 48% of the samples contained fragmented faunal remains versus 83% of the samples in Trench A. The discrepancy in the quantity of faunal remains may suggest differential access to meat, a greater number of scavengers that consumed and carried away the bones in Trench E, or better housecleaning habits in Trench A.

The distribution of chipped stone colors per locus type suggested that the tan chipped stone was used on a daily basis (with high concentrations in trash pits), whereas the dark brown stone was preferred for burials (indicated by the high density of micro-pieces in the burial fill) (Figure 7.7). The pink stone was highest in the samples taken from a hearth (a similar pattern was found in Building Unit 4 at Titriş, where concentrations of pink lithics corresponded with kitchen areas). None of these colors were found in the control samples. In sum, both Titriş and Tilbes demonstrated similar raw material preferences for agricultural versus domestic tasks.

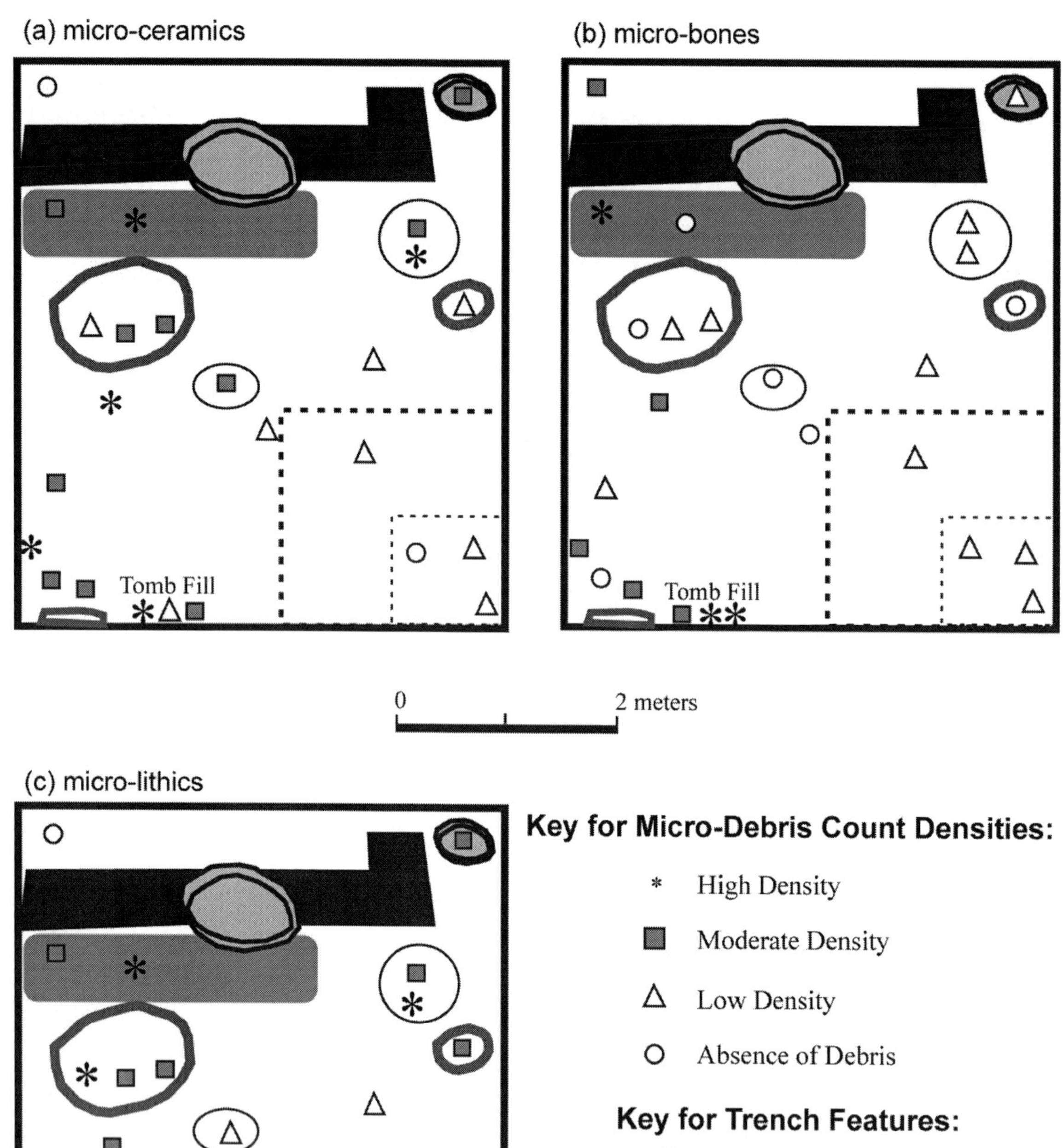

Figure 7.3. Distribution of micro-debris densities in Trench E, Tilbes.

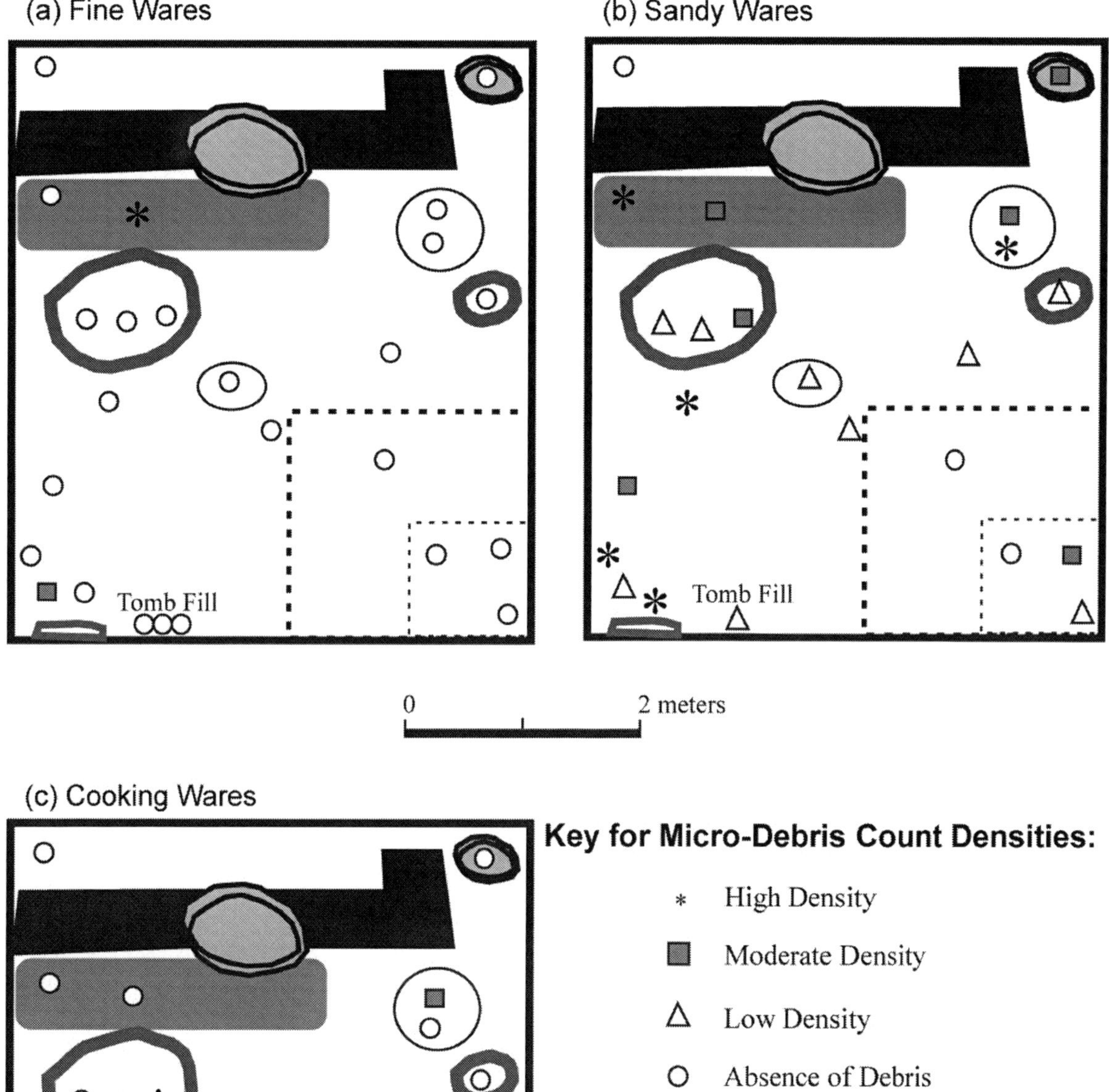

Figure 7.4. Distribution of micro-ceramic wares in Trench E, Tilbes.

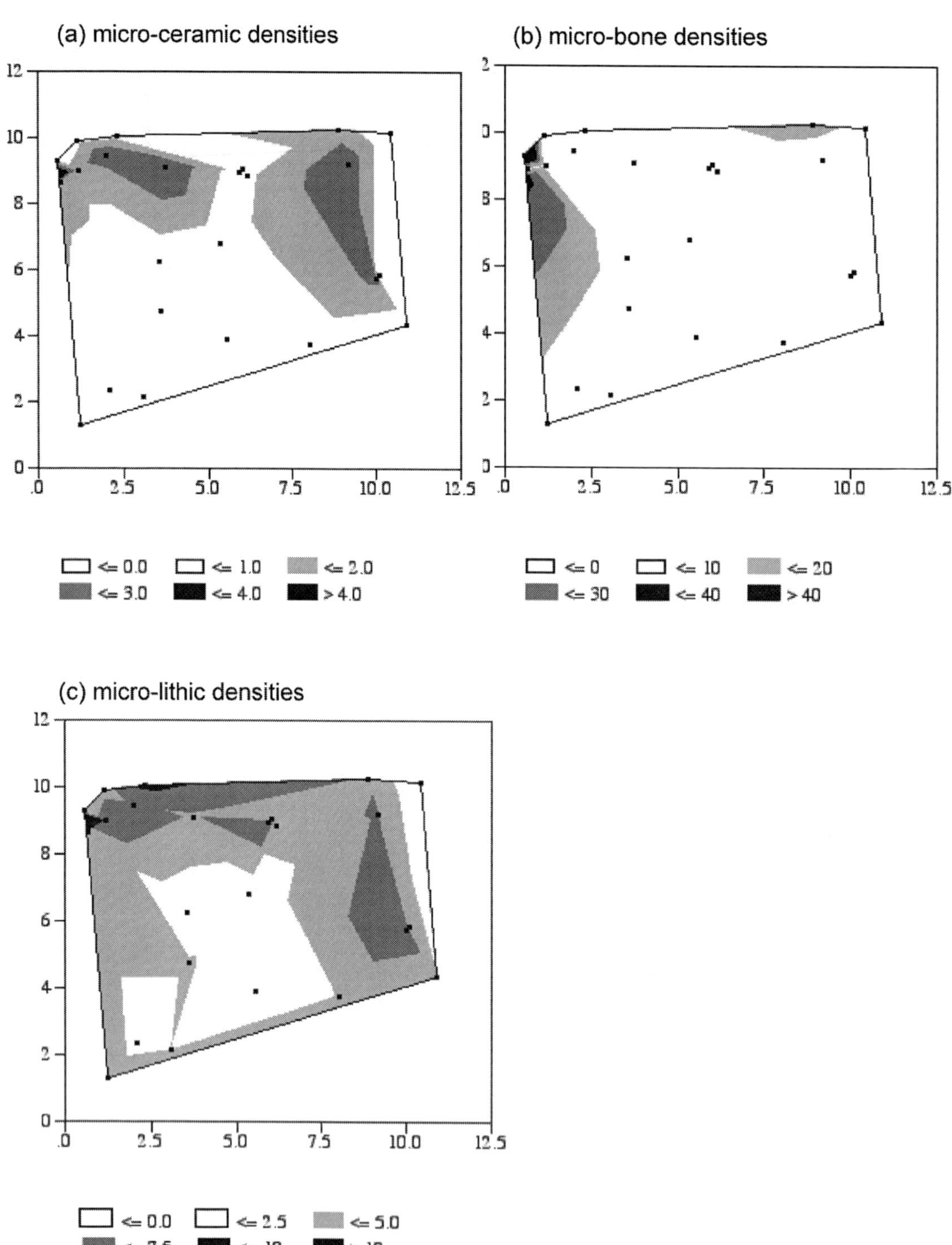

Figure 7.5. Micro-artifact density distributions in Trench E, Tilbes.

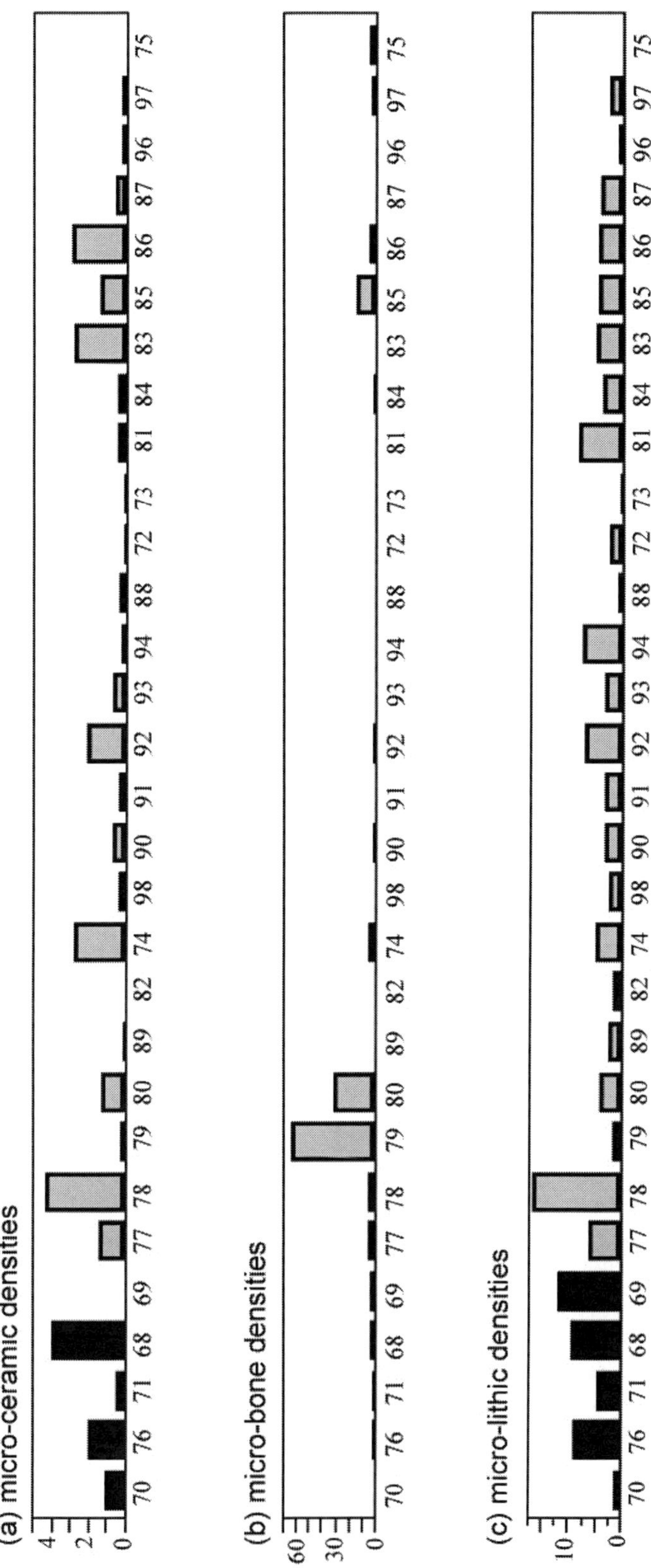

Figure 7.6. Micro-artifact densities from each sediment sample, Tilbes.

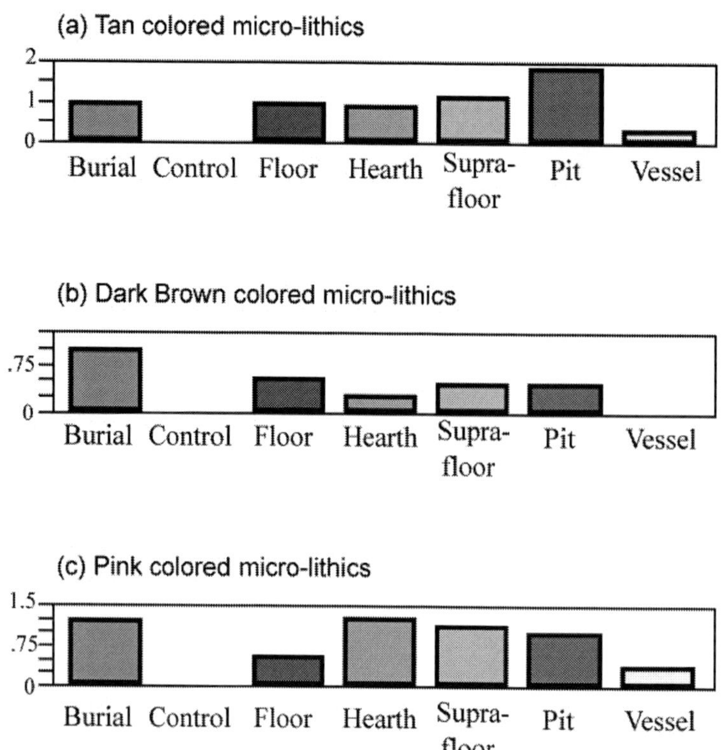

Figure 7.7. Distribution of lithic colors among locus types, Tilbes.

A Diversity of Village Types

Given the limited horizontal exposure at Tilbes and the lack of survey data to determine who and what Tilbes traded with, how are we to describe the village? One set of models comes from ethnographic researchers. For example, Kolars (1967: 69) classified modern Turkish villages based on their interactions and relationship to surrounding cities. In his "urban-directed villages" he included (1) Shadow, (2) Annexed, (3) Satellite, and (4) Summer dormitory types. In contrast, his "rural-directed villages" included (5) Market-seeking, (6) Market-recognizing, and (7) Market-ignoring.

Without further survey it is hard to place Tilbes into one of these categories. The lack of ceramic diversity at Tilbes, perhaps indicating a lack of regular economic exchange with nearby cities, suggests that Tilbes may have been a "market-ignoring" village. Conversely, in "market-recognizing" villages, a portion of the villagers produce crop surpluses. These surpluses can be used to barter for non-local goods. While the term "market" is probably anachronistic for the third millennium, we can imagine a continuum of ancient Anatolian villages that contained greater or lesser degrees of surplus and craft specialization. For example, the village site of Tell Raqa'i, in Syria, included silos, an area for processing grain, and a sanctuary (Curvers and Schwartz 1990).

Neutron activation analysis of sherds could determine whether or not vessels were produced from local clays or obtained from more distant sources. If clays were locally obtained, this would imply that a village potter produced the vessels, whereas the use of non-local clays to construct vessels would imply some form of an exchange system among sites (hopefully determinable from the clay sourcing). The limited results from the analysis of micro-wares at Tilbes suggests that sandy wares were much more prevalent at this rural site than at the contemporary urban site of Kazane. The sandy wares may correlate with a local clay source.

Kolars' village "types" also shed light on the diversity of populations at regional centers. For example, the "shadow" type may describe areas of Titriş: enclaves of a particular village that lived within a city. Kolars suggests that these rural migrants provided occupational specialties for the city. Perhaps the core area at Titriş is to be interpreted in this light. If the lithic workshop area was inhabited by village migrants, it would help explain both its peripheral location (outside of the city walls, see Figure 4.29a) and the apparently distinct architectural styles (see Figure 4.30c). The possibility of rural migrants living within urban centers should be explored further at third millennium cities.

Conclusion

The purpose of this brief chapter was to summarize ethnographic and micro-archaeological evidence for everyday life in Upper Mesopotamian villages. While limited in scope, the data suggests that "village societies" were not as homogeneous or socio-economically simplistic as sometimes assumed. While urbanites probably had more occupational choices, both to practice and to patronize, many city dwellers were engaged in agricultural activities, either through field ownership, management, or, for the lower classes, labor in surrounding fields. In addition, villages were not without specialists, albeit perhaps limited to potters, weavers, and knappers, rather than occupations such as goldsmiths, tanners, or jewelers.

Differences in social-economic scale and quality did exist between small villages and large cities. For example, a greater density of tablets have been found in urban centers, proving a greater amount of administrative complexity and coordination. In addition, it is likely that villages contained a larger proportion of lower classes and some middle classes (landowners), while the city contained a greater number of middle and upper classes, including, of course, kings, priests, and officials of various sorts. In short, both rural and urban settlements demonstrated a diversity of social, economic, religious, and political features.

In sum, we cannot understand Mesopotamian urbanism without studying the movement of populations, goods, and services between cities and villages. Unless we move beyond the urban-rural antithesis/dichotomy, we cannot fully understand the emergence and growth of urban centers and urbanization or the organization of the countryside.

Chapter 8: Concluding Remarks: building blocks

Daily life and the environs of individuals living in the early cities in southeastern Turkey have been the focus of this book. I have drawn upon a variety of types of evidence in order to study this everyday life: architectural features, macro- and micro-artifact densities, ethnographic studies, and texts. I have illustrated that a bottom-to-top perspective is valuable in interpreting the archaeological remains of houses, which represent the majority of the architectural remains at ancient cities. This "social history" must be integrated into economic and political models of ancient urbanism. While domestic concerns are frequently studied in "simple" societies, household archaeology is not commonly included in the analysis of "state-level" societies. I have argued that kinship relations and the household economy do not cease to be important in stratified and differentiated societies.

Urban Neighborhoods

This work has also highlighted the need to contextualize households within their immediate communities, or neighborhoods, and within the larger settlement, whether a city or a village. Contrary to many preconceived notions, I found evidence for extended families living side by side with smaller (although not necessarily poorer) nuclear families in ancient cities and evidence for self-sufficient households at village sites. In addition, different types of houses were found within neighborhoods, forcing us to rethink the conventional model of the ancient Near Eastern city that presumes neighborhood segregation by social and economic class. Instead, a diversity of house sizes, domestic activities, and, possibly, family types were found within urban neighborhoods. We should not expect household uniformity, in terms of family structure, craft activities, or socio-economic status within any given city, neighborhood, or village. Instead, a combination of family types, household compositions, community organizations, and site types characterized many ancient cities.

The Utility of Micro-Archaeology as a Complement to Traditional Techniques

The recovery of household activities was made possible through a new technique: micro-archaeology. The analysis of micro-artifacts and their distribution in space allows the identification of primary activity areas and, in turn, the investigation of variability of room use within Anatolian houses. This work has clearly demonstrated that macro-artifacts and features are not sufficient for understanding past domestic activities. While it is too early to present a complete program for the analysis and interpretation of micro-debris, the quantity and quality of micro-debris was invaluable in identifying socio-economic variability.

The next step will be to conduct ethnoarchaeological and micro-artifactual research in traditional cities: collecting micro-debris samples and analyzing the distribution of micro-artifacts on domestic and non-domestic surfaces in urban contexts. Of course, even in "traditional villages" (where a majority of the ethnoarchaeological work has been conducted to date), the introduction of metals, plastics, and numerous modern building materials and appliances produces different materials and patterns from the ancient samples. And contemporary urban settings are usually less "traditional" than villages. But an increased number of micro-debris samples taken from a wide variety of locus types, activity areas, rooms, structures, and sites will produce better interpretations of the patterns in the archaeological record.

Micro-debris provides a rare window into household *variability* in terms of room furnishings and artifact densities. In all urban societies people own belongings and they have a choice on how to "furnish" their homes. Karpat (1976) reports that even in Turkish squatter settlements, residents make an effort to bring and display objects from their family homesteads. In most cases, people attempt to re-establish links to home by replicating their former environs. Moreover, decorating practices produce a sense of place (Pred 1990: 16-22). But when our attention turns to ancient houses, we tend to ignore aberrant or singular features. For example, the late phase of Building Unit 4 at Titriş contained an unusual circular, limestone platform in the northeast corner of the main courtyard. Two lines of stones lay adjacent to the raised circle. Although it is difficult to recover the exact function of the feature, it may represent a bride's attempt to decorate her new house and/or to copy a feature found in her home (land). Or it may represent local variation or improvement to a "domestic preparation surface" (a circular, flat-lying, mudbrick surface possibly used for food processing and popular at Upper Mesopotamian sites). The study of micro-debris, although by no means conclusive, adds significantly to our understanding of the distribution of activities within ancient structures.

Activity Area Analysis

An important finding of this study is that multiple activities took place within any given room. Moreover, these activities were occasionally invisible at the macro-level. Instead, micro-artifacts were the only remaining trace of many daily activities such as stone tool retouching, food processing, and *in situ* vessels (removed upon abandonment but often chipped or broken through everyday use).

The process of taking sediment samples provided an additional, unexpected benefit beyond the analysis of micro-artifacts. Because the sediment samples were routinely taken from features and randomly sampled from interior and exterior surfaces, the micro-artifactual densities calculated for each sample provided a baseline for quantifying artifact variability and, in turn, locating ancient activity areas. In an ideal field project, the volume of all excavated sediments per feature/surface would be calculated. But at large urban sites it is very difficult to accurately estimate the density of artifacts per feature. The densities per sediment sample provide an unbiased, albeit limited, window into artifact densities from a large variety of activity areas.

Based on this preliminary study of micro-artifacts, I would suggest several modifications for the collection and analysis of micro-archaeological samples. First, a uniform collection and flotation system must be applied. While the quantity of sampled sediment does not have to be identical for each sample (because count and weight measurement can be expressed as densities), samples should be processed in a similar manner: Collect the sample (including any macro-artifacts that lay on or in the sediment), float the sediment, count and weigh all artifactual remains, both macro and micro. When this procedure is followed each sample will reveal a ratio of macro- to micro-artifacts and serve as a window into artifact densities across the site. Moreover, where micro-artifacts occur in high densities in otherwise "clean" surfaces (with a low macro-artifact density), the sampling strategy can be modified. For example, a room with few macro-artifacts but dense micro-artifacts may merit additional sampling.

In order for micro-archaeology to provide a more useful window into past activities, micro-debris samples should be taken from every excavated room, outdoor surface, and street. Features should also be regularly sampled. A large number of sampled areas provide a better baseline for determining "high" and "low" densities. While there is no objective, expected density of micro-debris per feature, comparing densities from a large number of samples, is useful (see Chapter 4).

Future activity area studies would also benefit from the geo-chemical, micro-morphological, and nuclear, and petrographic techniques discussed in Chapter 2.

Household Archaeology as a Necessary Complement to Urban Archaeology

The ancient Mesopotamians under discussion developed a variety of responses to cultural norms and ecological imperatives. These reactions were most often devised and implemented by the household decision-making unit, composed of at least one husband and wife and their children. In order to understand Early Bronze Age society, I explored several levels of analysis: the physical structure of the domestic unit, the people who comprised the household, family units (which may or may not reside in one household), and, clusters of households or neighborhood groupings. In these different levels of analysis I considered interactions between individuals and households. Just as community-level studies are necessarily built on the research of the building blocks (or individual houses), larger-scale political entities (such as government bureaucracies) cannot be understood without considering the communities that make up the larger system. For heuristic purposes I presented the analysis in a hierarchical fashion, from smallest unit of analysis (activity areas) to largest (cities and villages). This study exemplifies heterarchical frameworks as an approach to understanding how ancient people viewed and created order in their lives (see further Crumley 1995). This analysis, although it was conducted on a small scale, suggests that the state has little influence on daily socio-economic interactions within and between households. If so, there are considerable implications for our understanding of the functioning of Upper Mesopotamian states. In short, states do not control all aspects of socio-economic production. It is for this reason that we must study household activities as a field separate from state-level decision-making in order to understand fully ancient society.

Building Blocks for Understanding Upper Mesopotamian Society

Households cannot be understood in isolation as merely physical structures that contain families. Instead, we must analyze their societal context — in other words, the neighborhoods, cities, and villages in which they were situated and that they comprised. In this book, I examined several, nested, levels of analysis: activities within rooms, clusters of socio-economic activities within houses, types of houses within neighborhoods, and finally, the types of neighborhoods within urban and rural sites. Ideally, the sites would be contextualized within ancient Mesopotamia and its environs. Obviously, a comprehensive study of all Upper Mesopotamian sites is beyond the scope of this work. Still it is worth keeping in mind that sites were not closed systems. In addition to formal trading relations among sites, informal exchange of marriage partners, ideas, animals, and possibly household products (such as textiles, ceramics, and stone tools) no doubt occurred.

In order to gain a better understanding of the roles of households in Upper Mesopotamia, I investigated the form, variability, and distribution of structures and the activities performed within them. In Chapter 3, micro-debris signatures were identified for each sampled locus type. Combining micro-signatures and the patterning of features and architecture, activity areas were discerned within rooms. This, in turn, allowed me to recognize the diversity of activities that occurred within domestic and non-domestic rooms. Taken together, clusters of rooms were analyzed to determine the primary function of various structures. In Chapter 5, I compared the patterning of structures within two neighborhoods. And in Chapters 6 and 7, urban and rural settlements were investigated in order to better understand the former in Upper Mesopotamia.

The goal was not to create a typology of room functions or structure types, but rather to attach activities and structures to individuals and groups and to understand the social context in which daily activities occurred.

In conclusion, this study demonstrated how everyday domestic practices and activities can be identified and, in future research, integrated into our understanding of large-scale political and economic transformations. Household archaeology should not be treated as merely a "domestic inquiry." Rather, domestic economies must be included in any model of early urbanism. In turn, a more detailed study of domestic socio-economic activities will broaden our understanding of the emergence of Mesopotamian urbanism and the operation of the state.

APPENDIX A

List of Abbreviations Used in Appendices B - D

Column Heading		Explanation
No.		Sample number; assigned by the author, 1-370.
Area		Trench or area number.
Loc.		The type of locus (described and discussed in chapter 4).
	ndF, ndSF	Non-domestic floor and non-domestic supra-floor
	dF, dSF	Domestic-floor and domestic supra-floor
	extF	Exterior-floor
	St	Street
	Pit	Midden
	Hrth	Hearth
	DPS	Domestic preparation surface
	Mbk	Mudbrick
	Vess	Vessel
Liter		The number of liters of sediment collected and sampled.
c-cer		The count density of micro-ceramic remains within the sample.
c-bon		The count density of micro-faunal remains within the sample.
c-lit		The count density of micro-lithic remains within the sample.
w-cer		The weight density of micro-ceramic remains within the sample.
w-bon		The weight density of micro-faunal remains within the sample.
w-lit		The weight density of micro-lithic remains within the sample.
.		
fine		The count density of micro-fine-wares within the sample.
sand		The count density of micro-sandy-wares within the sample.
cook		The count density of micro-cooking-wares within the sample.
thin		The count density of micro-thin-wares within the sample.
med		The count density of micro-medium-wares within the sample.
thick		The count density of micro-thick-wares within the sample.
bbo		The count density of burnt bone within the sample.
rob		The count density of rodent bones within the sample.
tan		The count density of tan-colored chipped stone in the sample.
brown		The count density of brown-colored chipped stone in the sample.
gray		The count density of gray-colored chipped stone in the sample.
pink		The count density of pink-colored chipped stone in the sample.

Appendix B: Count densities from the Kazane Micro-Debris Samples

No.	Area	Locus	liter	.	c-cer	c-bon	c-lit	w-cer	w-bon	w-lit	.	fine	sand	cook	thin	med	thick	.	bbo	rob	.	tan	brown	gray	pink
1	C11	ndF	12	.	0.75	10.42	16.33	0.53	0.33	0.64	.	0.42	0.08	0.08	0.25	0.25	0.08	.	1.08	0.00	.	3.83	1.08	1.08	1.17
2	H15	dF	25	.	0.64	23.40	12.00	0.07	1.11	0.56	.	0.04	0.36	0.12	0.16	0.16	0.20	.	1.44	0.08	.	7.00	1.3	1.32	0.72
3	C11A	ndSF	6.5	.	0.00	7.54	5.23	0.00	1.00	0.06	.	0.00	0.00	0.00	0.00	0.00	0.00	.	1.23	0.15	.	2.15	0.9	0.92	0.15
4	C11A	Pit	6	.	0.67	18.83	8.50	0.72	0.57	0.58	.	0.00	0.67	0.00	0.33	0.33	0.00	.	2.00	0.00	.	3.83	1.2	1.17	1.00
5	D12	dSF	12	.	0.25	38.92	9.08	0.02	0.71	0.20	.	0.08	0.00	0.00	0.08	0.00	0.00	.	8.33	0.00	.	5.75	1	1.00	0.25
6	C11A	ndF	7.5	.	0.00	10.80	6.53	0.00	0.27	0.61	.	0.00	0.00	0.00	0.00	0.00	0.00	.	1.07	0.00	.	4.13	0.53	0.53	1.07
7	H15	dF	20	.	0.40	16.25	6.50	0.62	0.72	1.02	.	0.00	0.15	0.10	0.05	0.05	0.15	.	1.75	0.05	.	3.10	1.05	1.05	0.40
8	D12	Hrth	12.5	.	0.00	16.32	2.40	0.00	0.70	0.10	.	0.00	0.00	0.00	0.00	0.00	0.00	.	9.60	0.00	.	1.28	0.24	0.24	0.08
9	F14e	Hrth	35	.	1.00	8.40	4.00	0.81	0.67	0.71	.	0.17	0.66	0.03	0.54	0.23	0.09	.	0.86	0.29	.	1.66	0.29	0.29	0.46
10	F14b	Hrth	5	.	0.00	2.00	3.20	0.00	0.34	0.18	.	0.00	0.00	0.00	0.00	0.00	0.00	.	0.40	0.00	.	1.00	1.20	1.20	0.60
11	C11A	Hrth	3.5	.	0.00	15.43	3.14	0.00	0.71	0.03	.	0.00	0.00	0.00	0.00	0.00	0.00	.	5.71	0.00	.	1.14	1.14	1.14	0.57
12	C11A	ndSF	10	.	0.30	7.80	6.40	0.37	0.34	0.57	.	0.20	0.20	0.00	0.10	0.30	0.00	.	1.00	0.00	.	3.10	0.60	0.60	0.90
13	H15	dF	22	.	0.41	5.23	4.73	0.49	0.24	0.26	.	0.00	0.32	0.00	0.00	0.18	0.14	.	4.09	0.00	.	1.59	0.68	0.68	0.68
14	C11A	ndSF	10	.	0.00	9.70	3.20	0.00	0.30	0.19	.	0.00	0.00	0.00	0.00	0.00	0.00	.	1.80	0.00	.	0.70	0.80	0.80	1.00
15	C11A	ndF	20	.	0.60	12.05	4.05	0.26	0.72	0.32	.	0.15	0.45	0.00	0.55	0.05	0.00	.	1.75	0.00	.	2.10	0.50	0.50	0.30
16	C11A	ndF	4.5	.	0.22	16.22	13.11	0.40	0.53	0.69	.	0.00	0.22	0.00	0.00	0.22	0.00	.	2.67	0.22	.	8.00	1.11	1.11	0.67
17	C11A	ndF	6	.	0.50	26.83	12.67	0.02	0.87	0.90	.	0.17	0.33	0.00	0.17	0.33	0.00	.	3.50	0.00	.	7.50	0.67	0.67	0.67
18	C11A	ndF	23	.	1.48	7.43	18.83	0.99	0.28	0.81	.	0.43	0.70	0.00	1.09	0.04	0.00	.	1.74	0.00	.	11.74	1.74	1.74	2.17
19	E16	ndF	7.5	.	2.53	12.00	22.40	1.33	0.29	1.13	.	0.53	1.33	0.00	1.07	0.67	0.13	.	1.60	0.00	.	13.47	2.67	2.67	2.67
20	C11A	Hrth	10	.	0.00	20.00	14.10	0.00	0.61	0.87	.	0.00	0.00	0.00	0.00	0.00	0.00	.	2.00	0.00	.	9.80	1.10	1.10	1.20
21	C11A	ndF	4	.	2.25	100.00	16.00	0.60	2.58	0.25	.	0.50	1.75	0.00	1.75	0.50	0.00	.	3.25	0.00	.	12.25	1.00	1.00	0.75
22	C11A	ndSF	4	.	0.00	20.25	10.50	0.00	0.70	0.18	.	0.00	0.00	0.00	0.00	0.00	0.00	.	3.00	0.00	.	6.75	1.50	1.50	0.50
23	C11A	ndF	16	.	0.12	6.06	3.31	0.14	0.22	0.37	.	0.00	0.12	0.00	0.00	0.12	0.00	.	0.38	0.00	.	2.38	0.31	0.31	0.31
24	C11A	Hrth	6.5	.	0.62	13.69	8.00	0.51	0.63	0.57	.	0.15	0.46	0.00	0.00	0.46	0.15	.	2.31	0.00	.	4.62	0.77	0.77	0.46
25	C11A	Hrth	7.5	.	1.07	24.53	16.53	0.31	0.53	0.71	.	0.67	0.40	0.00	0.67	0.40	0.00	.	1.73	0.00	.	8.80	1.33	1.33	0.93
26	C11A	ndF	7.5	.	0.00	17.07	7.60	0.00	0.40	0.61	.	0.00	0.00	0.00	0.00	0.00	0.00	.	2.67	0.00	.	4.80	0.53	0.53	0.80
27	F14b	Hrth	5	.	0.20	3.80	5.00	0.01	0.22	0.36	.	0.00	0.20	0.00	0.20	0.00	0.00	.	0.80	0.00	.	2.60	0.40	0.40	0.40
28	C11A	Hrth	4	.	0.50	5.50	4.50	0.08	0.58	0.68	.	0.00	0.50	0.00	0.25	0.25	0.00	.	1.00	0.00	.	2.50	1.00	1.00	0.00
29	C11A	ndSF	2	.	0.00	24.50	5.50	0.00	1.45	0.03	.	0.00	0.00	0.00	0.00	0.00	0.00	.	8.00	0.00	.	2.50	0.50	0.50	1.00
30	F14a	dF	1	.	4.00	33.00	23.00	1.30	0.10	0.05	.	0.00	3.00	0.00	0.00	3.00	0.00	.	2.00	0.00	.	9.00	1.00	1.00	3.00
31	D17	dF	6	.	0.50	26.67	15.50	0.32	0.42	0.33	.	0.00	0.17	0.00	0.00	0.17	0.00	.	1.67	0.00	.	10.83	1.33	1.33	0.50
32	D16	Pit	6	.	0.33	33.33	6.33	0.17	1.62	0.05	.	0.17	0.17	0.00	0.17	0.17	0.00	.	3.00	0.00	.	4.00	0.83	0.83	0.50
33	D16	extF	9	.	0.67	19.33	4.67	0.02	1.57	0.19	.	0.33	0.22	0.00	0.56	0.00	0.00	.	4.44	0.00	.	4.00	0.44	0.44	0.22
34	D16	Pit	8	.	0.62	37.25	4.88	0.01	1.41	1.28	.	0.00	0.00	0.00	0.00	0.00	0.00	.	13.75	0.00	.	2.75	0.50	0.50	0.38
35	D16	extF	6	.	0.00	5.00	28.17	0.00	0.07	0.32	.	0.00	0.00	0.00	0.00	0.00	0.00	.	3.00	0.00	.	11.67	6.67	6.67	4.33
36	D17	dSF	5	.	0.00	33.00	24.00	0.00	1.20	0.46	.	0.00	0.00	0.00	0.00	0.00	0.00	.	3.80	0.00	.	11.40	1.60	1.60	1.60
37	D16	dSF	2	.	0.00	10.00	5.50	0.00	0.15	0.40	.	0.00	0.00	0.00	0.00	0.00	0.00	.	2.50	0.00	.	5.00	0.00	0.00	0.00
38	E16	ndF	2	.	1.50	17.50	11.50	0.05	0.35	0.25	.	0.50	1.00	0.00	1.50	0.00	0.00	.	2.50	0.00	.	6.00	2.50	2.50	0.50
39	D17	extF	5	.	0.00	16.60	10.60	0.00	0.30	0.28	.	0.00	0.00	0.00	0.00	0.00	0.00	.	1.60	0.00	.	8.00	0.00	0.00	0.60
40	F14a	dF	0.75	.	0.00	13.33	8.00	0.00	1.33	0.73	.	0.00	0.00	0.00	0.00	0.00	0.00	.	0.00	0.00	.	4.00	1.33	1.33	0.00

No.	Area	Locus	liter	.	c-cer	c-bon	c-lit	w-cer	w-bon	w-lit	.	fine	sand	cook	thin	med	thick	.	bbo	rob	.	tan	brown	gray	pink
41	F14c	dF	0.5	.	0.00	10.00	12.00	0.00	0.10	0.10	.	0.00	0.00	0.00	0.00	0.00	0.00	.	2.00	0.00	.	8.00	0.00	0.00	4.00
42	F14c	dF	0.75	.	4.00	20.00	21.33	0.67	0.93	0.47	.	0.00	2.67	0.00	0.00	2.67	0.00	.	0.00	0.00	.	13.33	1.33	1.33	0.00
43	C11A	Hrth	10	.	0.30	10.00	8.30	0.34	0.21	3.23	.	0.10	0.00	0.20	0.10	0.00	0.20	.	0.90	0.00	.	5.40	0.60	0.60	0.70
44	F14a	extSF	10	.	3.30	19.40	7.80	2.34	0.99	0.17	.	0.50	1.20	0.50	0.50	0.80	0.90	.	1.00	0.00	.	6.20	0.30	0.30	0.50
53	F14	extF	5	.	2.80	8.00	61.40	0.20	0.24	4.48	.	0.00	1.20	0.00	0.40	0.80	0.00	.	1.60	0.00	.	47.00	5.60	5.60	6.00
54	F14	dSF	5	.	0.80	20.00	3.20	1.90	2.20	0.08	.	0.20	0.60	0.00	0.00	0.40	0.40	.	3.00	0.00	.	1.60	0.40	0.40	0.20
55	D24	Vess	0.25	.	0.00	44.00	8.00	0.00	0.00	0.00	.	0.00	0.00	0.00	0.00	0.00	0.00	.	0.00	0.00	.	0.00	0.00	0.00	0.00
56	D24	Vess	0.5	.	0.00	26.00	10.00	0.00	0.00	0.00	.	0.00	0.00	0.00	0.00	0.00	0.00	.	0.00	0.00	.	0.00	0.00	0.00	0.00
360	C11A	Hrth	9	.	0.78	2.11	2.33	0.98	0.01	0.37	.	0.11	0.11	0.33	0.11	0.11	0.33	.	0.22	0.00	.	1.22	0.56	0.56	0.22
362	H15	extF	8	.	0.00	3.38	2.88	0.00	0.01	0.01	.	0.00	0.00	0.00	0.00	0.00	0.00	.	0.00	0.00	.	1.63	0.13	0.13	0.13
363	H15	dF	19	.	0.05	3.32	0.37	0.01	0.05	0.00	.	0.00	0.11	0.00	0.05	0.05	0.00	.	0.26	0.00	.	0.05	0.05	0.05	0.00

Appendix C: Count densities from the Tilbes Micro-Debris Samples

No.	Area	Locus	liter	c-cer	c-bon	c-lit	w-cer	w-bon	w-lit	fine	sand	cook	thin	med	thick	bbo	rob	tan	brown	gray	pink
68	A	extSF	3.25	4.00	3.38	9.54	1.32	0.03	0.40	0.00	4.00	0.00	0.00	3.69	0.31	0.62	0.31	2.46	0.62	0.62	0.92
69	A	extSF	3.75	0.00	3.47	12.00	0.00	0.05	0.13	0.00	0.00	0.00	0.00	0.00	0.00	0.00	0.00	1.87	2.13	2.13	4.27
70	A	St	13	1.15	0.69	1.54	1.31	0.11	0.22	0.00	1.08	0.08	0.54	0.23	0.38	0.31	0.00	0.54	0.23	0.23	0.38
71	A	dF	10.5	0.48	1.71	4.57	0.16	0.14	0.62	0.00	0.19	0.00	0.00	0.19	0.00	0.00	0.00	1.90	0.29	0.29	0.67
72	E	dSF	10	0.20	1.40	2.70	0.01	0.16	0.01	0.00	0.00	0.00	0.00	0.00	0.00	0.30	0.00	0.30	0.20	0.20	0.50
73	E	dSF	13	0.23	0.31	0.54	0.48	0.01	0.05	0.00	0.15	0.08	0.15	0.00	0.08	0.00	0.00	0.23	0.00	0.00	0.15
74	E	Hrth	5	2.80	5.80	5.20	0.80	0.14	0.14	0.00	2.20	0.60	0.60	1.60	0.60	1.80	0.00	0.60	0.20	0.20	2.60
75	E	extSF	0.5	0.00	6.00	0.00	0.00	0.00	0.00	0.00	0.00	0.00	0.00	0.00	0.00	0.00	0.00	0.00	0.00	0.00	0.00
76	A	St	4	2.00	3.25	9.25	2.08	0.13	0.08	0.00	2.00	0.00	0.50	1.25	0.25	0.25	0.00	2.75	0.50	0.50	2.50
77	E	Bur	4	1.50	5.75	6.50	1.10	0.13	0.13	0.00	1.50	0.00	0.50	0.75	0.25	0.00	0.00	1.75	0.25	0.25	2.00
78	E	Bur	2.5	4.40	6.00	16.80	2.32	0.08	0.48	0.00	3.60	0.00	1.60	1.60	0.40	0.00	0.00	1.20	4.00	4.00	2.80
79	E	Bur	6	0.33	64.33	2.00	0.43	1.98	0.05	0.00	0.17	0.00	0.00	0.00	0.17	0.00	0.00	0.33	0.33	0.33	0.17
80	E	Bur	3	1.33	32.00	4.33	1.17	0.80	0.07	0.00	1.33	0.00	0.67	0.33	0.33	0.00	0.67	1.67	0.33	0.33	1.00
81	E	dSF	3.5	0.57	1.14	8.29	1.09	0.23	0.26	0.00	0.57	0.00	0.00	0.00	0.57	0.29	0.00	0.86	0.00	0.00	1.14
82	E	Cntrl	3	0.00	1.33	1.67	0.00	0.00	0.03	0.00	0.00	0.00	0.00	0.00	0.00	0.33	0.00	0.00	0.00	0.00	0.00
83	E	extF	2.5	2.80	0.80	5.20	1.96	0.00	0.12	1.20	0.80	0.00	1.60	0.40	0.00	0.00	0.00	0.80	1.20	1.20	1.20
84	E	dSF	8	0.50	2.25	4.00	0.65	0.11	0.10	0.00	0.50	0.00	0.00	0.38	0.12	0.25	0.00	1.25	0.63	0.63	0.00
85	E	extF	6	1.50	15.33	4.83	2.25	0.23	0.13	0.00	1.50	0.00	0.00	1.17	0.33	0.00	0.17	0.67	0.83	0.83	0.83
86	E	extF	10	3.00	5.90	4.80	2.93	0.69	0.64	0.00	2.30	0.20	0.00	1.70	0.80	1.00	0.00	2.00	0.50	0.50	0.50
87	E	extF	10	0.60	1.00	4.20	1.42	0.07	0.32	0.10	0.40	0.00	0.00	0.10	0.40	0.10	0.00	1.30	0.60	0.60	0.90
88	E	Vess	5	0.40	0.60	1.00	0.46	0.00	0.08	0.00	0.40	0.00	0.00	0.20	0.20	0.00	0.00	0.40	0.00	0.00	0.40
89	E	Bur	5	0.20	0.00	2.60	0.14	0.00	0.06	0.00	0.20	0.00	0.00	0.20	0.00	0.00	0.00	0.20	0.20	0.20	0.40
90	E	Pit	8.5	0.71	2.71	3.65	1.20	0.04	0.11	0.00	0.59	0.12	0.00	0.12	0.59	0.00	0.00	0.82	0.94	0.94	0.47
91	E	Pit	11.5	0.43	1.04	3.30	0.21	0.09	0.30	0.00	0.17	0.00	0.17	0.00	0.00	0.00	0.00	1.74	0.00	0.00	0.35
92	E	Pit	5	2.20	1.80	7.20	1.82	0.04	0.40	0.00	1.40	0.00	0.00	0.60	0.80	0.00	0.00	2.80	0.00	0.00	2.60
93	E	Pit	5	0.80	1.40	3.60	1.24	0.06	0.12	0.00	0.60	0.20	0.20	0.00	0.60	0.00	0.20	0.80	0.80	0.80	0.40
94	E	Pit	3	0.33	0.00	7.33	0.50	0.00	0.30	0.00	0.33	0.00	0.00	0.00	0.33	0.00	0.00	3.33	0.67	0.67	1.33
96	E	extF	8	0.25	1.38	0.88	0.18	0.01	0.04	0.00	0.25	0.00	0.12	0.12	0.00	0.12	0.00	0.25	0.13	0.13	0.25
97	E	extF	10	0.30	3.60	2.50	0.20	0.02	0.14	0.00	0.30	0.00	0.00	0.20	0.10	0.00	0.00	0.60	0.80	0.80	0.10
98	E	Hrth	4.5	0.44	1.56	2.67	1.00	0.02	0.31	0.00	0.44	0.00	0.00	0.22	0.22	0.89	0.00	1.33	0.44	0.44	0.00

Appendix D: Count densities from the Titrish Micro-Debris Samples

No.	Area	Loc.	liter	c-cer	c-bon	c-lit	w-cer	w-bon	w-lit	fine	sand	cook	thin	med	thick	bbo	rob	tan	brwn	gray	pink
45	81/85	dSF	50	0.02	3.12	1.56	0.00	0.03	0.08	0.02	0.00	0.00	0.02	0.00	0.00	0.02	0.00	0.76	0.26	0.26	0.16
46	81/85	dSF	50	0.04	2.46	1.72	0.00	0.04	0.06	0.04	0.00	0.00	0.04	0.00	0.00	0.00	0.00	1.22	0.20	0.20	0.12
47	81/86	dSF	20	0.35	3.70	2.70	1.44	0.07	0.69	0.00	0.00	0.00	0.00	0.00	0.00	0.15	0.05	0.00	0.00	0.00	0.00
48	79/84	dSF	30	0.20	0.07	2.60	0.06	0.00	0.30	0.00	0.10	0.03	0.10	0.00	0.03	0.07	0.00	1.60	0.33	0.33	0.20
49	C-2	dF	3	0.67	0.33	6.67	0.03	0.00	0.10	0.00	0.67	0.00	0.33	0.33	0.00	0.00	0.00	3.33	0.00	0.00	0.67
50	C-2	St	3	0.33	2.67	18.33	0.50	0.00	0.73	0.00	0.33	0.00	0.00	0.33	0.00	0.00	0.00	14.67	1.67	1.67	0.67
51	C-2	St	3	2.33	4.33	7.67	1.50	0.07	1.17	0.00	2.33	0.00	2.00	0.33	0.00	0.00	0.00	4.33	0.67	0.67	0.33
52	C-1	dF	3	0.00	1.67	11.00	0.00	0.00	0.13	0.00	0.00	0.00	0.00	0.00	0.00	0.00	0.00	6.67	0.00	0.00	0.67
61	82/87	ndSF	0.8	0.00	0.00	16.25	0.00	0.00	0.50	0.00	0.00	0.00	0.00	0.00	0.00	0.00	0.00	6.25	3.75	3.75	2.50
62	82/87	ndSF	0.8	3.75	11.25	6.25	0.13	0.00	0.00	0.00	0.00	0.00	0.00	0.00	0.00	3.75	0.00	5.00	0.00	0.00	0.00
63	82/87	ndSF	0.8	0.00	5.00	5.00	0.00	0.00	0.13	0.00	0.00	0.00	0.00	0.00	0.00	0.00	0.00	2.50	0.00	0.00	0.00
64	82/87	ndSF	0.9	0.00	6.67	8.89	0.00	0.11	0.11	0.00	0.00	0.00	0.00	0.00	0.00	1.11	0.00	4.44	1.11	1.11	0.00
65	82/87	ndSF	0.8	1.25	15.00	1.25	0.25	0.25	0.00	0.00	1.25	0.00	1.25	0.00	0.00	11.25	0.00	0.00	0.00	0.00	0.00
66	82/87	ndSF	0.8	0.00	0.00	1.25	0.00	0.00	0.00	0.00	0.00	0.00	0.00	0.00	0.00	0.00	0.00	1.25	0.00	0.00	0.00
67	40/34	Hrth	2.1	2.38	7.14	12.38	1.43	0.57	0.24	0.00	1.43	0.00	0.48	0.48	0.48	1.90	0.00	6.19	0.00	0.00	0.95
99	82/86	dSF	50	0.22	2.88	2.66	0.20	0.03	0.07	0.06	0.14	0.02	0.18	0.02	0.02	0.10	0.10	1.56	0.16	0.16	0.04
100	34/13	dF	50	0.26	1.16	1.28	0.32	0.07	0.40	0.02	0.14	0.04	0.06	0.10	0.04	0.04	0.02	0.92	0.12	0.12	0.10
101	79/87	dF	7.5	0.93	1.07	2.00	0.53	0.04	0.11	0.67	0.00	0.00	0.40	0.27	0.00	0.00	0.00	1.07	0.13	0.13	0.00
102	34/11	dSF	50	0.38	2.30	3.84	0.07	0.23	1.07	0.08	0.30	0.00	0.38	0.00	0.00	0.00	0.04	2.96	0.30	0.30	0.04
103	81/86	dSF	50	0.16	2.98	2.98	0.01	0.43	0.79	0.06	0.10	0.00	0.16	0.00	0.00	0.02	0.04	2.10	0.30	0.30	0.10
104	C-5	Pit	5	0.00	0.80	132.00	0.00	0.02	21.70	0.00	0.00	0.00	0.00	0.00	0.00	0.00	0.00	122.60	2.60	2.60	0.00
105	C-5	Pit	5.5	0.36	3.82	8.91	1.46	0.62	1.00	0.18	0.18	0.00	0.00	0.36	0.00	0.18	0.00	5.27	1.09	1.09	0.55
106	C-5	extF	5	1.80	1.20	22.20	1.50	0.02	1.90	0.20	1.60	0.00	0.20	1.60	0.00	0.00	0.00	16.00	2.20	2.20	1.00
107	79/87	dF	6	0.83	2.50	5.33	0.45	0.03	0.70	0.00	0.83	0.00	0.67	0.17	0.00	0.33	0.00	3.17	0.33	0.33	0.00
108	79/87	dF	3	0.33	5.33	7.33	0.23	0.17	0.67	0.00	0.33	0.00	0.00	0.33	0.00	1.00	0.00	4.33	0.33	0.33	0.00
109	79/87	dF	5	0.00	0.20	0.60	0.00	0.00	0.02	0.00	0.00	0.00	0.00	0.00	0.00	0.00	0.00	0.20	0.00	0.00	0.00
110	80/87	dF	5	0.60	2.80	4.00	0.42	0.04	0.24	0.60	0.00	0.00	0.40	0.20	0.00	0.20	0.00	2.00	1.40	1.40	0.60
111	35/10	Pit	50	0.20	5.16	4.68	0.02	0.07	0.08	0.04	0.16	0.00	0.04	0.16	0.00	0.24	0.12	2.70	0.80	0.80	0.46
112	79/87	dF	6.5	1.85	3.08	3.38	1.68	0.17	0.74	0.62	1.23	0.00	0.46	1.23	0.15	0.00	0.00	1.23	0.92	0.92	0.00
113	79/87	dF	6	0.83	2.17	2.17	0.72	0.07	0.60	0.17	0.50	0.00	0.50	0.17	0.00	0.17	0.00	1.33	0.33	0.33	0.00
114	79/87	Pit	7	2.14	10.00	5.86	1.46	0.21	0.26	0.71	0.57	0.43	0.86	0.43	0.43	0.00	0.00	4.29	0.43	0.43	0.29
115	40/34	extF	10	0.60	2.00	8.40	0.09	0.15	0.33	0.30	0.30	0.00	0.40	0.20	0.00	0.00	0.00	5.10	0.70	0.70	0.80
116	79/87	dF	5.5	4.00	1.64	4.55	4.49	0.13	0.42	0.36	1.82	0.36	1.09	1.09	0.36	0.00	0.00	2.36	0.55	0.55	0.18
117	79/87	dF	6	0.17	2.33	2.83	0.95	0.05	0.18	0.00	0.00	0.17	0.00	0.00	0.17	0.00	0.00	1.67	0.83	0.83	0.00
118	33/12	dSF	20	0.35	3.15	4.00	0.47	0.14	0.30	0.10	0.15	0.00	0.15	0.05	0.05	0.10	0.05	0.00	0.60	0.60	0.20
119	79/87	Pit	0.3	0.00	16.67	33.33	0.00	0.00	0.33	0.00	0.00	0.00	0.00	0.00	0.00	0.00	0.00	20.00	3.33	3.33	0.00
120	79/87	Pit	7	0.71	5.57	9.00	1.10	0.11	0.54	0.00	0.71	0.00	0.43	0.00	0.29	0.29	0.14	6.86	0.57	0.57	0.71
121	79/87	Pit	1	1.00	2.00	5.00	0.00	0.00	0.60	1.00	0.00	0.00	1.00	0.00	0.00	0.00	0.00	2.00	0.00	0.00	0.00
122	79/87	Pit	0.1	0.00	20.00	0.00	0.00	0.00	0.00	0.00	0.00	0.00	0.00	0.00	0.00	0.00	0.00	0.00	0.00	0.00	0.00
123	40/34	Cntrl	1	0.00	0.00	0.00	0.00	0.00	0.00	0.00	0.00	0.00	0.00	0.00	0.00	0.00	0.00	0.00	0.00	0.00	0.00

No.	Area	Loc.	liter	c-cer	c-bon	c-lit	w-cer	w-bon	w-lit	fine	sand	cook	thin	med	thick	bbo	rob	tan	brwn	gray	pink
124	40/34	dSF	1	0.00	13.00	34.00	0.00	0.40	0.70	0.00	0.00	0.00	0.00	0.00	0.00	5.00	0.00	21.00	3.00	3.00	2.00
125	40/34	Mbk	2	0.00	1.00	3.00	0.00	0.00	0.05	0.00	0.00	0.00	0.00	0.00	0.00	0.00	0.00	2.00	0.00	0.00	0.00
126	40/34	Pit	26	1.08	1.12	6.65	0.85	0.05	0.99	0.04	0.42	0.19	0.27	0.15	0.23	0.08	0.00	2.58	0.19	0.19	0.35
127	40/34	extF	15	0.67	2.93	4.40	0.23	0.14	0.43	0.00	0.67	0.00	0.47	0.13	0.07	0.07	0.00	2.13	1.53	1.53	0.20
128	35/13	dSF	50	0.56	2.40	2.60	0.52	0.11	0.47	0.04	0.56	0.00	0.40	0.12	0.08	0.08	0.04	1.26	0.56	0.56	0.32
129	34/11	dSF	50	0.08	1.68	3.86	0.07	0.18	0.46	0.06	0.02	0.00	0.06	0.02	0.00	0.28	0.04	1.90	1.40	1.40	0.10
130	79/87	DPS	6	0.17	0.00	1.17	0.57	0.00	0.15	0.00	0.17	0.00	0.00	0.17	0.00	0.00	0.00	0.00	1.17	1.17	0.00
131	79/87	DPS	3	0.00	0.00	10.00	0.00	0.00	0.13	0.00	0.00	0.00	0.00	0.00	0.00	0.00	0.00	1.00	0.00	0.00	1.67
132	40/34	dF	75	0.51	1.93	2.80	0.59	0.07	0.69	0.00	0.00	0.00	0.00	0.00	0.00	0.00	0.00	1.69	0.37	0.37	0.11
133	80/87	dSF	6	0.67	5.33	5.17	0.27	0.07	0.62	0.17	0.50	0.00	0.33	0.33	0.00	0.67	0.00	2.33	1.50	1.50	0.00
134	40/34	dSF	60	0.12	1.08	1.88	0.02	0.04	0.25	0.07	0.02	0.00	0.03	0.05	0.00	0.03	0.00	1.07	0.33	0.33	0.08
135	40/34	dSF	20	0.45	2.70	3.00	0.30	0.09	0.33	0.15	0.30	0.00	0.15	0.25	0.05	0.10	0.00	1.75	0.85	0.85	0.05
136	40/34	dF	33	0.36	2.61	3.64	0.21	0.10	0.80	0.12	0.21	0.03	0.27	0.06	0.03	0.18	0.00	1.88	0.48	0.48	0.36
137	40/34	dF	40	0.45	2.73	3.27	0.16	0.12	0.40	0.05	0.23	0.10	0.05	0.20	0.12	0.12	0.00	1.55	0.50	0.50	0.65
138	40/34	dF	60	0.08	0.87	0.82	0.02	0.04	0.06	0.00	0.08	0.00	0.03	0.03	0.02	0.08	0.00	0.55	0.07	0.07	0.10
139	40/34	Hrth	25	0.84	5.16	2.28	0.57	0.33	0.79	0.00	0.44	0.32	0.16	0.04	0.56	0.92	0.00	1.48	0.16	0.16	0.08
140	40/34	dF	50	0.26	3.34	3.58	0.05	0.09	0.21	0.00	0.22	0.00	0.18	0.04	0.00	0.22	0.02	2.48	0.24	0.24	0.38
141	40/34	dF	4	0.50	3.50	9.00	0.23	0.05	0.68	0.00	0.50	0.00	0.50	0.00	0.00	0.25	0.00	4.75	0.75	0.75	1.50
142	40/34	dF	3	0.33	1.67	2.67	0.10	0.03	0.00	0.00	0.33	0.00	0.33	0.00	0.00	0.00	0.00	0.67	0.33	0.33	0.00
143	40/34	dF	50	0.34	1.82	2.74	0.04	0.05	0.17	0.10	0.24	0.00	0.24	0.10	0.00	0.20	0.08	1.20	0.36	0.36	0.30
144	40/34	extF	40	0.62	2.52	3.15	0.26	0.13	0.45	0.10	0.33	0.12	0.38	0.03	0.15	0.23	0.05	1.70	0.20	0.20	0.13
145	C-5	Pit	5	0.60	1.60	156.00	0.64	0.02	20.04	0.00	0.40	0.20	0.20	0.20	0.20	0.00	0.20	150.00	0.00	0.00	6.00
146	40/34	Hrth	50	0.78	5.82	2.52	1.15	0.41	0.53	0.00	0.62	0.16	0.32	0.20	0.26	0.60	0.00	1.24	0.16	0.16	0.30
147	80/87	dF	6	0.83	2.50	4.00	0.87	0.02	0.20	0.00	0.83	0.17	0.33	0.50	0.17	0.00	0.00	1.67	0.67	0.67	0.83
148	80/87	Mbk	0.1	0.00	0.00	0.00	0.00	0.00	0.00	0.00	0.00	0.00	0.00	0.00	0.00	0.00	0.00	0.00	0.00	0.00	0.00
150	79/87	dSF	6	0.50	1.67	2.50	1.22	0.13	1.57	0.17	0.17	0.17	0.33	0.00	0.17	0.00	0.00	1.33	0.50	0.50	0.00
151	82/87	Hrth	70	0.86	0.81	1.70	0.68	0.06	0.37	0.16	0.44	0.11	0.31	0.14	0.26	0.07	0.00	1.21	0.16	0.16	0.07
152	82/88	ndF	12	0.75	0.67	0.75	0.56	0.13	0.25	0.00	0.75	0.00	0.58	0.17	0.00	0.00	0.00	0.25	0.50	0.50	0.00
153	40/34	Hrth	50	0.12	0.50	1.26	0.14	0.09	0.24	0.00	0.12	0.00	0.06	0.04	0.02	0.12	0.00	0.56	0.06	0.06	0.10
154	82/87	ndSF	50	0.24	0.54	0.18	0.12	0.02	0.03	0.02	0.08	0.08	0.06	0.04	0.08	0.00	0.02	0.10	0.02	0.02	0.02
155	82/88	ndF	5	1.40	4.40	4.00	1.78	0.14	0.08	0.20	1.00	0.20	0.80	0.20	0.40	0.40	0.00	3.00	0.60	0.60	0.20
156	82/88	ndF	3	1.67	5.33	5.67	1.03	0.07	0.17	0.33	1.33	0.00	1.33	0.33	0.00	0.33	0.00	2.67	0.67	0.67	0.00
157	82/88	ndF	5	1.80	2.40	3.80	1.86	0.10	0.54	0.00	1.80	0.00	0.40	1.20	0.20	0.40	0.00	1.00	1.20	1.20	0.20
158	82/88	ndF	5	0.20	20.00	9.40	0.08	1.20	0.10	0.20	0.00	0.00	0.00	0.20	0.00	0.80	0.00	4.80	0.80	0.80	0.80
159	82/88	DPS	13	0.08	0.00	0.23	0.18	0.00	0.00	0.00	0.08	0.00	0.08	0.00	0.00	0.00	0.00	0.15	0.00	0.00	0.08
160	82/87	Bur	36	0.58	15.00	0.83	0.16	0.16	0.07	0.19	0.11	0.00	0.14	0.14	0.03	0.28	0.00	0.42	0.08	0.08	0.06
161	C-5	Pit	3	1.33	2.67	34.00	2.33	0.03	1.27	0.33	1.00	0.00	0.67	0.67	0.00	0.00	0.00	30.00	1.00	1.00	1.00
162	34/12	dSF	50	0.26	1.64	3.02	0.02	0.12	0.66	0.12	0.14	0.00	0.26	0.00	0.00	0.10	0.02	1.16	0.20	0.20	0.26
163	34/12	dSF	50	0.84	2.28	2.76	0.74	0.06	0.50	0.02	0.60	0.06	0.40	0.20	0.08	0.16	0.02	0.44	0.38	0.38	0.32
164	34/12	dSF	50	0.16	1.58	1.96	0.13	0.17	0.85	0.02	0.08	0.00	0.06	0.04	0.00	0.12	0.00	1.22	0.24	0.24	0.12
165	34/12	dSF	67	0.63	2.00	2.42	0.36	0.10	1.12	0.10	0.52	0.00	0.24	0.16	0.22	0.18	0.01	1.09	0.57	0.57	0.19

No.	Area	Loc.	liter	c-cer	c-bon	c-lit	w-cer	w-bon	w-lit	fine	sand	cook	thin	med	thick	bbo	rob	tan	brwn	gray	pink
166	82/88	ndSF	7	1.00	5.57	4.14	1.00	0.06	0.13	0.00	1.00	0.00	0.86	0.14	0.00	0.29	0.43	2.00	0.43	0.43	0.29
167	82/88	ndF	6	0.50	0.33	0.17	0.53	0.07	0.00	0.50	0.00	0.00	0.17	0.33	0.00	0.17	0.00	0.17	0.00	0.00	0.00
168	82/88	ndF	5.5	1.27	7.64	11.27	2.55	0.09	0.20	0.00	1.27	0.00	0.00	0.73	0.55	0.00	0.00	1.82	1.45	1.45	2.73
169	82/88	ndF	5.5	0.00	0.91	0.91	0.00	0.00	0.00	0.00	0.00	0.00	0.00	0.00	0.00	0.00	0.18	0.73	0.00	0.00	0.00
170	82/88	ndF	6	0.33	1.33	0.67	0.00	0.00	0.00	0.00	0.33	0.00	0.33	0.00	0.00	0.00	0.00	0.33	0.00	0.00	0.00
171	79/87	Pit	7.5	1.33	3.87	6.93	1.40	0.08	0.53	0.00	0.53	0.13	0.00	0.27	0.40	0.93	0.00	1.33	0.27	0.27	0.27
172	79/87	Pit	4	6.00	0.50	42.50	4.38	0.00	12.73	2.00	2.75	1.25	2.75	2.00	1.25	0.00	0.00	28.25	7.50	7.50	0.00
173	81/87	dSF	6	0.50	3.17	2.33	0.35	0.53	0.23	0.00	0.50	0.00	0.33	0.17	0.00	0.33	0.00	1.17	0.50	0.50	0.00
174	80/87	dSF	12	0.42	3.67	3.67	0.45	0.81	0.48	0.00	0.25	0.08	0.25	0.00	0.08	0.00	0.00	1.75	1.50	1.50	0.17
175	79/87	dSF	4.5	0.67	4.44	4.22	0.04	0.07	0.09	0.00	0.67	0.00	0.67	0.00	0.00	0.22	0.00	1.33	0.44	0.44	0.22
176	80/86	Mbk	50	0.20	1.68	1.82	0.29	0.19	0.51	0.00	0.18	0.02	0.12	0.04	0.04	0.08	0.18	1.06	0.28	0.28	0.20
177	82/87	ndSF	50	0.68	1.60	2.30	0.48	0.06	0.46	0.06	0.56	0.06	0.36	0.24	0.08	0.06	0.00	1.98	0.28	0.28	0.12
178	82/87	Hrth	50	0.82	0.64	1.58	0.72	0.03	0.42	0.10	0.58	0.14	0.24	0.30	0.28	0.06	0.00	0.86	0.32	0.32	0.10
179	82/87	ndSF	60	1.63	1.10	0.78	0.52	0.08	0.11	0.05	1.08	0.43	0.78	0.27	0.52	0.03	0.10	0.63	0.08	0.08	0.02
180	82/87	Vess	50	0.92	2.14	2.14	0.55	0.11	0.22	0.14	0.80	0.00	0.68	0.20	0.06	0.12	0.02	1.10	0.40	0.40	0.16
181	40/34	dSF	6	0.00	4.17	4.00	0.00	0.28	0.95	0.00	0.00	0.00	0.00	0.00	0.00	0.33	0.00	2.17	0.33	0.33	0.33
182	40/34	dF	6	0.17	2.00	3.17	0.02	0.08	0.13	0.00	0.17	0.00	0.00	0.17	0.00	0.17	0.00	1.50	0.33	0.33	0.50
183	40/34	Mbk	8	0.25	1.12	3.00	0.16	0.09	0.05	0.00	0.12	0.00	0.00	0.12	0.00	0.00	0.00	1.75	0.13	0.13	0.50
184	80/87	dSF	16	0.90	5.94	4.39	1.00	0.31	0.40	0.32	0.58	0.26	0.77	0.13	0.26	0.13	0.19	3.61	0.32	0.32	0.19
185	79/87	dF	5	0.40	4.00	2.40	0.78	0.04	0.02	0.40	0.00	0.00	0.20	0.20	0.00	0.00	0.00	1.20	0.00	0.00	0.00
186	79/87	dF	5	0.80	1.80	2.00	0.50	0.08	0.34	0.20	0.60	0.00	0.20	0.40	0.20	0.00	0.20	0.60	0.00	0.00	0.20
187	79/87	dF	5	0.20	2.40	2.80	0.00	0.02	0.08	0.00	0.00	0.00	0.00	0.00	0.00	0.00	0.00	1.80	0.00	0.00	0.00
188	79/87	dF	9	1.00	1.33	2.22	0.30	0.09	0.79	0.00	0.11	0.00	0.00	0.11	0.00	0.22	0.11	1.11	0.44	0.44	0.00
189	82/88	ndSF	6	0.00	3.00	3.17	0.00	0.02	0.38	0.00	0.00	0.00	0.00	0.00	0.00	0.00	0.00	1.67	0.50	0.50	0.17
191	80/87	dSF	7	0.00	2.57	3.86	0.00	0.03	0.84	0.00	0.00	0.00	0.00	0.00	0.00	0.14	0.14	2.29	1.14	1.14	0.43
192	80/87	dF	5	2.60	2.60	6.20	3.42	0.08	0.44	1.60	1.00	0.20	0.00	2.60	0.20	0.20	0.00	3.40	1.80	1.80	0.40
193	80/87	dF	5	1.00	0.80	8.20	0.66	0.02	0.82	0.00	0.80	0.00	0.00	0.80	0.00	0.20	0.00	3.40	2.60	2.60	1.00
194	80/87	dF	4	0.75	0.00	6.25	0.73	0.00	0.13	0.50	0.25	0.00	0.25	0.50	0.00	0.00	0.00	3.75	0.50	0.50	0.25
195	80/87	dF	4	0.25	0.75	1.00	0.23	0.03	0.03	0.00	0.00	0.00	0.00	0.00	0.00	0.00	0.00	0.00	0.00	0.00	0.25
196	80/87	dSF	6	1.33	3.33	6.00	2.00	0.07	0.13	0.67	0.33	0.17	0.50	0.50	0.17	0.00	0.17	4.33	0.17	0.17	0.00
197	80/87	dSF	6	0.83	2.00	4.50	0.80	0.02	0.23	0.50	0.83	0.00	0.33	1.00	0.00	0.00	0.17	1.83	0.50	0.50	0.17
198	80/87	Mbk	10	1.20	4.80	6.60	1.16	0.43	0.81	0.70	0.30	0.10	0.70	0.30	0.10	0.30	0.10	2.60	1.60	1.60	0.00
199	35/13	Vess	56	0.39	1.38	1.59	0.38	0.05	0.04	0.04	0.38	0.00	0.21	0.14	0.05	0.11	0.00	0.82	0.41	0.41	0.13
200	81/86	dF	50	0.14	26.00	1.40	0.10	0.61	0.06	0.06	0.06	0.02	0.06	0.06	0.02	0.18	0.00	0.78	0.16	0.16	0.06
201	81/86	dSF	50	0.04	0.46	1.76	0.00	0.01	0.10	0.02	0.02	0.00	0.04	0.00	0.00	0.04	0.00	0.82	0.36	0.36	0.12
202	34/13	dSF	50	0.26	1.94	2.18	0.02	0.04	0.12	0.08	0.18	0.00	0.26	0.00	0.00	0.12	0.04	1.26	0.46	0.46	0.14
203	81/86	dSF	40	0.17	5.88	1.00	0.01	0.21	0.05	0.03	0.15	0.00	0.15	0.03	0.00	0.00	0.00	0.33	0.18	0.18	0.13
204	79/84	Mbk	40	0.23	2.15	1.18	0.01	0.11	0.14	0.07	0.05	0.00	0.12	0.00	0.00	0.25	0.08	0.48	0.18	0.18	0.08
205	79/87	dSF	36	0.03	1.32	1.44	0.00	0.03	0.09	0.00	0.00	0.00	0.00	0.00	0.00	0.08	0.00	0.68	0.23	0.23	0.00
206	34/11	dSF	50	0.24	1.08	1.56	0.02	0.03	0.10	0.00	0.26	0.00	0.24	0.02	0.00	0.08	0.04	0.80	0.40	0.40	0.10
207	79/84	St	59	0.15	1.54	2.37	0.05	0.05	0.50	0.02	0.14	0.00	0.10	0.05	0.00	0.19	0.00	1.24	0.37	0.37	0.22

No.	Area	Loc.	liter .	c-cer	c-bon	c-lit	w-cer	w-bon	w-lit .	fine	sand	cook	thin	med	thick .	bbo	rob .	tan	brwn	gray	pink
208	80/84	dSF	50 .	0.08	0.72	0.88	0.01	0.02	0.07 .	0.02	0.06	0.00	0.06	0.02	0.00 .	0.04	0.00 .	0.50	0.22	0.22	0.00
209	80/87	dF	5 .	1.20	1.80	3.00	1.26	0.04	0.18 .	0.40	0.20	0.40	0.40	0.20	0.40 .	0.20	0.00 .	0.00	0.60	0.60	0.20
210	80/87	dF	5 .	2.40	0.80	3.00	2.66	0.06	0.06 .	1.80	0.60	0.00	1.60	0.80	0.00 .	0.00	0.00 .	2.20	0.00	0.00	0.00
211	80/87	dF	5 .	4.20	3.00	3.40	2.64	0.16	0.02 .	2.20	0.40	0.60	2.00	0.60	0.60 .	1.00	0.00 .	1.40	0.60	0.60	0.60
212	80/87	dF	5 .	0.40	3.40	2.20	0.26	0.04	0.56 .	0.40	0.00	0.00	0.40	0.00	0.00 .	0.60	0.60 .	1.40	0.00	0.00	0.00
213	C-5	dF	6 .	1.67	7.17	2.83	1.27	0.28	0.42 .	0.50	1.00	0.00	0.50	1.00	0.00 .	0.33	0.00 .	1.33	1.50	1.50	0.00
214	C-5	St	5 .	2.20	0.60	3.20	3.94	0.08	0.50 .	0.00	2.20	0.00	0.40	1.20	0.60 .	0.00	0.00 .	0.80	1.20	1.20	0.00
215	82/88	ndF	1 .	1.00	3.00	2.00	0.50	0.00	0.00 .	1.00	0.00	0.00	0.00	1.00	0.00 .	0.00	0.00 .	2.00	0.00	0.00	0.00
216	C-5	Bur	2.5 .	0.00	4.80	18.40	0.00	0.12	0.28 .	0.00	0.00	0.00	0.00	0.00	0.00 .	0.00	0.00 .	11.60	3.60	3.60	0.40
217	34/11	dSF	67 .	0.22	0.49	0.94	0.29	0.08	0.46 .	0.03	0.19	0.00	0.16	0.01	0.04 .	0.04	0.00 .	0.46	0.27	0.27	0.04
218	34/10	dSF	50 .	0.22	0.20	0.36	0.26	0.03	0.14 .	0.04	0.10	0.04	0.10	0.04	0.04 .	0.06	0.02 .	0.14	0.20	0.20	0.00
219	33/13	dSF	30 .	0.50	0.83	2.07	0.50	0.02	0.36 .	0.03	0.47	0.00	0.30	0.20	0.00 .	0.03	0.00 .	0.97	0.47	0.47	0.27
220	34/11	dSF	50 .	0.34	1.72	1.28	0.50	0.18	0.87 .	0.04	0.26	0.02	0.24	0.06	0.02 .	0.20	0.04 .	0.36	0.48	0.48	0.22
221	33/12	dSF	50 .	0.24	1.02	1.60	0.02	0.08	0.85 .	0.02	0.18	0.00	0.18	0.02	0.00 .	0.08	0.00 .	0.72	0.26	0.26	0.36
222	34/13	dF	50 .	0.22	0.56	0.94	0.02	0.01	0.04 .	0.00	0.22	0.00	0.22	0.00	0.00 .	0.02	0.00 .	0.52	0.16	0.16	0.06
223	80/84	Mbk	50 .	0.20	1.44	1.50	0.10	0.12	0.64 .	0.02	0.16	0.02	0.16	0.02	0.02 .	0.10	0.00 .	1.08	0.18	0.18	0.06
224	80/87	dSF	6 .	2.00	3.83	5.00	0.75	0.23	0.32 .	1.17	0.00	0.17	0.50	0.67	0.17 .	0.50	0.00 .	1.33	1.00	1.00	0.17
225	35/10	Pit	50 .	1.34	4.60	2.90	1.65	0.42	0.79 .	0.18	0.90	0.06	0.62	0.32	0.20 .	0.20	0.40 .	1.56	0.64	0.64	0.22
226	33/13	dSF	55 .	0.44	0.80	1.11	0.45	0.06	0.18 .	0.04	0.35	0.00	0.24	0.15	0.00 .	0.09	0.00 .	0.49	0.15	0.15	0.11
227	82/87	dSF	50 .	2.16	3.20	1.72	3.30	0.92	1.41 .	0.10	1.86	0.20	1.38	0.40	0.38 .	0.12	0.04 .	0.84	0.50	0.50	0.10
228	33/13	dSF	30 .	0.60	1.13	1.50	0.55	0.04	0.34 .	0.00	0.33	0.10	0.20	0.07	0.17 .	0.10	0.03 .	0.77	0.13	0.13	0.13
229	80/87	dSF	10 .	0.60	3.20	1.70	0.52	0.12	0.10 .	0.30	0.00	0.20	0.30	0.00	0.20 .	0.00	0.20 .	0.80	0.40	0.40	0.00
230	80/87	dF	5.5 .	1.64	7.64	2.91	2.29	0.42	0.24 .	0.36	0.55	0.00	0.55	0.36	0.00 .	0.91	0.00 .	1.64	0.18	0.18	0.36
232	80/87	dF	5 .	1.20	5.20	3.80	1.00	0.02	0.10 .	0.20	0.40	0.40	0.20	0.40	0.40 .	0.00	0.00 .	1.40	0.80	0.80	0.20
233	36/12	dSF	50 .	0.20	1.14	1.90	0.02	0.03	0.12 .	0.00	0.20	0.00	0.20	0.00	0.00 .	0.14	0.06 .	1.00	0.36	0.36	0.04
234	35/10	dSF	50 .	0.98	2.20	2.80	1.13	0.24	1.12 .	0.00	0.16	0.18	0.00	0.08	0.26 .	0.12	0.04 .	1.20	0.78	0.78	0.34
235	33/13	dSF	50 .	0.24	1.12	0.72	0.46	0.08	0.35 .	0.02	0.16	0.06	0.12	0.04	0.08 .	0.06	0.04 .	0.36	0.20	0.20	0.04
236	35/18	Bur	30 .	0.73	2.77	0.77	0.39	0.10	0.11 .	0.07	0.50	0.07	0.37	0.13	0.13 .	0.10	0.10 .	0.33	0.20	0.20	0.03
237	33/13	dSF	60 .	0.50	1.38	1.80	0.49	0.10	0.44 .	0.07	0.40	0.03	0.33	0.08	0.08 .	0.18	0.03 .	0.47	0.65	0.65	0.13
238	33/13	St	40 .	0.42	2.23	1.55	0.03	0.09	0.11 .	0.07	0.35	0.00	0.42	0.00	0.00 .	0.17	0.00 .	0.83	0.28	0.28	0.23
239	C-5	dSF	5 .	0.40	10.00	5.20	0.58	0.96	1.72 .	0.00	0.40	0.00	0.00	0.40	0.00 .	0.40	0.00 .	1.80	2.20	2.20	0.20
240	C-5	dSF	4.5 .	1.11	0.44	10.89	1.38	0.00	0.64 .	0.22	0.89	0.00	0.67	0.22	0.22 .	0.00	0.00 .	5.33	0.67	0.67	2.22
241	80/87	dF	6.5 .	1.08	1.08	3.85	0.88	0.17	0.49 .	0.77	0.15	0.15	0.62	0.31	0.15 .	0.00	0.00 .	2.92	0.00	0.00	0.00
242	80/87	dF	7 .	1.00	1.00	3.00	0.79	0.01	0.10 .	0.43	0.29	0.29	0.29	0.43	0.29 .	0.00	0.00 .	1.71	0.71	0.71	0.00
243	80/87	dF	6 .	0.83	1.67	2.50	0.55	0.02	0.07 .	0.83	0.50	0.17	0.17	1.17	0.17 .	0.17	0.00 .	1.00	0.17	0.17	0.50
244	81/87	dSF	5.5 .	1.64	2.73	3.64	1.71	0.42	0.60 .	0.00	1.64	0.00	0.55	0.73	0.36 .	0.55	0.00 .	2.18	0.36	0.36	0.00
245	35/13	Vess	25 .	0.16	1.60	1.92	0.02	0.04	0.11 .	0.00	0.12	0.00	0.12	0.00	0.00 .	0.08	0.00 .	0.76	0.40	0.40	0.12
246	80/87	Pit	7 .	1.00	2.71	4.14	0.54	0.06	0.21 .	0.71	0.14	0.00	0.57	0.29	0.00 .	0.00	0.00 .	1.14	1.00	1.00	0.43
247	80/87	dF	4.5 .	0.67	2.67	6.67	0.38	0.13	0.18 .	0.00	0.44	0.00	0.44	0.00	0.00 .	0.22	0.00 .	3.78	0.00	0.00	1.33
248	C-5	extF	3 .	0.00	4.33	23.67	0.00	0.03	2.47 .	0.00	0.00	0.00	0.00	0.00	0.00 .	0.00	0.00 .	17.33	3.33	3.33	0.67
249	81/87	St	5 .	1.80	6.40	6.20	1.50	0.06	0.90 .	0.40	1.40	0.00	0.80	0.80	0.20 .	0.40	0.00 .	3.20	0.60	0.60	0.60

No.	Area	Loc.	liter	.	c-cer	c-bon	c-lit	w-cer	w-bon	w-lit	.	fine	sand	cook	thin	med	thick	.	bbo	rob	.	tan	brwn	gray	pink
250	79/87	dF	5.5	.	1.64	3.82	7.82	1.95	0.18	0.07	.	0.18	0.73	0.55	0.55	0.36	0.55	.	0.00	0.00	.	6.00	0.00	0.00	0.36
251	79/87	dF	4	.	1.75	6.25	6.50	2.55	0.05	0.18	.	0.50	0.00	1.00	0.50	0.00	1.00	.	0.25	0.00	.	5.25	0.25	0.25	0.00
252	79/87	dF	5	.	1.40	2.40	5.40	1.38	0.04	0.12	.	0.00	1.20	0.20	0.00	1.00	0.40	.	0.20	0.00	.	3.80	0.40	0.40	0.40
253	79/87	Pit	6	.	6.17	9.33	6.50	9.28	0.58	0.52	.	2.33	5.00	0.50	4.83	2.00	1.00	.	0.17	0.33	.	4.00	1.00	1.00	0.50
254	80/87	Bur	5.5	.	0.73	3.27	2.18	0.24	0.06	0.05	.	0.55	0.00	0.00	0.00	0.55	0.00	.	0.00	0.00	.	1.82	0.00	0.00	0.00
255	79/87	dF	4	.	0.50	1.25	5.00	0.85	0.03	0.90	.	0.25	0.25	0.00	0.25	0.25	0.00	.	0.25	0.00	.	1.25	0.75	0.75	0.25
256	81/87	dF	6	.	1.33	1.00	5.67	1.18	0.05	0.60	.	0.00	0.83	0.00	0.17	0.33	0.33	.	0.00	0.00	.	3.50	0.50	0.50	0.50
257	34/11	dF	65	.	0.11	0.54	0.75	0.01	0.02	0.07	.	0.00	0.05	0.00	0.05	0.00	0.00	.	0.06	0.00	.	0.28	0.18	0.18	0.08
258	79/87	dSF	2.5	.	0.00	4.40	8.00	0.00	0.04	0.12	.	0.00	0.00	0.00	0.00	0.00	0.00	.	0.40	0.00	.	4.40	0.40	0.40	0.00
259	C-5	Pit	6	.	0.00	5.33	6.33	0.00	0.02	0.43	.	0.00	0.00	0.00	0.00	0.00	0.00	.	0.00	0.33	.	2.67	1.83	1.83	0.33
260	C-5	dF	4	.	0.00	1.50	6.75	0.00	0.03	0.53	.	0.00	0.00	0.00	0.00	0.00	0.00	.	0.00	0.00	.	5.00	0.75	0.75	0.00
261	C-5	dF	4.5	.	0.22	2.67	4.89	0.04	0.11	0.71	.	0.22	0.00	0.00	0.22	0.00	0.00	.	0.00	0.22	.	1.56	2.00	2.00	0.22
262	34/16	dSF	35	.	2.49	6.23	6.51	0.94	0.30	0.61	.	0.37	0.46	0.06	0.37	0.40	0.11	.	0.06	0.00	.	4.06	0.80	0.80	0.54
263	36/12	St	10	.	0.90	4.50	3.30	0.08	0.17	0.19	.	0.10	0.40	0.00	0.40	0.10	0.00	.	0.30	0.00	.	2.00	0.30	0.30	0.40
264	35/13	Vess	25	.	1.00	1.36	1.64	0.92	0.14	0.40	.	0.12	0.40	0.00	0.08	0.36	0.08	.	0.16	0.00	.	0.96	0.24	0.24	0.12
265	34/12	St	50	.	0.16	0.40	0.70	0.05	0.01	0.09	.	0.00	0.02	0.02	0.00	0.02	0.02	.	0.00	0.00	.	0.40	0.10	0.10	0.06
266	34/11	dSF	15	.	1.60	0.67	1.27	1.97	0.03	0.55	.	0.00	1.27	0.33	0.20	0.93	0.47	.	0.13	0.00	.	0.67	0.27	0.27	0.00
267	34/12	dSF	10	.	0.50	0.80	1.90	0.04	0.02	0.51	.	0.00	0.40	0.10	0.40	0.00	0.10	.	0.00	0.00	.	1.10	0.20	0.20	0.10
268	79/87	dF	4.5	.	0.67	0.67	1.56	0.69	0.00	0.04	.	0.67	0.00	0.00	0.00	0.67	0.00	.	0.00	0.00	.	0.22	0.22	0.22	0.00
269	79/87	dF	5	.	1.20	2.60	3.40	1.18	0.10	0.14	.	0.00	1.00	0.20	0.80	0.20	0.20	.	0.00	0.00	.	1.80	0.60	0.60	0.20
270	34/11	dF	50	.	0.20	0.46	0.96	0.06	0.02	0.09	.	0.02	0.12	0.00	0.10	0.04	0.00	.	0.02	0.00	.	0.26	0.56	0.56	0.06
271	35/13	dSF	50	.	0.08	0.30	0.42	0.01	0.01	0.02	.	0.02	0.06	0.00	0.08	0.00	0.00	.	0.02	0.00	.	0.20	0.12	0.12	0.02
272	35/12	St	45	.	0.42	2.04	1.93	0.02	0.07	0.12	.	0.07	0.29	0.00	0.31	0.04	0.00	.	0.04	0.09	.	1.09	0.31	0.31	0.20
273	35/12	dSF	30	.	0.30	0.90	0.87	0.56	0.04	0.40	.	0.00	0.30	0.03	0.17	0.07	0.10	.	0.13	0.00	.	0.30	0.27	0.27	0.10
274	35/12	dSF	30	.	0.70	1.17	2.90	1.36	0.17	1.32	.	0.00	0.63	0.00	0.37	0.23	0.03	.	0.03	0.00	.	1.43	0.93	0.93	0.30
275	35/12	dSF	40	.	0.28	0.85	1.45	0.00	0.08	0.32	.	0.07	0.12	0.00	0.17	0.03	0.00	.	0.05	0.00	.	0.98	0.28	0.28	0.05
276	81/87	dSF	6	.	0.67	3.67	2.33	0.48	0.12	0.75	.	0.17	0.50	0.00	0.50	0.17	0.00	.	0.17	0.00	.	1.17	0.33	0.33	0.00
277	81/87	St	6	.	2.00	2.00	2.33	1.12	0.07	0.98	.	0.50	1.33	0.00	1.00	0.50	0.33	.	0.17	0.00	.	1.33	0.33	0.33	0.17
278	80/87	Pit	10	.	1.00	1.50	1.50	0.64	0.04	0.12	.	0.60	0.00	0.40	0.50	0.10	0.40	.	0.30	0.00	.	0.20	0.30	0.30	0.00
279	80/87	Mbk	5	.	1.20	2.40	8.00	0.82	0.30	0.32	.	0.60	0.20	0.40	0.60	0.20	0.40	.	0.00	0.00	.	5.20	1.40	1.40	0.00
280	80/87	dF	6	.	1.00	1.33	7.33	0.75	0.08	0.58	.	0.83	0.00	0.17	0.83	0.00	0.17	.	0.00	0.00	.	4.17	1.00	1.00	0.00
281	80/87	dF	6	.	0.50	5.83	6.67	0.22	0.28	0.20	.	0.17	0.00	0.17	0.17	0.00	0.17	.	0.33	0.17	.	4.83	1.33	1.33	0.00
282	80/87	dF	6	.	3.67	4.00	6.17	1.88	0.20	0.82	.	2.83	0.17	0.00	0.67	2.33	0.00	.	0.17	0.00	.	4.00	0.67	0.67	0.50
283	80/87	dF	5	.	1.60	2.00	7.60	1.02	0.02	1.02	.	1.00	0.00	0.20	0.40	0.60	0.20	.	0.20	0.00	.	4.20	0.80	0.80	0.20
284	80/87	dF	5	.	0.80	3.80	9.20	0.64	0.10	0.56	.	0.60	0.00	0.20	0.40	0.20	0.20	.	0.00	0.00	.	7.60	0.60	0.60	0.00
285	80/87	dF	5.5	.	1.27	3.09	7.27	0.42	0.07	0.51	.	1.09	0.00	0.00	0.73	0.36	0.00	.	0.00	0.00	.	3.64	1.45	1.45	0.73
286	80/87	dF	5	.	2.20	5.40	4.80	1.86	0.52	0.32	.	0.60	1.60	0.00	0.60	1.60	0.00	.	0.00	0.00	.	2.40	1.00	1.00	0.00
287	80/87	dF	5	.	1.20	21.80	8.00	0.92	1.18	0.20	.	0.60	0.20	0.20	0.60	0.20	0.20	.	0.00	0.00	.	4.60	1.40	1.40	0.00
288	80/88	dSF	6	.	1.00	1.50	2.33	1.05	0.13	0.08	.	0.00	1.00	0.00	0.50	0.50	0.00	.	0.17	0.17	.	1.00	0.50	0.50	0.00
289	80/88	dSF	6	.	1.50	2.00	5.17	1.18	0.07	0.22	.	0.50	0.50	0.17	0.00	1.00	0.17	.	0.00	0.00	.	1.83	1.17	1.17	0.17
290	79/87	Pit	50	.	0.68	0.76	1.02	0.97	0.05	0.30	.	0.12	0.48	0.06	0.34	0.26	0.06	.	0.16	0.00	.	0.72	0.12	0.12	0.02

No.	Area	Loc.	liter	c-cer	c-bon	c-lit	w-cer	w-bon	w-lit	fine	sand	cook	thin	med	thick	bbo	rob	tan	brwn	gray	pink
291	80/87	Bur	4	0.75	1.75	2.75	0.23	0.15	0.18	0.50	0.00	0.00	0.50	0.00	0.00	0.25	0.00	1.50	0.50	0.50	0.00
292	81/87	dSF	6	0.50	1.17	1.33	0.30	0.00	0.17	0.17	0.33	0.00	0.33	0.00	0.17	0.17	0.00	0.50	0.67	0.67	0.17
293	81/87	dSF	7	1.29	0.86	5.71	1.29	0.01	0.91	0.00	1.14	0.00	0.29	0.57	0.29	0.00	0.14	2.57	0.43	0.43	0.29
294	C-5	extF	4.5	0.89	1.11	22.67	1.02	0.00	1.18	0.00	0.89	0.00	0.22	0.44	0.22	0.22	0.00	17.78	1.56	1.56	1.11
295	C-5	St	6	2.33	4.50	15.50	27.02	0.78	8.25	6.33	16.67	1.00	10.17	9.83	4.00	0.00	0.00	12.00	2.50	2.50	0.17
296	C-5	St	6	23.50	2.83	23.83	32.02	1.28	11.27	6.17	17.33	0.00	11.00	10.17	2.33	0.00	0.00	16.33	3.83	3.83	0.00
297	C-5	St	5	29.80	4.20	40.00	36.36	0.90	7.14	5.20	24.00	2.60	11.60	13.80	6.40	0.00	0.00	31.60	2.60	2.60	0.60
298	C-5	extF	6	2.33	0.33	4.50	2.68	0.02	0.77	0.67	0.67	1.00	0.67	0.50	1.17	0.00	0.00	3.17	1.17	1.17	0.00
299	C-5	St	4	4.00	0.00	8.75	6.88	0.00	1.03	0.50	2.75	0.75	1.50	1.00	1.50	0.00	0.00	5.75	1.25	1.25	1.25
300	80/88	dSF	6	0.67	1.83	1.67	0.82	0.13	0.22	0.17	0.17	0.33	0.17	0.17	0.33	0.00	0.00	0.33	0.83	0.83	0.00
301	80/88	Hrth	5	0.80	1.40	2.20	0.72	0.20	0.10	0.20	0.60	0.00	0.00	0.80	0.00	0.00	0.00	0.40	1.00	1.00	0.20
302	80/88	DPS	4	1.50	3.50	5.25	2.90	0.10	1.73	0.50	0.50	0.25	0.75	0.25	0.25	0.00	0.00	1.50	0.00	0.00	0.25
303	80/87	dSF	10	1.40	3.80	4.70	1.33	0.09	0.92	0.40	0.70	0.20	0.50	0.60	0.20	0.20	0.10	2.80	0.60	0.60	0.20
304	80/87	dSF	5	0.40	1.20	3.40	0.48	0.06	0.46	0.20	0.00	0.20	0.00	0.20	0.20	0.00	0.00	1.80	0.60	0.60	0.00
305	79/87	dF	4	1.00	4.00	1.25	0.80	0.33	0.15	0.00	0.75	0.25	0.50	0.25	0.25	0.00	0.50	1.00	0.00	0.00	0.00
306	79/87	dF	6	0.00	0.33	0.83	0.00	0.00	0.07	0.00	0.00	0.00	0.00	0.00	0.00	0.17	0.00	0.17	0.00	0.00	0.00
307	79/87	dF	6	0.00	0.67	1.17	0.00	0.00	0.22	0.00	0.00	0.00	0.00	0.00	0.00	0.00	0.00	0.67	0.17	0.17	0.17
308	79/87	dF	4.5	0.22	0.00	0.89	0.42	0.00	0.16	0.22	0.00	0.00	0.00	0.22	0.00	0.00	0.00	0.22	0.00	0.00	0.22
309	80/88	dSF	7	2.14	4.57	2.29	2.11	0.04	0.20	0.43	1.71	0.00	0.57	1.29	0.29	0.14	0.29	0.57	0.43	0.43	0.29
310	79/87	Pit	50	1.76	2.90	1.10	2.41	0.53	0.43	0.20	1.40	0.16	0.88	0.72	0.16	0.00	0.00	0.72	0.12	0.12	0.04
311	82/87	ndSF	50	0.80	0.78	0.82	0.76	0.04	0.43	0.02	0.68	0.02	0.44	0.16	0.12	0.04	0.02	0.54	0.06	0.06	0.02
312	79/87	dSF	50	0.16	0.54	1.00	0.02	0.01	0.05	0.04	0.06	0.00	0.04	0.06	0.00	0.08	0.00	0.78	0.06	0.06	0.06
313	35/10	dSF	50	0.06	1.56	1.16	0.01	0.04	0.07	0.00	0.02	0.00	0.02	0.00	0.00	0.12	0.08	0.46	0.10	0.10	0.32
314	36/12	dSF	15	1.13	9.87	7.93	0.14	0.43	0.55	0.27	0.40	0.07	0.53	0.13	0.07	0.20	0.00	4.53	1.40	1.40	0.67
315	35/13	dSF	30	0.63	1.43	1.63	0.89	0.08	0.31	0.03	0.53	0.03	0.33	0.17	0.10	0.03	0.07	1.03	0.13	0.13	0.13
316	C-5	Pit	3	0.00	8.33	17.00	0.00	0.00	0.27	0.00	0.00	0.00	0.00	0.00	0.00	0.00	0.00	10.67	2.00	2.00	2.00
317	80/87	dF	5.5	2.36	5.45	0.36	1.64	0.11	0.82	0.73	0.73	0.00	0.73	0.73	0.00	0.00	0.55	0.18	0.18	0.18	0.00
318	80/87	dF	4	2.25	5.00	2.25	2.15	0.23	0.10	0.50	1.75	0.00	1.00	1.25	0.00	0.25	0.00	0.75	0.50	0.50	0.00
319	80/87	dF	6	1.50	2.67	2.33	0.27	0.07	0.08	0.33	0.33	0.33	0.33	0.33	0.33	0.00	0.33	2.00	0.00	0.00	0.00
320	80/87	DPS	4	1.50	0.00	2.75	2.55	0.00	0.78	1.00	0.00	3.50	1.00	0.00	3.50	0.00	0.00	0.50	1.00	1.00	0.00
321	80/87	dF	4.5	0.44	3.11	4.22	0.38	0.27	0.04	0.00	0.44	0.00	0.44	0.00	0.00	0.00	0.00	2.67	0.89	0.89	0.00
322	80/87	dF	5	0.40	9.40	2.80	0.28	0.04	0.04	0.00	0.00	0.40	0.00	0.00	0.40	0.00	0.40	1.80	0.00	0.00	0.00
323	80/87	dF	4.5	0.44	2.22	1.33	1.47	0.13	0.02	0.00	0.00	0.44	0.00	0.00	0.44	0.00	0.22	0.22	0.00	0.00	0.44
324	80/87	dSF	6	1.17	1.00	2.17	0.58	0.02	0.07	0.17	0.83	0.17	0.50	0.50	0.17	0.00	0.00	1.67	0.33	0.33	0.00
325	80/87	dF	4.5	1.33	1.33	4.00	1.09	0.02	0.47	0.44	0.89	0.00	0.67	0.67	0.00	0.22	0.00	1.11	0.67	0.67	0.22
326	80/87	dF	5	1.20	1.00	2.80	0.60	0.02	0.02	0.40	0.40	0.40	0.80	0.00	0.40	0.20	0.00	1.80	0.00	0.00	0.20
327	80/87	dF	5.5	0.55	2.00	1.64	0.24	0.02	0.09	0.55	0.00	0.00	0.36	0.18	0.00	0.00	0.00	0.73	0.55	0.55	0.00
328	80/87	Hrth	5	1.20	4.80	4.20	0.50	0.04	1.18	0.60	0.00	0.00	0.60	0.00	0.00	0.20	0.00	1.80	0.80	0.80	0.00
329	80/88	St	4	28.00	4.75	10.25	25.48	0.23	2.68	4.25	18.75	3.75	8.25	14.00	4.50	0.00	0.00	3.00	4.00	4.00	0.50
330	80/88	St	3.5	15.14	9.43	5.71	21.94	0.94	1.03	4.86	8.57	1.71	6.86	5.71	2.57	0.00	0.57	3.14	0.86	0.86	0.00
331	80/88	dF	4	1.50	1.25	2.25	1.83	0.03	0.45	0.25	0.50	0.00	0.50	0.00	0.25	0.00	0.00	1.00	0.00	0.00	0.25

No.	Area	Loc.	liter	c-cer	c-bon	c-lit	w-cer	w-bon	w-lit	fine	sand	cook	thin	med	thick	bbo	rob	tan	brwn	gray	pink
332	80/88	dF	4	0.00	0.75	2.00	0.00	0.00	0.08	0.00	0.00	0.00	0.00	0.00	0.00	0.00	0.00	0.50	0.00	0.00	0.25
333	80/88	dSF	4	1.25	2.75	3.00	0.98	0.03	0.43	0.00	0.50	0.75	0.50	0.00	0.75	0.00	0.00	0.25	0.25	0.25	0.50
334	80/88	dF	5	1.00	5.60	2.80	0.78	0.02	0.32	0.60	0.00	0.40	0.60	0.00	0.40	0.00	0.00	0.60	0.20	0.20	0.20
335	80/88	dF	5	1.60	3.80	2.60	2.02	0.22	0.10	0.60	1.00	0.00	0.60	1.00	0.00	0.20	0.00	0.80	0.40	0.40	0.40
336	80/88	dF	3	7.00	4.00	5.00	7.13	0.07	0.27	4.00	3.00	0.00	3.00	4.00	0.00	0.00	0.00	1.33	1.33	1.33	0.00
337	80/88	dF	5	1.60	4.80	3.00	1.46	0.10	0.52	0.00	1.40	0.20	1.00	0.00	0.60	0.00	0.00	0.80	0.60	0.60	0.00
338	80/88	dF	3.5	0.00	0.00	0.00	0.00	0.00	0.00	0.00	0.00	0.00	0.00	0.00	0.00	0.00	0.00	0.00	0.00	0.00	0.00
339	81/87	St	3	0.67	2.33	2.00	0.20	0.10	1.63	0.00	0.67	0.00	0.33	0.33	0.00	0.33	0.00	0.33	0.33	0.33	0.00
340	81/87	dSF	6	0.17	2.00	2.83	0.33	0.03	0.05	0.00	0.17	0.00	0.00	0.17	0.00	0.00	0.33	1.83	0.33	0.33	0.00
341	81/87	dSF	6	0.33	2.50	4.00	0.45	0.02	0.67	0.00	0.33	0.00	0.00	0.00	0.33	0.00	0.00	2.67	0.67	0.67	0.17
342	81/87	dF	4.5	0.00	1.11	2.22	0.00	0.00	0.16	0.00	0.00	0.00	0.00	0.00	0.00	0.22	0.00	1.11	0.44	0.44	0.00
343	81/87	dF	5	0.80	5.60	2.00	0.28	0.04	0.16	0.40	0.40	0.00	0.60	0.20	0.00	0.60	0.00	1.40	0.00	0.00	1.00
344	81/87	dF	5	0.80	1.80	2.20	0.80	0.06	0.32	0.00	0.20	0.60	0.00	0.20	0.60	0.00	0.00	1.20	0.60	0.60	0.00
345	81/87	dF	2.5	2.80	0.40	4.40	1.76	0.08	1.16	0.80	0.80	1.20	0.40	1.20	1.20	0.00	0.00	2.40	1.20	1.20	0.00
346	81/87	St	3.5	1.71	2.00	4.29	1.54	0.14	0.40	0.00	0.86	0.86	0.29	0.57	0.86	0.00	0.29	2.57	0.57	0.57	0.00
347	81/87	St	4	0.75	2.50	6.75	0.33	0.03	0.23	0.50	0.00	0.00	0.50	0.00	0.00	0.00	0.00	2.50	1.25	1.25	0.00
348	81/87	St	4	11.75	4.00	7.25	14.85	0.40	3.65	1.50	10.25	0.00	4.00	5.75	2.00	0.50	0.00	3.50	2.00	2.00	0.75
349	81/87	DPS	4	8.00	0.00	2.00	12.45	0.00	1.33	0.75	7.25	0.00	1.25	4.75	2.00	0.00	0.00	1.00	0.50	0.50	0.25
350	81/87	dF	3.5	1.14	0.00	3.43	0.60	0.00	1.97	0.00	0.86	0.29	0.57	0.29	0.29	0.00	0.00	1.71	0.57	0.57	0.00
351	81/87	dSF	4	0.75	3.00	0.25	1.30	0.00	0.10	0.00	0.50	0.25	0.00	0.25	0.50	0.00	0.50	0.00	0.25	0.25	0.00
352	79/87	dF	4	0.00	1.25	2.50	0.00	0.03	0.88	0.00	0.00	0.00	0.00	0.00	0.00	0.00	0.00	0.75	0.75	0.75	0.00
353	79/87	Hrth	2	0.00	0.00	1.50	0.00	0.00	0.95	0.00	0.00	0.00	0.00	0.00	0.00	0.50	0.00	1.00	0.00	0.00	0.50
354	79/87	dF	5	0.20	10.40	1.40	0.02	0.10	0.02	0.00	0.20	0.00	0.20	0.00	0.00	0.00	0.00	0.20	0.60	0.60	0.00
355	79/87	dF	4	0.75	4.75	4.75	1.05	0.10	0.03	0.25	0.50	0.00	0.00	0.75	0.00	1.25	0.00	3.25	0.00	0.00	0.50
356	79/87	dF	4	12.75	0.00	3.25	23.13	0.00	1.48	1.25	6.75	4.75	2.25	4.50	6.00	0.00	0.00	2.25	0.50	0.50	0.00
357	79/87	DPS	4	5.00	0.25	4.25	0.73	0.00	0.80	2.00	0.00	0.25	2.00	0.00	0.25	0.00	0.00	0.25	0.25	0.25	0.75
358	79/87	Hrth	2.5	0.80	1.20	3.60	2.40	0.00	1.08	0.00	0.40	0.40	0.00	0.40	0.40	0.00	0.00	2.00	1.20	1.20	0.00
359	80/87	Vess	7	1.14	19.57	2.29	0.57	0.71	0.07	0.14	0.00	0.14	0.14	0.00	0.14	0.00	0.00	1.29	0.43	0.43	0.29

References Cited

Abu-Lughod, J. L.
1971 *Cairo: 1001 Years of the City Victorious.* Princeton: Princeton University Press.

1987 The Islamic City – Historic Myth, Islamic Essence, and Contemporary Relevance. *International Journal of Middle East Studies* 19: 2: 155-76.

Adams, R. McC.
1966 *The Evolution of Urban Society: Early Mesopotamia and Prehispanic Mexico.* Chicago: Aldine.

1981 *Heartland of Cities: Surveys of Ancient Settlement and Land Use on the Central Floodplain of the Euphrates.* Chicago: University of Chicago Press.

Adams, R. McC. and H. Nissen
1972 *Uruk Countryside: the natural setting of urban societies.* Chicago: University of Chicago Press.

Akkermans, P.M.M.G.
1989 *Excavations at Tell Sabi Abyad, Northern Syria.* British Archaeological Reports No. 468. Oxford: Archaeopress.

Alcock, S., R. Van Dyke, and N.H. Keeble, editors
2003 *Archaeologies of Memory.* Oxford: Blackwell.

Aldenderfer, M. S. and R. K. Blashfield
1984 *Cluster Analysis.* London: Sage University Papers.

Algaze, G.
1986 The Chicago Euphrates Archaeological Project, 1980-1984: An Interim Report. *Anatolica* 13: 54-60.

1993a *The Uruk World System.* Chicago: University of Chicago Press.

1993b Expansionary Dynamics of Some Early Pristine States. *American Anthropologist* 95: 2: 304-333.

Algaze, G., editor
1990 *Town and Country in Southeastern Anatolia.* University of Chicago Oriental Institute publications, v. 109-110. Chicago: Oriental Institute.

Algaze, G., R. Breuninger, J. Knudstad
1994 Tigris-Euphrates Archaeological Research Project: Report of the Birecik and Carchemish Dam Survey Areas. *Anatolica* 20: 1-95.

Algaze, G., P. Goldberg, D. Honça, T. Matney, A. Mısır, A. Miller Rosen, D. Schlee, and L. Somers
1995 Titriş Höyük, A Small Early Bronze Age Urban Center in Southeastern Anatolia: The 1994 Season. *Anatolica* 21: 13-64.

Algaze, G., B. Hartenberger, T. Matney, J. Pournelle, L. Rainville, E. Rupley, and R. Vallet
2001 Research at Titriş Höyük in Southeastern Turkey: A Preliminary Report of the 1999 Season. *Anatolica* 27: 23-106.

Algaze, G., T. Matney, D. Schlee, and J. Kelly
1996 Late EBA Urban Structure at Titriş Höyük, Southeastern Turkey: the 1995 Season. *Anatolica* 22: 129-143.

Algaze, G. and A. Mısır
1994 Excavations at Titriş Höyük, a Small Mid-Late Third Millennium Urban Center in Southeastern Anatolia, 1992. *Kazı Sonuçları Toplantısı* 15: 153-170. Ankara: Anitler ve Müzeler Genel Müdürlügü.

1995a Titriş Höyük: An Early Bronze Age Urban Center in Southeastern Anatolia, 1993. *Kazı Sonuçları Toplantısı* 16: 107-120. Ankara: Anitler ve Müzeler Genel Müdürlügü.

1995b Titriş Höyük, A Small EBA Urban Center in Southeastern Anatolia: The 1994 Season. *Anatolica* 21: 129-150.

Algaze, G., A. Mısır, and T.J. Wilkinson
1992 Sanliurfa Museum/University of California Excavations and Surveys at Titriş Höyük, 1991: A Preliminary Report. *Anatolica* 18: 33-60.

Allentuck, A.
2004 *Production, Distribution and Consumption of Early Bronze Age Titriş Höyük, Southeastern Turkey: A Zooarchaeological Approach.* M.A. Thesis. University of Manitoba.

Allison, P. M., editor
1999 *The Archaeology of Household Activities.* London: Routledge.

Antoun, R.
1972 *Arab Village: A Social Structural Study of a Trans-Jordanian Peasant Community*. Bloomington: Indiana University Press.

Aurenche, O.
1981 *La Maison Orientale l'architecture du Proche Orient Ancien des Origines au Milieu du Quatrième Millénaire*. Series Bibliotheque Archéologique et Historique, No. 109. Paris: Librairie orientalists P. Guethner.

Aurenche, O., M. Bazin, and S. Dadler
1997 *Villages Engloutis: enquête ethnoarchéologique à Cafer Höyük (vallée de l'Euphrate)*. Travaux de la Maison de l'Orient Méditerranéen, 26. Lyon and Paris: Maison de l'Orient Méditerranéen/Diffusion de Brocard.

Baker, C. M.
1978 The Size Effect: An Explanation of Variability in Surface Artifact Assemblage Content. *American Antiquity* 43: 288-93.

Banning, E. and B.F. Byrd
1987 Houses and the Changing Residential Unit: Domestic Architecture at PPNB 'Ain Ghazal, Jordan. *Proceedings of the Prehistoric Society* 53: 309-325.

Barth, F.
1981 *Process and Form in Social Life: Selected Essays of Fredrik Barth: Volume I*. London, Boston, and Henley: Routledge and Kegan Paul.

Battini-Villard, L.
1999 *L'espace domestique en Mésopotamie de la IIIe dynastie d'Ur à l'époque paléo-Babylonienne*. British Archaeological Reports International Series No. 767, 2 volumes. Oxford: Archaeopress.

Baumler, M. F. and C. Downum
1989 Between Micro and Macro: a study in the interpretation of small-sized lithic debitage. In, *Experiments in Lithic Technology*. Edited by Daniel S. Amick and Raymond P. Mauldin, pp. 101-116. British Archaeological Reports International Series No. 528. Oxford: Archaeopress.

Beaudry, M.
1999 House and Household: The Archaeology of Domestic Life in Early America. In, *Old and New Worlds*. Edited by Geoff Egan and R. L. Michael, pp. 117-26. Oxford: Oxbow Books.

Bermann, M.
1990 *Prehispanic Household and Empire at Lukurmata, Bolivia*. Ph.D. Dissertation, Department of Anthropology, University of Michigan.

1994 *Lukurmata: Household Archaeology in Prehispanic Bolivia*. Princeton: Princeton University Press.

Binford, L.
1978 Dimensional Analysis of Behavior and Site Structure: Learning from an Eskimo Hunting Stand. *American Antiquity* 43: 330-361.

1987 Research Ambiguity: Frames of Reference and Site Structure. In, *Method and Theory for Activity Area Research: An Ethnoarchaeological Approach*. Edited by S. Kent, pp. 449-512. New York: Columbia University Press.

Blackman, M. James, G. J. Stein, and P. B. Vandiver
1993 The Standardization Hypothesis and Ceramic Mass Production: Technological, Compositional, and Metric Indexes of Craft Specialization at Tell Leilan, Syria. *American Antiquity* 58: 1: 60-80.

Blanton R.E.
1994 *Houses and Households: A Comparative Study*. New York: Plenum.

Blanton, R. E., S.A. Kowalweski, G. Feinman, and J. Appel
1981 *Ancient Mesoamerica*. Cambridge: Cambridge University Press.

Boivin, N.
2000 Life Rhythms and Floor Sequences: excavating time in rural Rajasthan and Neolithic Catalhöyük. *World Archaeology* 31: 3: 367-88.

Bottéro, J.
1952 *La Religion babylonienne*. Paris: Presses Universitaires de France.

1985 The Cuisine of Ancient Mesopotamia. *Biblical Archaeologist* 48: 1: 36-47.

1992 [1995] *Mesopotamia: Writing, Reasoning, and the Gods*. Chicago and London: The University of Chicago Press.

Bourdieu, P.
1973 The Berber House. In, *Rules and Meanings*. Edited by M. Douglas, pp. 98-110. Harmondsworth: Penguin Books.

Bradley, R. and M. Fulford
1980 Sherd Size in the Analysis of Occupation Debris. *Bulletin of the Institute of Archaeology of London* 17: 85-94.

Braidwood, R. J. and L. S. Braidwood
1960 *Excavations in the Plain of Antioch I*. Oriental Institute Publications No. 61. Chicago: University of Chicago Press.

Brice, W. C.
1966 *South-west Asia: A Systematic Regional Geography*. London: University of London Press.

1978 *The Environmental History of the Near and Middle East Since the Last Ice Age*. London and New York: Academic Press.

Brinkman, J.A.
1977 Appendix: Chronology of the Historical Period. In, *Ancient Mesopotamia*. Edited by A. L. Oppenheim. Chicago: University of Chicago Press.

Brumfiel, E.
1991 Weaving and Cooking: Women's Production in Aztec Mexico. In, *Engendering Archaeology*. Edited by J.M. Gero and M.W. Conkey, pp. 224-51. Oxford: Basil Blackwell.

Brumfiel, E. and T. Earle, editors
1987 *Specialization, Exchange, and Complex Societies*. Cambridge: Cambridge University Press.

Brusasco, P.
1999-2000 'Family archives and the social use of space in Old Babylonian houses at Ur." *Mesopotamia* 34-5: 1-173.

Bullock, P.N., N. Fédoroff, A. Jongerius, G. Stoops, and T. Tursina
1985 *Handbook for Soil Thin Section Description*. Wolverhampton: Waine Research Publications.

Burgess, E.
1926 *The Urban Community*. Selected Papers from the Proceedings of the American Sociological Society. Chicago: The University of Chicago Press.

Cameron, C.
1991 Structure Abandonment in Villages. In, *Archaeological Method and Theory* 3. Edited by M.B. Schiffer, pp. 155-94. Tucson, AZ: University Arizona Press.

Carsten, J. and S. Hugh-Jones, editors
1995 *About the House: Lévi-Strauss and beyond*. Cambridge: Cambridge University Press.

Cauvin, M.-C.
1996 L'obsidienne dans le Proche-Orient préhistorique: état des recherches en 1996. *Anatolica* 22: 3-31.

Cessford, C.
2003 Microartifactual Floor Patterning: The Case at Çatal Höyük. *Assemblage 7*. Electronic Document available at, www.shef.ac.uk/assem/issue7/cessford.html.

Çevik, A.
1995 Social Meanings of Household Spaces: A Modern Material Culture Study in an Anatolian Village. *Archaeological Dialogues* 1995: 39-50.

Chang, K.-C.
1958 Study of the Neolithic Social Grouping: examples from the New World. *American Anthropologist* 60: 2: 298-334.

Charpin, D.
1995 The History of Ancient Mesopotamia: An Overview. In, *Civilizations of the Ancient Near East*, volume 2. Edited by J. Sasson, pp. 807-829. New York: Charles Scribner's Sons.

Childe, V.G.
1951 *Man Makes Himself*. New York: New American Library.

Ciolek-Torrello, R.S.
1984 An Alternative Model of Room Function from Grasshopper Pueblo, Arizona. In, *Intrasite Spatial Analysis in Archaeology*. Edited by H.J. Hietala, pp. 127-53. Cambridge: Cambridge University Press.

Clark, J.
1986 Another Look at Small Debitage and Microdebitage. *Lithic Technology* 15: 1: 21-33.

Clutton-Brock, J.
1978 The Levant During the Prepottery Neolithic. In, *The Environmental History of the Near and Middle East Since the Last Ice Age*. Edited by W. C. Brice, pp. 29-40. London and New York: Academic Press.

Comaroff, J. L., editor
1980 *The Meaning of Marriage Payments*. London and New York: Academic Press.

Cook, S.F. and A.E. Treganza
1947 The Quantitative Investigations of Aboriginal Sites: Comparative Physical and Chemical Analysis of Two Californian Indian Mounds. *American Anthropologist* 13: 135-142.

1950 *The Quantitative Investigation of Indian Mounds, with special reference to the relation of the physical components to the probable material culture.* Berkeley: University of California Press.

Costin, C. L.
1991 Craft Specialization: Issues in Defining, Documenting, and Explaining the Organization of Production. *Archaeological Method and Theory* 3: 1-56.

Courty, M.-A., P. Goldberg, and R. I. Macphail
1989 *Soils and Micromorphology in Archaeology*. Cambridge: Cambridge University Press.

Courty, M.-A., R.I. Macphail, and J. Wattez
1991 Soils and Micromorphological Indicators of Pastoralism; with special reference to Arene Candide, Finale Ligure, Italy. *Rivista di studi Liguri* .LVII: 1-4: 127-150.

Cowgill, G.
1993 Beyond Criticizing New Archeology. *American Anthropologist* 95: 3: 551-73.

Crawford, H.
1977 *The Architecture of Iraq in the Third Millennium BC.* Mesopotamia 5. Copenhagen: Akademisk Forlag.

1991 [1994] *Sumer and the Sumerians.* Cambridge: Cambridge University Press.

Crumley, C. L.
1995 Heterarchy and the Analysis of Complex Societies. In, *Heterarchy and the Analysis of Complex Societies.* Edited by R.M. Ehrenreich, C.L. Crumley, and J.E. Levy, pp. 1-5. Archaeological Papers of the American Anthropological Association No. 6. Arlington.

Curvers, H. and G. Schwartz
1990 Excavations at Tell al-Raqa'i: a small rural site of early urban Northern Mesopotamia. *American Journal of Archaeology* 94: 1: 3-23.

Dalley, S.
1980 Old Babylonian Dowries. *Iraq* 42: 53-73.

D'Altroy, T. and C. Hastorf
1984 The Distribution and Contents of Inca State Storehouses in the Xauxa Region of Peru. *American Antiquity* 49: 334-49.

David, N. and C. Kramer
2001 *Ethnoarchaeology in Action.* Cambridge: Cambridge University Press.

Davidson, D.A., S.P. Carter, and T.A. Quine
1992 An Evaluation of Micromorphology as an Aid to Archaeological Interpretation. *Geoarchaeology* 7: 1: 55-65.

Deal, M.
1985 Household Pottery Disposal in the Maya Highlands: An Ethno-archaeological Interpretation. *Journal of Anthropological Archaeology* 4: 243-91.

DeBoer, W. R. and D.W. Lathrop
1979 The Making and Breaking of Shipbo-Conibo Ceramics. In, *Ethnoarchaeology: Implications of Ethnography for Archaeology.* Edited by C. Kramer, pp. 102-138. New York: Columbia University Press.

Deetz, J.
1982 Households: A Structural Key to Archaeological Explanation. *American Behavioral Scientist* 25: 6: 717-24.

Delaney, C.
1991 *The Seed and the Soil: Gender and Cosmology in Turkish Village Society.* Berkeley, Los Angeles, and Oxford: University of California Press.

Delougaz, P. H. Hill, and S. Lloyd
1967 *Private Houses and Graves in the Diyala Region.* The University of Chicago Oriental Institute Publications No. 88. Chicago: University of Chicago Press.

Diakonoff, I. M.
1974 Structure of Society and State in Early Dynastic Sumer. *Monographs on the Ancient Near East* 1: 3. Malibu: Undena.

1976 Slaves, Helots, and Peasants in Early Antiquity. In, *Wirtschaft und Gesellschaft im alten Vorderasien.* Edited by J. Hamatta and G. Komoroczy, pp. 47-78. Budapest: Akademia Kiado.

1991 General Outline of the First Period of the History of the Ancient World and the Problem of the Ways of Development. In, *Early Antiquity.* Edited by I.M. Diakonoff and P.L. Kohl, pp. 27-66. Chicago and London: The University of Chicago Press.

Dunnell, R.C. and J.K. Stein
1989 Theoretical Issues in the Interpretation of Microartifacts. *Geoarchaeology* 4: 31-42.

Ehrich, R. W., editor
1992 *Chronologies in Old World Archaeology*. Chicago: University of Chicago Press. Third Edition.

Eickelman, D.
1974 Is There an Islamic City? The Making of a Quarter in a Moroccan Town. *International Journal of Middle East Studies* 5: 3: 274-94.

1994 The Comparative Studies of 'Islamic' Cities. In, *Urbanism in Islam*. Edited by Y. Tadeshi, pp. 309-19. Tokyo: Research Project "Urbanism in Islam" and the Middle East Culture Center in Japan.

Ember, M. and C. Ember, editors
1983 *Marriage, Family, and Kinship: comparative studies of social organization*. New Haven, CT: HRAF Press.

Emberling, G.
1995 *Ethnicity and the State in Early Third Millennium Mesopotamia*. Ph.D. Dissertation, Department of Anthropology, University of Michigan.

1997 The Origins of Ethnicity in Complex Societies. *Journal of Archaeological Research* 5: 4: 295-344.

1999 The Value of Tradition: The Development of Social Identities in Early Mesopotamian States. In, *Material Symbols*. Edited by J. Robb, pp. 277-301. Center for Archaeological Investigations, Occasional Paper No. 26. Carbondale, IL: Southern Illinois University.

Emberling, G., J. Cheng, T. E. Larsen, H. Pittman, T. B.B. Skuldboel, J. Weber, and H. T. Wright
1999 Excavations at Tell Brak 1998: Preliminary Report. *Iraq* 61: 1-41.

English, P. W.
1966 *City and Village in Iran: Settlement and Economy in the Kirman Basin*. Madison, Milwaukee, and London: The University of Wisconsin Press.

1973 The Traditional City of Herat, Afghanistan. In, *From Medina to Metropolis: Heritage and Change in the Near Eastern City*. Edited by L. C. Brown, pp. 73-89. Princeton, NJ: Darwin Press.

Englund, R. K. and J.-P. Grégoire
1991 *The Proto-Cuneiform Texts from Jemdet Nasr*. Berlin: Gebr. Mann Verlag.

Erdentug, N.
1959 *A Study on the Social Structure of a Turkish Village*. Ankara: Ayyilidiz Matbaasi.

Erinç, S.
1978 Changes in the Physical Environment in Turkey Since the End of the Last Glacial. In, *The Environmental History of the Near and Middle East Since the Last Ice Age*. Edited by W. C. Brice, pp. 87-110. London and New York: Academic Press.

Eslick, C.
1988 Hacilar to Karatas: Social Organization in South-Western Anatolia. *Meditarch* 1: 10-40.

Evin, J.
1995 Possibilité et Nécessité de la Calibration des Datations c-14 de l'archéologie du Proche-Orient. *Paléorient* 1: 1: 5-16.

Falconer, S. E.
1991 Village Economy and Society in the Jordan Valley: A Study of Bronze Age Rural Complexity. In, *Archaeological Views from the Countryside*. Edited by G. Schwartz and S. Falconer, pp. 121-42. Washington and London: Smithsonian Institution Press.

1995 Rural Responses to Early Urbanism: Bronze Age Household and Village Economy at Tell el-Hayyat, Jordan. *Journal of Field Archaeology* 22: 399-419.

Falconer, S. E. and S. H. Savage
1995 Heartlands and Hinterlands: Alternative Trajectories of Early Urbanization in Mesopotamia and the Southern Levant. *American Antiquity* 60: 1: 37-58.

Fales, M.
1990 The Rural Landscape of the Neo-Assyrian Empire: A Survey. *State Archives of Assyria Bulletin* IV: 2: 81-142.

Fathy, H.
1986 *Natural Energy and Vernacular Architecture*. Chicago: University of Chicago Press.

Fehon, J. R. and S. C. Scholtz
1978 A Conceptual Framework for the Study of Artifact Loss. *American Antiquity* 43: 271-73.

Finkelstein, J. J.
1962 Mesopotamia. *Journal of Near Eastern Studies* 21: 2: 73-92.

Fladmark, K.R.
1982 Microdebitage Analysis: Initial Considerations. *Journal of Archaeological Science* 9: 205-220.

Flannery, K.
1976 Analyzing Household Activities. In, *The Early Mesoamerican Village*. Edited by K. Flannery, pp. 34-47. New York: Academic Press.

Forest, J.-D.
1999 *Les premiers temples de Mésopotamie.* British Archaeological Reports International Series No. 765. Oxford: Archaeopress.

Fortes, M.
1971 Introduction. In, *The Developmental Cycle in Domestic Groups*. Edited by J. Goody, pp. 1-14. Cambridge Papers in Social Anthropology. New York: Cambridge University Press.

Franke, J. A.
1987 *Artifact Patterning and Functional Variability in the Urban Dwelling: Old Babylonian Nippur, Iraq*. Ph.D. Dissertation, Department of Anthropology, University of Chicago.

Frankfort, H.
1934 *Iraq excavations of the Oriental Institute, 1932-33: third preliminary report of the Iraq Expedition.* Oriental Institute Communications, No. 17. Chicago: University of Chicago Press.

1950 Town Planning in Ancient Mesopotamia. *Town Planning Review* 21: 98-115.

1954 *The Art and Architecture of the Ancient Orient*. Harmondsworth: Penguin Books.

French, D.H., G.C. Hillman, S. Payne, and R.J. Payne
1972 Excavations at Can Hansan III 1969-1970. In, *Papers in Economic Prehistory*. Edited by E.S. Higgs, pp. 181-90. Cambridge: Cambridge University Press.

Friedman, K.
1984 Households as Income-Pooling Units. In, *Households and the World Economy*. Edited by J. Smith, I. Wallerstein, and H.D. Evers, pp. 37-55. London: Sage Publications.

Fuensanta, J.G., M. S. Rothman, and E. Bucak
1999 1997 Salvage Excavations at Tilbes Höyük. *Kazı Sonuçları Toplantısı* 20: 207-18.

Fuensanta, J.G., M. S. Rothman, and E. Bucak
2000 Salvage Excavations at Tilbes Höyük, 1998. *Kazı Sonuçları Toplantısı* 21: 157-66.

Gelb, I.
1979 Household and Family in Early Mesopotamia. In, *State and Temple Economy in the Ancient Near East.* Edited by E. Lipinski, pp. 1-98. Leuven: Departement Oriëntalistiek.

Ghirshman, R.
1954 *Iran: From the Earliest Times to the Islamic Conquest.* Harmondsworth: Penguin Books.

Giddens, A.
1984 *The Constitution of Society: Outline of a Theory of Structuration.* Cambridge: Polity Press.

Gifford, D.P.
1978 Ethnoarchaeological Observations of Natural Processes Affecting Cultural Materials. In, *Explorations in Ethnoarchaeology.* Edited by R.P. Gould, pp. 77-101. Albuquerque, NM: University of New Mexico Press.

Gifford, E. W.
1916 *Composition of California Shell-Mounds.* University of California Publications in American Archaeology and Ethnology, Vol 12. No. 1. Berkeley.

Gifford-Gonzalez, D., D. Damrosch, D. Damrosch, J. Pryor, and R. Thunen
1985 The Third Dimension in Site Structure: an experiment in trampling and vertical dispersal. *American Antiquity* 50: 803-818.

Gilbert, A. S.
1995 The Flora and Fauna of the Ancient Near East. In, *Civilizations of the Ancient Near East.* Edited by J. Sasson, pp. 153-74. New York: Charles Scribner's Sons.

Glassner, J.-J.
1985 Aspects du don, d l'échange et formes d'appropriation du sol dans la Mésopotamie du IIIe millénaire, avant la fondation de l'empire d'Ur. *Journal Asiatique* 273: 11-59.

1996 From Sumer to Babylon: Families as Landowners and Families as Rulers. In, *A History of the Family.* Edited by A. Burguiére, C. Klapisch-Zuber, M. Segalen, and F.

Zonabend, pp. 92-127. Cambridge: Belknap Press of Harvard University.

Gnivecki, P.
1987 On the Quantitative Derivation of Household Spatial Organization from Archaeological Residues in Ancient Mesopotamia. In, *Method and Theory for Activity Area Research: An Ethnoarchaeological Approach*. Edited by S. Kent, pp. 176-235. New York: Columbia University Press.

Goldberg, P.
1980 Micromorphology in Archaeology and Prehistory. *Paléorient* 6: 159-64.

1987 Soils, Sediments, and Acheulian Artifacts at Berekhat Ram, Golan Heights. In, *Micromorphologie des Sols - Soil Micromorphology*. Edited by N. Fedoroff, L.M. Bresson, and M.A. Courty, pp. 583-90. Plaisir: Association Française pour l'Étude du Sol.

Goldberg, P. and S.C. Sherwood
1994 Micromorphology of Dust Cave sediments: some preliminary results. *Journal of Alabama Archaeology*, 40: 57-65.

Goldberg, P. and I. Whitbread
1993 Micromophological Study of a Bedouin Tent Floor. In, *Formation Processes in Archaeological Context.* Monographs in World Archaeology No. 17. Edited by P. Goldberg, D.T. Nash, and M.D. Petraglia, pp. 165-188. Madison, WI: Prehistory Press.

Goldberg, P., D. T. Nash, and M. D. Petraglia, editors
1993 *Formation Processes in Archaeological Context.* Monographs in World Archaeology No. 17. Madison, WI: Prehistory Press.

Goody, J., editor
1971[1958] *The Developmental Cycle in Domestic Groups*. Cambridge Papers in Social Anthropology No. 17. Cambridge: Cambridge University Press.

Greenshields, T.H.
1980 "Quarters" and Ethnicity. In, *The Changing Middle Eastern City*. Edited by G.H. Blake and R.I. Lawless, pp. 120-40. London: Croom Helm.

Gulick, J.
1967 *Tripoli: A Modern Arab City*. Cambridge: Cambridge University Press.

Guyer, J. I. and P. E. Peters, editors
1987 *Conceptualizing the Household: Issues of Theory and Policy in Africa. Development and Change* 18: 2.

Hallo, W. W. and W. K. Simpson
1971 *The Ancient Near East: A History*. New York: Harcourt Brace Jovanovich College Publishers.

Hammel, E.A.
1980 Household Structure in Fourteenth-Century Macedonia. *Journal of Family History* 5: 242-73.

Harris, R.
1975 *Ancient Sippar: A Demographic Study of an Old-Babylonian City*. Istanbul: Netherlands Historisch-Archaeologisch Instituut.

Hartenberger, B.
2003 *A Study of Craft Specialization and the Organization of Chipped Stone Production at Early Bronze Age Titriş, Southeastern Turkey.* Ph.D. Dissertation, Department of Archaeology, Boston University.

Hartenberger, B., S. Rosen, and T. Matney
2000 The Early Bronze Age Blade Workshop at Titriş Höyük: Lithic Specialization in an Urban Context. *Near Eastern Archaeologist* 63: 1: 51-58.

Hassan, F.A.
1978 Sediments in Archaeology: Methods and Implications for Palaeoenvironmental and Cultural Analysis. *Journal of Field Archaeology* 5: 197-213.

Hastorf, C.
1990 The Effect of the Inka State on Sausa Agricultural Production and Crop Consumption. *American Antiquity* 55: 2: 262-90.

Hauptmann, H.
1982 Lidar Höyük. *Anatolian Studies* 32: 17-18.

1993 Vier Jahrtausende Siedlungsgeschichte am mittleren Euphrat. *Archäologie in Deutschland* 1: 10-15.

Hayden, B. and A. Cannon
1983 Where the Garbage Goes: Refuse Disposal in the Maya Highlands. *Journal of Anthropological Archaeology* 2: 117-163.

Healan, D.
1983 Excavation and Preliminary Analysis of an Obsidian Workshop in Tula, Hidalgo, Mexico. *Journal of Field Archaeology* 10: 127-45.

Heizer, R. G.
1960 Physical Analysis of Habitation Residues. In, *The Application of Quantitative Methods in Archaeology*. Edited by R. Heizer and S. Cook, pp. 93-157. Viking Fund Publications in Anthropology No 28. New York.

Heinrich, E.
1982 *Die Tempel und Heiligtümer im alten Mesopotamien: Typologie, Morphologie und Geschichte*. Deutsches Archäologishes Institut, Denkmäler der antiker Architecktuir 14. 2 volumes. Berlin: Walter de Gruyter.

Helbaek, H.
1972 Samarran Irrigation Agriculture at Choga Mami in Iraq. *Iraq* 34: 35-48.

Hendon, J.
1996 Archaeological Approaches to the Organization of Domestic Labor: Household Practice and Domestic Relations. *Annual Review of Anthropology* 25: 50-61.

1999 Multiple Sources of Prestige and the Social Evaluation of Women in Prehispanic Mesoamerica. In, *Material Symbols*. Edited by J. Robb, pp. 257-76. Center for Archaeological Investigations, Occasional Paper No. 26. Carbondale, IL: Southern Illinois University.

Henrickson, E.F.
1981 Non-Religious Residential Settlement Patterning in the Late Early Dynastic of the Diyala Region. *Mesopotamia* 16: 43-140.

1982 Functional Analysis of Elite Residences in the Late Early Dynastic of the Diyala Region: House D and the Walled Quarter at Khafajah and the Palaces at Tell Asmar. *Mesopotamia* 17: 5-35.

Henry, D.O., C.V. Haynes, and B. Bradley
1976 Quantitative Variations in Flaked Stone Debitage. *Plains Anthropologist* 21: 71: 57-61.

Hill, H.
1967 Tell Asmar: The Private House Area. In, *Private Houses and Graves in the Diyala Region*. Edited by P. Delougaz, H. Hill, and S. Lloyd, pp. 143-209. Chicago: University of Chicago Press.

Hillier, B. and J. Hanson
1984 *The Social Logic of Space*. Cambridge: Cambridge University Press.

Hodder, I.
1987 The Contextual Analysis of Symbolic Meanings. In, *The Archaeology of Contextual Meanings*. Edited by I. Hodder, pp. 1-10. Cambridge: Cambridge University Press.

Hodder, I. and C. Cessford
2004 Daily Practice and Social Memory at Çatalhöyük. *American Antiquity* 69:17-40.

Hole, F.
1983 Symbols of Religion and Social Organization at Susa. In, *The Hilly Flanks and Beyond: essays on the prehistory of southwestern Asia*. Edited by T. C. Young, P. E. Smith, and P. Mortensen. Studies in Ancient Oriental Civilization No. 36. Chicago: University of Chicago Press.

Hole, F., J. Neely, and K. Flannery
1969 *Prehistory and Human Ecology of the Deh Luran Plain*. Memoirs of the Museum of Anthropology No. 1. Ann Arbor, MI: University of Michigan.

Horne, L.
1994 *Village Spaces: Settlement and Society in Northern Iran*. Washington, DC: Smithsonian Institution Press.

Hourani, A. H.
1970 Introduction: The Islamic City in the Light of Recent Research. In, *The Islamic City*. Edited by A.H. Hourani and S.M. Stern, pp. 9-24. Oxford: Bruno Cassirer and University of Pennsylvania Press.

1991 *A History of the Arab Peoples*. New York: MJF Books.

Hoyt, H.
1933 *One Hundred Years of Land Values in Chicago*. New York: Arno Press.

Hull, K.L.
1987 Identification of Cultural Site Formation Processes through Microdebitage Analysis. *American Antiquity* 52: 772-83.

Isaac, G.L.
1967 Towards an Interpretation of Occupational Debris. *Kroeber Anthropological Society Papers* 37: 31-55.

Ismail, F., W. Sallaberger, P. Talon, and K. Van Lerberghe
1996 *Administrative Documents from Tell Beydar: Seasons 1993-1995.* Turnhout, Belgium: Brepols Publishers.

Jacobs, L.
1979 Tell-i Nun: Archaeological Implications of a Village in Transition. In, *Ethnoarchaeology.* Edited by C. Kramer, pp 175-91. New York: Columbia University Press.

Jacobsen, T.
1970 Early Political Development in Mesopotamia. Reprinted in, *Toward the Image of the Tammuz.* Edited by W. Morgan, pp. 132-56. Cambridge.

1976 *The Treasures of Darkness: a History of Mesopotamian Religion.* New Haven: Yale University Press.

Jasim, S. A.
1983 Excavations at Tell Abada: A preliminary report. *Iraq* XLV: II: 165-186.

1985 *The 'Ubaid Period in Iraq: recent excavations in the Hamrin Region.* British Archaeological Reports International Series No. 267. Oxford: Archaeopress.

Jawad, A.
1965 *The Advent of the Era of Townships in Northern Mesopotamia.* Leiden: E.J. Brill.

Johnson, G.
1973 *Local Exchange and Early State Development in SW Iran.* Museum of Anthropology, Anthropological Papers No. 51. Ann Arbor, MI: University of Michigan.

Joyce, R. and S. Gillespie, editors
2000 *Beyond Kinship: Social and Material Reproduction in House Societies.* Philadelphia: University of Pennsylvania Press.

Kamp, K.
1982 *Architectural Indices of Socio-Economic Variability: An Ethnoarchaeological Case Study from Syria.* Ph.D. Dissertation, Department of Anthropology, University of Arizona.

Kandiyoti, D.
1974 Social Change and Social Stratification in a Turkish Village. *Journal of Peasant Studies* 2: 206-19.

Karpat, K. H.
1975 *The Gecekondu: rural migration and urbanization.* Cambridge: Cambridge University Press.

Keith, K.
1999 *Cities, Neighborhoods, and Houses: Urban Spatial Organizations in Old Babylonian Mesopotamia.* Ph.D. Dissertation, Department of Anthropology, University of Michigan.

2003 The Spatial Patterns of Everyday Life in Old Babylonian Neighborhoods. In, *The Social Construction of Ancient Cities.* Edited by M. L. Smith, pp. 56-80. Washington: Smithsonian Press.

Keller, S.
1968 *The Urban Neighborhood: A Sociological Perspective.* New York: Random House.

Kemp, B. J., D. Samuel, and R. Luff
1994 Food for an Egyptian City: Tell el-Amarna. In, *Whither Environmental Archaeology?* Edited by R. Luff and P. Rowley Conwy, pp. 133-70. Oxford: Oxbow Books.

Kent, S.
1984 *Analyzing Activity Areas.* Albuquerque, NM: University New Mexico Press.

Kent, S., editor
1990 *Domestic Architecture and the Use of Space.* Cambridge: Cambridge University Press.

Kepinski-Lecomte, C.
1992 *Haradum I: Une ville nouvelle sur le Moyen-Euphrate.* Paris: Editions Recherche sur les Civilisations

Kirkby, A. and M.J. Kirkby
1976 Geomorphic Processes and the Surface Survey of Archaeological Sites in Semi-arid Areas. In, *Geoarchaeology: Earth Science and the Past.* Edited by D.A. Davidson and M.L. Shackley, pp. 229-53. Boulder, CO: Westview Press.

Klucas, E. E.
1996 *The Village Larder: Village Level Production and Exchange in an Early State.* Ph.D. Dissertation, Department of Anthropology, University of Arizona.

Knapp, A. B.
1988 *The History and Culture of Ancient Western Asia and Egypt.* Chicago: Dorsey Press.

Kolars, J. F.
1967 Types of Rural Development. In, *Four*

Studies on the Economic Development of Turkey. Edited by F. C. Shorter, pp. 63-87. London: Frank Cass & Co., Ltd.

Kozyreva, N.V.
1991 The Old Babylonian Period. In, *Early Antiquity*. Edited by I.M. Diakonoff and P. L. Kohl, pp. 98-123. Chicago and London: The University of Chicago Press.

Kramer, C., editor
1979a *Ethnoarchaeology: Implications of Ethnography for Archaeology*. New York: Columbia University Press.

Kramer, C.
1979b Introduction. In, *Ethnoarchaeology*. Edited by C. Kramer, pp. 1-20. New York: Columbia University Press.

1979c An Archaeological View of a Contemporary Kurdish Village: domestic architecture, household size, and wealth. In, *Ethnoarchaeology*. Edited by C. Kramer, pp. 139-63. New York: Columbia University Press.

1980 Estimating Prehistoric Populations: An Ethnoarchaeological Approach. In, *L'Archéologie de l'Iraq du Début del'Epoque Neolithique à 333 Avant Notre Ere*. Edited by M.T. Barralet, 315-23. Paris: C.N.R.S.

1982a *Village Ethnoarchaeology: rural Iran in archaeological perspective*. New York: Academic Press.

1982b Ethnographic Households and Archaeological Interpretation. *American Behavioral Scientist* 25: 6: 663-75.

Kramer, S. N.
1963 *The Sumerians: their history, culture, and character*. Chicago: The University of Chicago Press.

Kuhrt, A.
1995 *The Ancient Near East, c. 3000-330 B.C.*, 2 Volumes. London and New York: Routledge.

Kubba, S.A.A.
1987 *Mesopotamian Architecture and Town Planning from the Mesolithic to the End of the Proto-historic Period, 10,000 - 3,500 B.C.* British Archaeological Reports International Series No. 367, 2 volumes. Oxford: Archaeopress.

Küçükerman, Ö.
1992 *Das Alttürkische Wohnhaus: auf der suche nach der Räumlichen identität.* Istanbul: Cömertler Matbaacilik.

Kuper, A.
1982 *Wives for Cattle*. London: Routledge and Kegan Paul.

Lamberg-Karlovsky, C.C.
1999 The Archaeological Evidence for International Commerce: Public and/or Private Enterprise in Mesopotamia. In, *Privatization in the Ancient Near East and Classical World*. Edited by M. Hudson and B. A. Levine, pp. 73-108. Peabody Museum Bulletin No. 5. Cambridge: Harvard University.

LaMotta, V. and M. Schiffer
1999 Formation Processes of House Floor Assemblages. In, *The Archaeology of Household Activities*. Edited by P. Allison, pp. 19-29. London and New York: Routledge.

Lampl, P.
1968 *Cities and Planning in the Ancient Near East*. New York: George Braziller.

Lane, E. W.
1836 *An Account of the Manners and Customs of the Modern Egyptians*. London: Charles Knight & Co.

Laneri, N.
1999 Intramural Tombs - a Funerary Tradition of the Middle Euphrates Valley During the IIIrd Millennium B.C. *Anatolica* 25: 221-41.

Lange, F.W. and C.R. Rydberg
1972 Abandonment and Post-Abandonment Behavior at a Rural Central American House-Site. *American Antiquity* 37: 419-32.

Lapidus, I.M.
1967 *Muslim Cities in the Later Middle Ages*. Cambridge: Harvard University Press.

1973 Traditional Muslim Cities: Structure and Change. In, *From Madina to Metropolis*. Edited by L. C. Brown, pp. 51-69. Princeton: Darwin Press.

1986 Cities and Societies: A Comparative Study of the Emergence of Urban Civilization in Mesopotamia and Greece. *Journal of Urban History* 12: 3: 257-92.

Larsen, C. E.
1975 The Mesopotamian Delta Region. *Journal of the American Oriental Society* 95: 1: 43-58.

Larsen, C. E. and G. Evans
1978 The Holocene Geological History of the Tigris-Euphrates-Karun Delta. In, *The Environmental History of the Near and Middle East Since the Last Ice Age*. Edited by W. C. Brice, pp. 227-44. London and New York: Academic Press.

Larsen, M.T.
1979 The Tradition of empire in Mesopotamia. In, *Power and Propaganda. A Symposium on Ancient Empires*. Edited by M.T. Larsen, pp. 75-103. Mesopotamia Copenhagen Studies in Assyriology No. 7. Copenhagen: Akademisk Forlag.

Laslett, P. and R. Wall
1972 *Household and Family in Past Time.* Cambridge: Cambridge University Press.

Lees, G.M. and N.L. Falcon
1952 The Geographical History of the Mesopotamian Plains. *Geographical Journal* 118: 24-39.

LeTourneau, R.
1949 *Fez avant le Protectorat*. Casablanca: SMLE.

1961 *Fez in the Age of the Marinides*. Norman: University of Oklahoma Press.

Lloyd, S.
1940 Iraq Government Soundings at Sinjar. *Iraq* 7: 13-21.

1984 [1978] *The Archaeology of Mesopotamia from the Old Stone Age to the Persian Conquest.* London: Thames and Hudson.

Lupton, A.
1996 *Stability and Change: Socio-Political Development in North Mesopotamia and South-East Anatolia, 4000-2700 B.C.* British Archaeological Reports International Series No. 627. Oxford: Archaeopress.

Madanipour, A.
1998 *Tehran: The Making of a Metropolis.* New York: John Wiley & Sons.

Madsen, M.E. and Dunnell, R.C.
1989 The Role of Microartifacts in Deducing Land Use from Low Density Records in Plowed Surfaces. Paper presented at the 54th Annual Meeting of the Society for American Archaeology, Atlanta, Georgia.

Maekawa, K.
1980 Female Weavers and their Children in Lagash - Pre-Sargonic and Ur III. *Acta Sumerologica* 2: 82-125.

1996 The Governor's Family and the 'Temple Households' in Ur III Girsu. In, *Houses and Households in Ancient Mesopotamia.* Edited by K.R. Veenhof, pp. 171-80. Istanbul: Nederland Historisch-Archaeologisch Intituut.

Maisels, C. K.
1990 *The Emergence of Civilization: From Hunting and Gathering to Agriculture, Cities, and the State in the Near East.* London: Routledge.

1993 *The Near East: Archaeology in the 'Cradle of Civilization.'* London and New York: Routledge.

Makal, M.
1954 *A Village in Anatolia.* Translated by W. Deedes. London: Valentine, Mitchell.

Mann, P. H.
1970 The Neighborhood. In, *Neighborhood, City, and Metropolis.* Edited by R. Gutman and D. Popenoe, pp. 568-83. New York: Random House.

Manzanilla, L.
1996 Corporate Groups and Domestic Activities at Teotihuacan. *Latin American Antiquity* 7: 3: 228-246.

1997 *Emergence and Change in Early Urban Societies.* New York: Plenum.

Manzanilla, L. and L. Barba
1990 The Study of Activities in Classic Households: Two case studies from Coba and Teotihuacan. *Ancient Mesoamerica* 1: 41-49.

Marçais, W.
1928 L'Islamisme et la vie urbaine. In, *L'Académie des Inscriptions et Belles-Lêttres. Comptes Rendus*, pp. 86-100. Paris.

Marçais, G.
1945 La conception des villes dans l'Islam. *Revue d'Alger* 2: 517-33.

Marcus, J.
1983 On the Nature of Mesoamerican Cities. In, *Prehistoric Settlement Patterns: Essays in Honor of C.G. Willey.* Edited by E. Voight and R. Leventhal, pp. 195-242. Albuquerque, NM: University of New Mexico Press.

Marfoe, L., et al.
1986 The Chicago Euphrates Archaeological Project 1980-1984: An Interim Report. *Anatolica* 13: 37-148.

Margueron, J.
1982 Mari: Originalité ou Dépendance? *Seb* V: 121-44.

1989 Architecture et Société à l'époque d'Obeid. In, *Upon This Foundation*. Edited by E. Henrickson and E. Thuesen, pp. 43-77. Carsten Niebuhr Institute of Ancient Near East Studies. Copenhagen: Museum Tusculanum Press.

Martin, H.
1988 *Fara: A Reconstruction of the Ancient Mesopotamian City of Shuruppak*. Birmingham, UK: Harriet P. Martin.

Martin, H., J. Moon, and N.J. Postgate
1985 *Graves 1-99. Abu Salabikh Excavations*. London: British School of Archaeology in Iraq.

Matney, T.
1993 *A Semantic Model for the Analysis of Architecture from Late Third Millennium BC Mesopotamia*. Ph.D. Dissertation, Department of Anthropology, University of Pennsylvania.

Matney, T. and G. Algaze
1995 Urban Development at Mid-Late Early Bronze Age Titriş Höyük in Southeastern Anatolia. *Bulletin of the American Schools of Oriental Research* 299/300: 33-52.

Matney, T., G. Algaze, and H. Pittman
1997 Excavations at Titriş Höyük in Southeastern Turkey: A Preliminary Report of the 1996 Season. *Anatolica* 23: 61-84.

Matney, T., G. Algaze, and S. Rosen, with contributions by S. Aricanli and B. Hartenberger
1999 Early Bronze Age Urban Structure at Titriş Höyük, Southeastern Turkey: the 1998 season. *Anatolica* 25: 185-201.

Matthews, W.
1992 *The Micromorphology of Occupational Sequences and the Use of Space in a Sumerian City*. Ph.D. Dissertation, University of Cambridge.

1995 Micromorphological Characterisation and Interpretation of Occupation Deposits and Microstratigraphc Sequences at Abu Salabikh, Iraq. In, *Archaeological Sediments and Soils, Analysis, Interpretation and Management*. Edited by A.J. Barham and R.I. Macphail, pp. 41-76. London: Archetype Books.

1997 Activities inside the temple: the evidence of microstratigraphy. In, *The Dilmun Temple at Saar*. Edited by H. Crawford, R. Killick, and J. Moon, pp. 31-46, Plates 178-204. London: Kegan Paul International.

2001 Methdological approaches in microstratigraphic anlaysis of uses and concepts of space at Tell Brak. In, *Recherches en archéométrie*. Edited by M. Fortin, pp. 177-97. Quebec: CELAT.

2003 Microstratigraphic sequences: indications of uses and concepts of space. In, *Excavations at Tell Brak, Vol. 4*. Edited by R. Matthews, pp. 377-388. Cambridge: McDonald Institute for Archaeological Research, and, London: the British School of Archaeology in Iraq.

2004 Micromorphological and Microstratigraphic Traces of Uses and Concepts of Space. In, *Çatalhöyük 1995-1999*. Edited by I. Hodder. Cambridge: McDonald Institute Monorgraphs and Ankara: British Institute of Archaeology.

Matthews, W. and J.N. Postgate, with S. Payne, M.P. Charles, and K. Dobney
1994 The Imprint of Living in a Mesopotamian City: questions and answers. In, *Whither Environmental Archaeology?* Edited by R. Luff and P. Rowley-Conwy, pp. 171-212. Oxford: Oxbow Books.

Matthews, W., C.A.I. French, T. Lawrence, D.F. Cutler
1996 Multiple Surfaces: the micromorphology. In, *On the Surface: Çatal Höyük, 1993-95*. Edited by I. Hodder, pp. 301-42. Cambridge: McDonald Institute for Archaeological Research and British Institute of Archaeology at Ankara.

Matthews, W., C.A.I. French, T. Lawrence, D.F. Cutler, and M.K. Jones
1997 Microstratigraphic Traces of Site Formation Processes and Human Activities. High Definition Archaeology: threads through the past. *World Archaeology* 29: 2: 281-308.

Matthiae, P.
1980 *Ebla: An Empire Rediscovered*. London: Hodder and Stoughton.

McCown, D. and R.C.Haines, assisted by D.P. Hansen
1967 *Nippur I: Temple of Enlil, Scribal Quarter, and Soundings*. Chicago: Oriental Institute Publication No. 78. Chicago: University of Chicago Press.

McGovern, P.
1990 *Organic Contents of Ancient Vessels: materials analysis and archaeological investigation.* Philadelphia: MASCA, the University Museum of Archaeology and Anthropology, University of Pennsylvania.

McGuire, R.
1991 Critical Traditions in Contemporary Archaeology. *American Anthropologist* 93: 737-8.

Meighan, C.W., N.E. Coles, F.D. Davis, G.M. Greenwood, W.M. Harrison, and E.H.MacBain
1956 *Archaeological Excavations in Iron County, Utah.* Anthropological Papers No. 25. Salt Lake City: University of Utah.

Mellaart, J.
1970 *Excavations at Hacilar.* 2 volumes. Edinburgh: University Press.

Merpert, N. and R. Munchaev
1987 The Earliest Levels at Yarim Tepe I and Yarim Tepe II in Northern Iraq. *Iraq* 49: 1-36.

Metcalfe, D. and K. M. Heath
1990 Microrefuse and Site Structure: The Hearths and Floors of the Heartbreak Hotel. *American Antiquity* 55: 4: 781-796.

Middle East Technical University
1965 *Yassi Höyük: A Village Study.* Ankara: Middle East Technical University.

Meyers, E. M. , editor
1997 *The Oxford Encyclopedia of Archaeology in the Near East.* New York: Oxford University Press.

Michalowski, P.
1987 Charisma and Control: On Continuity and Change in Early Mesopotamian Bureaucratic Systems. In, *The Organization of Power.* Edited by M. Gibson and R. Biggs, pp. 55-67. Chicago: Oriental Institute of the University of Chicago.

1998 Cuneiform Texts from Kazane Höyük. *Journal of Cuneiform Studies* 50: 53-58.

Middleton, W.
1998 *Craft Specialization at Ejutla, Oaxaca, Mexico: An Archaeometric Study of the Organization of Household Craft Production.* Ph.D. Dissertation, Department of Anthropology, University of Wisconsin.

Middleton, W. and T. D. Price
1996 Chemical Analysis of Modern and Archaeological House Floors by Means of Inductively Coupled Plasma-Atomic Emission Spectroscopy. *Journal of Archaeological Science* 23: 5: 673-87.

Miglus, P. A.
1996 Die Räumliche Organisation des altbabylonischen Hofhauses. In, *Houses and Households in Ancient Mesopotamia.* Edited by K.R.Veenhof, pp. 211-220. Istanbul: Nederlands Historisch-Archaeologisch Intituut.

Milano, L.
1995 Ebla: A Third-Millennium City-State in Ancient Syria. In, *Civilizations of the Ancient Near East.* Edited by J. Sasson, pp. 1219-30. New York: Charles Scribner's Sons.

Miller, R.
1986 Flaked Stone Manufacture and Use at Busra from the Epipaleolithic to Early Islamic Times. *Berytus* 32: 149-58.

Miller, N.
1986 Vegetation and Land Use. In, Marfoe, et al., The Chicago Euphrates Archaeological Project 1980-1984. *Anatolica* 13, pp. 85-89.

Moholy-Nagy, H.
1990 The Misidentification of Mesoamerican Lithic Workshops. *Latin American Antiquity* 1: 3: 268-279.

1992 Lithic Deposits as Waste Management. *Latin American Antiquity* 3: 3: 249-51.

Moorey, P.R.S.
1982 *Ur 'of the Chaldees': A Revised and Updated Edition of Sir Leonard Woolley's Excavations at Ur.* Ithaca, NY: Cornell University Press.

1994 *Ancient Mesopotamian Materials and Industries: the archaeological evidence.* Oxford: Clarendon Press.

Murray, P.
1980 Discard Location: the Ethnographic Data. *American Antiquity* 45: 3: 490-500.

Naroll, R.
1962 Floor Area and Settlement Population. *American Antiquity* 27: 4: 587-89.

Nass, J. P. and R. W. Yerkes
1995 Social Differentiation at Cahokia and in Its Hinterlands. In, *Mississippian Communities and Households.* Edited by J. D. Rogers and B. Smith, pp. 58-80. Tuscaloosa, AL: University of Alabama Press.

Nemet-Nejat, K. R.
1998 *Daily Life in Ancient Mesopotamia.* Westport, CT: Greenwood Press.

Netting, R., R. Wilk, and E. Arnould, editors
1984 *Households: Comparative and Historical Studies of the Domestic Group.* Los Angeles: University of California Press.

Nevett, L.
1999 *House and Society in the Ancient Greek World.* Cambridge: Cambridge University Press.

Nielsen, A.E.
1991 Trampling in the Archaeological Record: An Experimental Study. *American Antiquity* 56: 483-503.

Nissen, H. J.
1988 *The Early History of the Ancient Near East, 9000-2000 B.C.* Chicago and London: The University of Chicago Press.

Nissen, H.J., P. Damerow, and R.K. Englund
1990 *Frühe Schrift und Techniken der Wirtschaftsverwaltung im alten Vorderen Orient.* Berlin: Franzbecker.

O'Connell, J.F.
1987 Alyawara Site Structure and its Archaeological Implications. *American Antiquity* 52: 74-108.

Oates, D.
1987 Excavations at Tell Brak, 1985-1986. *Iraq* 49: 173-191.

Oates, J.
1960 Ur and Eridu, the Prehistory. *Iraq* 22: 32-50.

1978 Mesopotamian Social Organization: archaeological and philological evidence. In, *The Evolution of Social Systems.* Edited by J. Friedman and M. Rowlands, pp. 457-485. Pittsburgh: University of Pittsburgh Press.

1986 [1979] *Babylon.* London: Thames and Hudson.

Oates, J. and S.A. Jasim
1986 Early Tokens and Tablets in Mesopotamia: new information from Tell Abada and Tell Brak. *World Archaeology* 17: 348-62.

Oates, J. and D. Oates
1976a *The Rise of Civilization.* Oxford: Elsevier-Phaidon.

1976b Early Irrigation Agriculture in Mesopotamia. In, *Problems in Social and Economic Archaeology*. Edited by G. Sieveking, I.H. Longworth, and K.E. Wilson, pp. 109-35. London: Duckworth.

Oppenheim, A.L.
1964 *Mesopotamia: Portrait of a Dead Civilization.* Chicago: University of Chicago Press.

1969 Mesopotamia: Land of Many Cities. In, *Middle Eastern Cities.* Edited by I. Lapidus, pp. 3-18. Berkeley: University of California Press.

Ören, I.
1997 Continuity and Development Trends in Housing and Traditional Environments. A paper given at the "Culture and Space in Home Environment" Symposium, Istanbul.

Ortner, S. B.
1984 Theory in Anthropology since the Sixties. *Society for Comparative Study of Society and History* 26: 126-166.

Özbal, R.
2000 Microartifact Analysis. In, Tell Kurdu Excavations 1999, Yener et al., *Anatolica* 26, pp. 49-55.

Parrot, A.
1959 *Le Palais.* Paris: Guethner.

Pearson, M. P. and C. Richards
1994 *Architecture and Order: Approaches to Social Space.* London and New York: Routledge.

Pettinato, G.
1981 *The Archives of Ebla: An Empire Inscribed in Clay.* Garden City, NJ: Doubleday.

Pfalzner, P.
2001 *Haus and Haushalt: Wohnformen des dritten Jahrtausends vor Christus in Nordmesopotamien* Damaszener Forschungen Band No. 9. Mainz am Rhein: P. von Zabern

Pierce, J. E.
1964 *Life in a Turkish Village.* New York: Holt, Rinehart, and Winston.

Pitard, W. T.
1987 *Ancient Damascus.* Winona Lake, IN: Eisenbrauns.

Pollock, S.
1991 Women in a Men's World: Images of Sumerian Women. In, *Engendering Archaeology*. Edited by J. Gero and M. Conkey, pp. 366-87. Oxford: Blackwells.

1999 *Ancient Mesopotamia: The Eden that Never Was*. Cambridge: Cambridge University Press.

Pollock, S. and C. Coursey
1995 Ceramics from Hacinebi Tepe: Chronology and Connections. *Anatolica* 21: 101-41.

Porada, E.
1965 The Relative Chronology of Mesopotamia. In, *Chronologies in Old World Archaeology*. Edited by R. W. Ehrich, pp. 177-79. Chicago: University of Chicago Press.

Postgate, J.N.
1980 Early Dynastic Burial Customs at Abu Salabikh. *Sumer* 36: 1-2: 65-81.

1990 Excavations at Abu Salabikh, 1988-89. *Iraq* 52: 95-106.

1992 *Early Mesopotamia: Society and Economy at the Dawn of History*. London: Routledge.

1994 How Many Sumerians per Hectare? Probing the Anatomy of an Early City. *Cambridge Archaeological Journal* 4: 47-65.

Potts, D. T.
1997 *Mesopotamian Civilization: The Material Foundations*. London: The Athlone Press.

Pournelle, J.
2001 Titris and its hinterland: The EBA landscape of the city. In, Research at Titris Höyük in southeastern Turkey: The 1999 Season., pp. 58-106, *Anatolica* 24: 23-106.

Pred, A. R.
1990 *Making Histories and Constructing Human Geographies: the local transformation of practice, power relations, and consciousness*. Boulder: Westview Press.

Rainville, L.
In press Daily Life and Micro-Debris: Micro-Archaeology in a South Indian Village. To appear in a volume dedicated to formation processes, published by Deccan College, India.

2003a Micro-Debris Analysis. In, Excavations at Ziyaret Tepe, Turkey, 2002. By T. Matney, et al. *Anatolica* 29: 194-197, 218.

2003b Results from Micro-Archaeology in 2001 and 2002. In, Excavations at Tell Brak, 2001-2002. By G. Emberling and H. McDonald, et al. *Iraq* 64: 63-73.

2001 Micro-Debris based functional analyses of late EBA houses. In, Research at Titris Höyük in Southeastern Turkey: A Preliminary Report of the 1999 Season. By G. Algaze, et al., *Anatolica* 27: 30-33 and 86-87.

2000 Microdebris Analysis in Early Bronze Age Mesopotamian Households. *Antiquity* 74: 284.

Rapoport, A.
1969 *House Form and Culture*. Englewood Cliffs, NJ: Prentice Hall.

1980 Vernacular Architecture and the Cultural Determinants of Form. In, *Buildings and Society: Essays on the Social Development of the Built Environment*. Edited by A. King, pp. 283-305. London: Routledge and Kegan Paul.

1990 Systems of Activities and Systems of Settings. In, *Domestic Architecture and the Use of Space*. Edited by S. Kent, pp. 9-20. Cambridge: Cambridge University Press.

Rapoport, A., editor
1982 *The Meaning of the Built Environment: A Non-Verbal Communication Approach*. Beverly Hills, CA: Sage Publications.

Rathje, W.
1979 Modern Material Cultural Studies. In, *Advances in Archaeological Methods*, volume 2. Edited by M.B. Schiffer, pp. 1-37. New York: Academic Press.

Raymond, A.
1984 *The Great Arab Cities in the 16th-18th Centuries: An Introduction*. New York and London: New York University Press.

Reade, J.
1968 Preliminary Reports on Tell Taya. *Iraq* 30: 234-64.

1971 Preliminary Reports on Tell Taya. *Iraq* 33: 87-100.

1973 Tell Taya (1972-73): Summary Report. *Iraq* 35: 155-87.

1982 Tell Taya. In, *Fifty Years of Mesopotamian Discovery*. Edited by John Curtis, pp. 72-8. The British School of Archaeology in Iraq. Hertford, England: Stephen Austin and Sons Ltd.

Redman, C. L., M. Berman, F. Curtin, W. Langhorne, N. Versaggi, and J. Wanser
1978 *Social Archaeology: Beyond Subsistence and Dating*. New York: Academic Press.

Renger, J. M.
1973 Who are all those people? *Orientalia* 42: 359-73.

1995 Institutional, Communal, and Individual Ownership or Possession of Arable Land in Ancient Mesopotamia from the End of the Fourth to the End of the First Millennium BC. Symposium on Ancient Law, Economics, and Society. Edited by J. Lindgren, L. Mayali, and G. P. Miller. *Chicago-Kent Law Review* 71: 1: 2: 269-319.

Roaf, M.
1989 Social Organization and Social Activities at Tell Madhhur. In, *Upon this Foundation*. Edited by E. Henrickson and I. Thuesen, pp. 91-146. CNI Publications No. 10. Copenhagen: Museum Tusculanum Press.

1990 *Cultural Atlas of Ancient Mesopotamia and the Ancient Near East*. New York, NY: Facts on File.

Rosen, A.
1986 *Cities of Clay: The Geoarchaeology of Tells*. Chicago: University of Chicago Press.

1989a Ancient Town and City Sites: a view from the microscope. *American Antiquity* 54: 564-578.

1989b Environmental Change at the end of Early Bronze Age Palestine. In, *L'urbanisation de la Palestine à l'âge du Bronze ancien*. Edited by P. Miroschedji, pp. 247-55. British Archaeological Reports, International Series No. 527, volume ii. Oxford: Archaeopress.

1991 Microartifacts and the Study of Ancient Societies. *Biblical Archaeologist* 54: 97-103.

1993 Microartifacts as a Reflection of Cultural Factors in Site Formation. In, *Formation Processes in Archaeological Context*. Edited by P. Goldberg, D. T. Nash, and M.D. Petraglia, pp. 141-48. Monographs in World Archaeology No. 17. Madison, WI: Prehistory Press.

Rosen, S.
1989 The Analysis of Early Bronze Age Chipped Stone Industries: A Summary Statement. In, *L'urbanisation de la Palestine à l'âge du Bronze ancien*. Edited by P Miroschedji, pp. 199-222. British Archaeological Reports International Series No. 527, volume i. Oxford: Archaeopress.

Rothschild, N.
1991 Incorporating the Outdoors as Living Space. *Expedition* 33: 1: 24-32.

Roux, G.
1992[1964] *Ancient Iraq*. London: Penguin Books.

Rowton, M. B.
1976 Dimorphic Structure and Topology. *Oriens Antiquus* 15: 17-31.

Rupley, E. S.A.
2003 ^{14}C AMS determinations of the fourth millennium BC from Tell Brak. In, Excavations at Tell Brak, 2001-2002, pp. 33-41. By G. Emberling and H. McDonald, et al. *Iraq* LXV: 1-75.

Safar, F., M. A. Mustafa, and S. Lloyd
1981 *Eridu*. Baghdad: State Organization of Antiquities and Heritage.

Saggs, H. W. F.
1995 *Babylonians*. Norman, OK: University of Oklahoma.

Sahlins, M.
1971 The Intensity of Domestic Production in Primitive Societies: Social Inflections of the Chayanov Slope. In, *Studies in Economic Anthropology*. Edited by G. Dalton, pp. 30-51. Anthropological Studies No. 7. Washington: American Anthropological Association.

1972 *Stone Age Economics*. Chicago: Adline.

Santley, R. S.
1983 Obsidian Trade and Teotihuacan Influence in Mesoamerica. In, *Interdisciplinary Approaches to the Study of Highland-Lowland Interaction*. Edited by A. Miller, pp. 69-123. Washington: Dumbarton Oaks.

Scanlon, G.T.
1970 Housing and Sanitation: Some Aspects of Medieval Public Service. In, *The Islamic City: A Colloquium*. Edited by A.H. Hourani and S.M. Stern, pp. 179-94. Oxford: Bruno Cassirer Ltd. and Philadelphia: University of Pennsylvania Press.

Schiffer, M. B.
1972 Archaeological Context and Systemic Context. *American Antiquity* 37: 2: 156-65.

1983 Toward the Identification of Formation Processes. *American Antiquity* 48: 675-706.

1995 *Behavioral Archaeology: First Principles*. Salt Lake City: University of Utah Press.

1996 [1987] *Formation Processes of the Archaeological Record.* Salt Lake City: University of Utah Press.

Schmandt-Besserat, D.
1992 *Before Writing*. Austin: University of Texas Press.

Schmidt, J.
1964 Strassen in Altorientalischen Wohngebieten: Eine Studie zur Geschichte des Städtebaues in Mesopotamien und Syrien. *Baghdader Mitteilungen* 3: 125-147.

Schutz, A.
1964 The Problem of Rationality in the Social World. In, *Collected Papers: Studies in Social Theory*. Edited by A. Brodersen, pp. 64-88. The Hague: Martinus Nijhoff.

Schwartz, G.
1987 The Ninevite V Period and the Development of Complex Society in Northern Mesopotamia. *Paléorient* 13: 2: 93-100.

Scurlock, J. A.
1995 Death and the Afterlife in Ancient Mesopotamian Thought. In, *Civilizations of the Ancient Near East*. Edited by J. Sasson, pp. 1883-93. New York: Charles Scribner's Sons.

Sharer, R. J. and W. Ashmore
1987 *Archaeology: Discovering our Past.* Mountain View, CA: Mayfield Publishing Company.

Shea, J. J. and J. D. Klenck
1993 An Experimental Investigation of the Effects of Trampling on the Results of Lithic Microwear Analysis. *Journal of Archaeological Science* 20: 175-194.

Shennan, S. J.
1991 Tradition, Rationality, and Cultural Transmission. In, *Processual and Postprocessual Archaeologies*. Edited by R. Preucel, pp. 197-208. Carbondale: Southern Illinois University.

Sherwood, S.
2001a *The Geoarchaeology of Dust Cave: A Late Paleoindian through Middle Archaic Site in the Middle Tennessee River Valley*. PhD Dissertation, University of Tennessee, Knoxville.

2001b Microartifacts. In, *Earth Sciences and Archaeology*. Edited by P. Goldberg, V. T. Holliday, and C. R. Ferring. pp. 327-351. New York: Kluwer Academic/Plenum Publishers.

Sherwood, S., J. Simek, and R. Polhemus
1995 Artifact Size and Spatial Process: macro and microartifacts in a Mississippian House. *Geoarchaeology* 10: 6: 429-55.

Shunnaq, M. S. and W. A. Schwab
2000 Continuity and Change in a Middle Eastern City: the social ecology of Irbid City, Jordan. *Urban Anthropology* 29: 1: 69-96.

Silverblatt, I.
1995 Lessons of Gender and Ethnohistory in Mesoamerica. *Ethnohistory* 42: 4: 639-50.

Simms, S. R.
1988 The Archaeological Structure of a Bedouin Camp. *Journal of Archaeological Science* 15: 197-211.

Simms, S. R. and K. M. Heath
1990 Site Structure of the Orbit Inn: An Application of Ethnoarchaeology. *American Antiquity* 55: 4: 797-813.

Sinopoli, C.
1994 Political Choices and Economic Strategies in the Vijayanagara Empire. In, *The Economic Anthropology of the State*. Edited by E. M. Brumfiel, pp. 223-43. Monographs in Economic Anthropology. Lanham, MD: University Press of America.

Sjoberg, G.
1960 *The Preindustrial City: Past and Present.* New York: Free Press.

Snell, D. C.
1997 *Life in the Ancient Near East, 3100-332 B.C.E.*. New Haven and London: Yale University Press.

Snyder, A. B.
2000 Re-constructing the Anatolian Village: Revisiting Alishar. *Anatolica* 26: 173-91.

Southall, A.
1998 *The City in Time and Space*. Cambridge: Cambridge University Press.

Steadman, S.

1996 Recent Research in the Archaeology of Architecture: Beyond the Foundations. *Journal of Anthropological Research* 4: 1: 51-93.

2000 Spatial Patterning and Social Complexity on Prehistoric Anatolian Tell Sites: Models for Mounds. *Journal of Anthropological Archaeology* 19: 164-99.

Stein, G.

1987 Regional Economic Integration in Early State Societies: Third Millennium B.C. Pastoral Production at Gritille, Southeast Turkey. *Paléorient* 13: 2: 101-11.

1999 *Rethinking World-Systems: Diasporas, Colonies, and Interaction in Uruk Mesopotamia.* Tucson, AZ: The University of Arizona Press.

Stein, J. K.

1987 Deposits for Archaeologists. In, *Advances in Archaeological Method and Theory*, volume 11. Edited by M.B. Schiffer, pp. 337-95. New York: Academic Press.

Steinkeller, P.

1987a The Administrative and Economic Organization of the Ur III State: The Core and Periphery. In, *The Organization of Power: Aspects of Bureaucracy in the Ancient Near East.* Edited by M. Gibson, and R.D. Biggs, pp. 19-41. Chicago: The Oriental Institute of the University of Chicago.

1987b The Foresters of Umma: Toward a Definition of Ur III Labor. In, *Labor in the Ancient Near East.* Edited by M.A. Powell, pp. 73-115. New Haven: American Oriental Society.

1996 The Organization of Crafts in Third Millennium Babylonia: The Case of Potters. *Altorientalische Forschungen* 23: 2: 232-53.

Stevenson, T. B.

1985 *Social Change in a Yemeni Highlands Town.* Salt Lake City: University of Utah Press.

Stirling, P.

1953 Social Rank in a Turkish Village. *British Journal of Sociology* IV: 1.

1965 *Turkish Village.* London: Weidenfeld and Nicholson.

Stone, E. C.

1981 Texts, Architecture, and Ethnographic Analogy: Patterns of Residence in Old Babylonian Nippur. *Iraq* 43: 1: 19-33.

1987 *Nippur Neighborhoods.* Studies in Ancient Oriental Civilization No. 44. Chicago: Oriental Institute of the University of Chicago.

1990 The Tell Abu Duwari Project, Iraq, 1987. *Journal of Field Archaeology* 17: 141-162.

1991 The Spatial Organization of Mesopotamian Cities. *Aula Orientalis* 9: 235-242.

1995 The Development of Cities in Ancient Mesopotamia. In, *Civilizations of the Ancient Near East.* Edited by J. Sasson, pp. 235-48. New York: Charles Scribner's Sons.

1996 Houses, Households, and Neighborhoods in the OB Period. In, *Houses and Households in Ancient Mesopotamia.* Edited by K. Veenhof, pp. 229-236. Leiden: Nederlands Historisch-Archeologisch Instituut te Istanbul.

Stone, E. and P. Zimansky

1992 Mashkan-shapir and the Anatomy of an Old Babylonian City. *Biblical Archaeologist* 55: 4: 212-218.

1994 The Tell Abu Duwari Project, 1988-1990. *Journal of Field Archaeology* 21: 437-55.

2004 *The Anatomy of a Mesopotamian City Survey and Soundings at Mashkan-shapir.* Winona Lake, IN: Eisenbrauns.

Strommenger, E.

1980 *Habuba Kabira. Eine Stadt vor 5000 Jahren.* Mainz: Phillip von Zabern.

Sumner, W. M.

1972 *Cultural Developments in the Kur River Basin.* Ph.D. Dissertation, Department of Anthropology, University of Pennsylvania.

1979 Estimating Population by Analogy. In, *Ethnoarchaeology.* Edited by C. Kramer, pp. 164-74. New York: Columbia University Press.

1985 The Proto-Elamite City Wall at Tal-i Malyan. *Iran* 33: 153-61.

Sweet, L. E.

1974 *Tell Toqaan: A Syrian Village.* Anthropological Papers No. 14. Museum of Anthropology Ann Arbor, MI: University of Michigan.

Urfa

1967 *Köy Envanter Etüdlerine Göre* (Village Inventory Survey, in Urfa Province). Urkiyede Köy Gerçekleri ve ihtiyaç guruplari serisi: 17.

Konya Yildiz Basimevi.

Tobler, A.
1950 *Excavations at Tepe Gawra.* Philadelphia: University of Pennsylvania Press.

Torraca, G., G. Chiari, and G. Gullini
1972 Report on Mud Brick Preservation. *Mesopotamia* 7: 259-86.

Tringham, R.
1991 Households with Faces: the challenge of gender in prehistoric architectural remains. In, *Engendering Archaeology.* Edited by J.M. Gero and M.W. Conkey, pp. 93-131. Oxford: Basil Blackwell.

1995 Archaeological Houses, Households, Housework and the Home. In, *The Home: words, interpretations, meanings, and environments.* Edited by D. N. Benjamin, pp. 79-107. Aldershot, UK: Avebury.

Vallet, R.
1997 Habuba Kébira Sud, Approche Morphologique de l'Habitat. In, *La Maison dans le Syria antique de IIIe millenaire aux débuts de l'Islam.* Edited by C. Castel, pp. 105-119. Actes du colloque de Damas (Juin 1992). IFAPO.

Van De Mieroop, M.
1986 The Administration of Crafts in the Early Isin Period. In, *Cuneiform Archives and Libraries: Papers read at the 30e Recontre Assyriologique Internationale.* Edited by K.R. Veenhof, pp. 88-95. Istanbul: Nederlands Historisch-Archaeologisch Instituut.

1987 *Crafts in the Early Isin Period: A Study of the Isin Craft Archive from the Reigns of Ishbi-Erra and Shu-ilishu.* Orientalia Lovaniensia Analecta 24. Leuven: Departement Oriëntalistiek.

1992 *Society and Enterprise in Old Babylonian Ur.* Berlin: Dietrich Beimer Verlag.

1999 [1997] *The Ancient Mesopotamian City.* Oxford: Oxford University Press.

Van der Toorn, K.
1996a *Family Religion in Babylonia, Syria, and Israel: Continuity and Change in the Forms of Religious Life.* Leiden, New York, and Köln: E.J. Brill.

1996b Domestic Religion in Ancient Mesopotamia. In, *Houses and Households in Ancient Mesopotamia.* Edited by K. Veenhof. pp. 69-77. Leiden: Nederlands Historisch-Archeologisch Instituut te Istanbul.

Van Driel, G.
2000 The Mesopotamian North: Land Use, An Attempt. In, *Rainfall and Agriculture in Northern Mesopotamia* (MOS Studies No. 3). Edited by R.M. Jas, pp. 265-99. Istanbul: Nederlands Historisch-Archaeologisch Instituut te Istanbul.

Van Driel, G. and C. Van Driel-Murray
1983 Jebel Aruda, the 1982 Season of Excavations, Interim Report. *Akkadica* 33: 1-26.

Veenhof, K. R.
1996 *Houses and Households in Ancient Mesopotamia.* Istanbul: Nederlands Historisch-Archaeologisch Instituut.

Verhaaren, B. T.
1989 *Architecture and Archaeological Analysis: Between the Early and Middle Bronze Ages at Kurban Höyük, Turkey.* Ph.D. Dissertation, Department of Near Eastern Languages and Civilizations, University of Chicago.

von Soden, W.
1985 *The Ancient Orient.* Grand Rapids, MI: William B. Eerdmans Publishing Company.

Waetzoldt, H.
1987 Compensation of Craft Workers and Officials in the Ur III Period. In, *Labor in the Ancient Near East.* Edited by M.A. Powell, pp. 117-43. New Haven, CT: The American Oriental Society.

Watson, P. J.
1966 Clues to Iranian Prehistory in Modern Village Life. *Expedition* 8: 9-19.

1978 Architectural Differentiation in Some Near Eastern Communities, Prehistoric and Contemporary. In, *Social Archaeology: Beyond Subsistence and Dating.* Edited by C.F. Redman et al., pp. 131-58. New York: Academic Press.

1979 *Archaeological Ethnography in Western Iran.* Viking Fund Publications in Anthropology No. 57. Tucson, AZ: University of Arizona Press.

Wattenmaker, P.
1987a Town and Village Economies in an Early State Society. *Paléorient* 13: 2: 113-22.
1987b The Organization of Production and

Consumption in a Complex Society: A Study of a Village Site in Southeast Turkey. *MASCA Journal* 4: 191-203.

1991 State Formation and the Organization of Domestic Craft Production at Third Millennium B.C. Kurban Höyük, Southeast Turkey. In, *Archaeological Views from the Countryside*. Edited by G. Schwartz and S. Falconer, pp. 109-120. Washington and London: Smithsonian Institution Press.

1994a Political Fluctuations and Local Exchange Systems: Evidence from the Early Bronze Age Settlements at Kurban Höyük. In, *Chiefdoms and Early States in the Near East: The Organizational Dynamics of Complexity*. Edited by G. Stein and M. Rothman, pp. 193-208. Madison, WI: Prehistory Press.

1994b Household Economy in Early State Society: Material Value, Productive Context and Spheres of Exchange. In, *Economic Anthropology of the State*. Edited by E. Brumfiel, pp. 93-118. Lanham, MD: University Press of America.

1997 Kazane Höyük, 1995: Excavations of an Early City. *Kazı Sonuçları Toplantısı* 18: 1: 177-92.

1998a *Household and State in Upper Mesopotamia: Specialized Economy and the Social Uses of Goods in an Early Complex Society*. Washington and London: Smithsonian Institution Press.

1998b Craft Production and Social Identity in Northwest Mesopotamia. In, *Craft and Social Identity*. Edited by C. Costin and R. Wright, pp. 47-56. Archaeological Papers of the AAA, No. 8. Arlington, VA: American Anthropological Association.

Wattenmaker, P. and A. Mısır

1994 Excavations at Kazane Höyük - 1992. *Kazı Sonuçları Toplantısı* 15: 177-187.

Wattenmaker, P. and G. Stein

1986 Early Pastoral production in SE Anatolia: Faunal Remains from Kurban Höyük and Gritille Höyük. *Anatolica* 13: 38-46.

Weber, M.

1958 *The City*. Glencoe, IL: The Free Press.

Weiss, H., editor

1986 *The Origins of Cities in Dry-Farming Syria and Mesopotamia in the Third Millennium B.C.* Guilford, CT: Four Quarters.

Weiss, H.

1983 Excavations at Tell Leilan and the Origins of North Mesopotamian Cities in the Third Millennium B.C. *Paléorient* 9: 39-52.

Westenholz, A.

1984 The Sargonic Period. In, *Circulation of Goods in Non-Palatial Contexts in the Ancient Near East*. Edited by A. Archi, pp. 17-30. Rome: Ateneo.

Whallon, R.

1979 *An Archaeological Survey of the Keban Reservoir Area of East-Central Turkey*. Memoirs of the Museum of Anthropology. University of Michigan. No. 11. Ann Arbor, MI: University of Michigan Press.

1984 Unconstrained Clustering for the Analysis of Spatial Distributions in Archaeology. In, *Intrasite Spatial Analysis in Archaeology*. Edited by H.J. Hietala, pp. 242-77. Cambridge: Cambridge University Press.

Wilk, R. and W. Ashmore, editors

1988 *Household and Community in the Mesoamerican Past*. Albuquerque, NM: University of New Mexico Press.

Wilk, R. and W. Rathje

1982 Household Archaeology. *American Behavioral Scientist* 25: 6: 617-39.

Wilk, R. and M. Schiffer

1979 The Archaeology of Vacant Lots in Tucson, AZ. *American Antiquity* 44: 3: 530-36.

Wilkinson, T. J.

1986 Environmental Change and Local Settlement History (Kurban Höyük). *Anatolica* 13: 90-96.

1990 The Development of Settlement in the North Jazira between the 7th and 1st Millennia B.C. *Iraq* 52: 49-62.

1994 The Structure and Dynamics of Dry-Farming States in Upper Mesopotamia. *Current Anthropology* 35: 5: 483-520.

1998 Water and Human Settlement in the Balikh Valley, Syria: Investigations from 1992-1995. *Journal of Field Archaeology* 25: 63-87.

2000 Regional Approaches to Mesopotamian Archaeology: The Contribution of Archaeological Surveys. *Journal of*

Anthropological Research 8: 3: 219-67.

2003 *Archaeological Landscapes of the Near East*. Tucson, AZ: University of Arizona Press.

Willey, G. R., editor
1956 *Prehistoric Settlement Patterns in the New World*. Viking Fund Publications in Anthropology No 23. New York: Wenner-Gren Foundation for Anthropological Research.

Wirth, L.
1938 Urbanism as a Way of Life. *American Journal of Sociology* 44: 1-24.

Woolley, C. L.
1929 *Ur of the Chaldees*. Harmondsworth: Penguin Books.

1954 *Excavations at Ur: A Record of Twelve Years' Work*. London: Ernest Benn Limited.

1965 *The Sumerians*. New York: W.W. Norton and Company.

Wright, H. T.
1977 Recent Research on the Origin of the State. *Annual Review of Anthropology* 6: 379-397.

1980 Problems of Absolute Chronology in Protohistoric Mesopotamia. *Paléorient* 6: 93-98.

1986 The Evolution of Civilizations. In, *American Archaeology*. Edited by D. Meltzer, pp. 323-365. Washington: Smithsonian Institution Press.

Wright, H. T., N. Miller, and R. Redding
1980 Time and Process in an Uruk Rural Center. In, *L'Archéologie de l'Iraq: Perspectives et Limites de l'Interprétation Anthropologique des Documents*, pp. 265-284. No. 580. Paris: C.N.R.S.

Wright, H. and E. Rupley
2001 Calibrated Radiocarbon Age Determinations of Uruk-Related Assemblages. In, *Uruk Mesopotamia and Its Neighbors*, pp. 85-122. Edited by M. Rothman. Santa Fe: School of American Research Press.

Wright, R.
1998 Crafting Social Identity in Ur III Southern Mesopotamia. In, *Craft and Social Identity*. Edited by C. Costin and R. Wright, pp. 57-69. Archaeological Papers of the AAA, No. 8. Arlington, VA: American Anthropological Association.

Yakar, J.
2000 *Ethnoarchaeology of Anatolia: Rural Socio-Economy in the Bronze and Iron Age*. Monograph Series of the Sonia and Marco Nadler Institute of Archaeology. Tel Aviv: Institute of Archaeology.

Yanagisako, S.
1979 Family and Household: The Analysis of Domestic Groups. *Annual Review of Anthropology* 8: 161-205.

Yener, K. Aslihan, C. Edens, J. Casana, B. Diebold, H.Ekstrom, M. Loyet, and R. Özbal
2000 Tell Kurdu Excavations 1999. *Anatolica* 26: 31-116.

Yoffee, N.
1986 The Process of Ruralization in Social Evolutionary Theory. Paper presented at the 51st Annual Meeting of the Society for American Archaeology.

1993 Too Many Chiefs? (or Safe Texts for the 90s). In, *For Archaeological Theory: Who Sets the Agenda?*, pp. 60-78. Cambridge: Cambridge University Press.

1995 Political Economy in Early Mesopotamian States. *Annual Review of Anthropology* 24: 281-311.

1997 The Obvious and the Chimerical: City-States in Archaeological Perspective. In, *The Archaeology of City-States: Cross-cultural Approaches*. Edited by D. Nichols and T. Charlton, pp. 255-263. Washington, D.C.: Smithsonian Institution Press.

Zeder, M.
1991 *Feeding Cities: Specialized Animal Economy in the Ancient Near East*. Washington: Smithsonian Institution Press.